IDOL *dreams*

& ART BY
ANEMURA

1

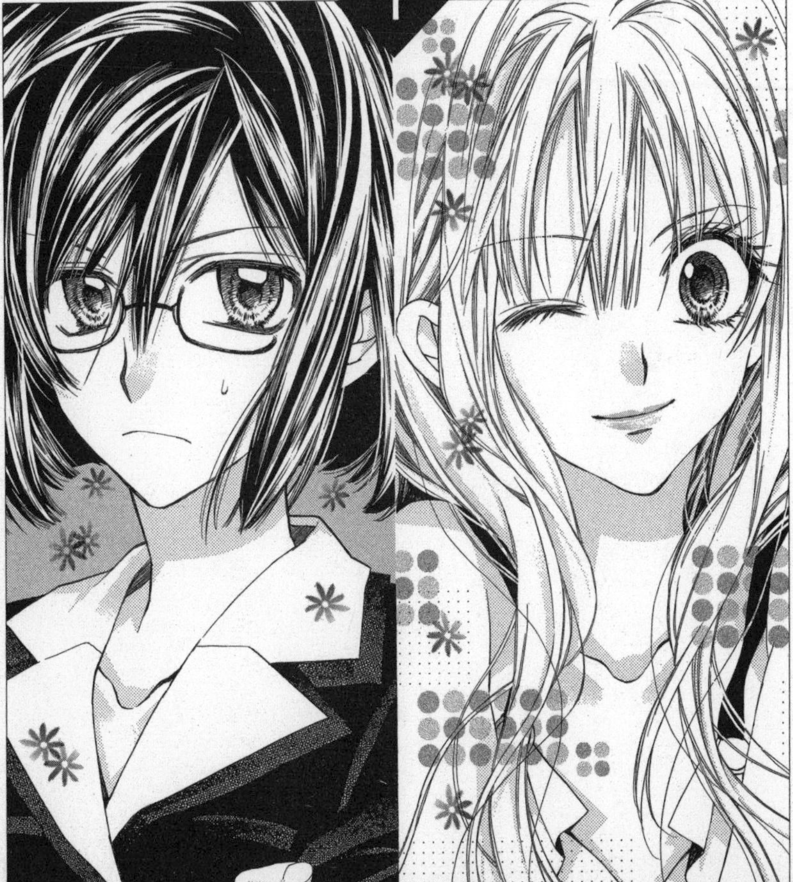

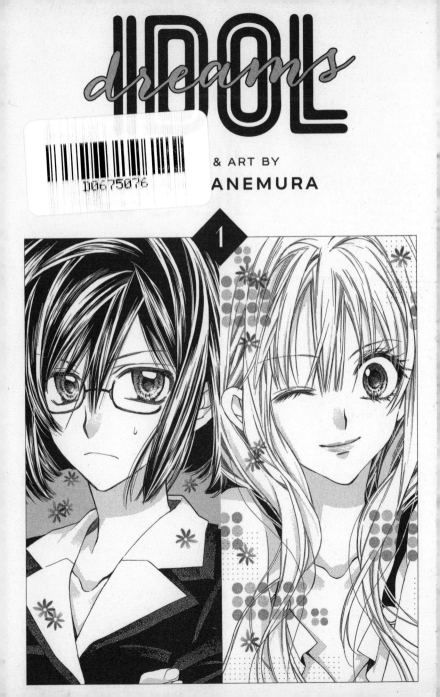

IDOL dreams 1

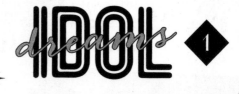

CONTENTS

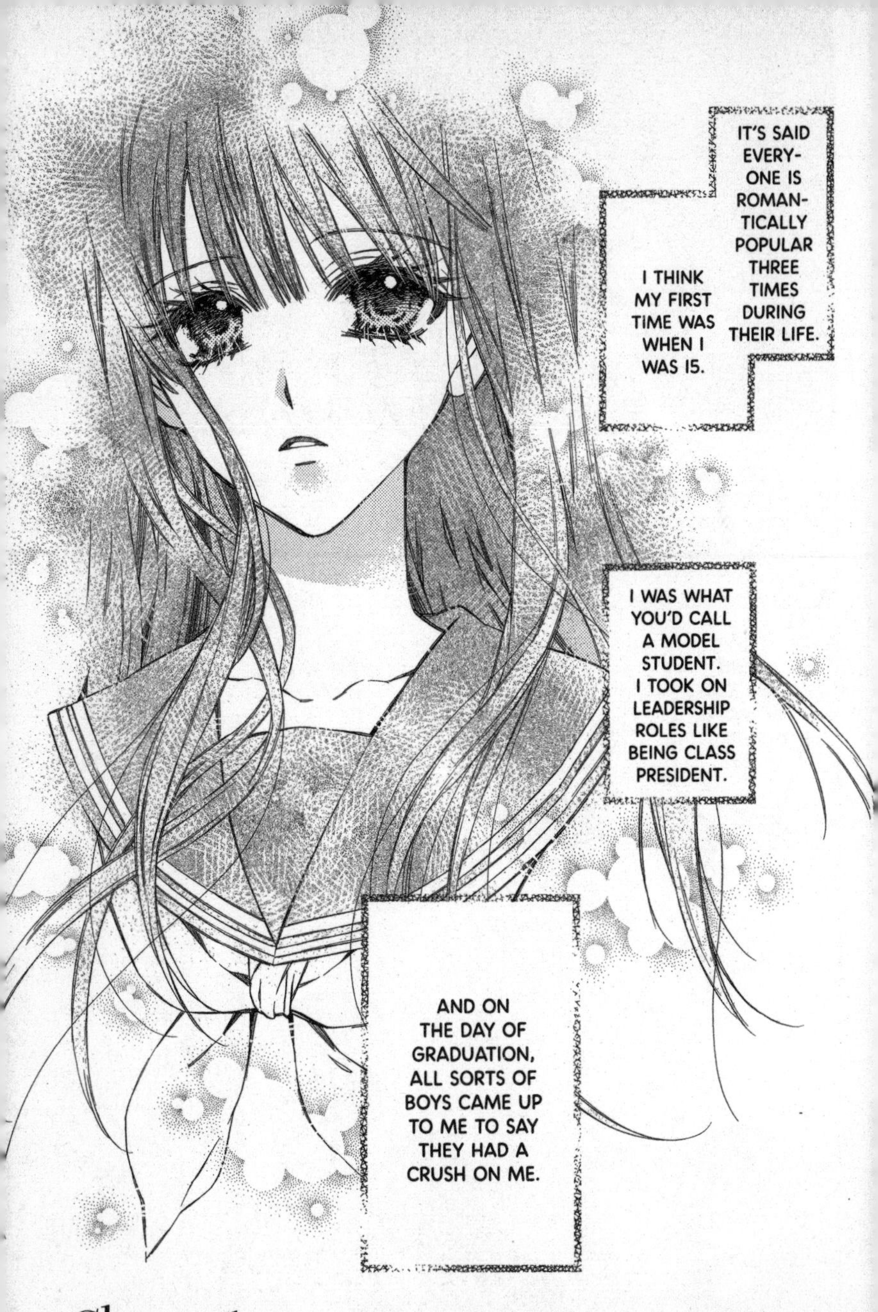
IT'S SAID EVERYONE IS ROMANTICALLY POPULAR THREE TIMES DURING THEIR LIFE.
I THINK MY FIRST TIME WAS WHEN I WAS 15.
I WAS WHAT YOU'D CALL A MODEL STUDENT. I TOOK ON LEADERSHIP ROLES LIKE BEING CLASS PRESIDENT.
AND ON THE DAY OF GRADUATION, ALL SORTS OF BOYS CAME UP TO ME TO SAY THEY HAD A CRUSH ON ME.

Chapter 1

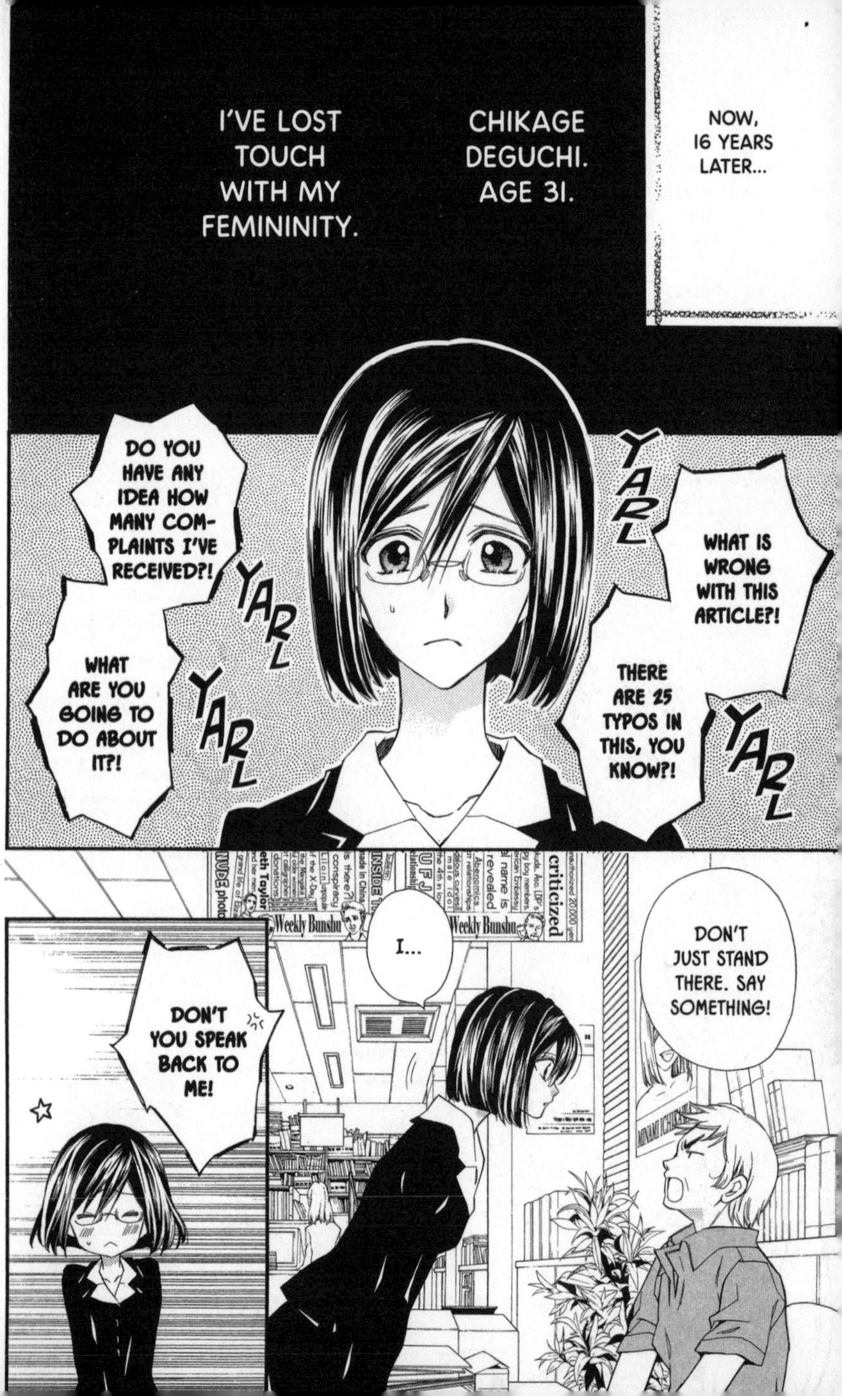
NOW, 16 YEARS LATER...
CHIKAGE DEGUCHI. AGE 31.
I'VE LOST TOUCH WITH MY FEMININITY.
YARL
WHAT IS WRONG WITH THIS ARTICLE?!
THERE ARE 25 TYPOS IN THIS, YOU KNOW?!
YARL
DO YOU HAVE ANY IDEA HOW MANY COM-PLAINTS I'VE RECEIVED?!
YARL
WHAT ARE YOU GOING TO DO ABOUT IT?!
YARL
DON'T JUST STAND THERE. SAY SOMETHING!
I...
DON'T YOU SPEAK BACK TO ME!

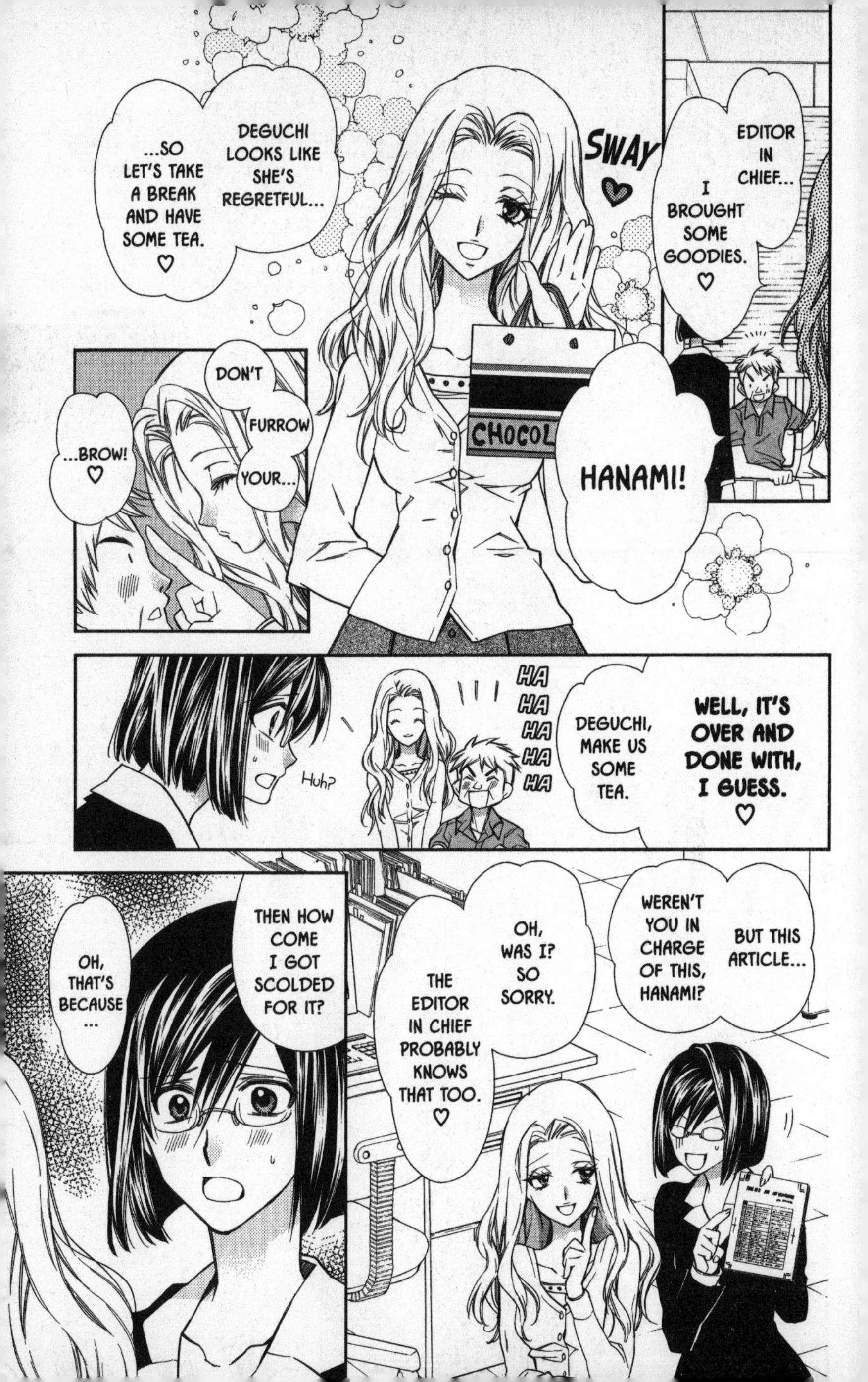

EDITOR IN CHIEF... I BROUGHT SOME GOODIES. ♡
SWAY ♡
HANAMI!
CHOCOL
DEGUCHI LOOKS LIKE SHE'S REGRETFUL...
...SO LET'S TAKE A BREAK AND HAVE SOME TEA. ♡
DON'T
FURROW
YOUR...
...BROW! ♡
WELL, IT'S OVER AND DONE WITH, I GUESS. ♡
DEGUCHI, MAKE US SOME TEA.
HA HA HA HA HA HA
Huh?
BUT THIS ARTICLE...
WEREN'T YOU IN CHARGE OF THIS, HANAMI?
OH, WAS I? SO SORRY.
THE EDITOR IN CHIEF PROBABLY KNOWS THAT TOO. ♡
THEN HOW COME I GOT SCOLDED FOR IT?
OH, THAT'S BECAUSE ...

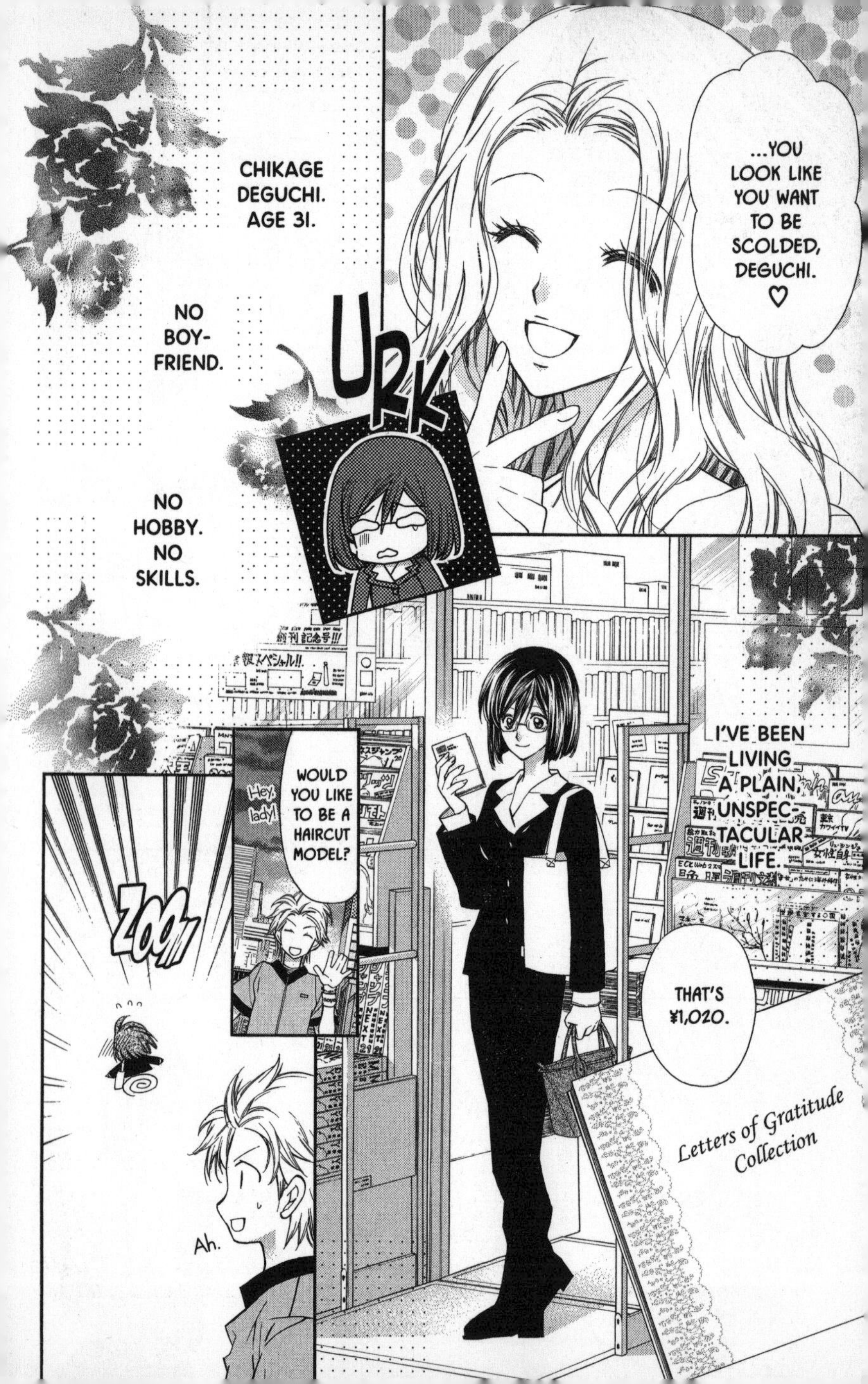
...YOU LOOK LIKE YOU WANT TO BE SCOLDED, DEGUCHI. ♡
URK
CHIKAGE DEGUCHI. AGE 31.
NO BOY-FRIEND.
NO HOBBY. NO SKILLS.
I'VE BEEN LIVING A PLAIN, UNSPEC-TACULAR LIFE.
THAT'S ¥1,020.
Letters of Gratitude Collection
Hey, lady!
WOULD YOU LIKE TO BE A HAIRCUT MODEL?
ZOOM
Ah.

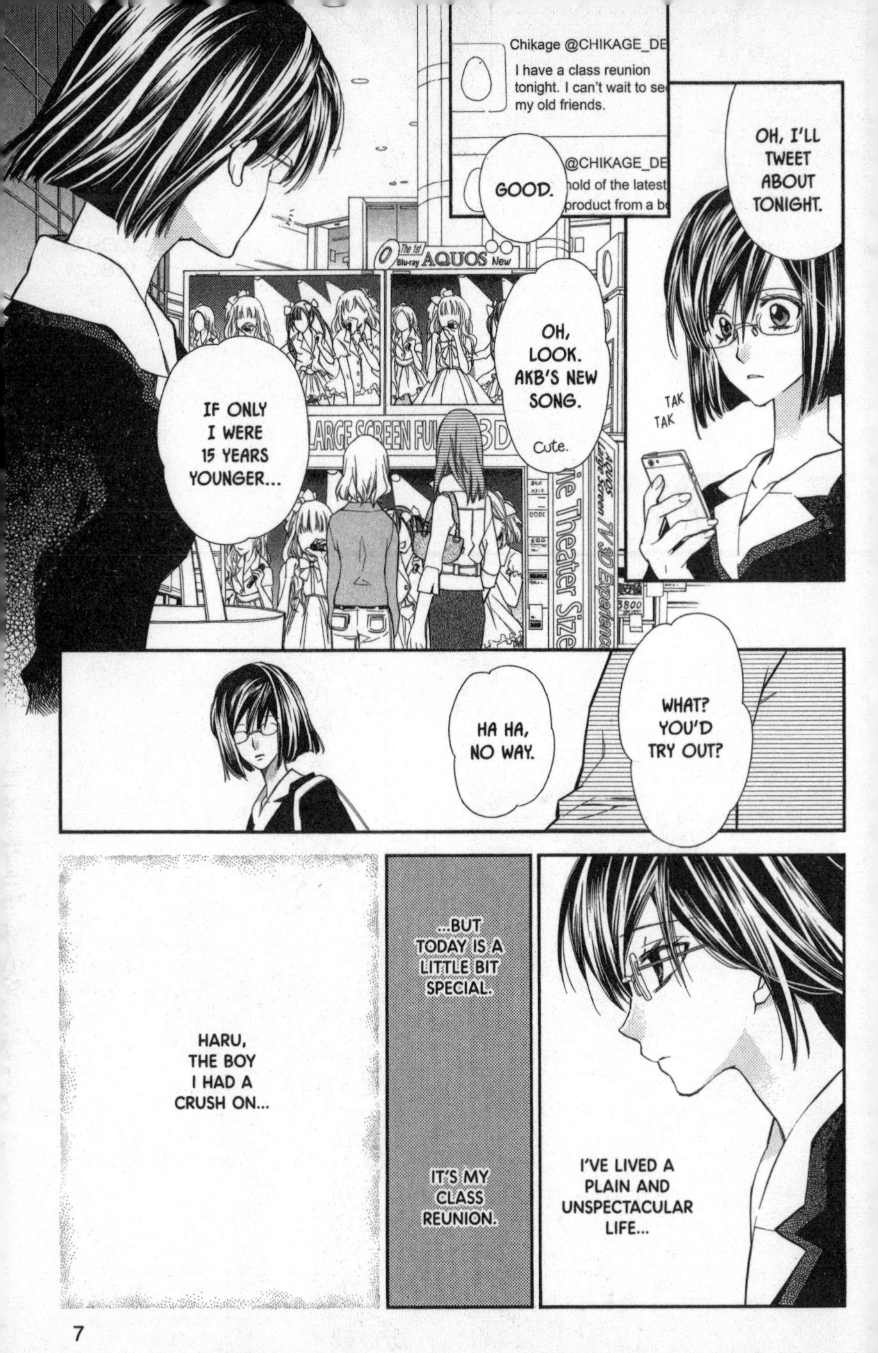
OH, I'LL TWEET ABOUT TONIGHT.
TAK TAK
Chikage @CHIKAGE_DE
I have a class reunion tonight. I can't wait to se
my old friends.
@CHIKAGE_DE
hold of the latest
product from a b
GOOD.
The 1st Blu-ray AQUOS New
OH, LOOK. AKB'S NEW SONG.
Cute.
AQUOS Large Screen TV 3D Experience
IF ONLY I WERE 15 YEARS YOUNGER...
WHAT? YOU'D TRY OUT?
HA HA, NO WAY.
I'VE LIVED A PLAIN AND UNSPECTACULAR LIFE...
...BUT TODAY IS A LITTLE BIT SPECIAL.
IT'S MY CLASS REUNION.
HARU, THE BOY I HAD A CRUSH ON...

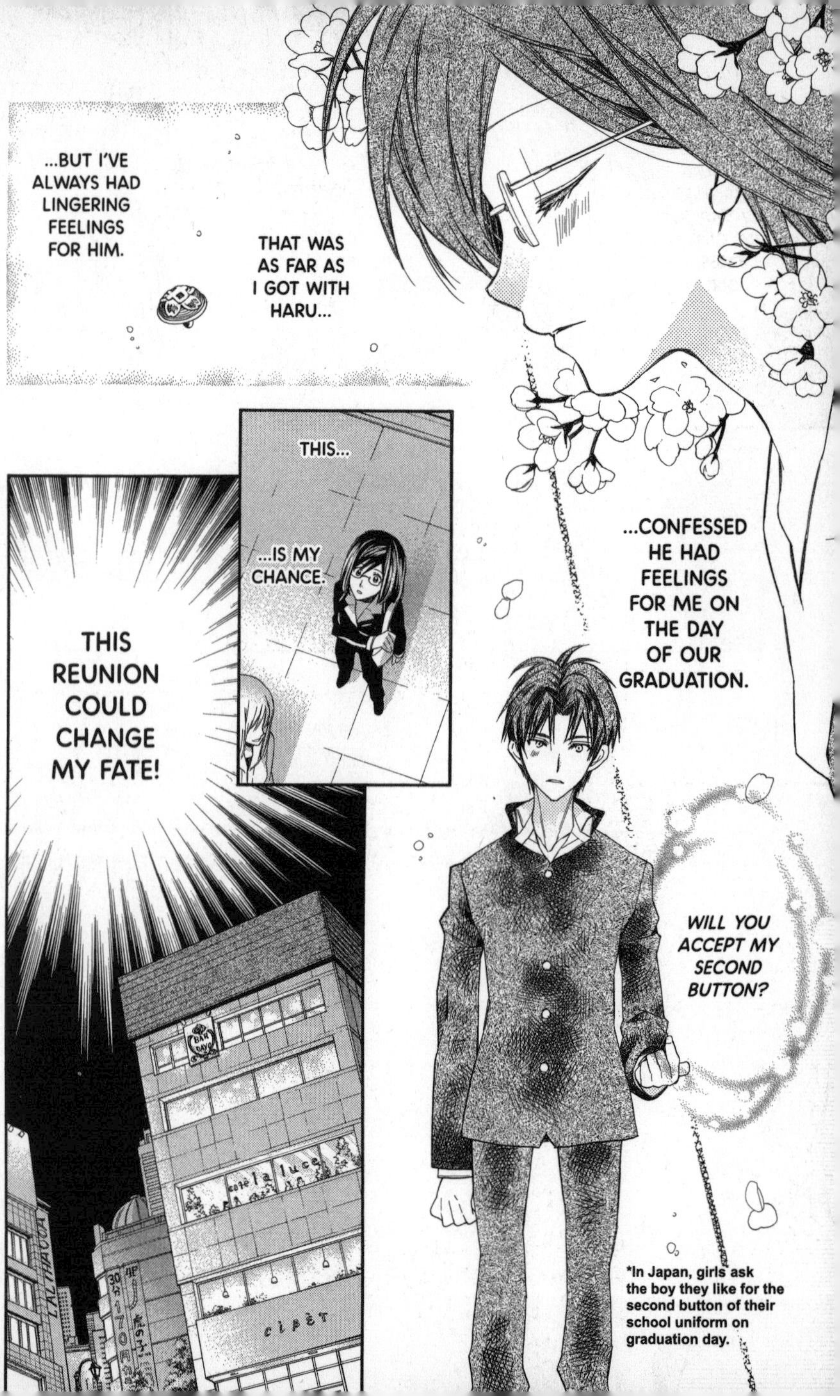
...CONFESSED HE HAD FEELINGS FOR ME ON THE DAY OF OUR GRADUATION.
WILL YOU ACCEPT MY SECOND BUTTON?
THAT WAS AS FAR AS I GOT WITH HARU...
...BUT I'VE ALWAYS HAD LINGERING FEELINGS FOR HIM.
THIS...
...IS MY CHANCE.
THIS REUNION COULD CHANGE MY FATE!

*In Japan, girls ask the boy they like for the second button of their school uniform on graduation day.

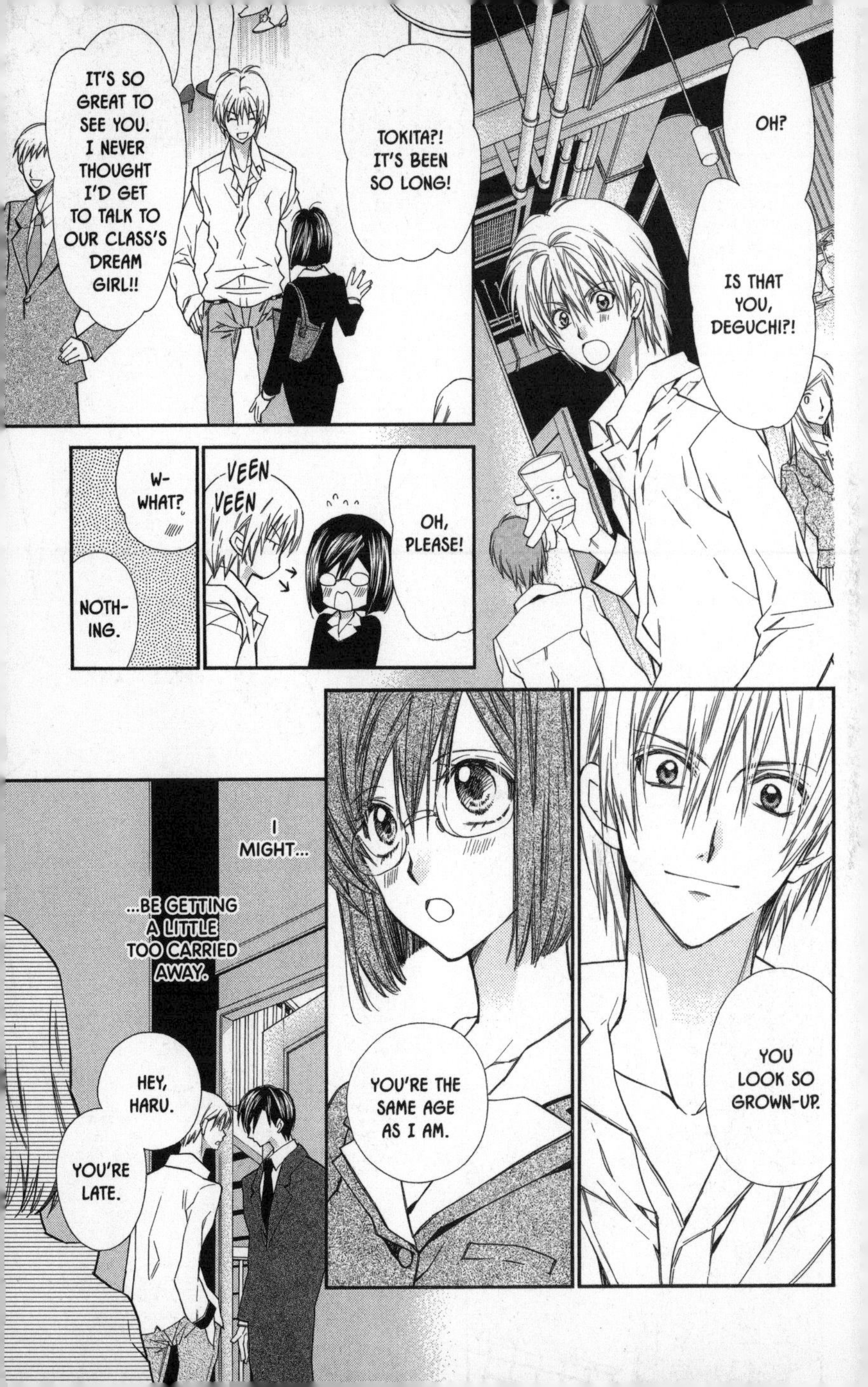
OH?
IS THAT YOU, DEGUCHI?!
TOKITA?! IT'S BEEN SO LONG!
IT'S SO GREAT TO SEE YOU. I NEVER THOUGHT I'D GET TO TALK TO OUR CLASS'S DREAM GIRL!!
OH, PLEASE!
VEEN VEEN
W-WHAT?
NOTHING.
YOU LOOK SO GROWN-UP.
YOU'RE THE SAME AGE AS I AM.
I MIGHT...
...BE GETTING A LITTLE TOO CARRIED AWAY.
HEY, HARU.
YOU'RE LATE.

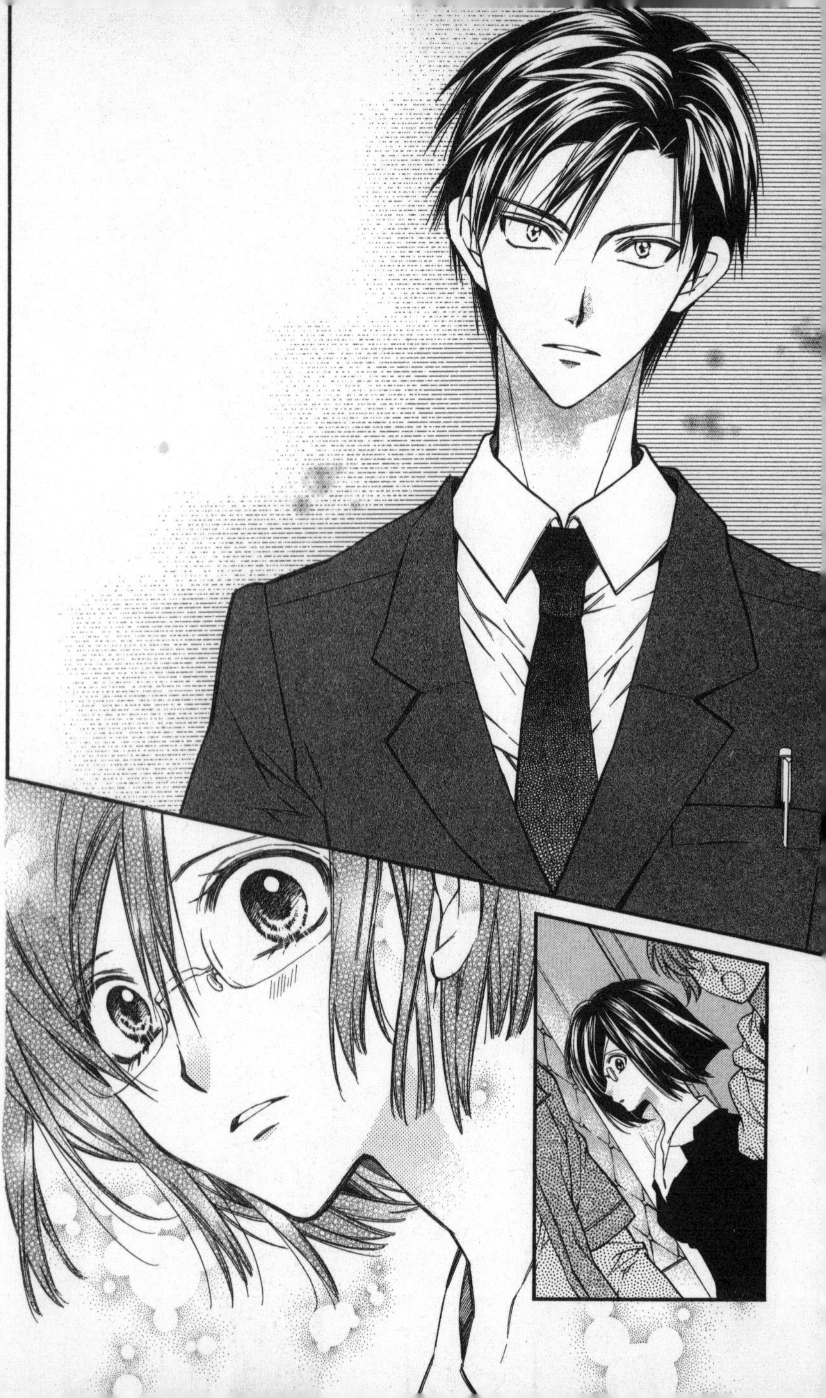

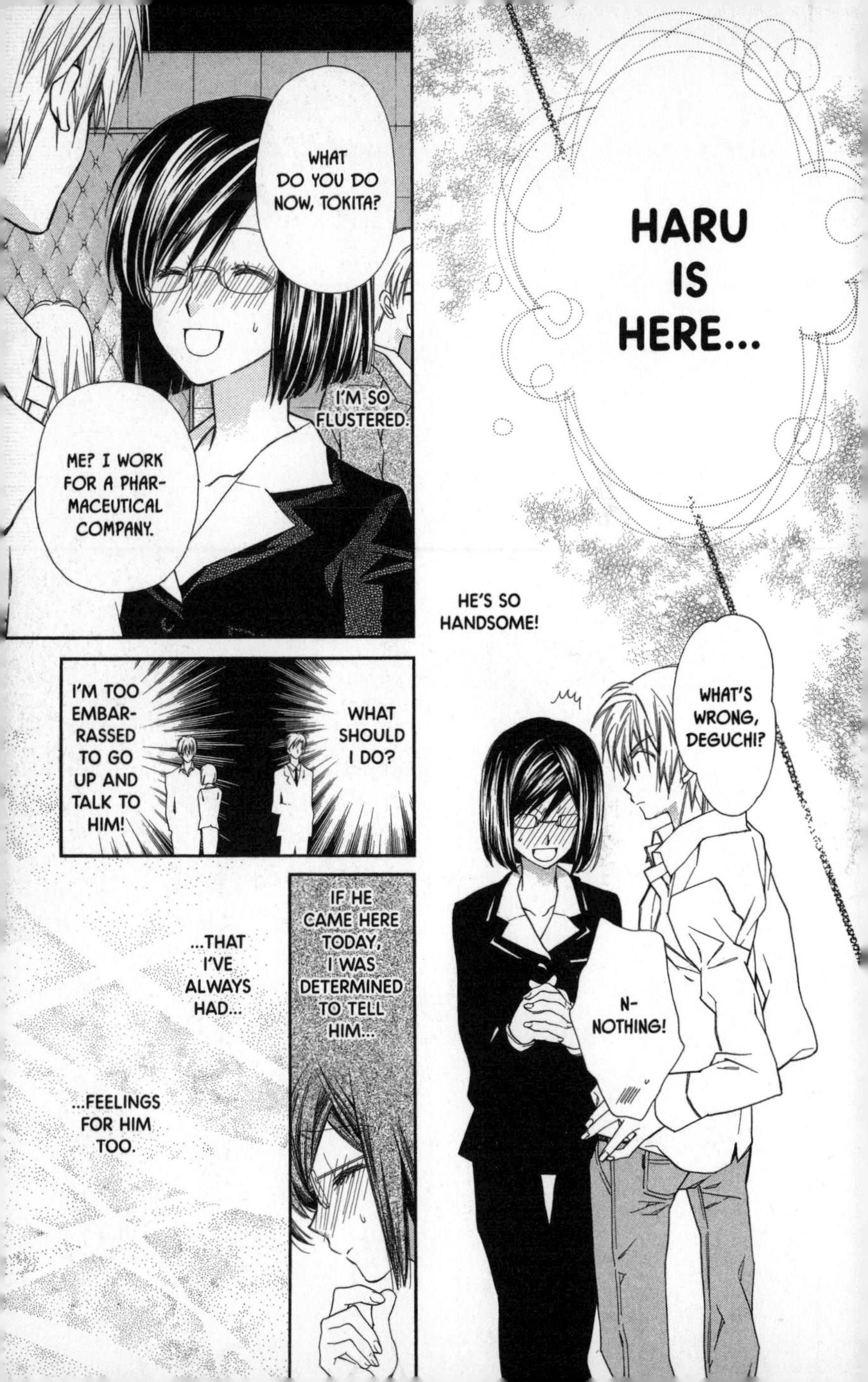
HARU IS HERE...
HE'S SO HANDSOME!
WHAT'S WRONG, DEGUCHI?
N-NOTHING!
WHAT DO YOU DO NOW, TOKITA?
I'M SO FLUSTERED.
ME? I WORK FOR A PHAR-MACEUTICAL COMPANY.
WHAT SHOULD I DO?
I'M TOO EMBAR-RASSED TO GO UP AND TALK TO HIM!
IF HE CAME HERE TODAY, I WAS DETERMINED TO TELL HIM...
...THAT I'VE ALWAYS HAD...
...FEELINGS FOR HIM TOO.

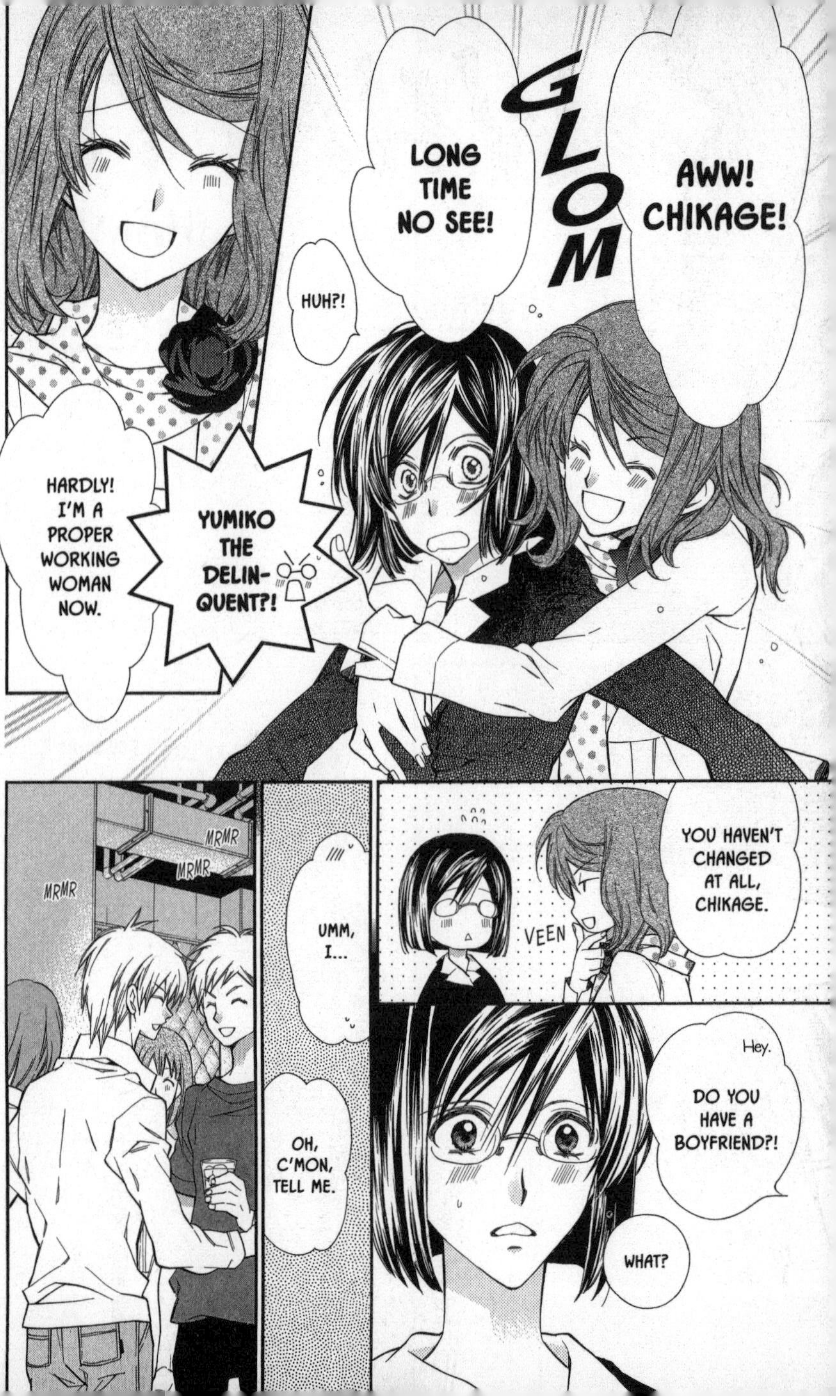
AWW! CHIKAGE!
GLOM
LONG TIME NO SEE!
HUH?!
YUMIKO THE DELIN-QUENT?!
HARDLY! I'M A PROPER WORKING WOMAN NOW.
YOU HAVEN'T CHANGED AT ALL, CHIKAGE.
VEEN
Hey.
DO YOU HAVE A BOYFRIEND?!
WHAT?
UMM, I...
OH, C'MON, TELL ME.
MRMR
MRMR
MRMR

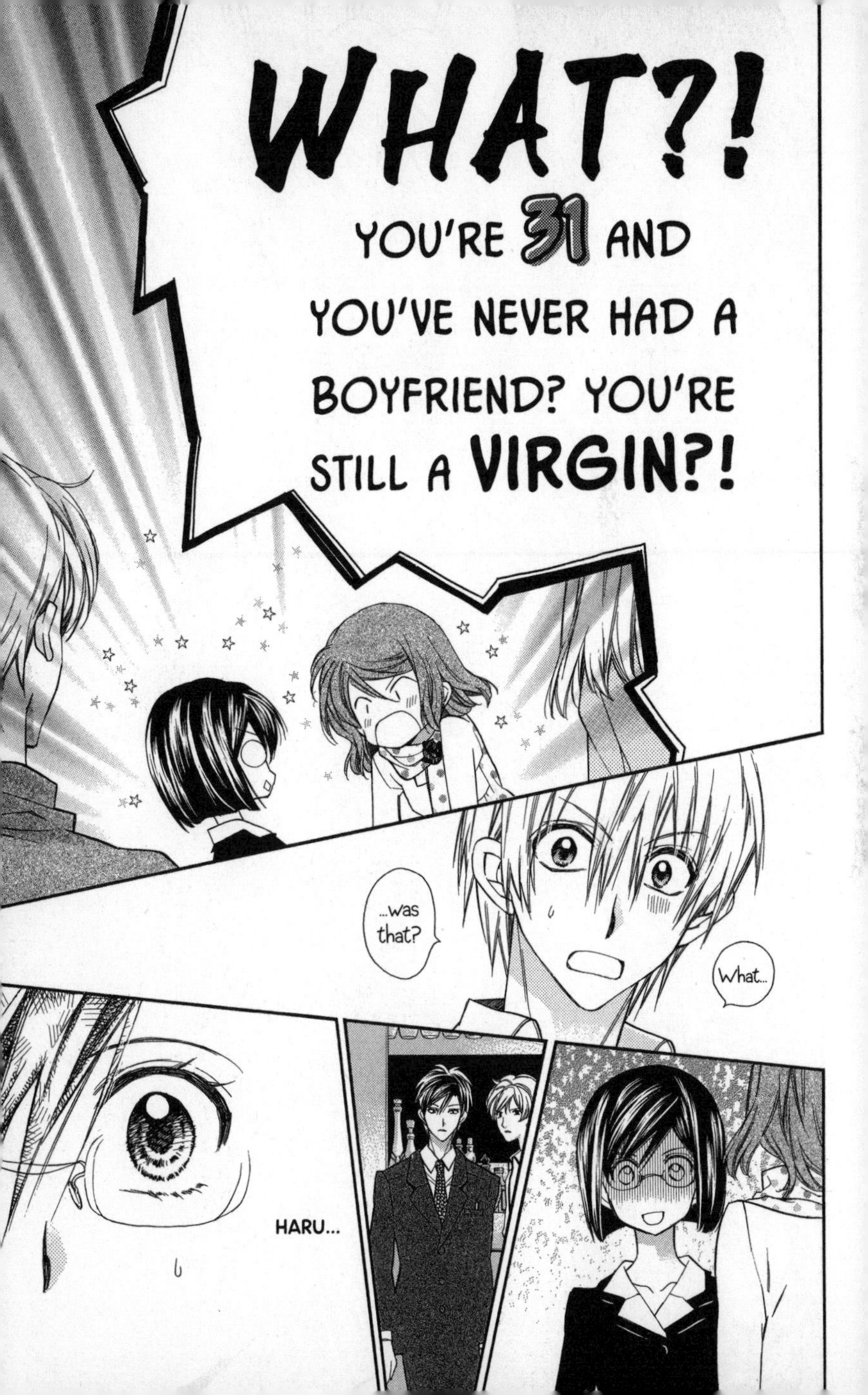
WHAT?!
YOU'RE 31 AND YOU'VE NEVER HAD A BOYFRIEND? YOU'RE STILL A VIRGIN?!
What...
...was that?
HARU...

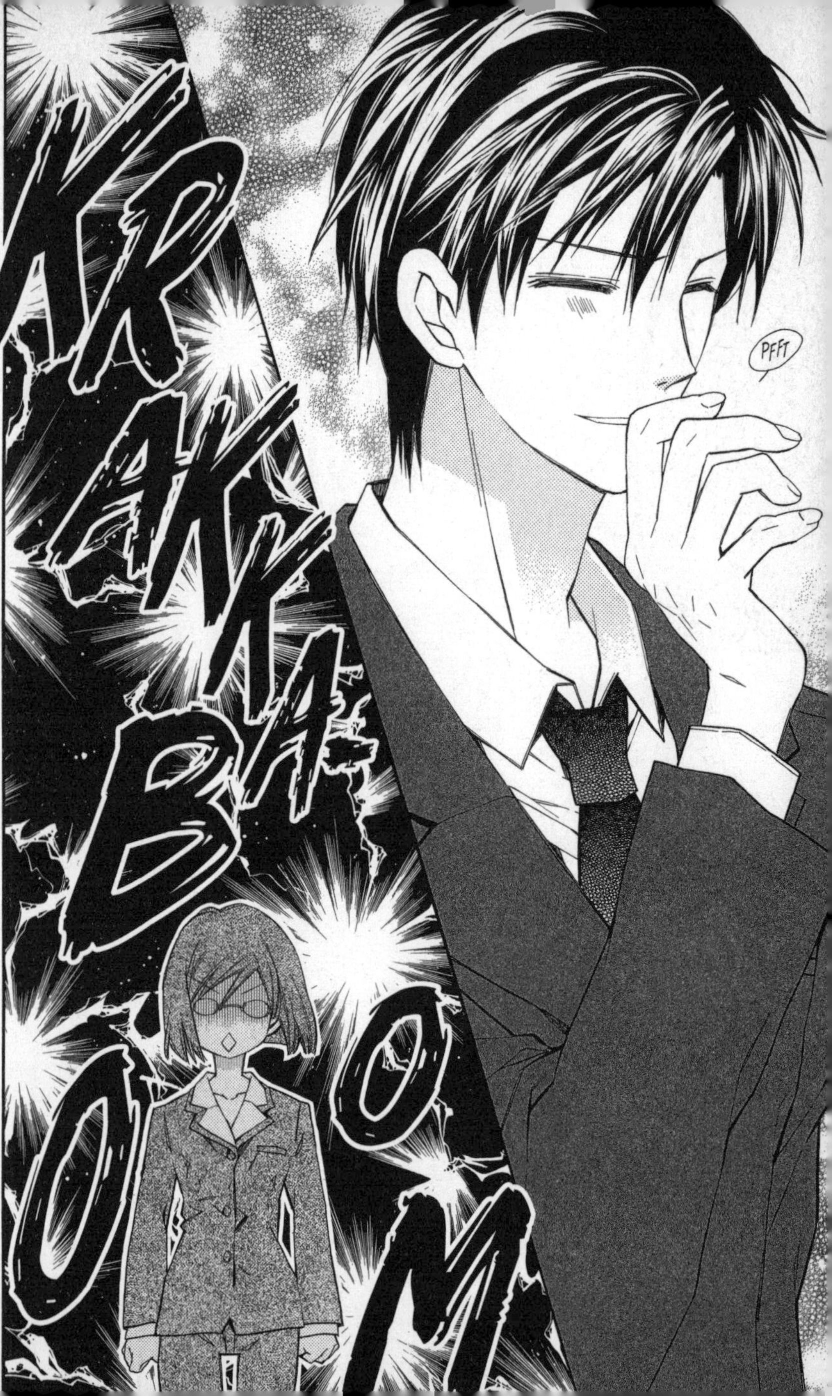
PFFT
KRAKA-BOOM

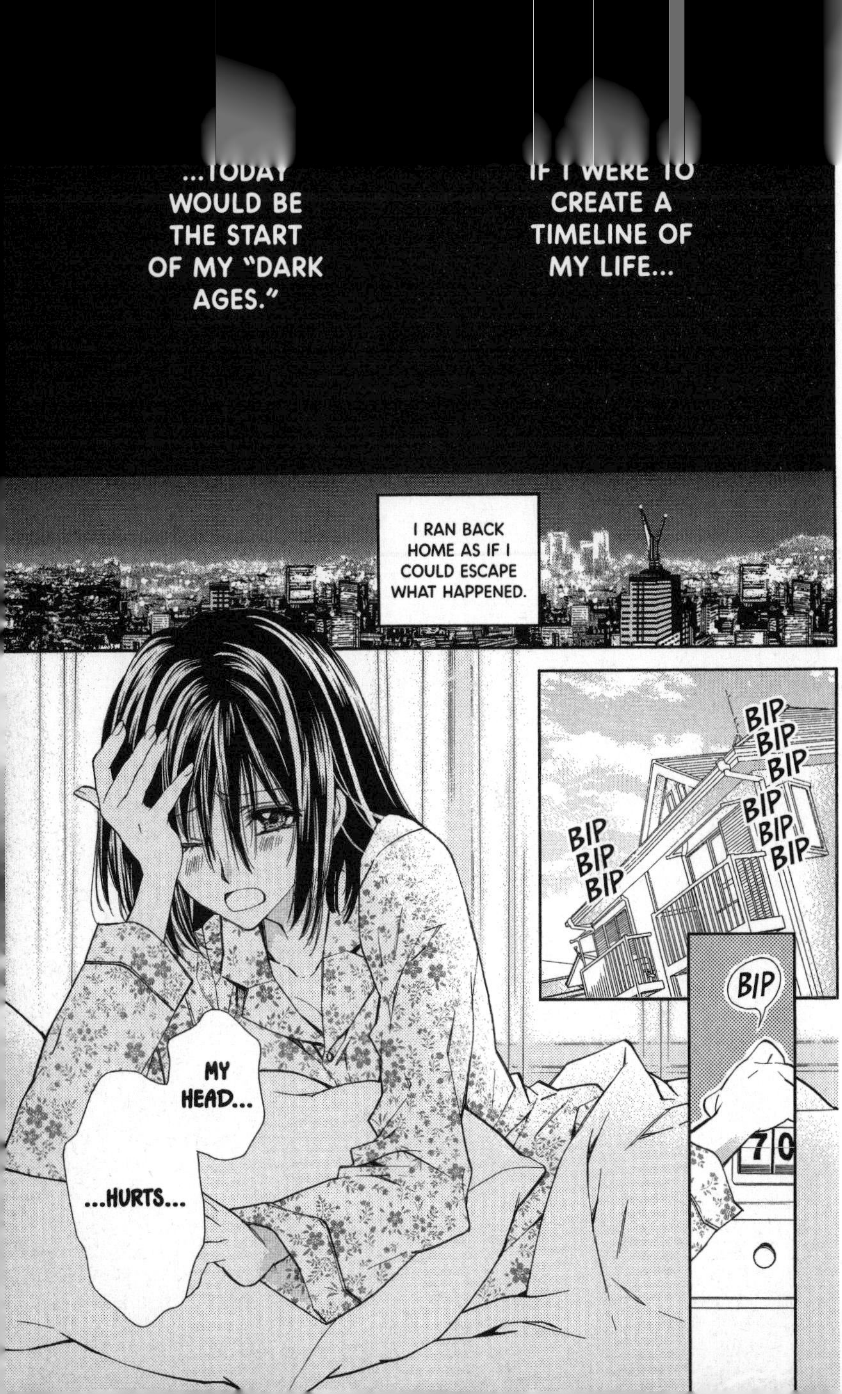
IF I WERE TO CREATE A TIMELINE OF MY LIFE...
...TODAY WOULD BE THE START OF MY "DARK AGES."
I RAN BACK HOME AS IF I COULD ESCAPE WHAT HAPPENED.
BIP BIP BIP BIP BIP BIP
BIP BIP BIP
BIP
MY HEAD...
...HURTS...

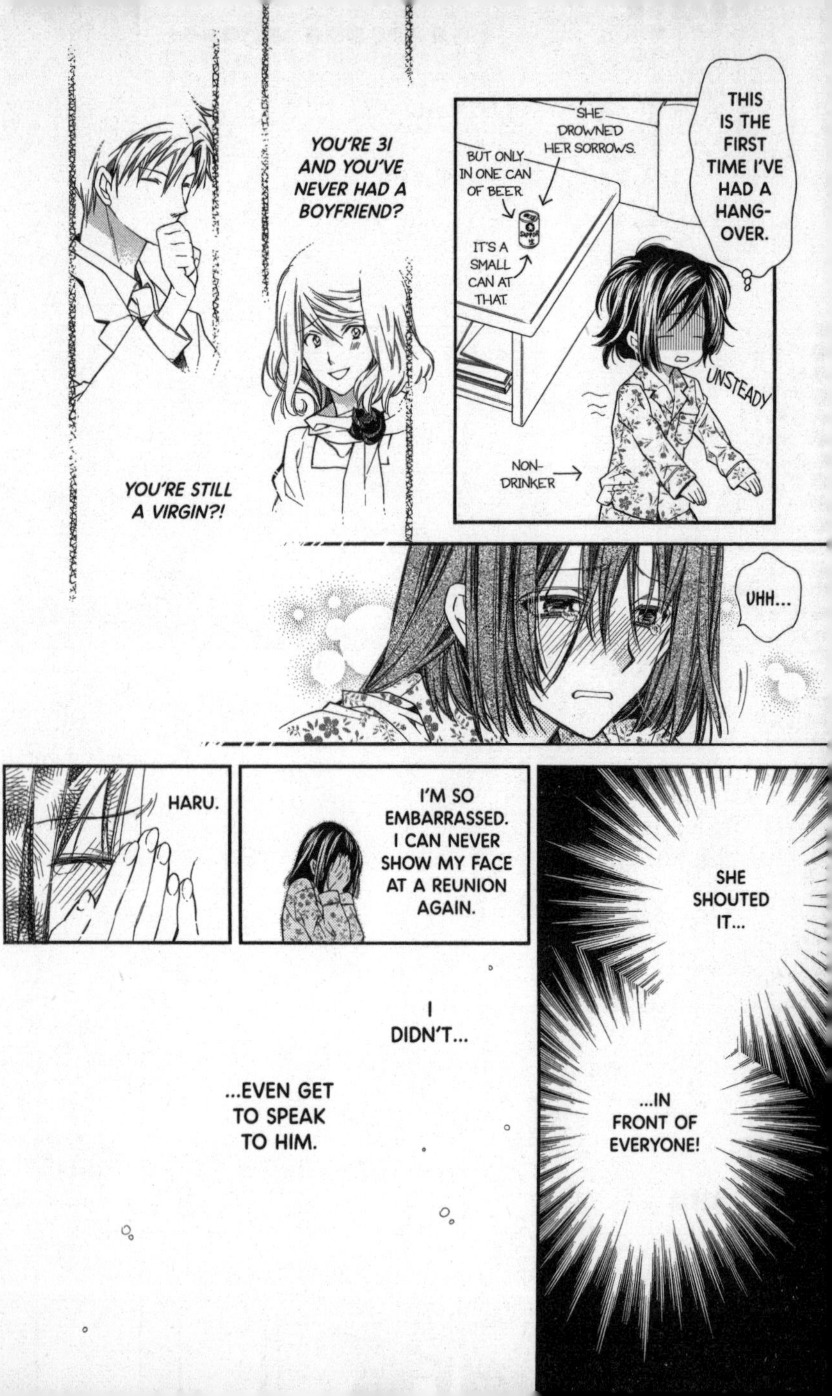
THIS IS THE FIRST TIME I'VE HAD A HANGOVER.
SHE DROWNED HER SORROWS.
BUT ONLY IN ONE CAN OF BEER.
IT'S A SMALL CAN AT THAT.
UNSTEADY
NON-DRINKER
YOU'RE 31 AND YOU'VE NEVER HAD A BOYFRIEND?
YOU'RE STILL A VIRGIN?!
UHH...
SHE SHOUTED IT...
...IN FRONT OF EVERYONE!
I'M SO EMBARRASSED. I CAN NEVER SHOW MY FACE AT A REUNION AGAIN.
HARU.
I DIDN'T...
...EVEN GET TO SPEAK TO HIM.

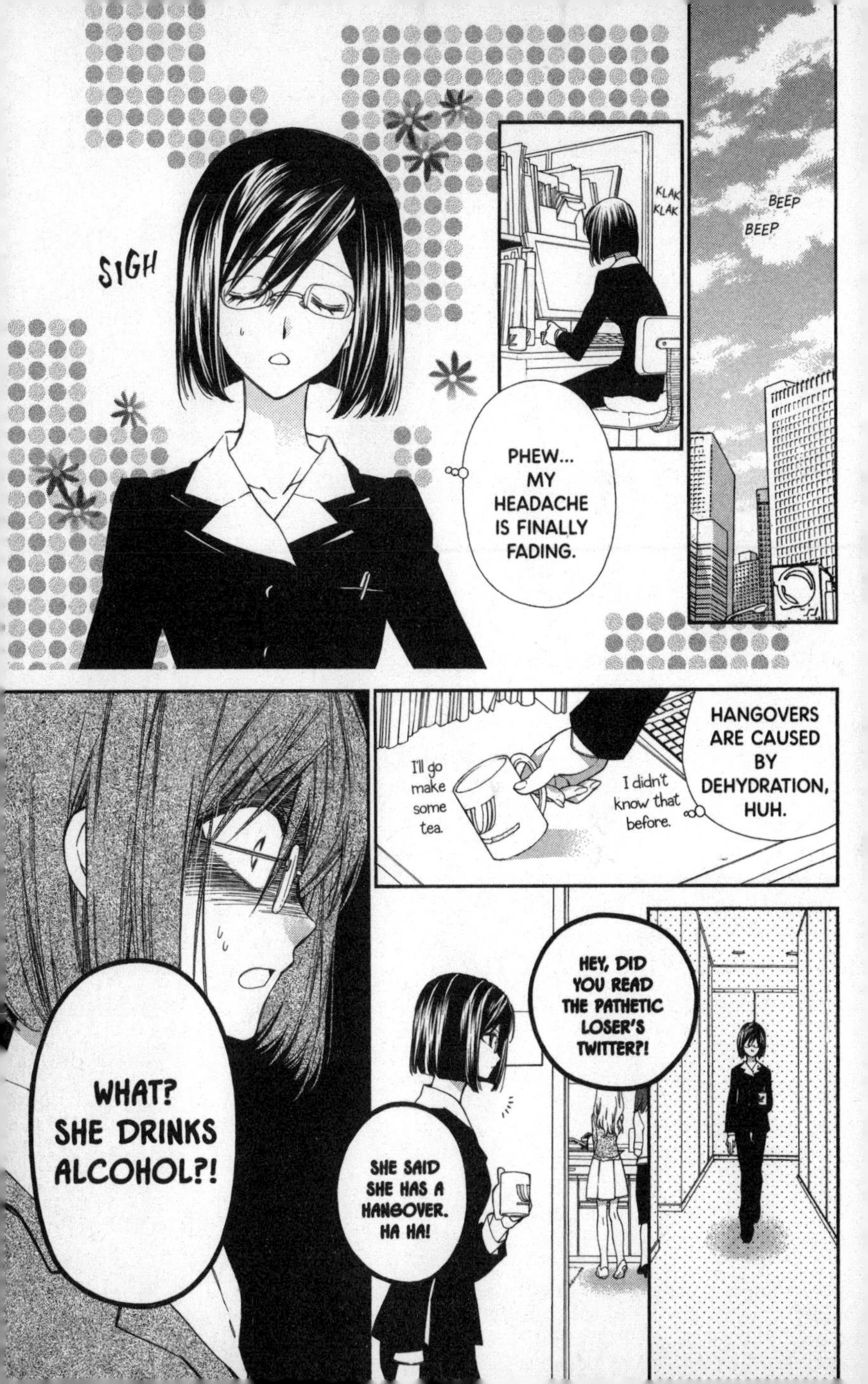
BEEP
BEEP
KLAK
KLAK
PHEW... MY HEADACHE IS FINALLY FADING.
SIGH
HANGOVERS ARE CAUSED BY DEHYDRATION, HUH.
I didn't know that before.
I'll go make some tea.
HEY, DID YOU READ THE PATHETIC LOSER'S TWITTER?!
SHE SAID SHE HAS A HANGOVER. HA HA!
WHAT? SHE DRINKS ALCOHOL?!

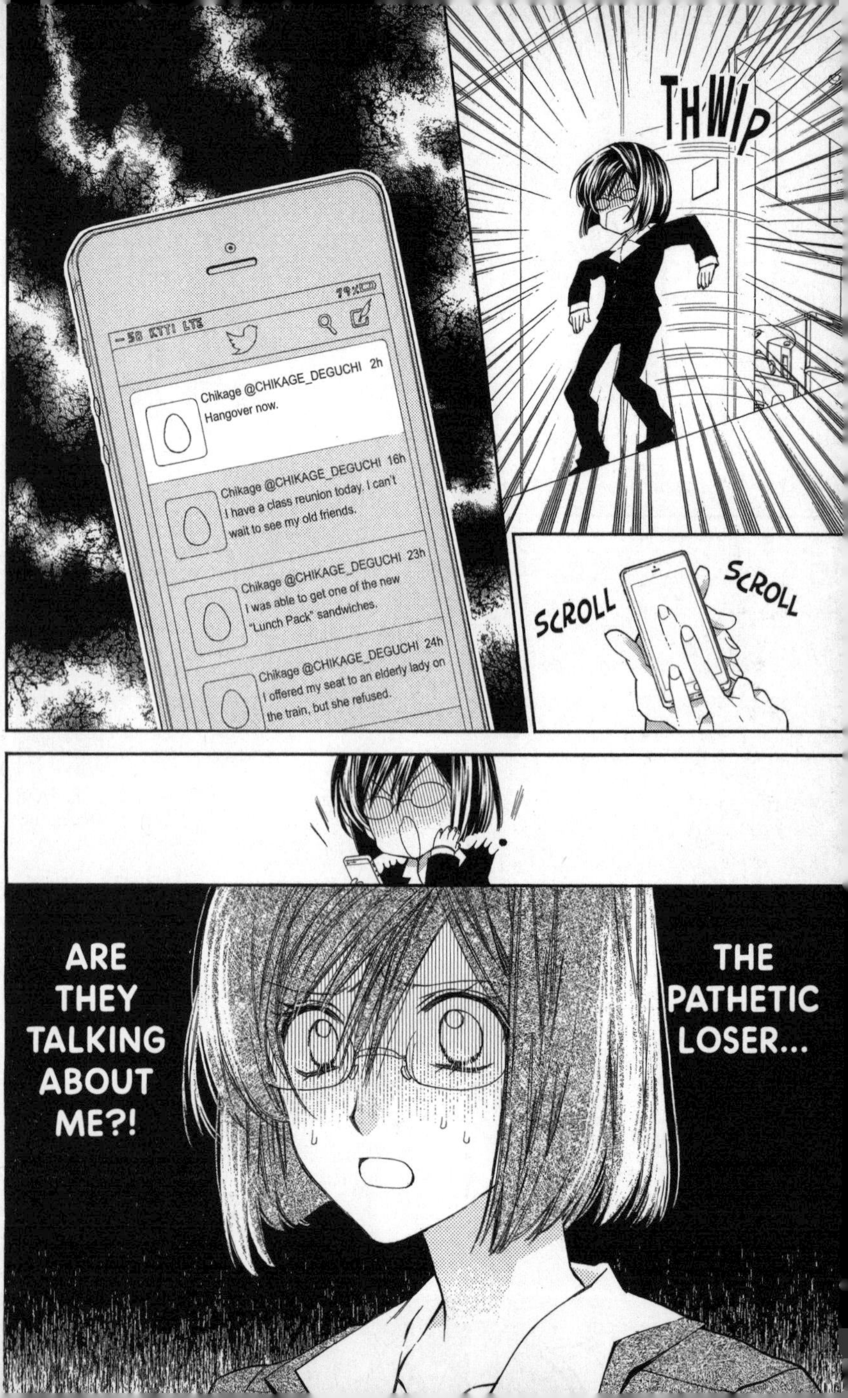
THWIP
SCROLL
SCROLL
Chikage @CHIKAGE_DEGUCHI 2h
Hangover now.
Chikage @CHIKAGE_DEGUCHI 16h
I have a class reunion today. I can't wait to see my old friends.
Chikage @CHIKAGE_DEGUCHI 23h
I was able to get one of the new "Lunch Pack" sandwiches.
Chikage @CHIKAGE_DEGUCHI 24h
I offered my seat to an elderly lady on the train, but she refused.
THE PATHETIC LOSER...
ARE THEY TALKING ABOUT ME?!

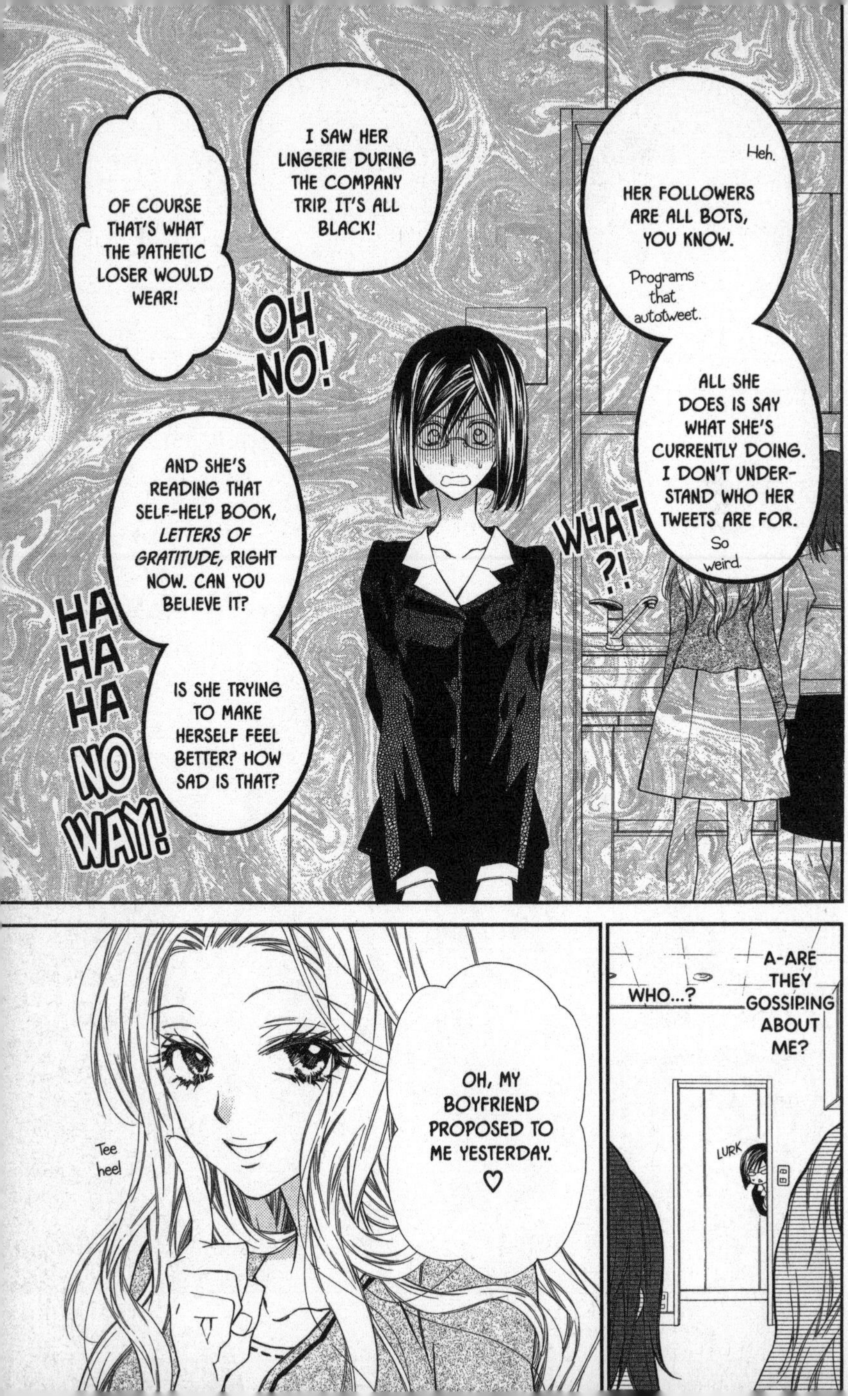
Heh.
HER FOLLOWERS ARE ALL BOTS, YOU KNOW.
Programs that autotweet.
ALL SHE DOES IS SAY WHAT SHE'S CURRENTLY DOING. I DON'T UNDER-STAND WHO HER TWEETS ARE FOR.
So weird.
WHAT?!
I SAW HER LINGERIE DURING THE COMPANY TRIP. IT'S ALL BLACK!
OF COURSE THAT'S WHAT THE PATHETIC LOSER WOULD WEAR!
OH NO!
AND SHE'S READING THAT SELF-HELP BOOK, *LETTERS OF GRATITUDE,* RIGHT NOW. CAN YOU BELIEVE IT?
IS SHE TRYING TO MAKE HERSELF FEEL BETTER? HOW SAD IS THAT?
HA HA HA NO WAY!
A-ARE THEY GOSSIPING ABOUT ME?
WHO...?
LURK
OH, MY BOYFRIEND PROPOSED TO ME YESTERDAY. ♡
Tee hee!

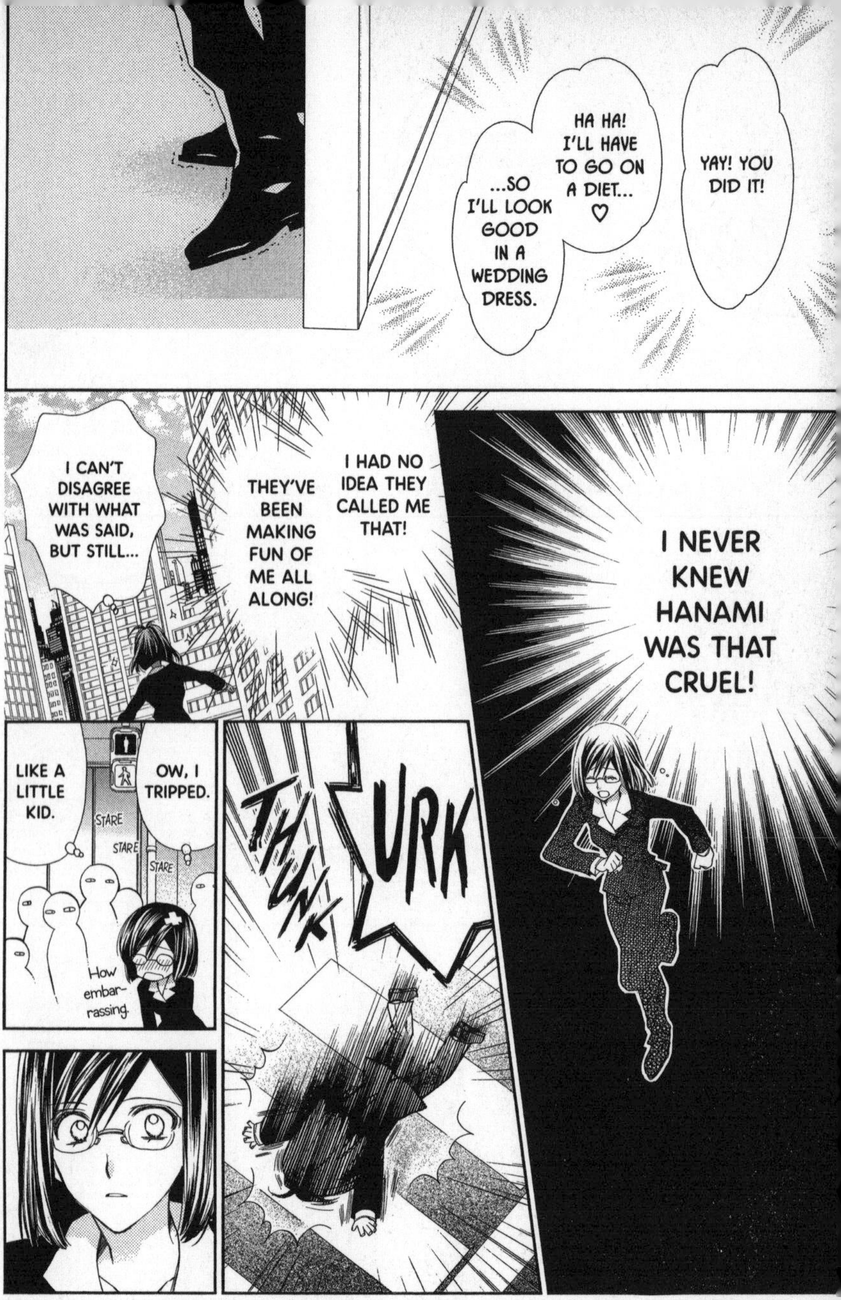
YAY! YOU DID IT!
HA HA! I'LL HAVE TO GO ON A DIET... ♡
...SO I'LL LOOK GOOD IN A WEDDING DRESS.
I NEVER KNEW HANAMI WAS THAT CRUEL!
I HAD NO IDEA THEY CALLED ME THAT!
THEY'VE BEEN MAKING FUN OF ME ALL ALONG!
I CAN'T DISAGREE WITH WHAT WAS SAID, BUT STILL...
URK
THUNK
OW, I TRIPPED.
LIKE A LITTLE KID.
STARE
STARE
STARE
How embarrassing.

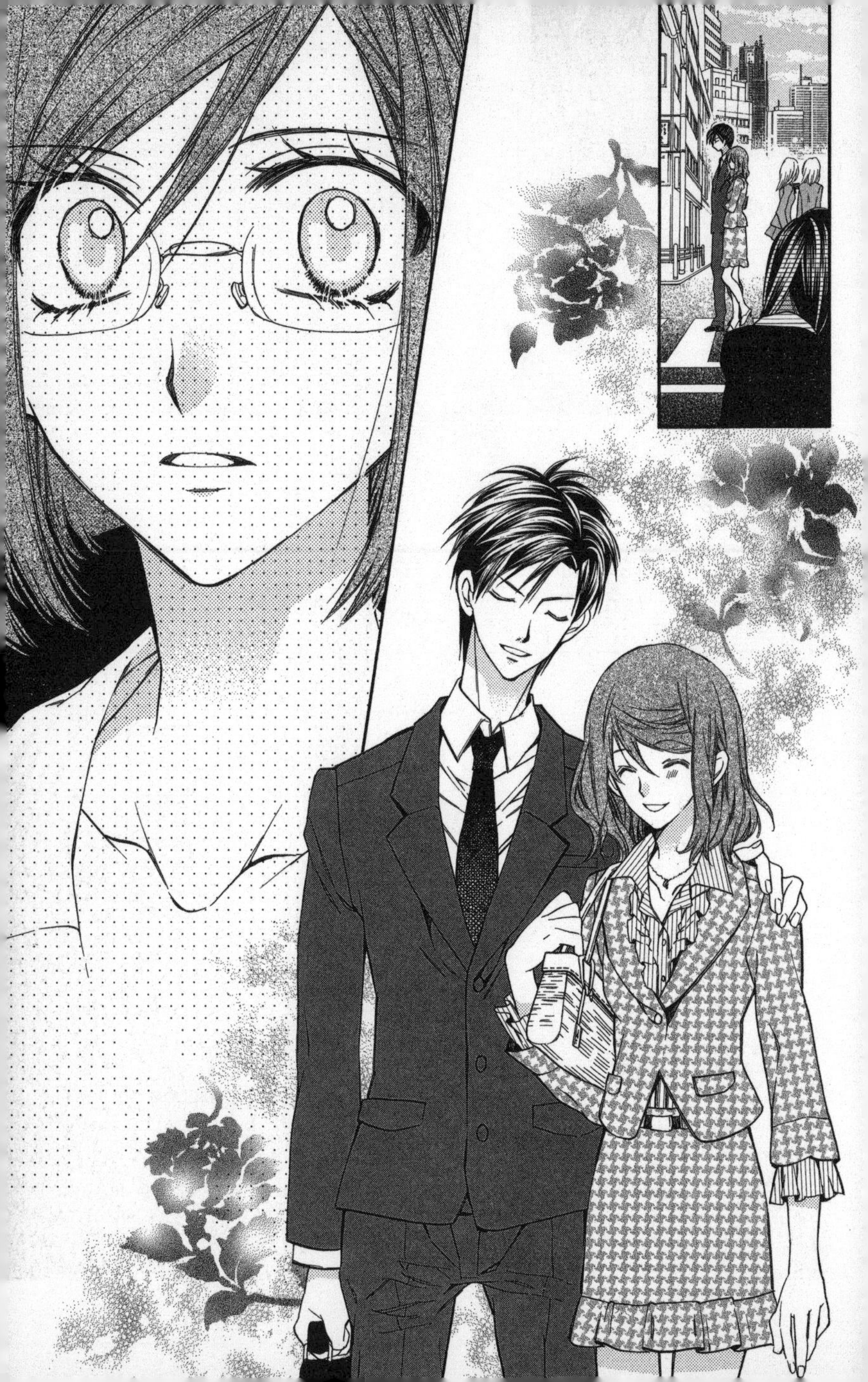

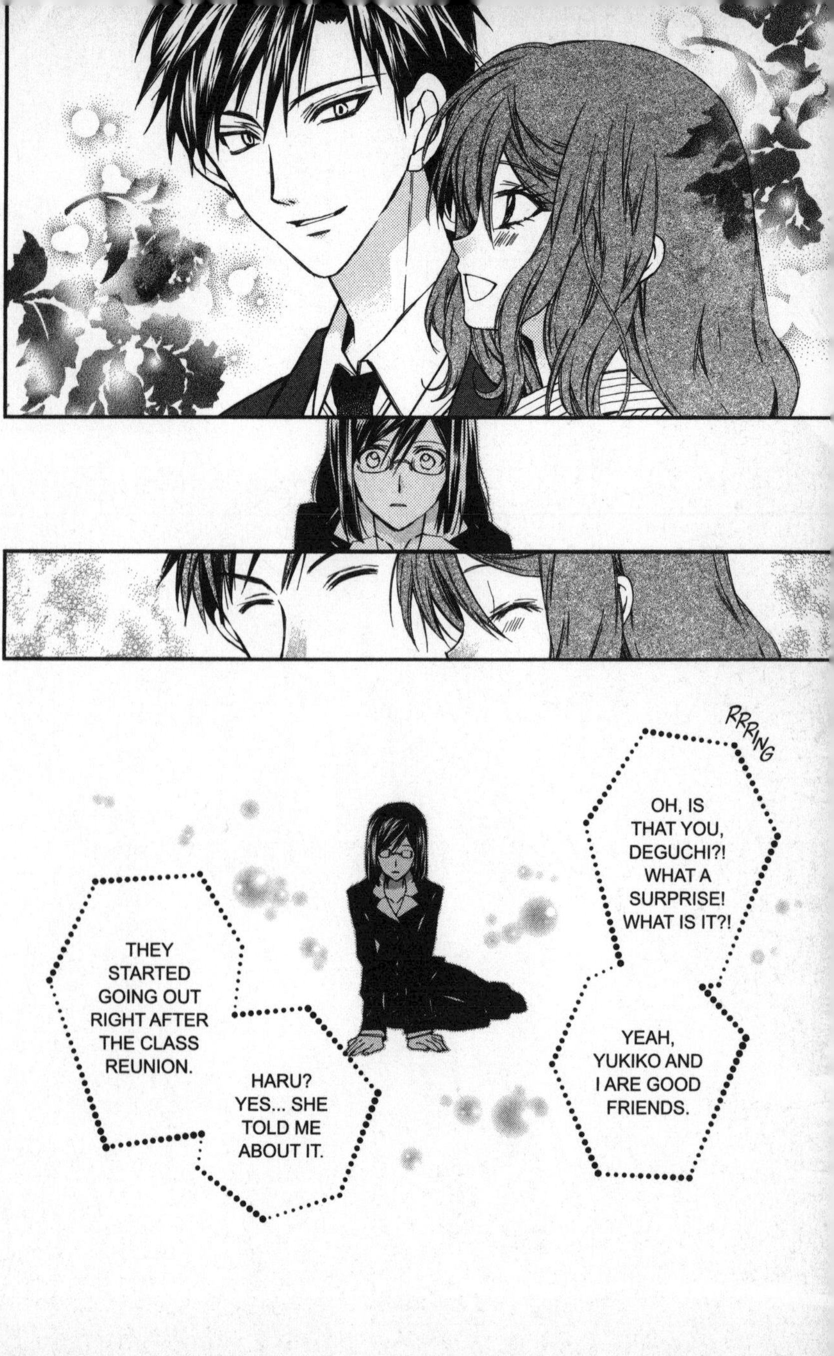
RRRING
OH, IS THAT YOU, DEGUCHI?! WHAT A SURPRISE! WHAT IS IT?!
YEAH, YUKIKO AND I ARE GOOD FRIENDS.
HARU? YES... SHE TOLD ME ABOUT IT.
THEY STARTED GOING OUT RIGHT AFTER THE CLASS REUNION.

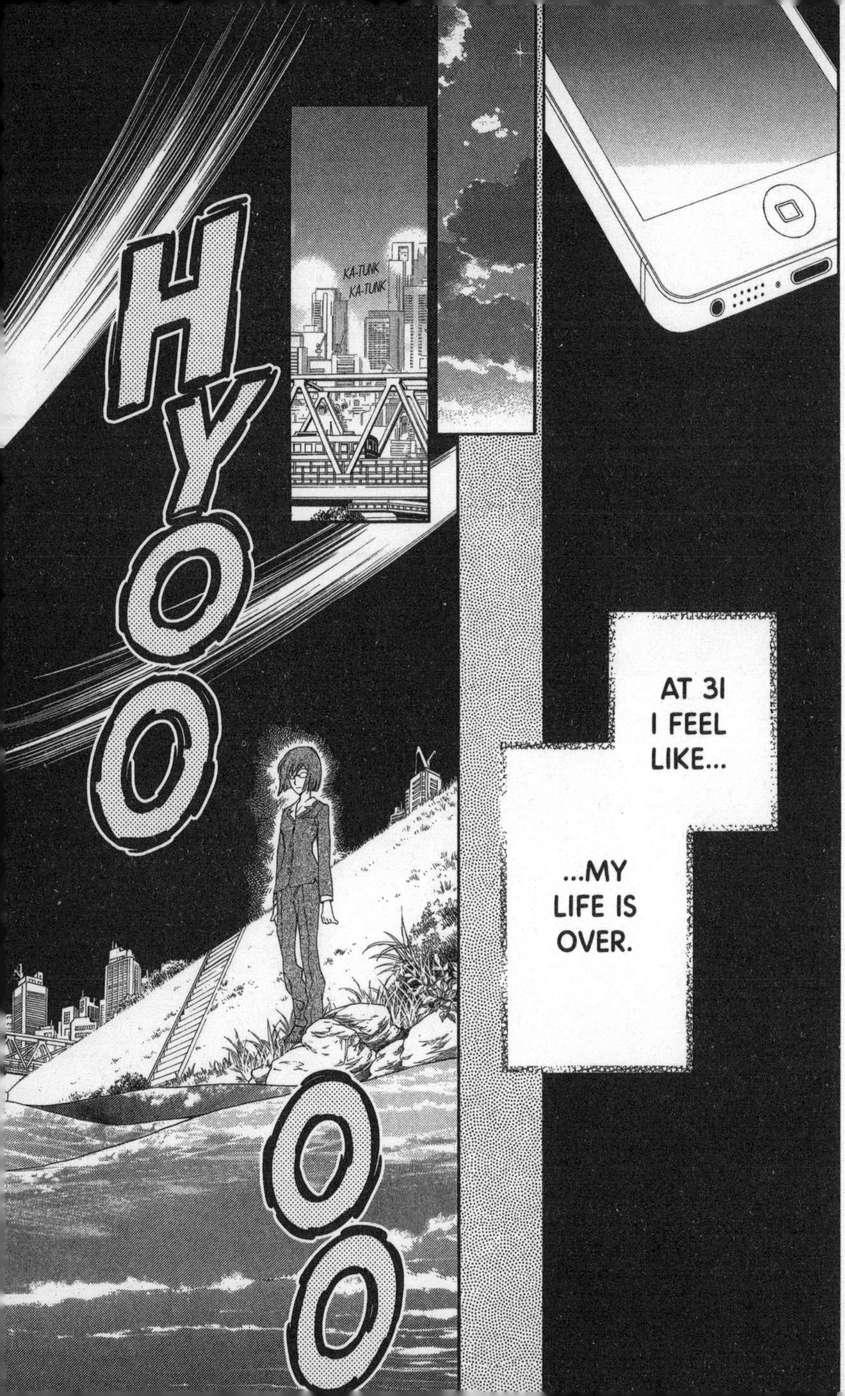
KA-TUNK
KA-TUNK
AT 31 I FEEL LIKE...
...MY LIFE IS OVER.
HYOOOOO

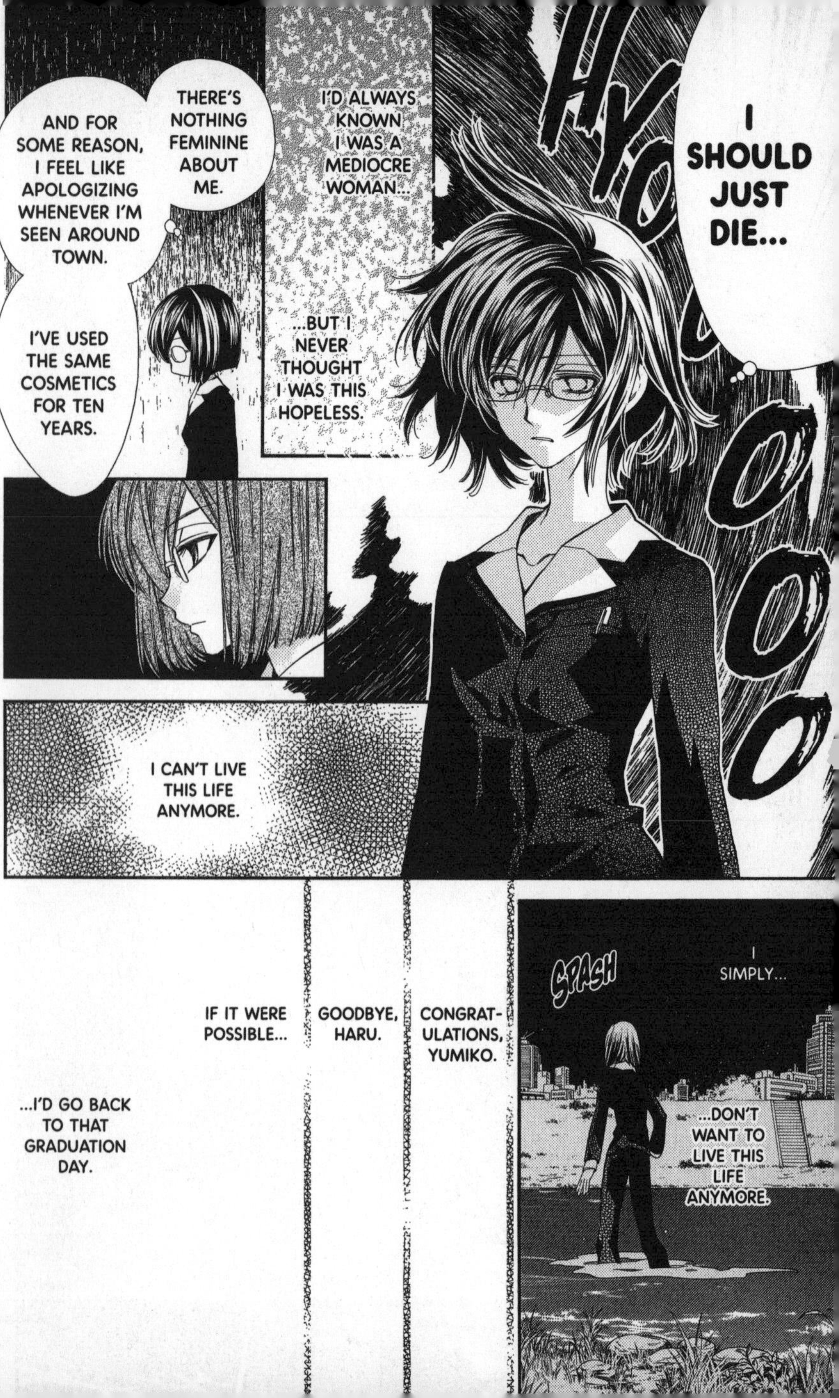
HYOOOOOOO
I SHOULD JUST DIE...
I'D ALWAYS KNOWN I WAS A MEDIOCRE WOMAN...
...BUT I NEVER THOUGHT I WAS THIS HOPELESS.
THERE'S NOTHING FEMININE ABOUT ME.
AND FOR SOME REASON, I FEEL LIKE APOLOGIZING WHENEVER I'M SEEN AROUND TOWN.
I'VE USED THE SAME COSMETICS FOR TEN YEARS.
I CAN'T LIVE THIS LIFE ANYMORE.
I SIMPLY...
SPASH
...DON'T WANT TO LIVE THIS LIFE ANYMORE.
CONGRAT-ULATIONS, YUMIKO.
GOODBYE, HARU.
IF IT WERE POSSIBLE...
...I'D GO BACK TO THAT GRADUATION DAY.

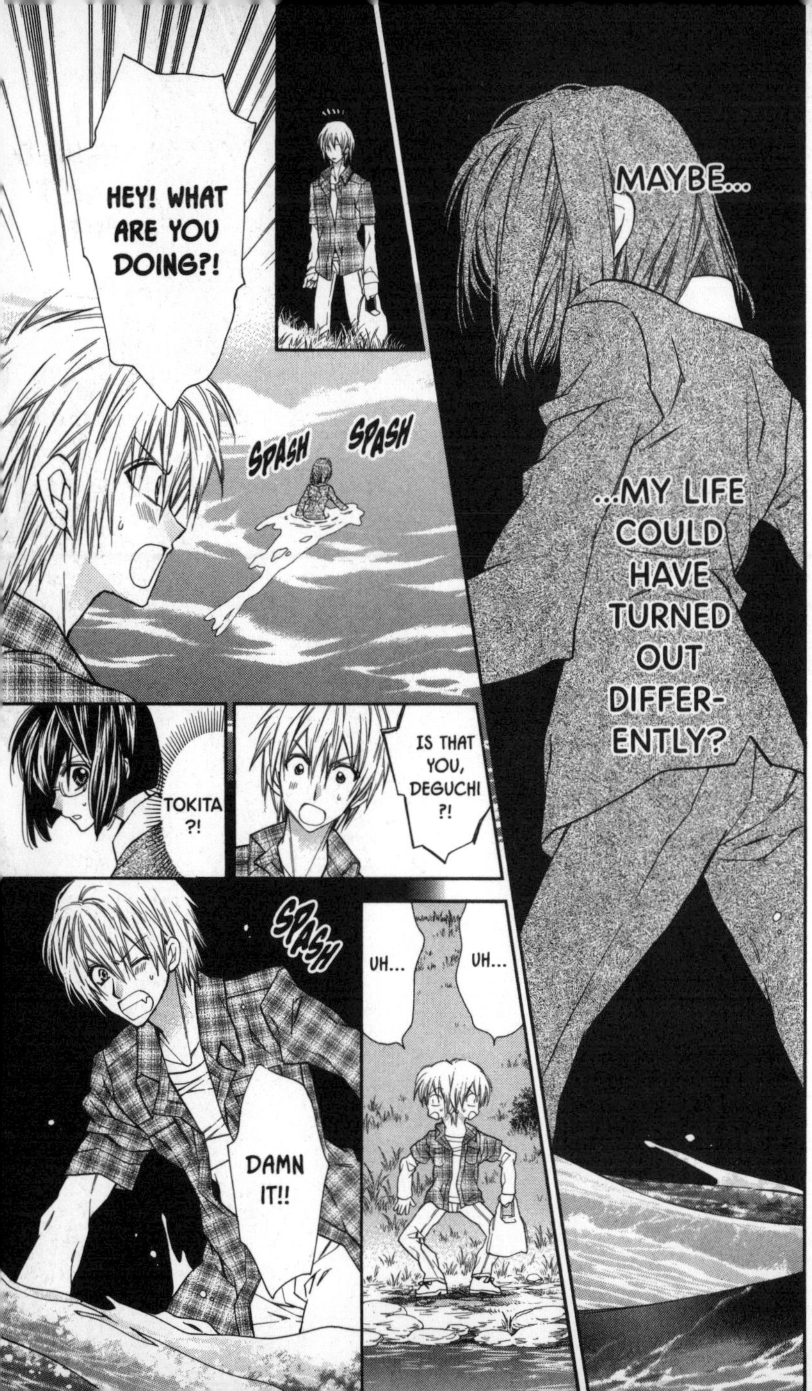
MAYBE...
...MY LIFE COULD HAVE TURNED OUT DIFFER-ENTLY?
HEY! WHAT ARE YOU DOING?!
SPASH
SPASH
IS THAT YOU, DEGUCHI?!
TOKITA?!
UH...
UH...
SPASH
DAMN IT!!

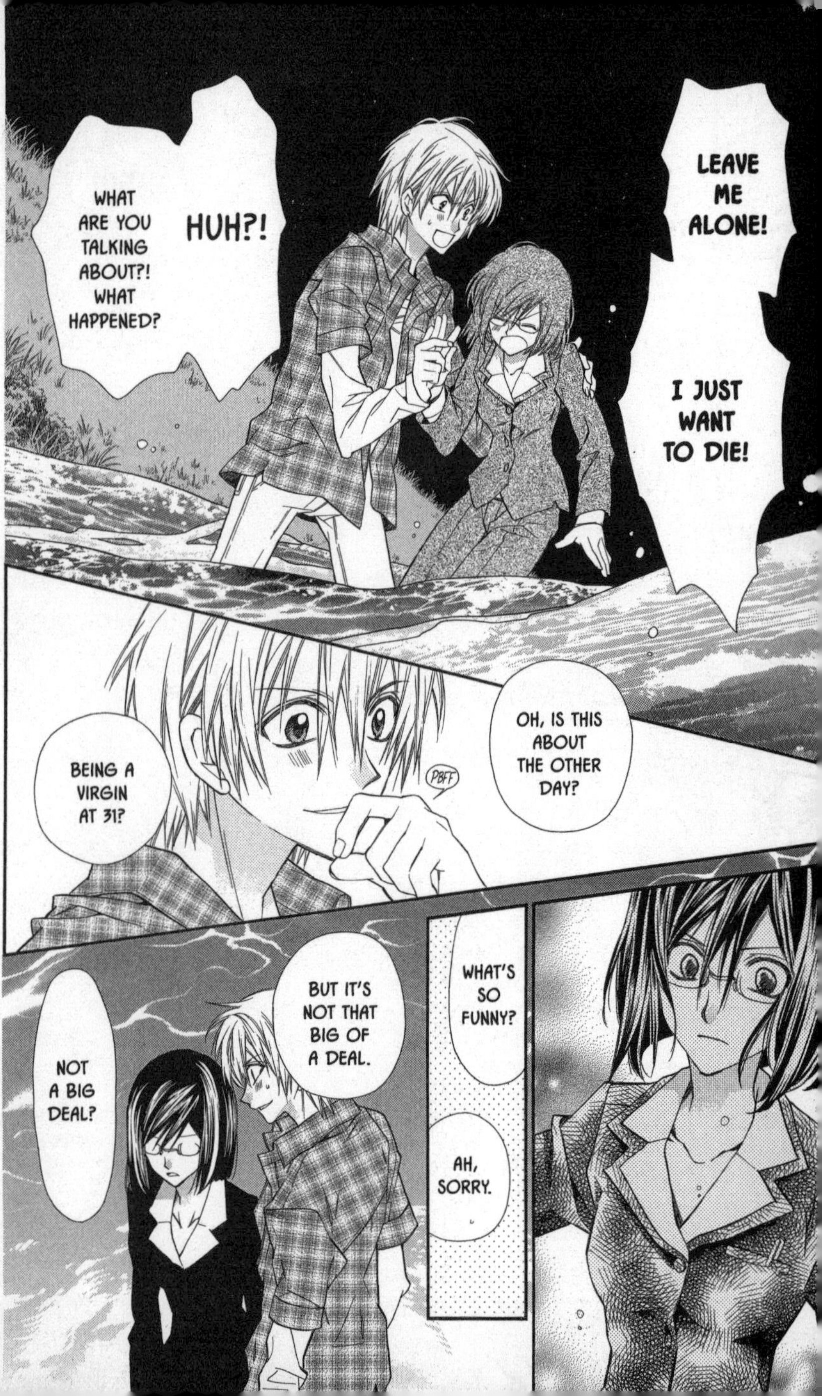
LEAVE ME ALONE!
I JUST WANT TO DIE!
HUH?!
WHAT ARE YOU TALKING ABOUT?! WHAT HAPPENED?
OH, IS THIS ABOUT THE OTHER DAY?
PBFF
BEING A VIRGIN AT 31?
WHAT'S SO FUNNY?
AH, SORRY.
BUT IT'S NOT THAT BIG OF A DEAL.
NOT A BIG DEAL?

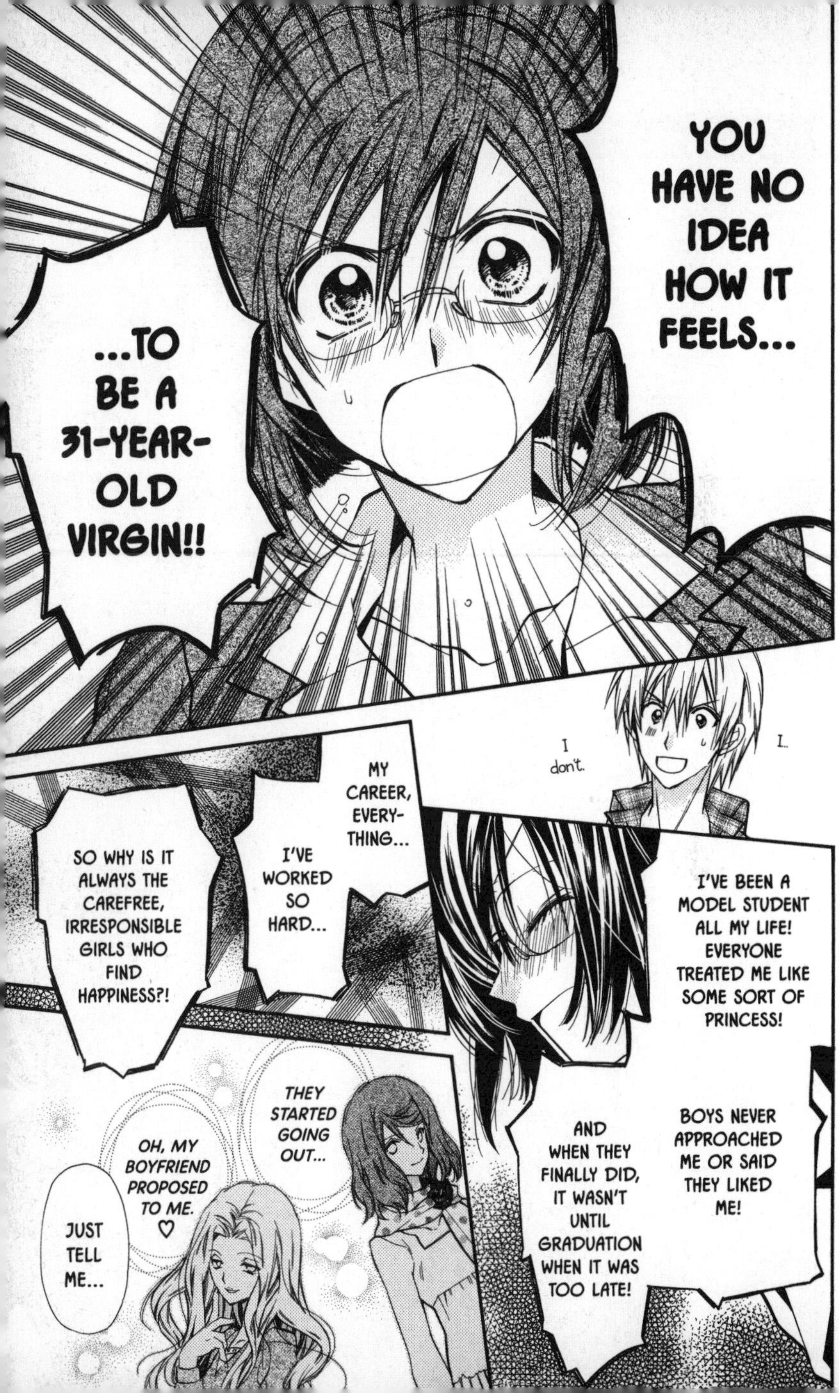

YOU HAVE NO IDEA HOW IT FEELS...
...TO BE A 31-YEAR-OLD VIRGIN!!
I...
I don't.
I'VE BEEN A MODEL STUDENT ALL MY LIFE! EVERYONE TREATED ME LIKE SOME SORT OF PRINCESS!
BOYS NEVER APPROACHED ME OR SAID THEY LIKED ME!
AND WHEN THEY FINALLY DID, IT WASN'T UNTIL GRADUATION WHEN IT WAS TOO LATE!
MY CAREER, EVERYTHING...
I'VE WORKED SO HARD...
SO WHY IS IT ALWAYS THE CAREFREE, IRRESPONSIBLE GIRLS WHO FIND HAPPINESS?!
THEY STARTED GOING OUT...
OH, MY BOYFRIEND PROPOSED TO ME. ♡
JUST TELL ME...

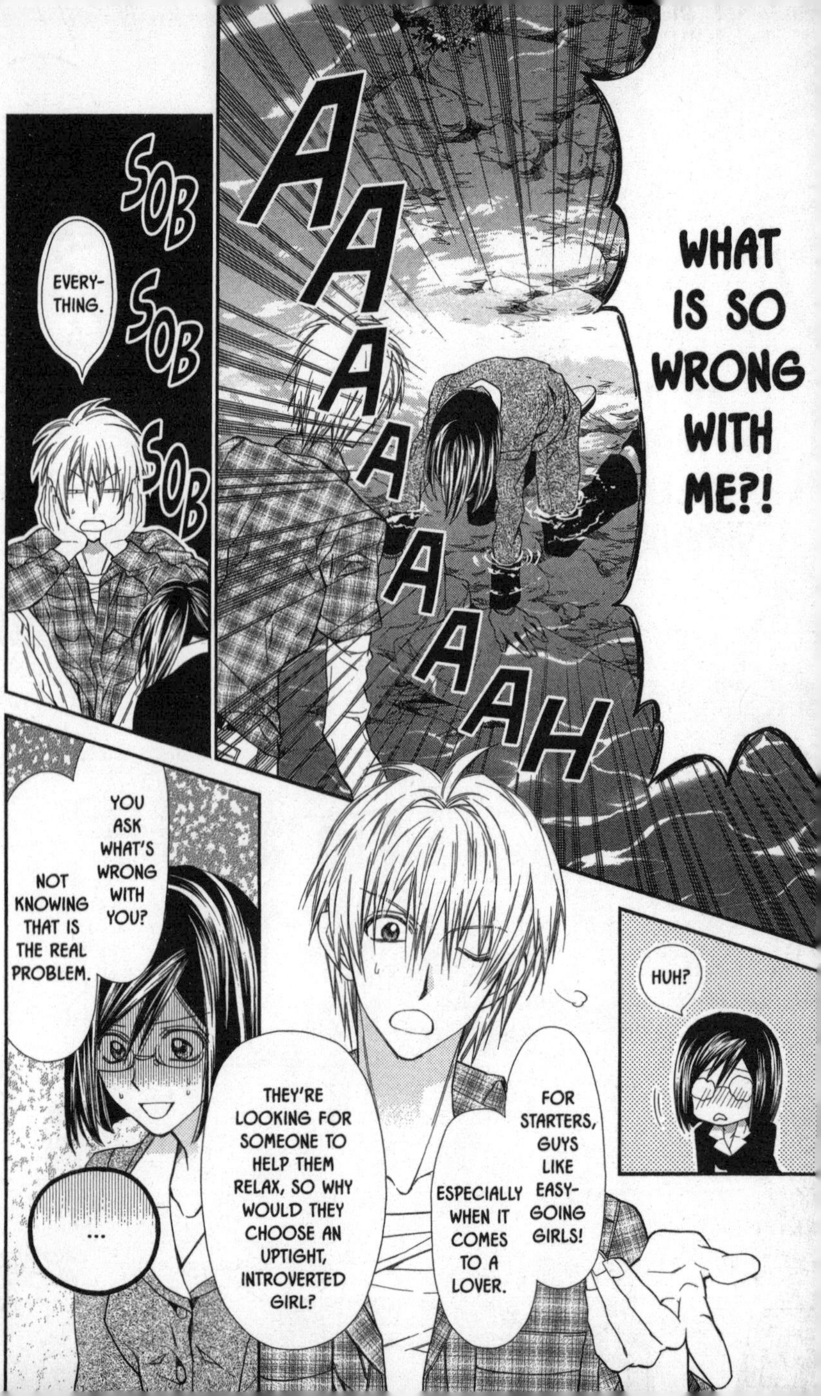
WHAT IS SO WRONG WITH ME?!
AAAAAAAAH
SOB SOB SOB
EVERY-THING.
HUH?
FOR STARTERS, GUYS LIKE EASY-GOING GIRLS!
ESPECIALLY WHEN IT COMES TO A LOVER.
THEY'RE LOOKING FOR SOMEONE TO HELP THEM RELAX, SO WHY WOULD THEY CHOOSE AN UPTIGHT, INTROVERTED GIRL?
YOU ASK WHAT'S WRONG WITH YOU?
NOT KNOWING THAT IS THE REAL PROBLEM.
...

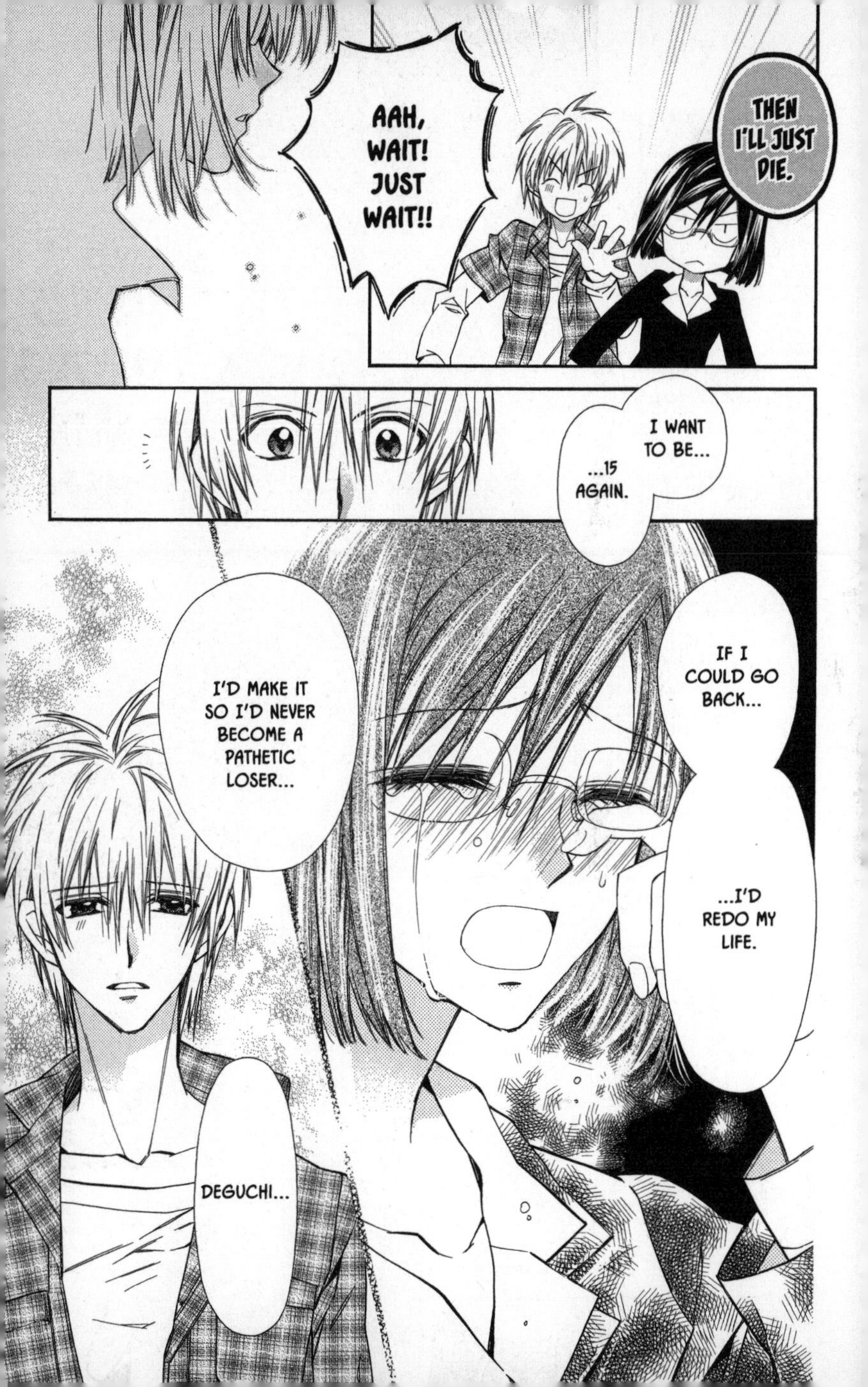
THEN I'LL JUST DIE.
AAH, WAIT! JUST WAIT!!
I WANT TO BE...
...15 AGAIN.
IF I COULD GO BACK...
...I'D REDO MY LIFE.
I'D MAKE IT SO I'D NEVER BECOME A PATHETIC LOSER...
DEGUCHI...

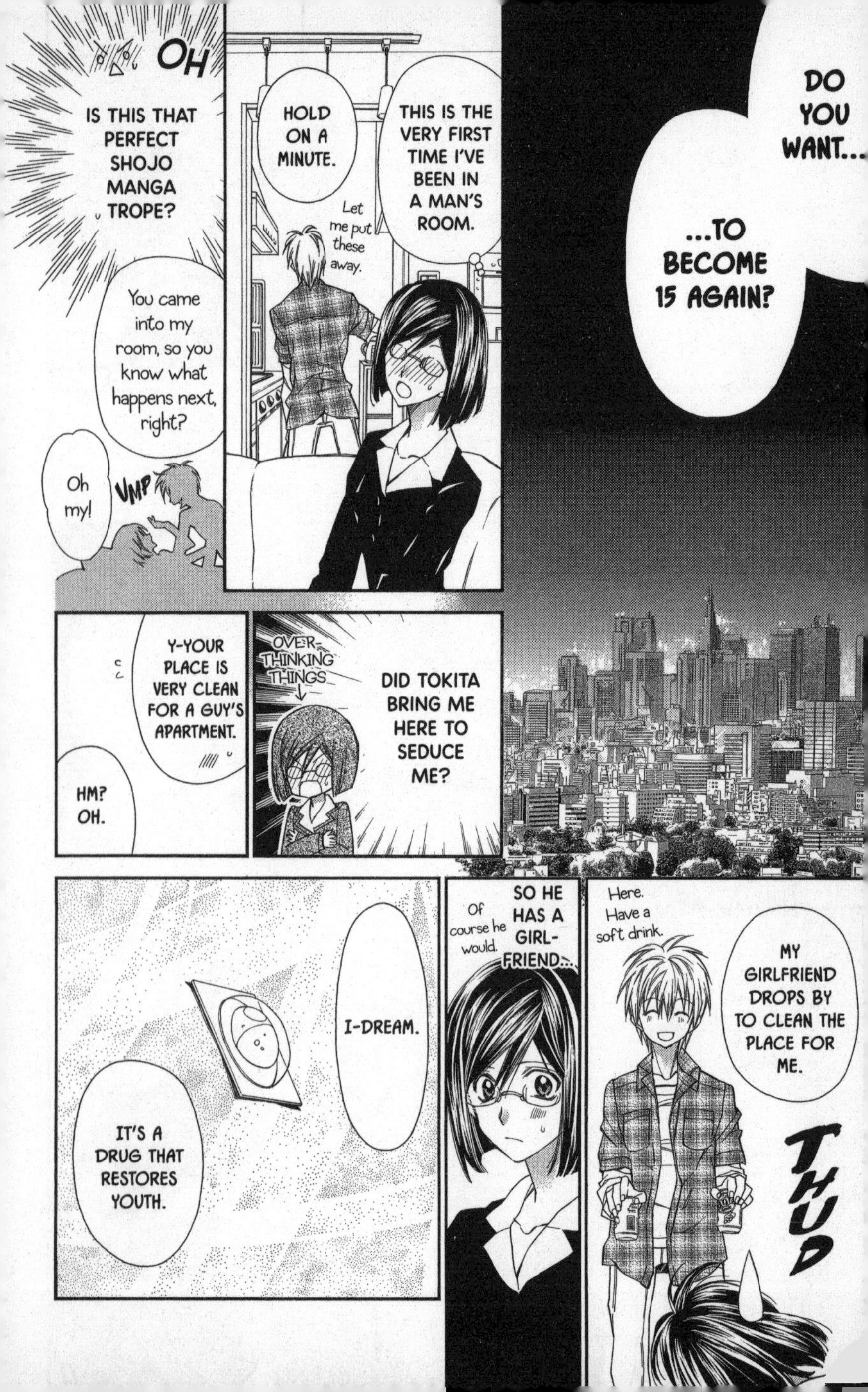
DO YOU WANT...
...TO BECOME 15 AGAIN?
THIS IS THE VERY FIRST TIME I'VE BEEN IN A MAN'S ROOM.
HOLD ON A MINUTE.
Let me put these away.
OH
IS THIS THAT PERFECT SHOJO MANGA TROPE?
You came into my room, so you know what happens next, right?
UMP
Oh my!
DID TOKITA BRING ME HERE TO SEDUCE ME?
OVER-THINKING THINGS
Y-YOUR PLACE IS VERY CLEAN FOR A GUY'S APARTMENT.
HM? OH.
Here. Have a soft drink.
MY GIRLFRIEND DROPS BY TO CLEAN THE PLACE FOR ME.
THUD
SO HE HAS A GIRLFRIEND...
Of course he would.
I-DREAM.
IT'S A DRUG THAT RESTORES YOUTH.

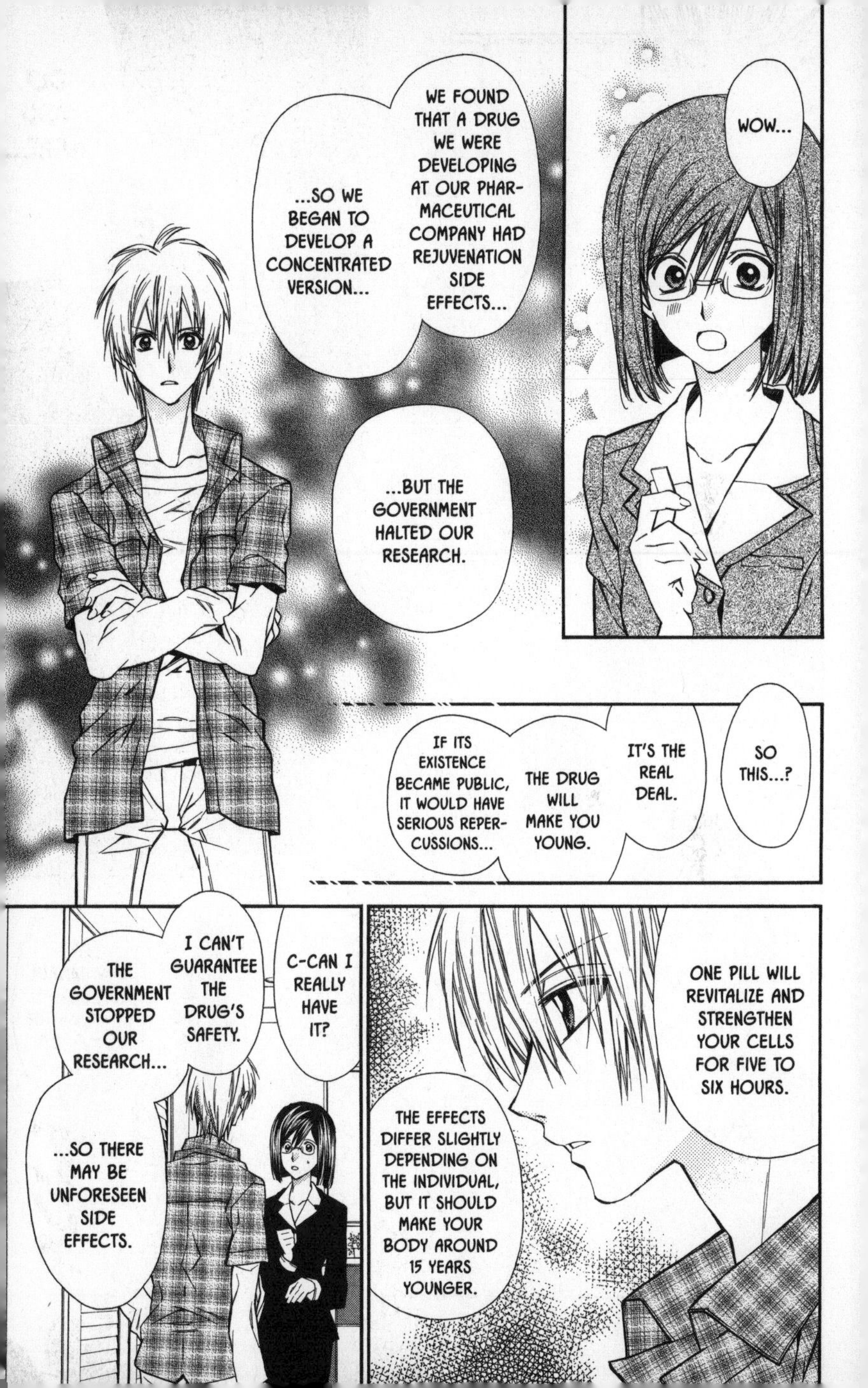
WOW...
SO THIS...?
IT'S THE REAL DEAL.
THE DRUG WILL MAKE YOU YOUNG.
IF ITS EXISTENCE BECAME PUBLIC, IT WOULD HAVE SERIOUS REPERCUSSIONS...
WE FOUND THAT A DRUG WE WERE DEVELOPING AT OUR PHARMACEUTICAL COMPANY HAD REJUVENATION SIDE EFFECTS...
...SO WE BEGAN TO DEVELOP A CONCENTRATED VERSION...
...BUT THE GOVERNMENT HALTED OUR RESEARCH.
ONE PILL WILL REVITALIZE AND STRENGTHEN YOUR CELLS FOR FIVE TO SIX HOURS.
THE EFFECTS DIFFER SLIGHTLY DEPENDING ON THE INDIVIDUAL, BUT IT SHOULD MAKE YOUR BODY AROUND 15 YEARS YOUNGER.
C-CAN I REALLY HAVE IT?
I CAN'T GUARANTEE THE DRUG'S SAFETY.
THE GOVERNMENT STOPPED OUR RESEARCH...
...SO THERE MAY BE UNFORESEEN SIDE EFFECTS.

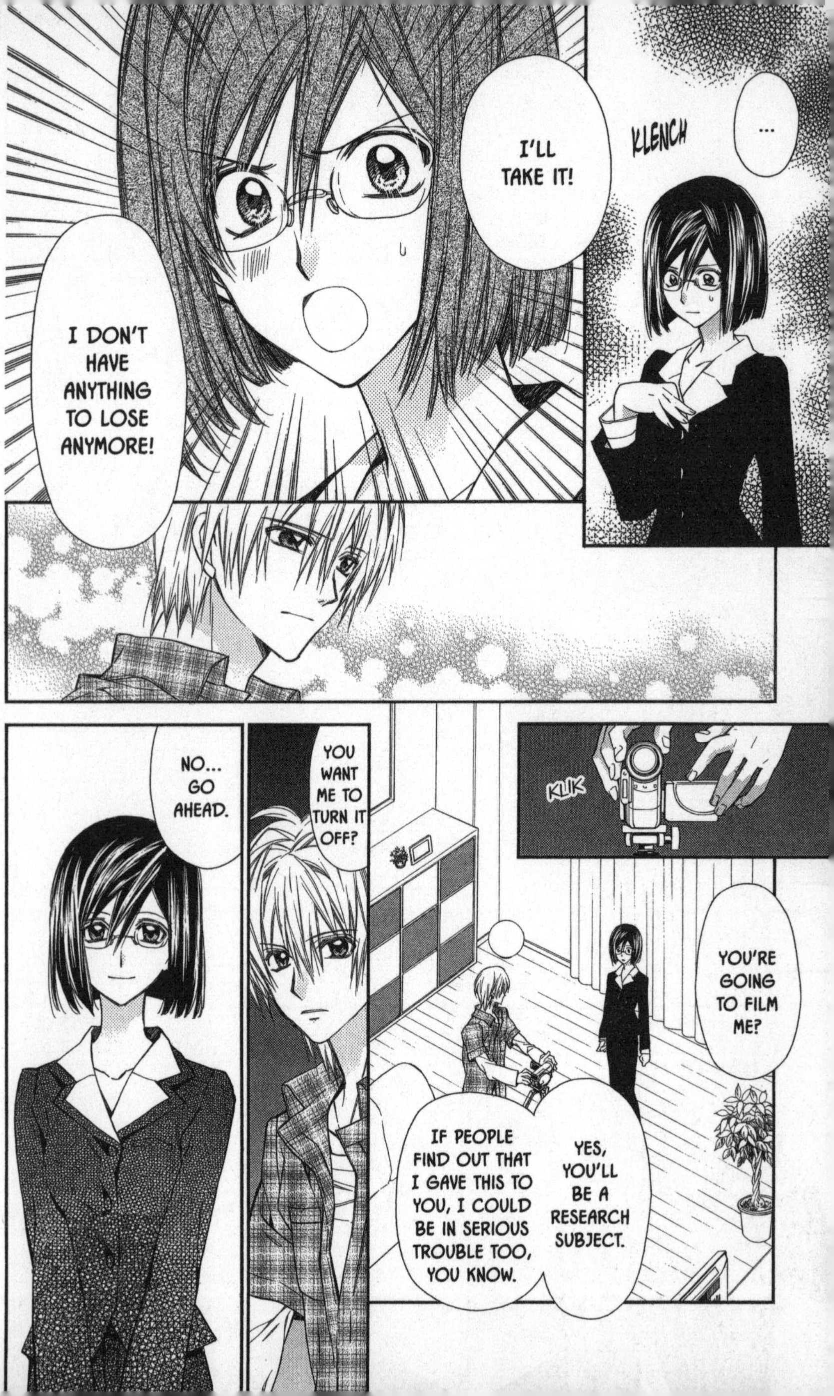
...
KLENCH
I'LL TAKE IT!
I DON'T HAVE ANYTHING TO LOSE ANYMORE!
KLIK
YOU'RE GOING TO FILM ME?
YES, YOU'LL BE A RESEARCH SUBJECT.
IF PEOPLE FIND OUT THAT I GAVE THIS TO YOU, I COULD BE IN SERIOUS TROUBLE TOO, YOU KNOW.
YOU WANT ME TO TURN IT OFF?
NO... GO AHEAD.

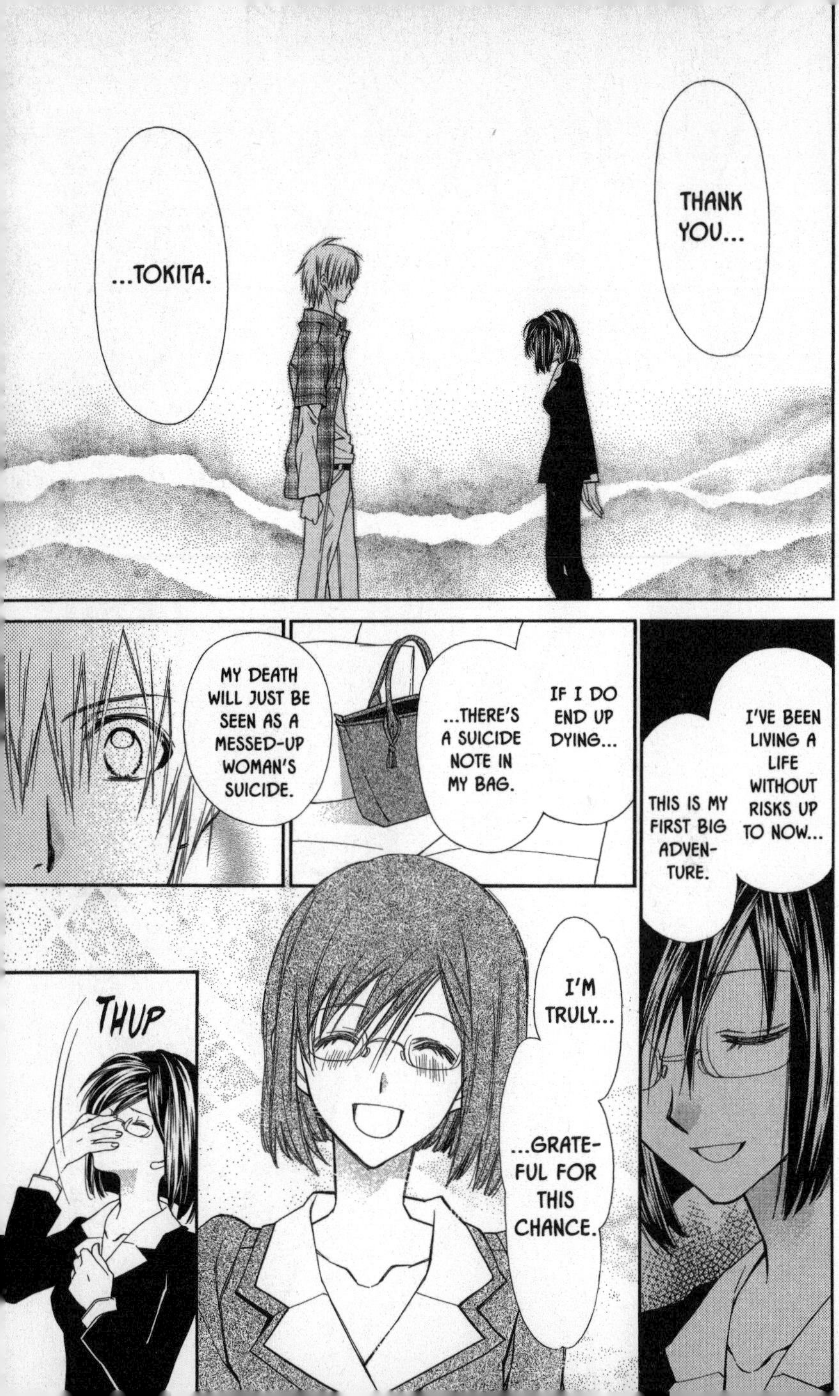
THANK YOU...
...TOKITA.
I'VE BEEN LIVING A LIFE WITHOUT RISKS UP TO NOW...
THIS IS MY FIRST BIG ADVEN-TURE.
IF I DO END UP DYING...
...THERE'S A SUICIDE NOTE IN MY BAG.
MY DEATH WILL JUST BE SEEN AS A MESSED-UP WOMAN'S SUICIDE.
I'M TRULY...
...GRATE-FUL FOR THIS CHANCE.
THUP

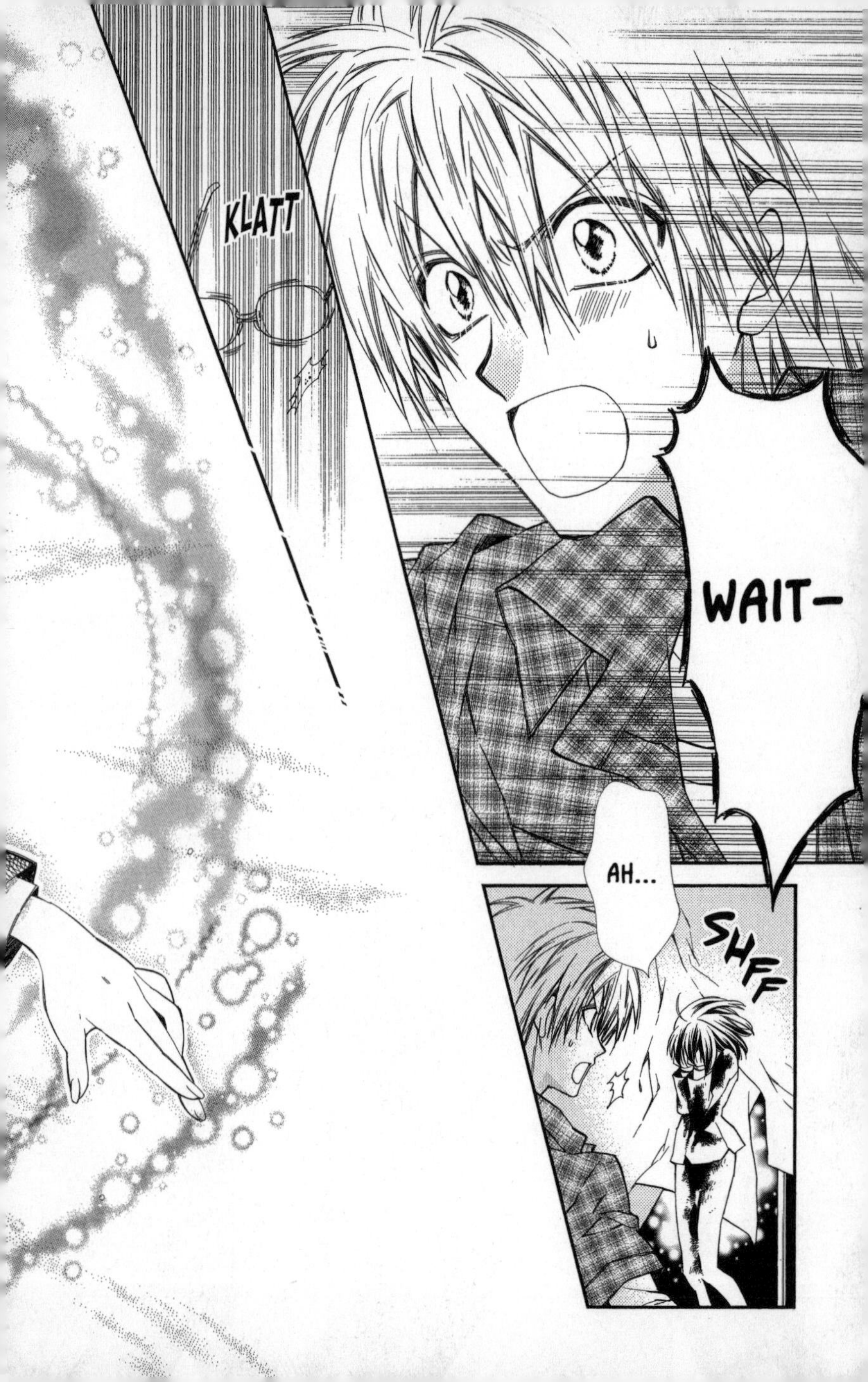
WAIT-
AH...
SHFF
KLATT

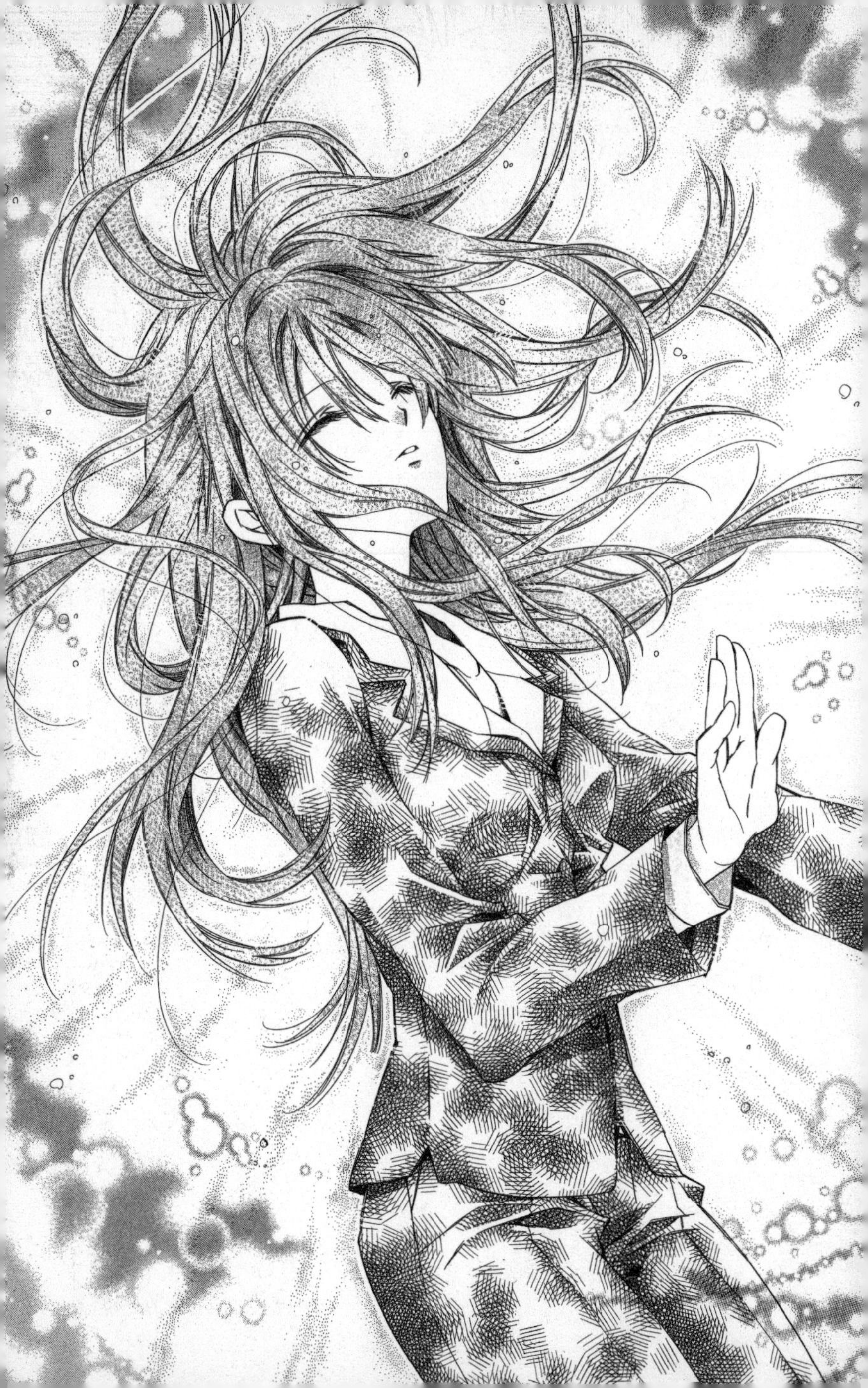

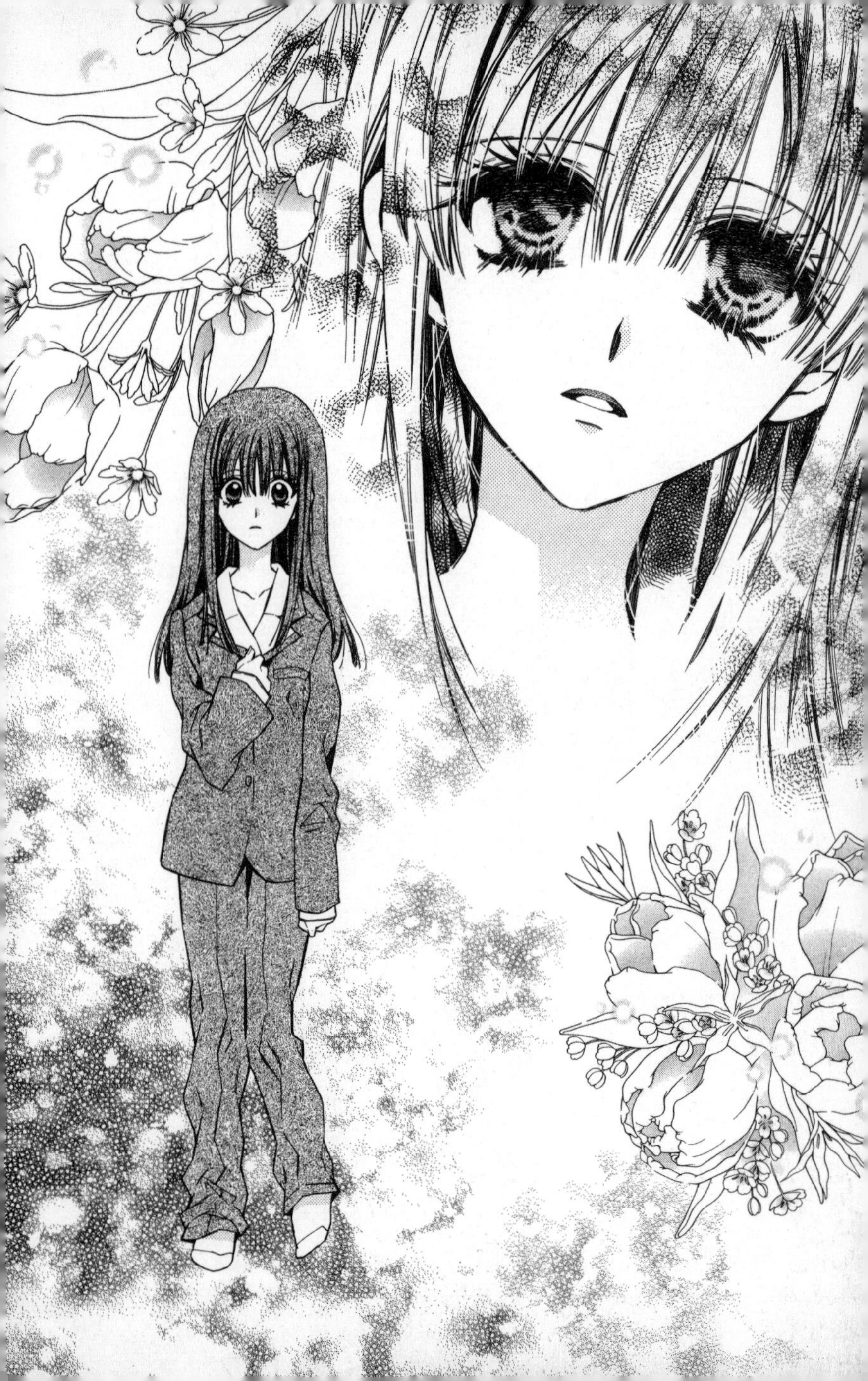

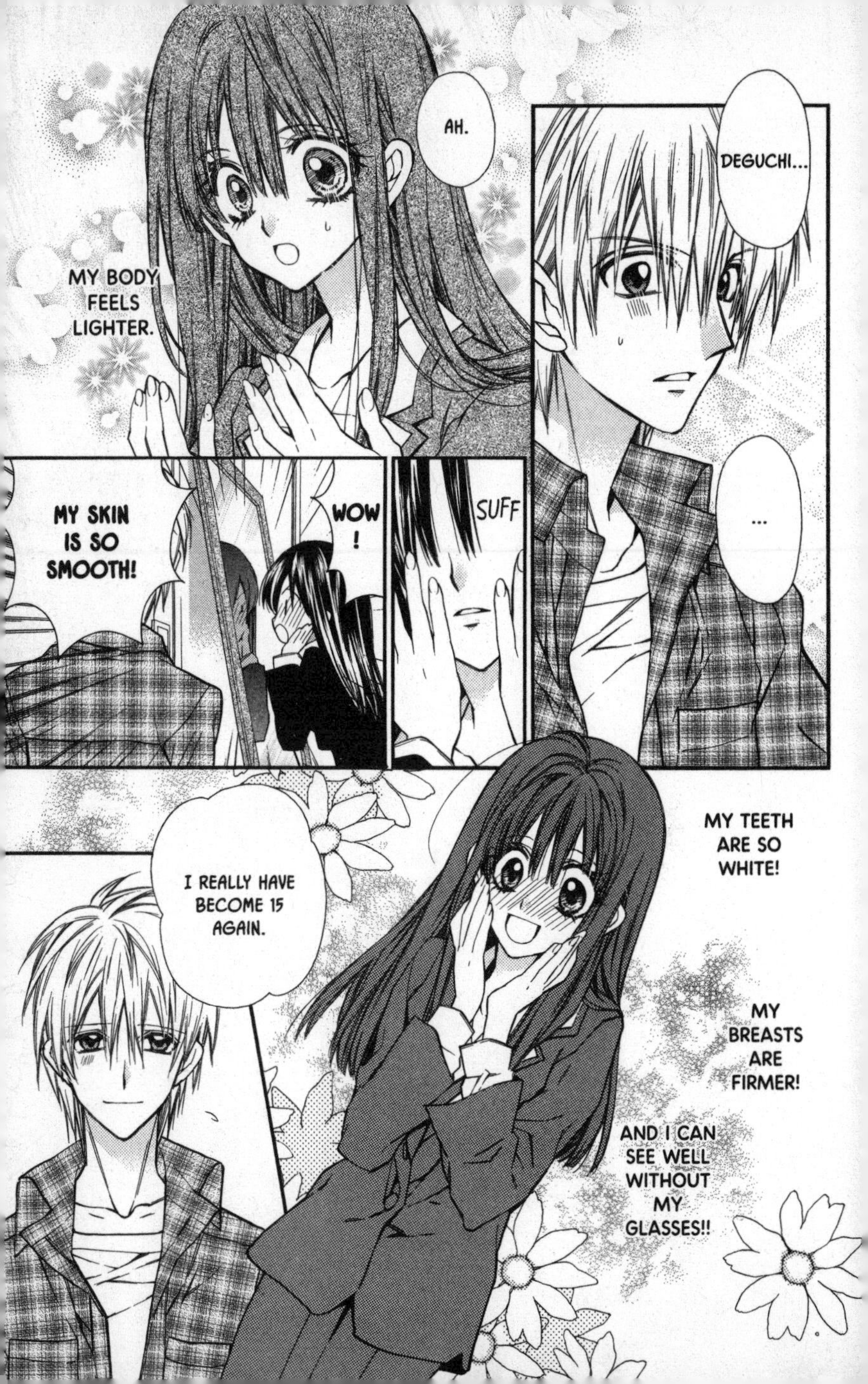
DEGUCHI...
...
AH.
MY BODY FEELS LIGHTER.
SUFF
WOW!
MY SKIN IS SO SMOOTH!
MY TEETH ARE SO WHITE!
MY BREASTS ARE FIRMER!
AND I CAN SEE WELL WITHOUT MY GLASSES!!
I REALLY HAVE BECOME 15 AGAIN.

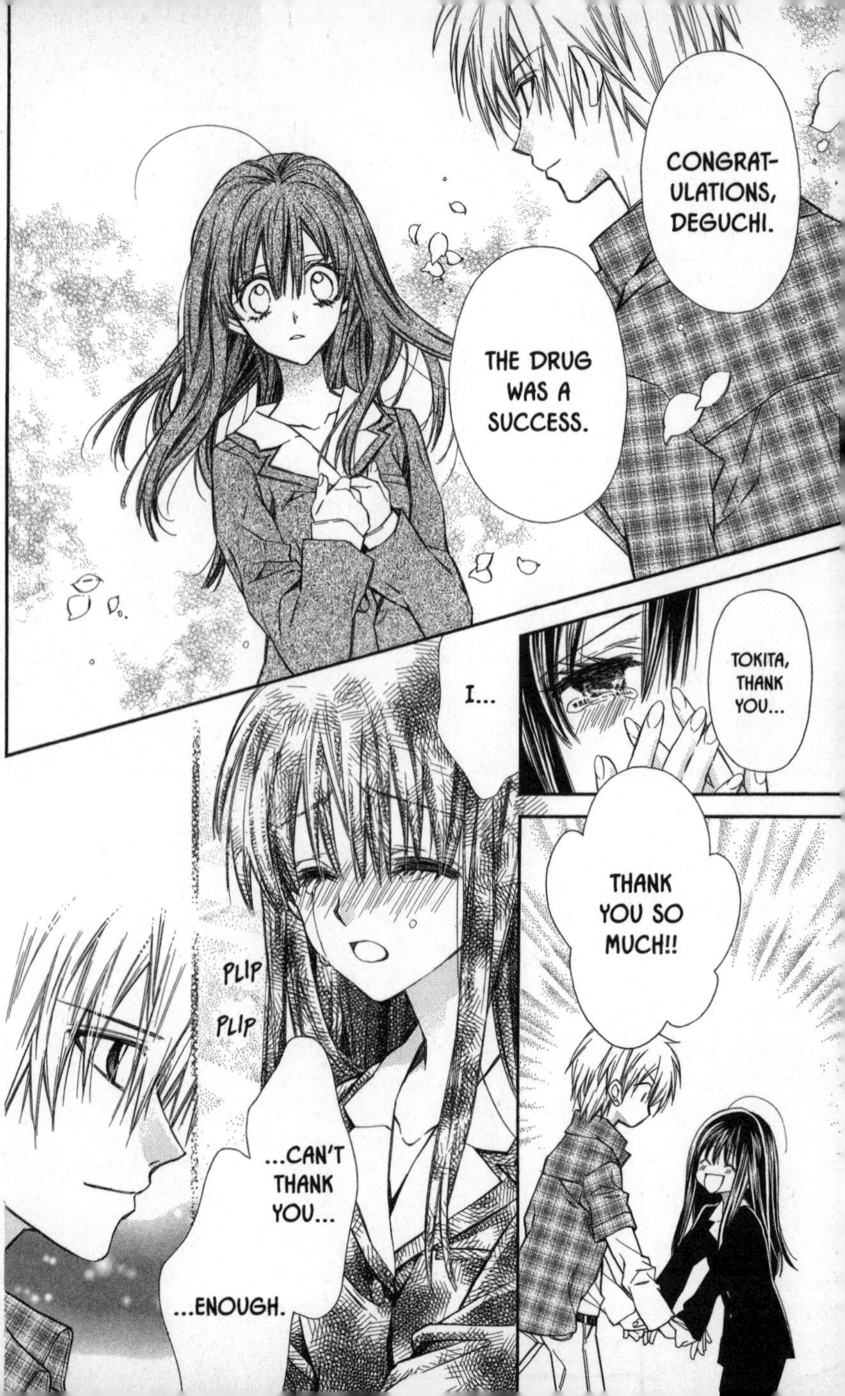
CONGRAT-ULATIONS, DEGUCHI.
THE DRUG WAS A SUCCESS.
TOKITA, THANK YOU...
THANK YOU SO MUCH!!
I...
PLIP
PLIP
...CAN'T THANK YOU...
...ENOUGH.

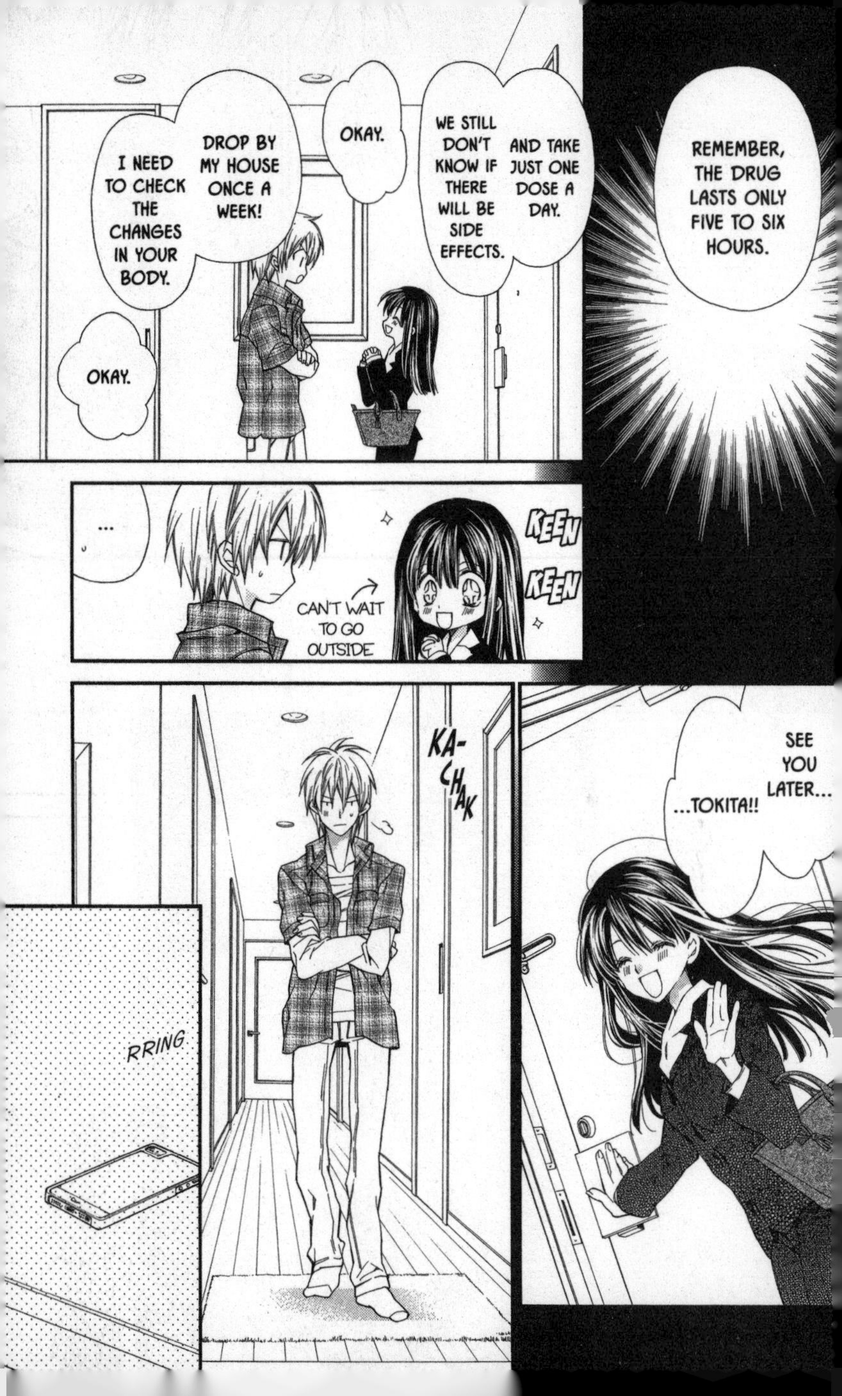
REMEMBER, THE DRUG LASTS ONLY FIVE TO SIX HOURS.
AND TAKE JUST ONE DOSE A DAY.
WE STILL DON'T KNOW IF THERE WILL BE SIDE EFFECTS.
OKAY.
DROP BY MY HOUSE ONCE A WEEK!
I NEED TO CHECK THE CHANGES IN YOUR BODY.
OKAY.
KEEN
KEEN
CAN'T WAIT TO GO OUTSIDE
...
SEE YOU LATER...
...TOKITA!!
KA-CHAK
RRING

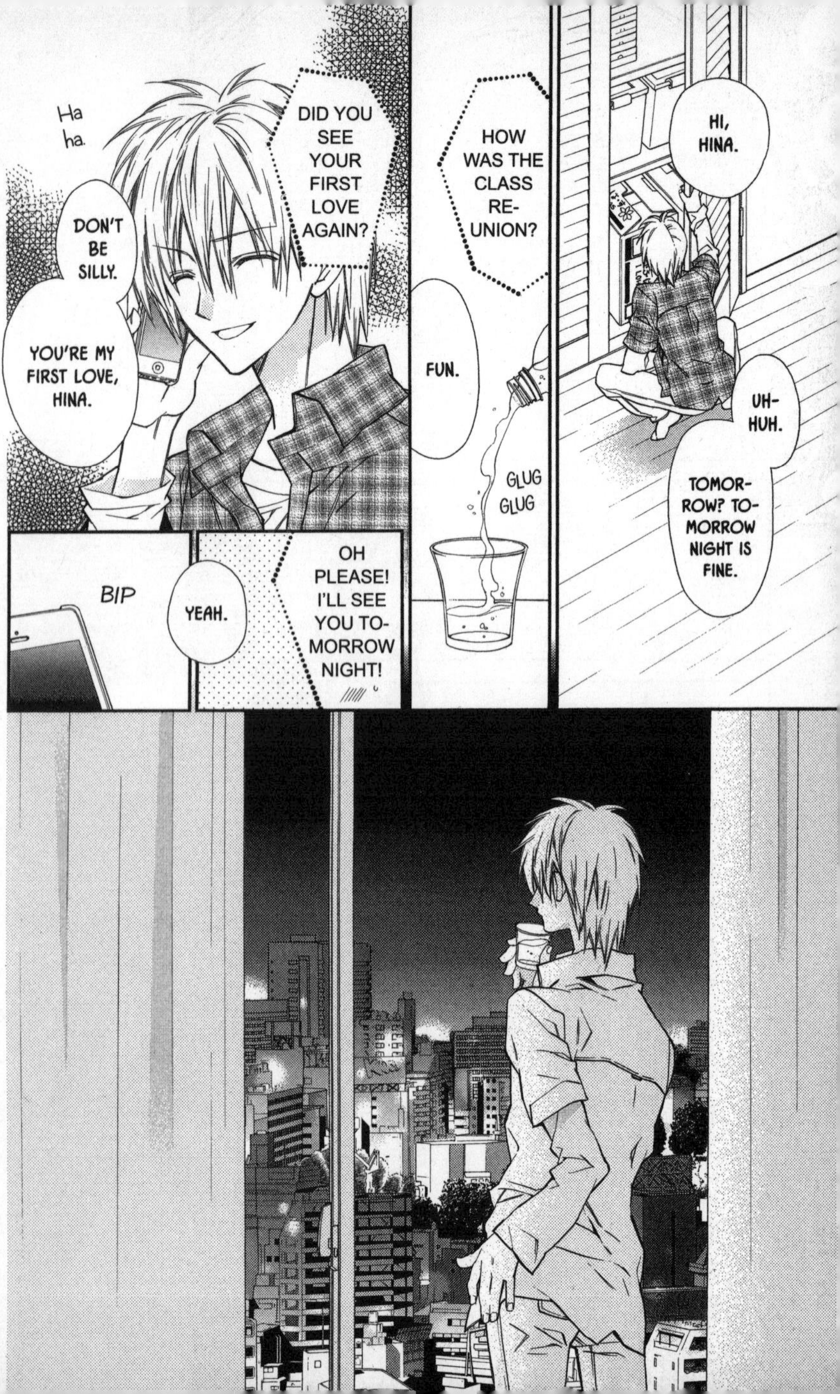
HI, HINA.
UH-HUH.
TOMOR-ROW? TO-MORROW NIGHT IS FINE.
HOW WAS THE CLASS RE-UNION?
FUN.
GLUG GLUG
DID YOU SEE YOUR FIRST LOVE AGAIN?
Ha ha.
DON'T BE SILLY.
YOU'RE MY FIRST LOVE, HINA.
OH PLEASE! I'LL SEE YOU TO-MORROW NIGHT!
YEAH.
BIP

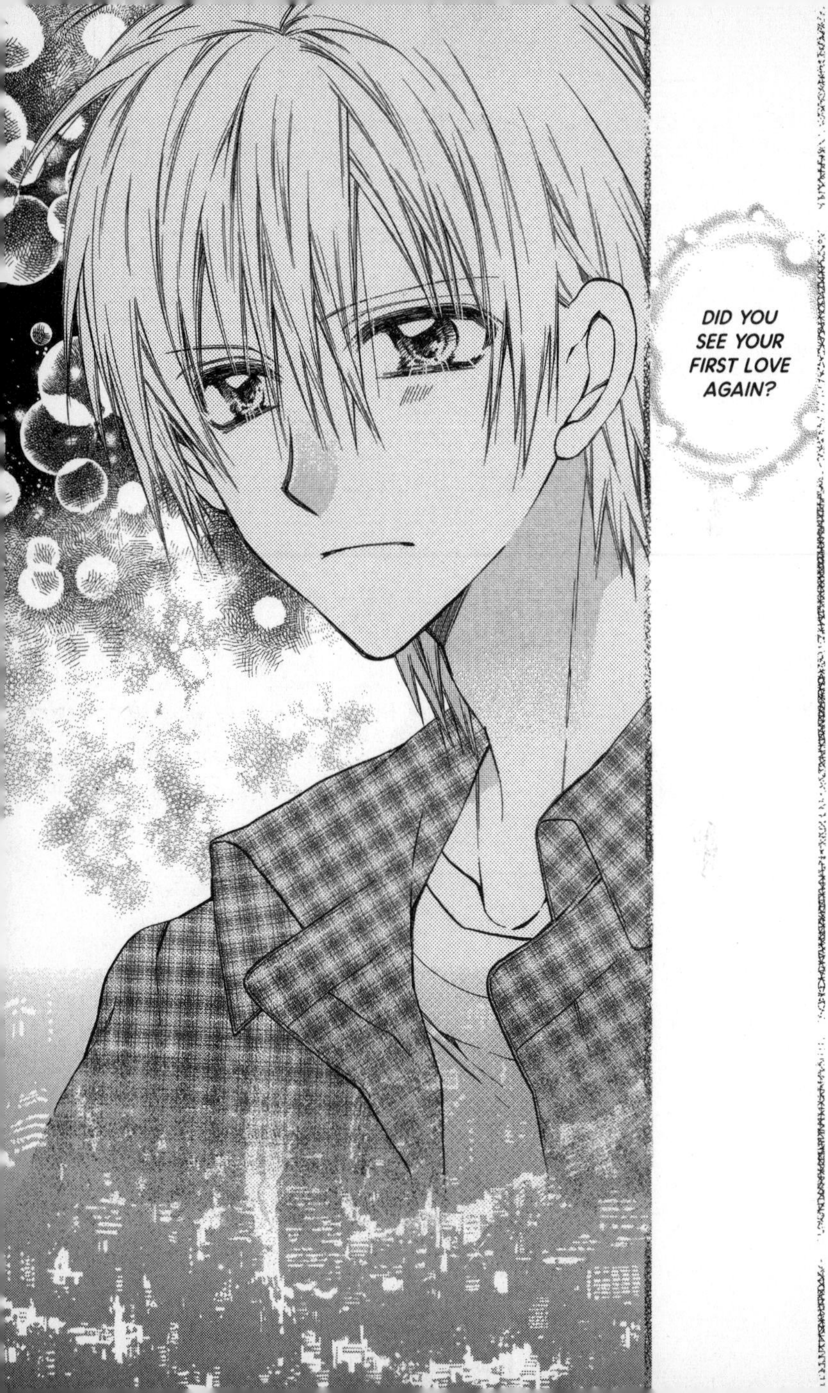
DID YOU SEE YOUR FIRST LOVE AGAIN?

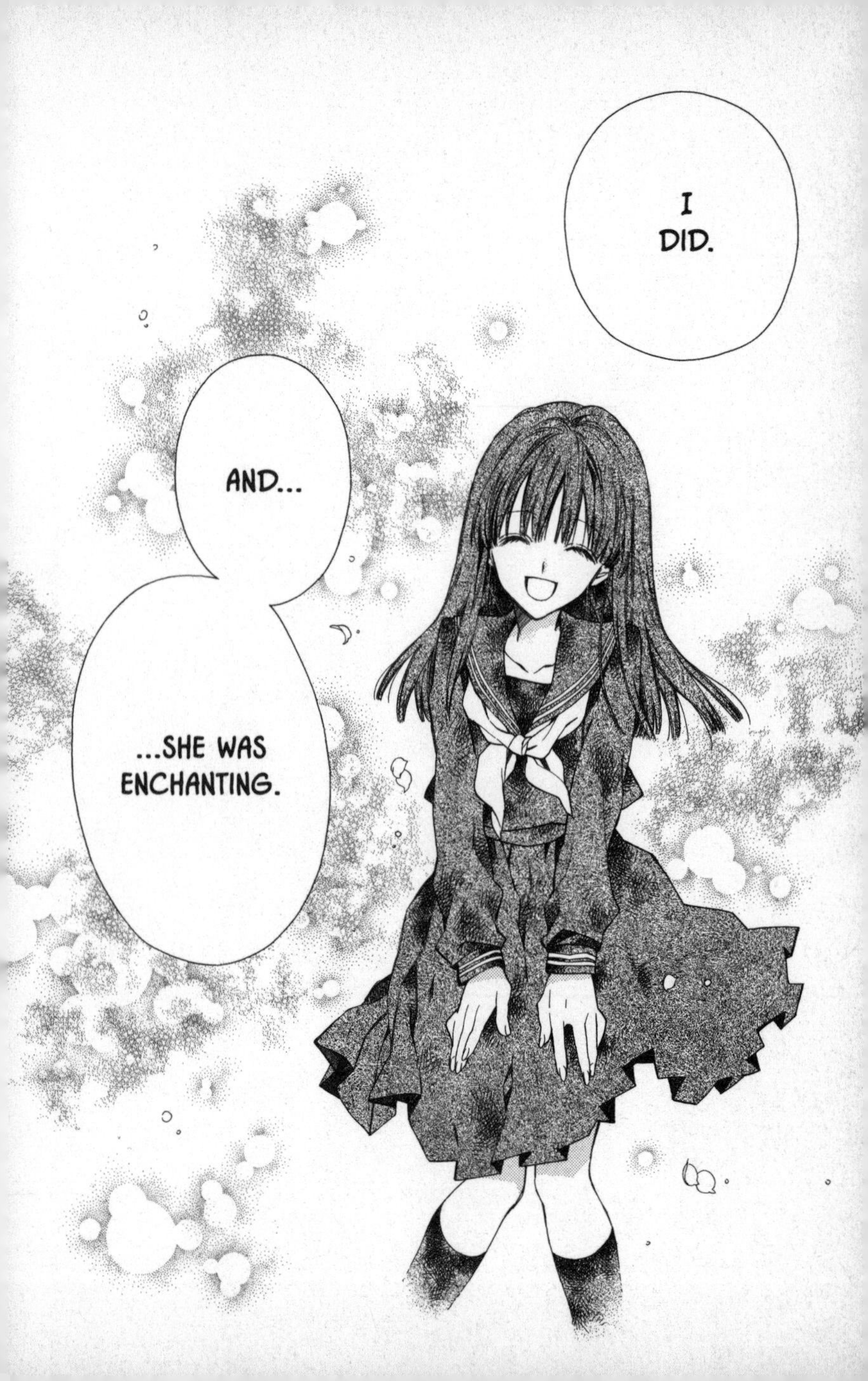
I DID.
AND...
...SHE WAS ENCHANTING.

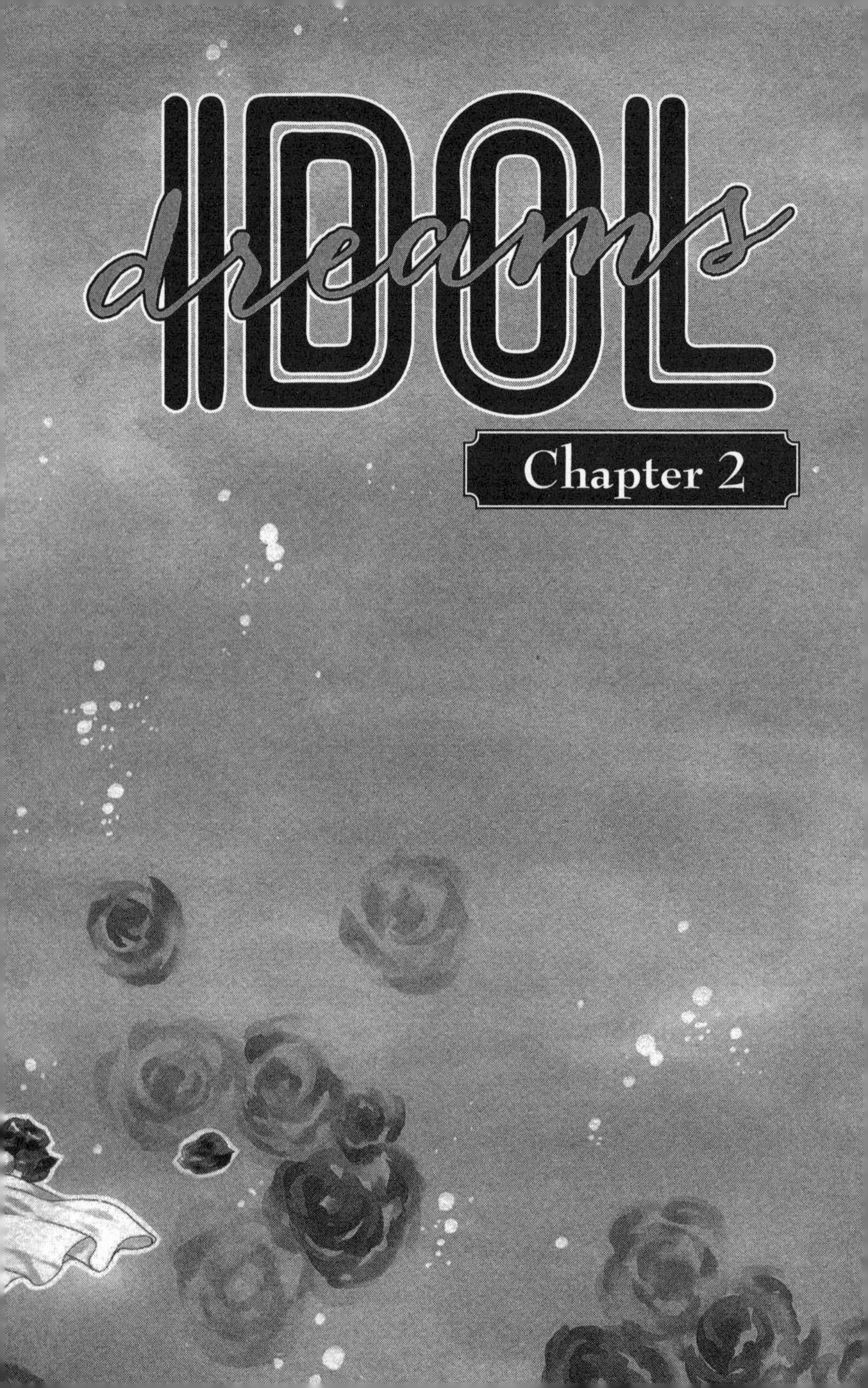
IDOL dreams
Chapter 2

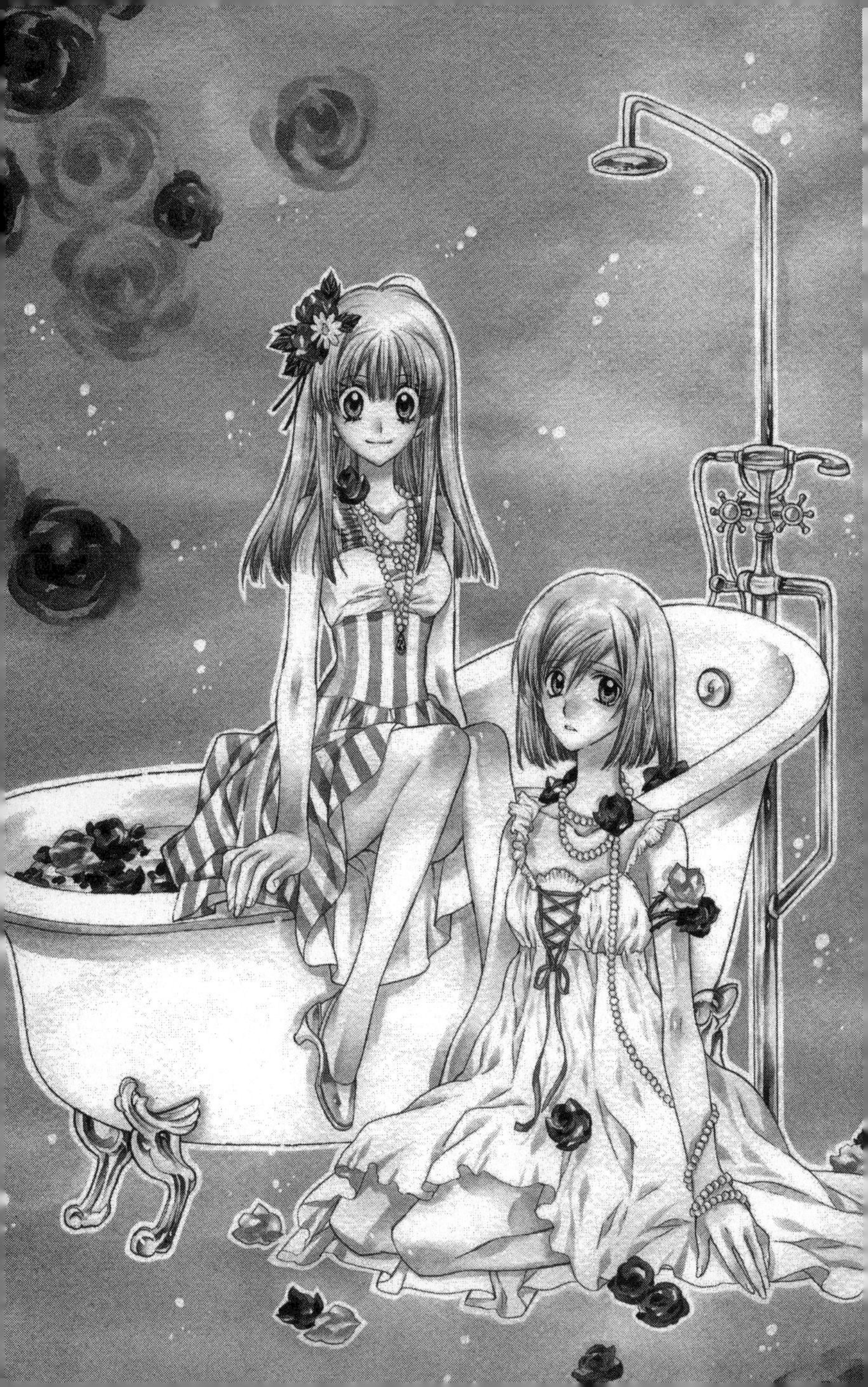

IDOL dreams

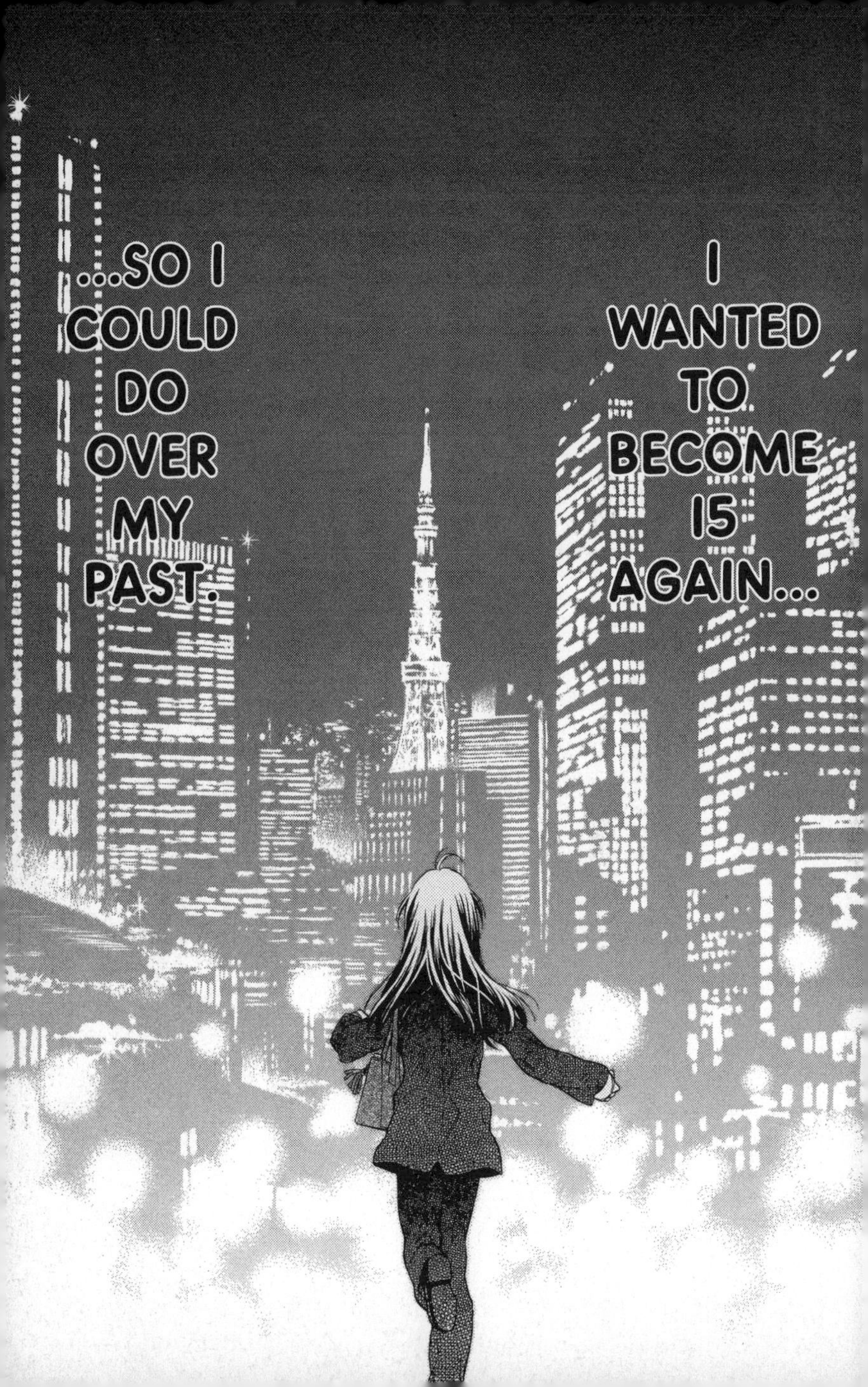
I WANTED TO BECOME 15 AGAIN...
...SO I COULD DO OVER MY PAST.

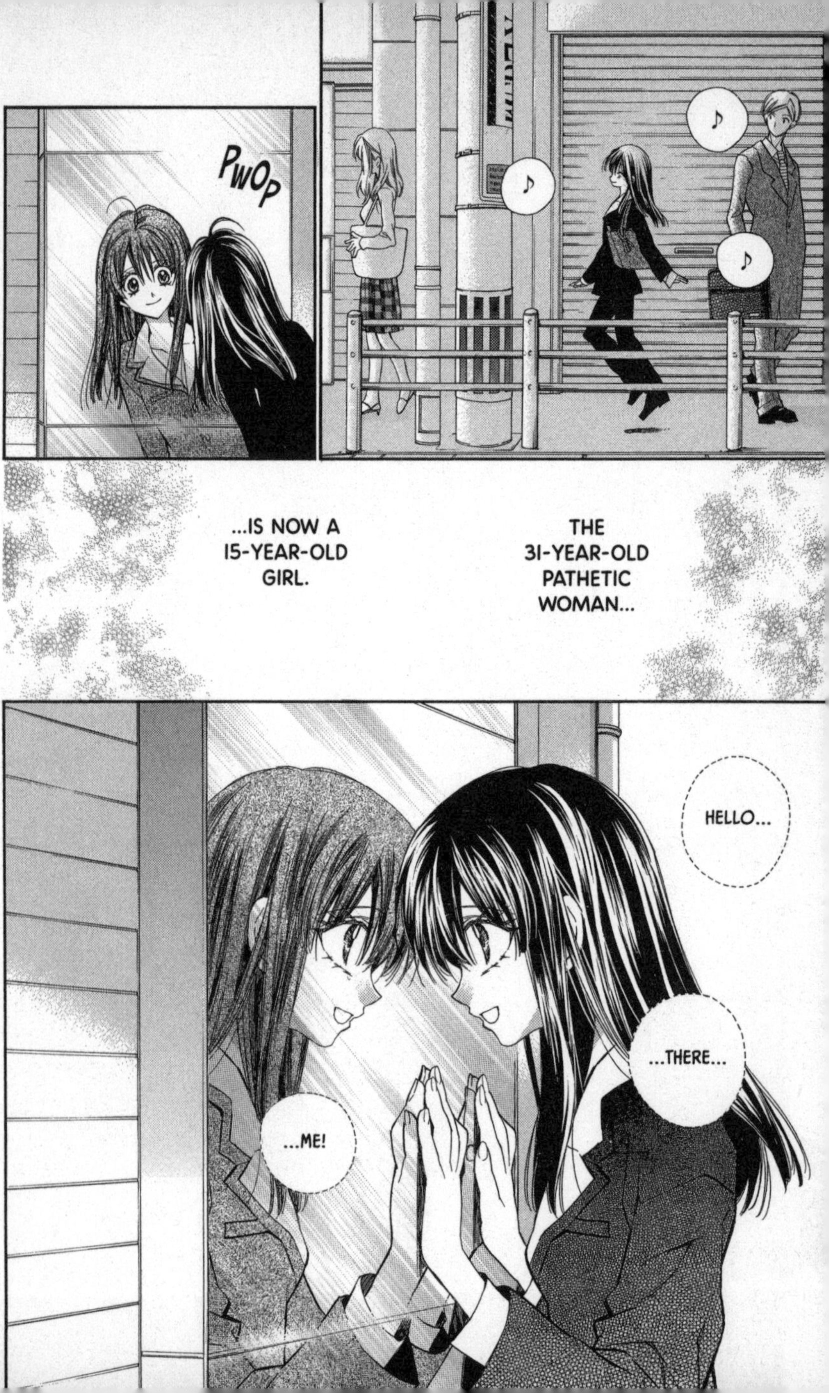
PWOP
THE 31-YEAR-OLD PATHETIC WOMAN...
...IS NOW A 15-YEAR-OLD GIRL.
HELLO...
...THERE...
...ME!

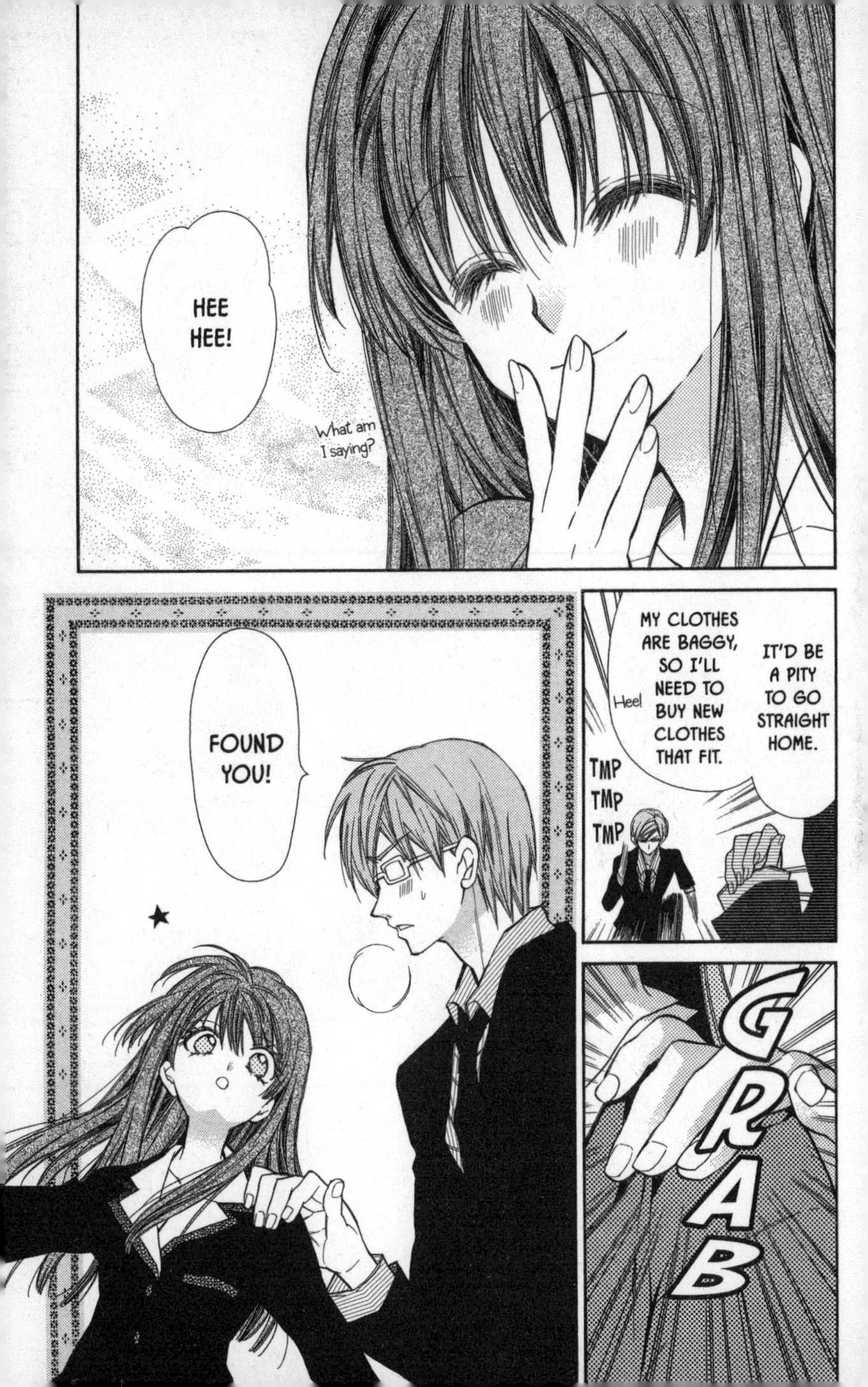
HEE HEE!
What am I saying?
IT'D BE A PITY TO GO STRAIGHT HOME.
MY CLOTHES ARE BAGGY, SO I'LL NEED TO BUY NEW CLOTHES THAT FIT.
Hee!
TMP TMP TMP
GRAB
FOUND YOU!

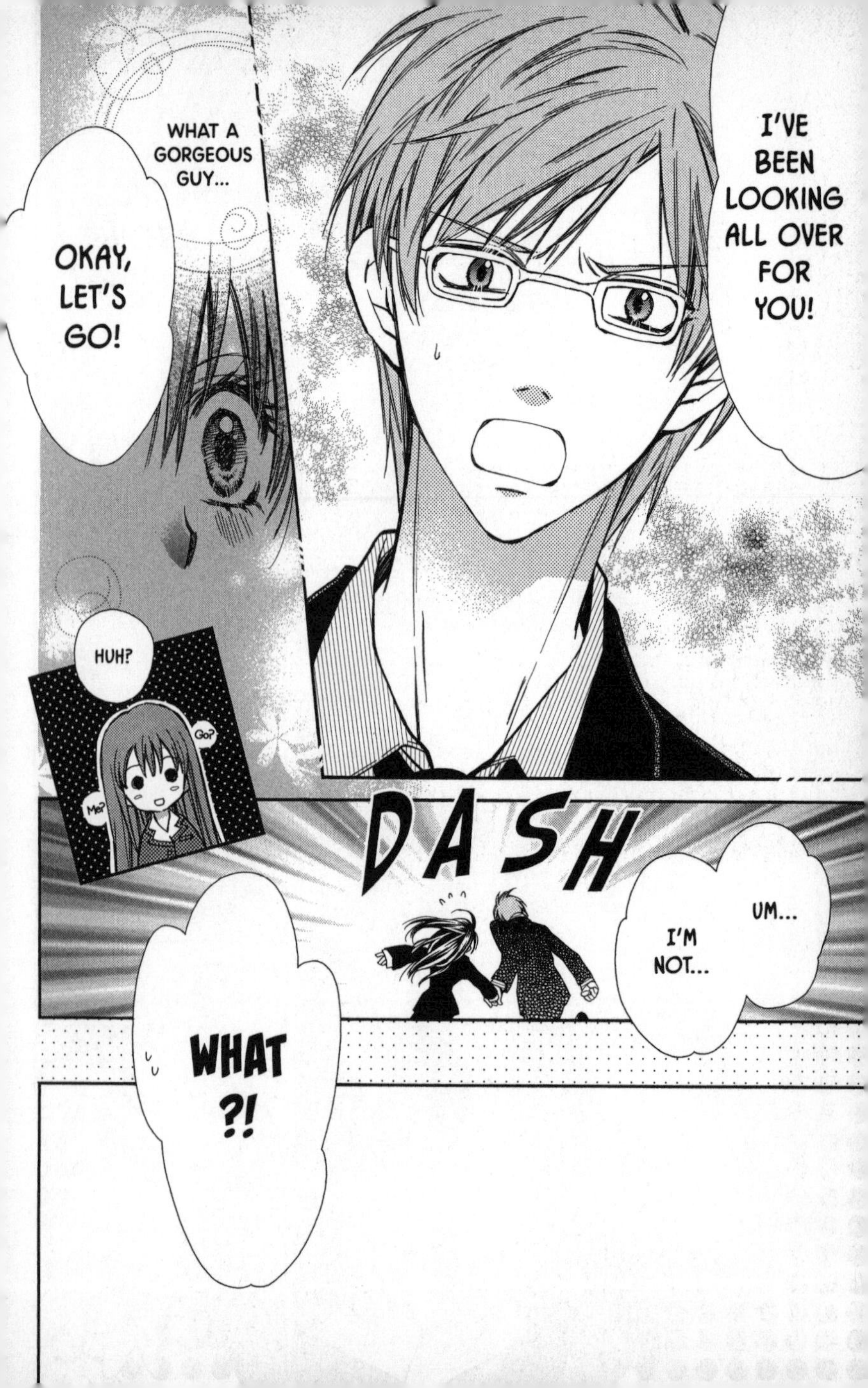
I'VE BEEN LOOKING ALL OVER FOR YOU!
WHAT A GORGEOUS GUY...
OKAY, LET'S GO!
HUH?
Go?
Me?
DASH
UM...
I'M NOT...
WHAT ?!

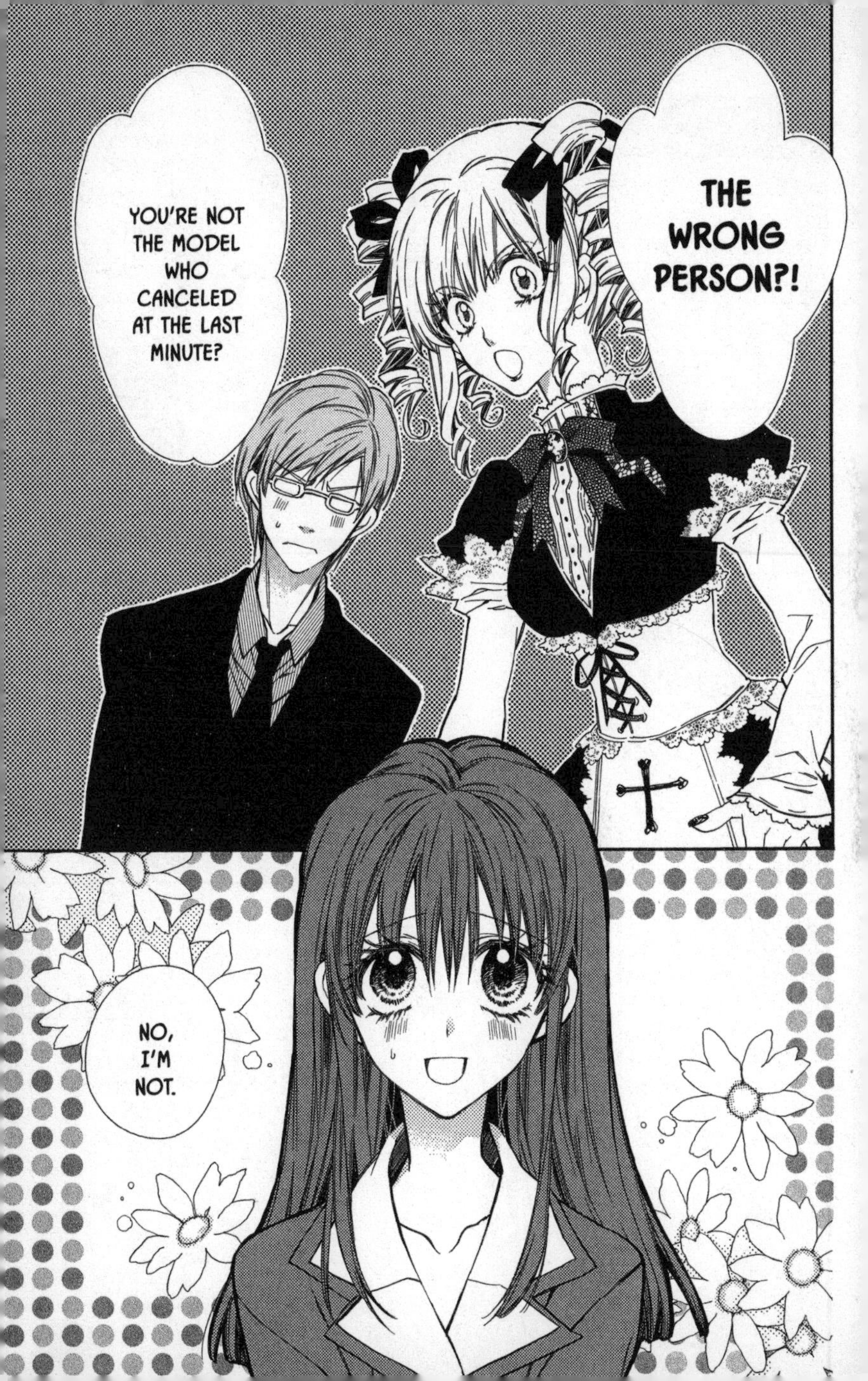
THE WRONG PERSON?!
YOU'RE NOT THE MODEL WHO CANCELED AT THE LAST MINUTE?
NO, I'M NOT.

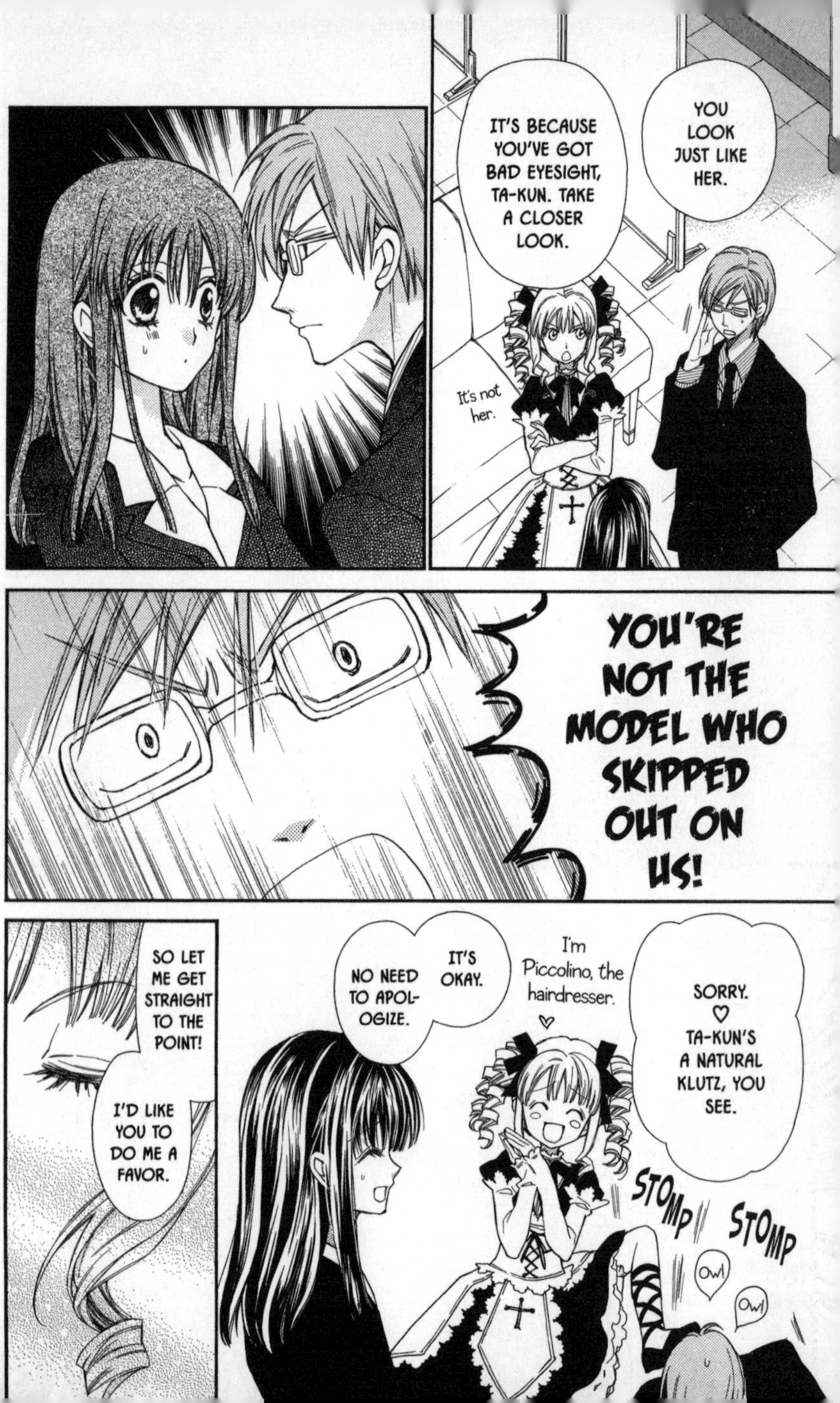
YOU LOOK JUST LIKE HER.
IT'S BECAUSE YOU'VE GOT BAD EYESIGHT, TA-KUN. TAKE A CLOSER LOOK.
It's not her.
YOU'RE NOT THE MODEL WHO SKIPPED OUT ON US!
SORRY. ♡ TA-KUN'S A NATURAL KLUTZ, YOU SEE.
I'm Piccolino, the hairdresser. ♡
IT'S OKAY.
NO NEED TO APOLOGIZE.
STOMP
STOMP
OW!
OW!
SO LET ME GET STRAIGHT TO THE POINT!
I'D LIKE YOU TO DO ME A FAVOR.

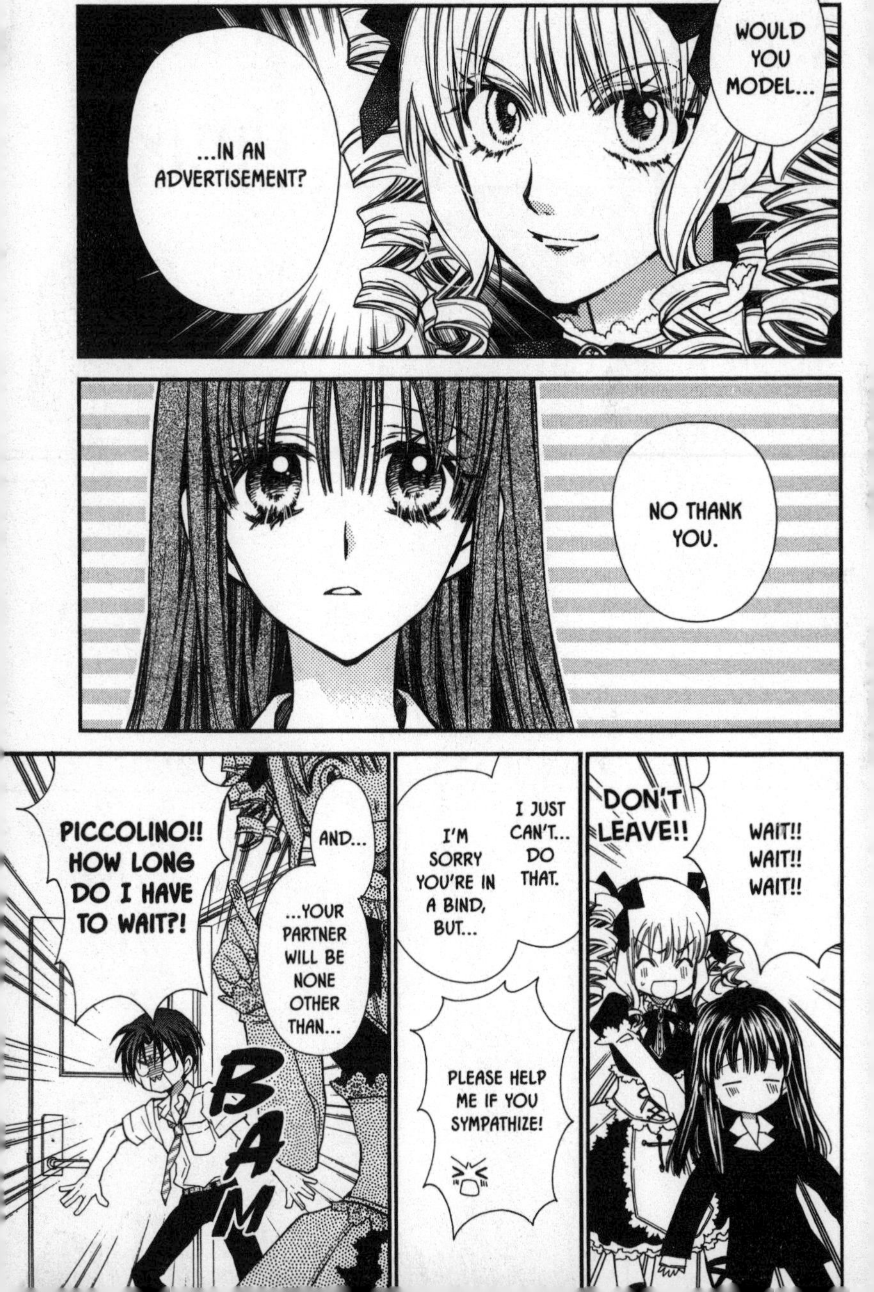
WOULD YOU MODEL...
...IN AN ADVERTISEMENT?
NO THANK YOU.
DON'T LEAVE!!
WAIT!! WAIT!! WAIT!!
I JUST CAN'T... DO THAT.
I'M SORRY YOU'RE IN A BIND, BUT...
PLEASE HELP ME IF YOU SYMPATHIZE!
AND...
...YOUR PARTNER WILL BE NONE OTHER THAN...
PICCOLINO!! HOW LONG DO I HAVE TO WAIT?!
BAM

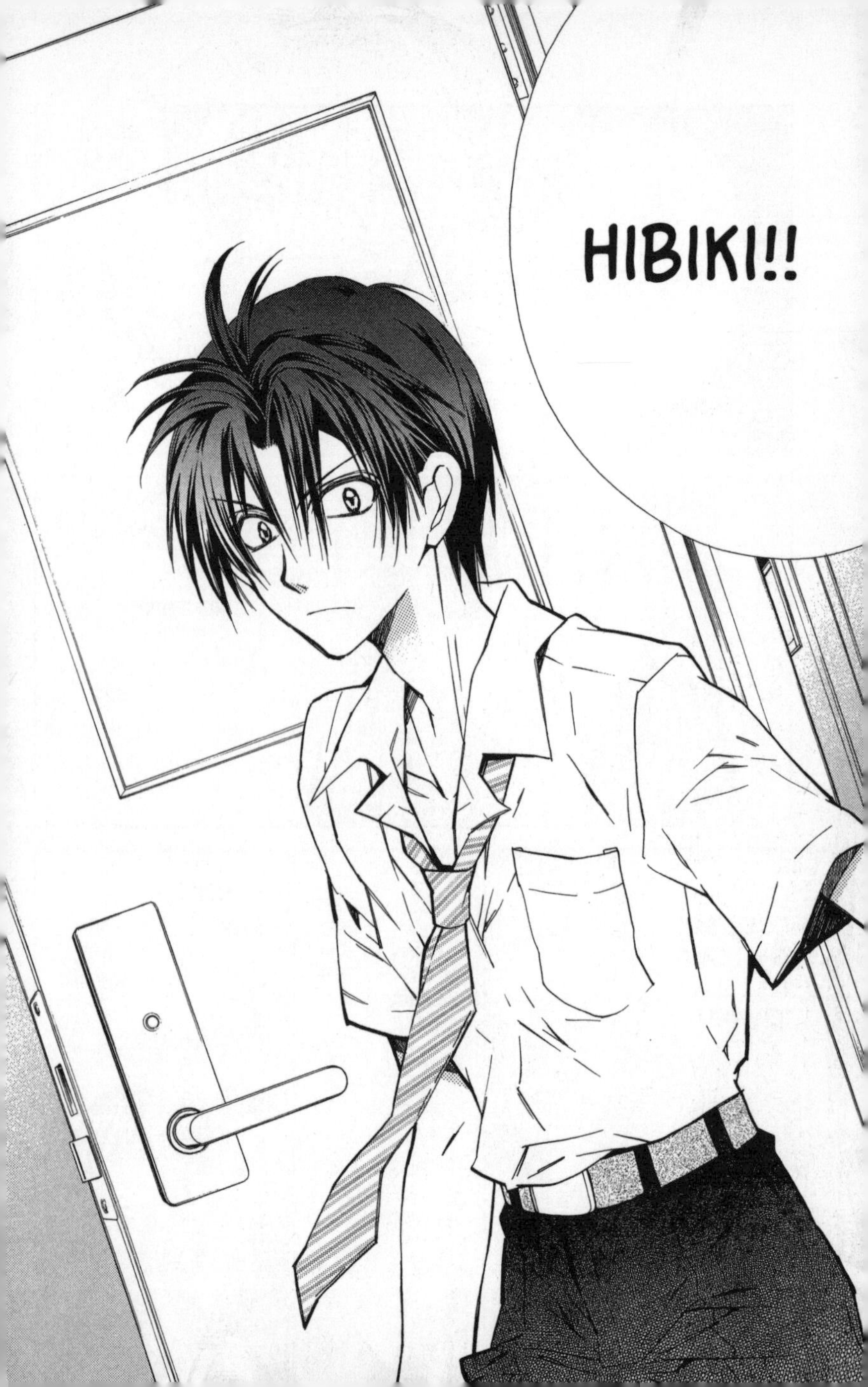
HIBIKI!!

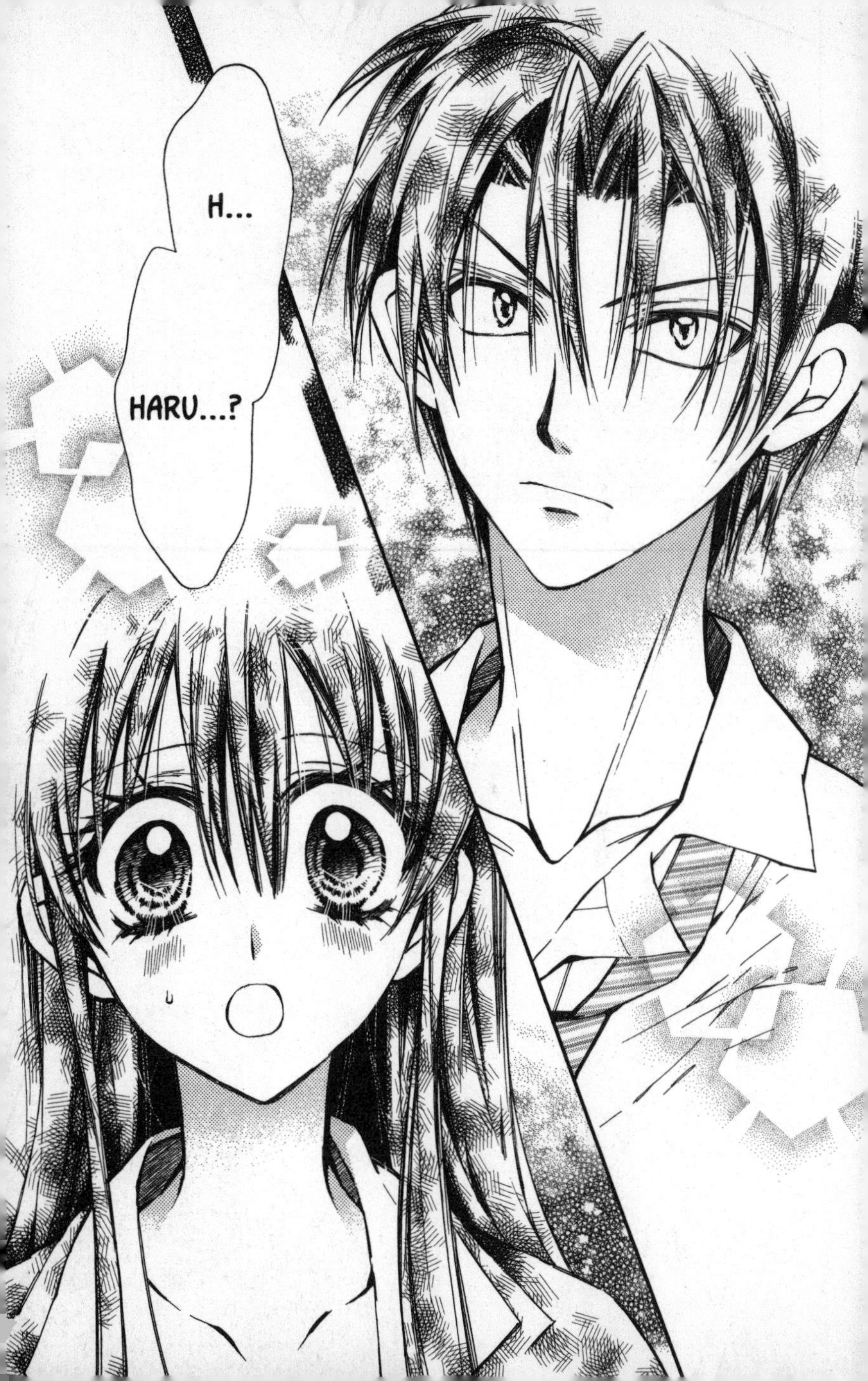
H...
HARU...?

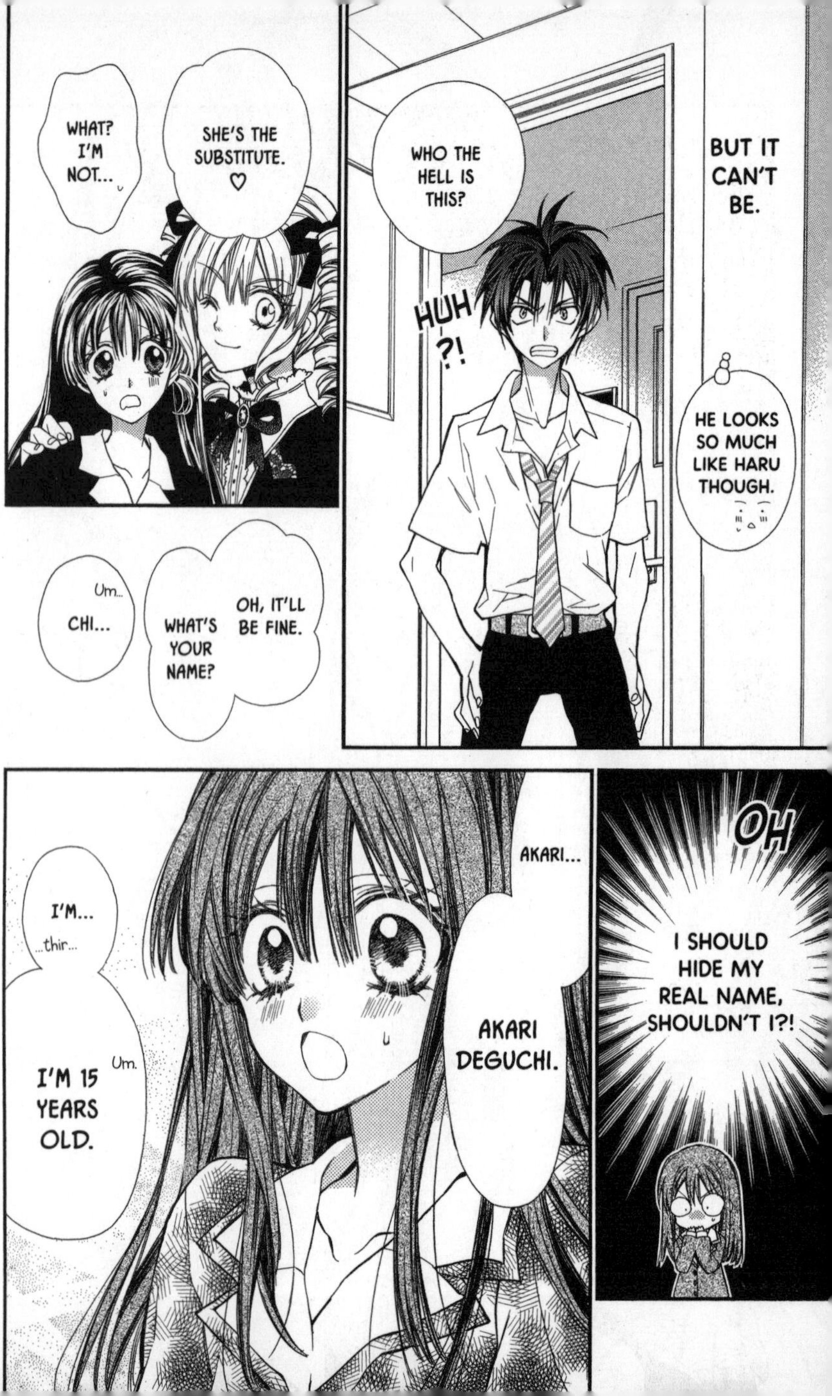
BUT IT CAN'T BE.
WHO THE HELL IS THIS?
HUH ?!
HE LOOKS SO MUCH LIKE HARU THOUGH.
SHE'S THE SUBSTITUTE. ♡
WHAT? I'M NOT...
OH, IT'LL BE FINE.
WHAT'S YOUR NAME?
Um...
CHI...
OH
I SHOULD HIDE MY REAL NAME, SHOULDN'T I?!
AKARI...
AKARI DEGUCHI.
I'M...
...thir...
Um.
I'M 15 YEARS OLD.

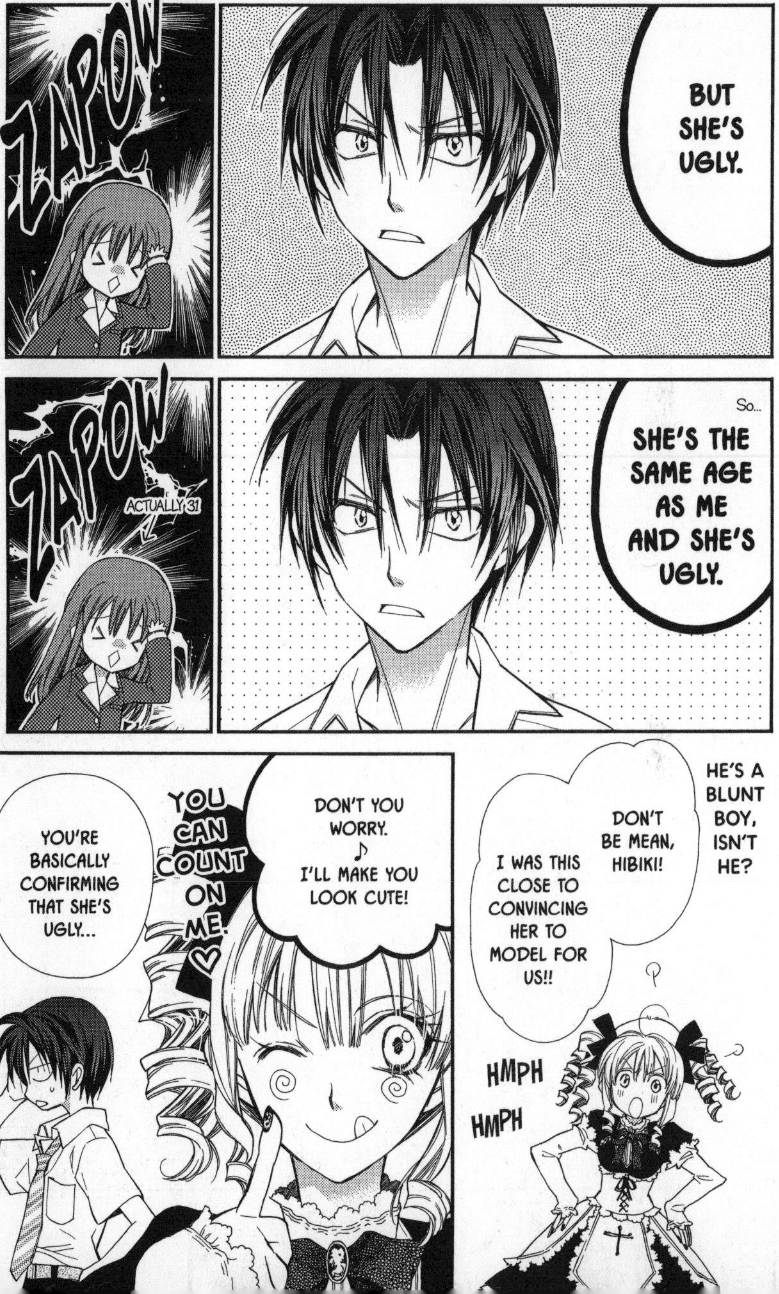
BUT SHE'S UGLY.
ZAPOW
So...
SHE'S THE SAME AGE AS ME AND SHE'S UGLY.
ZAPOW
ACTUALLY 31
HE'S A BLUNT BOY, ISN'T HE?
DON'T BE MEAN, HIBIKI!
I WAS THIS CLOSE TO CONVINCING HER TO MODEL FOR US!!
HMPH
HMPH
DON'T YOU WORRY. ♪ I'LL MAKE YOU LOOK CUTE!
YOU CAN COUNT ON ME. ♡
YOU'RE BASICALLY CONFIRMING THAT SHE'S UGLY...

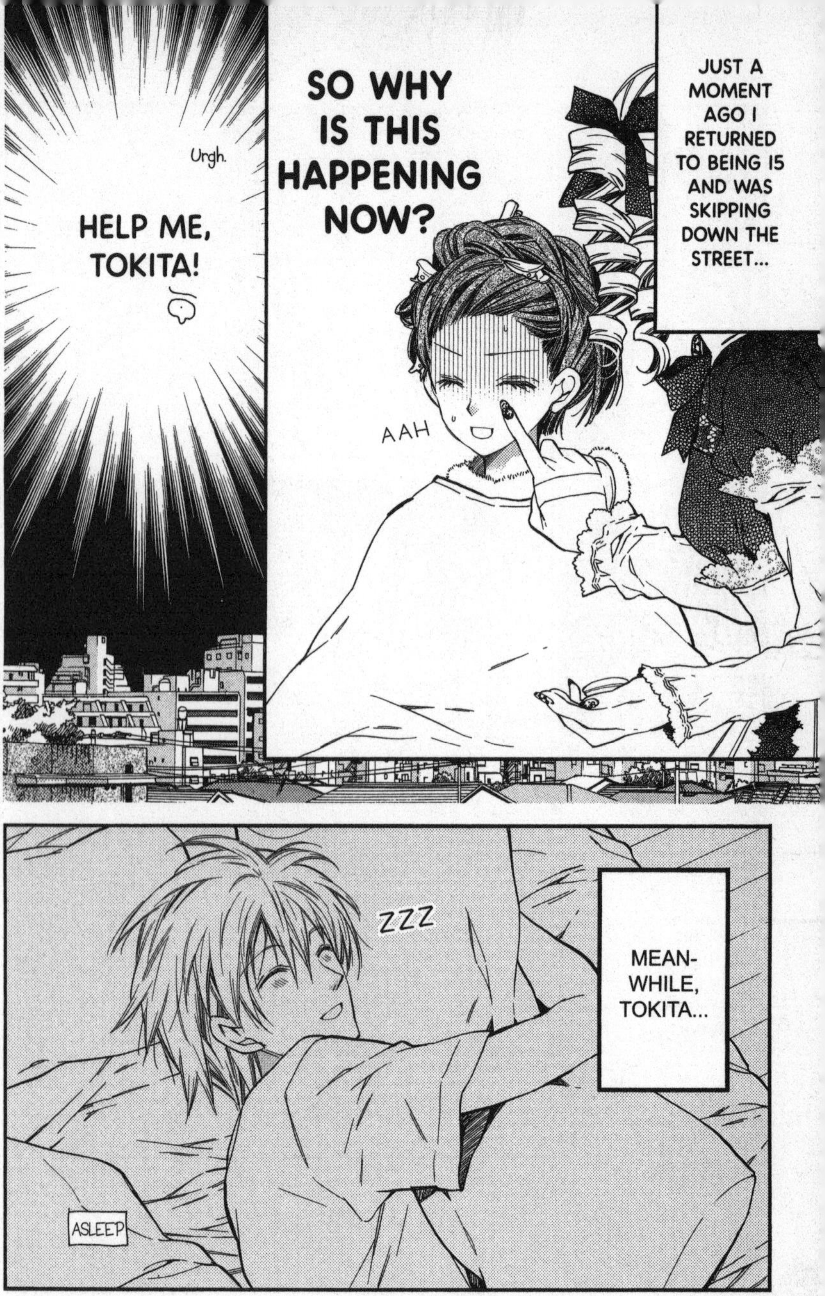
JUST A MOMENT AGO I RETURNED TO BEING 15 AND WAS SKIPPING DOWN THE STREET...
SO WHY IS THIS HAPPENING NOW?
AAH
Urgh.
HELP ME, TOKITA!
MEAN-WHILE, TOKITA...
ZZZ
ASLEEP

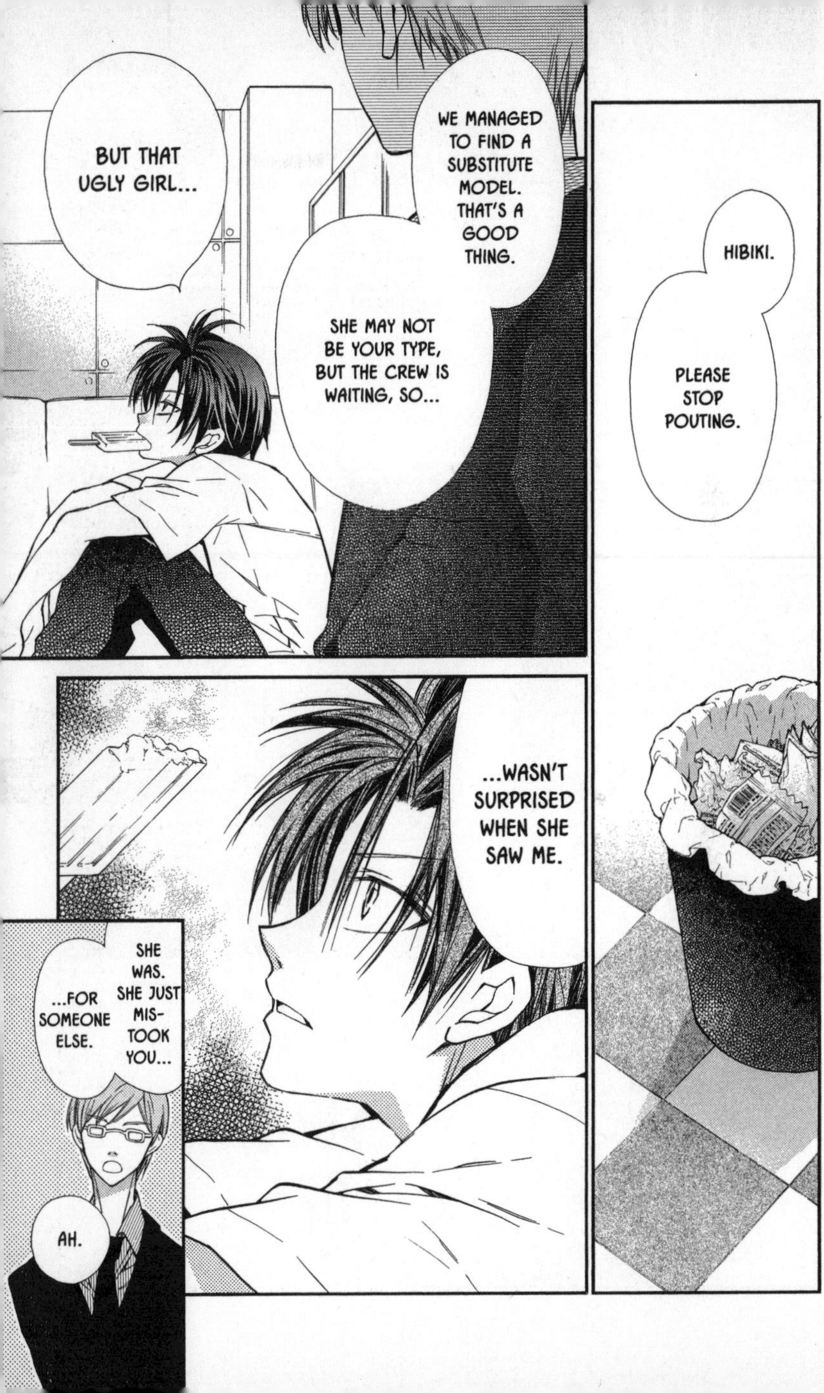
HIBIKI.
PLEASE STOP POUTING.
WE MANAGED TO FIND A SUBSTITUTE MODEL. THAT'S A GOOD THING.
SHE MAY NOT BE YOUR TYPE, BUT THE CREW IS WAITING, SO...
BUT THAT UGLY GIRL...
...WASN'T SURPRISED WHEN SHE SAW ME.
SHE WAS. SHE JUST MIS-TOOK YOU...
...FOR SOMEONE ELSE.
AH.

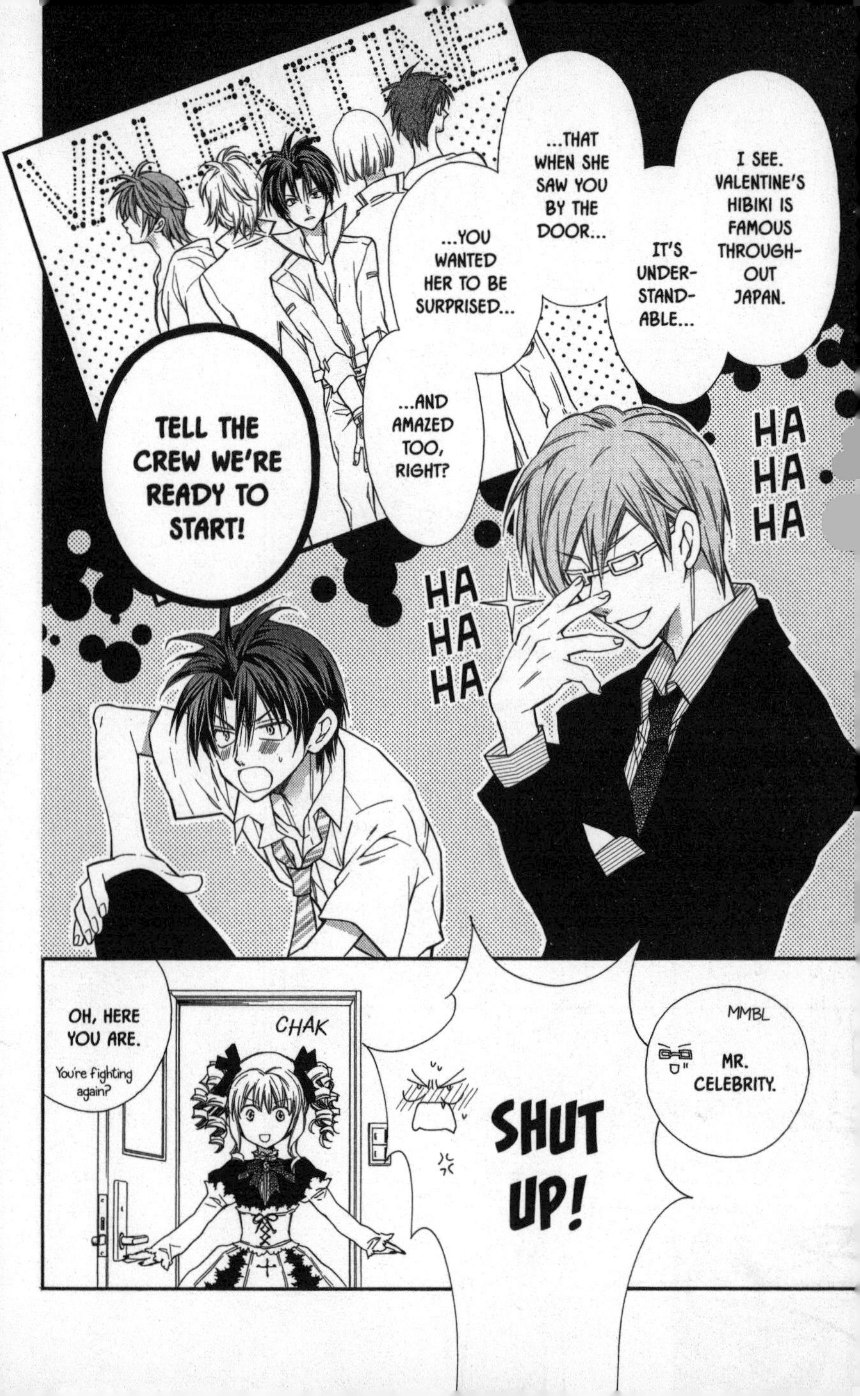
VALENTINE
I SEE. VALENTINE'S HIBIKI IS FAMOUS THROUGH-OUT JAPAN.
IT'S UNDER-STAND-ABLE...
...THAT WHEN SHE SAW YOU BY THE DOOR...
...YOU WANTED HER TO BE SURPRISED...
...AND AMAZED TOO, RIGHT?
HA HA HA
HA HA HA
TELL THE CREW WE'RE READY TO START!
MMBL
MR. CELEBRITY.
SHUT UP!
CHAK
OH, HERE YOU ARE.
You're fighting again?

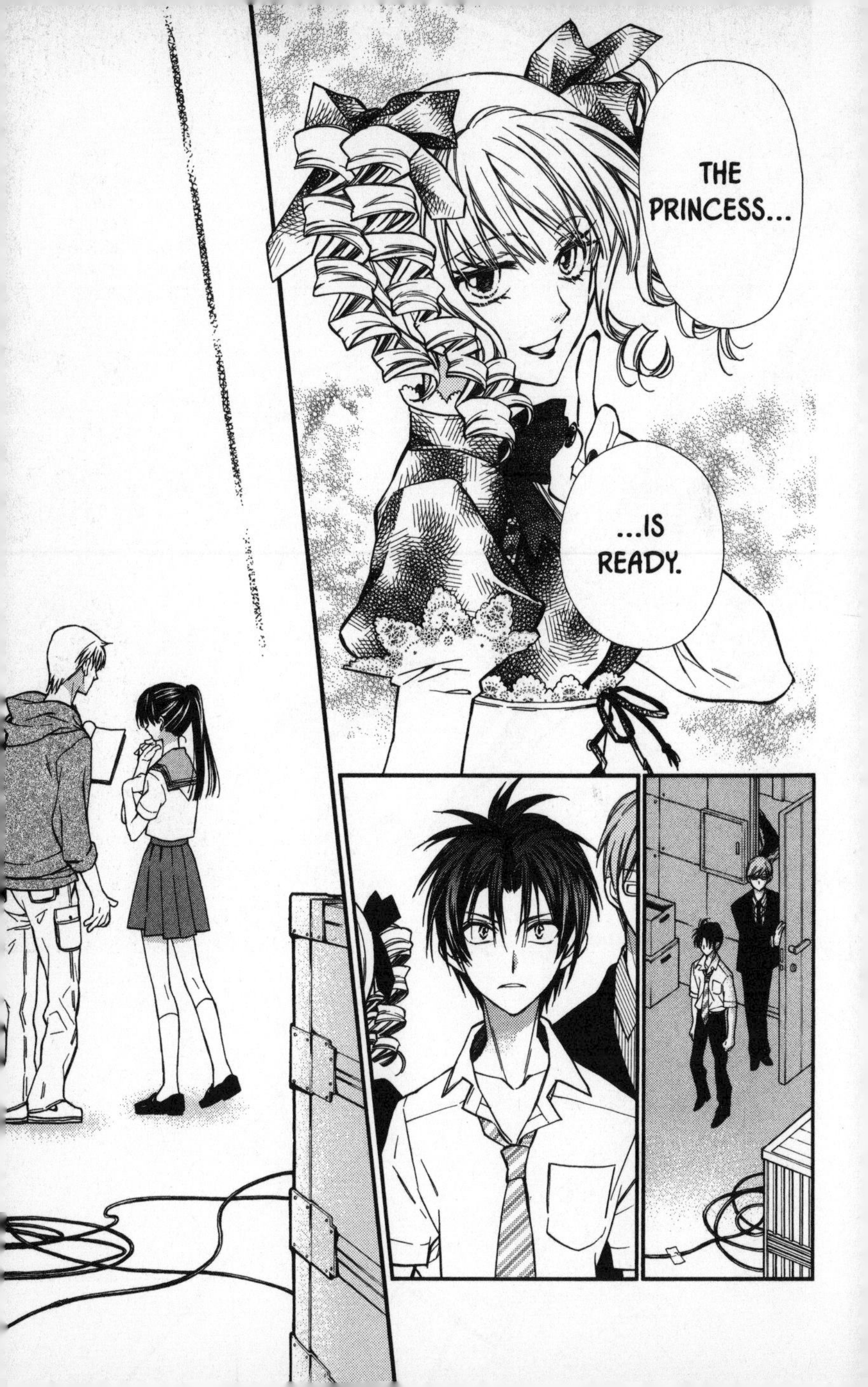
THE PRINCESS...
...IS READY.

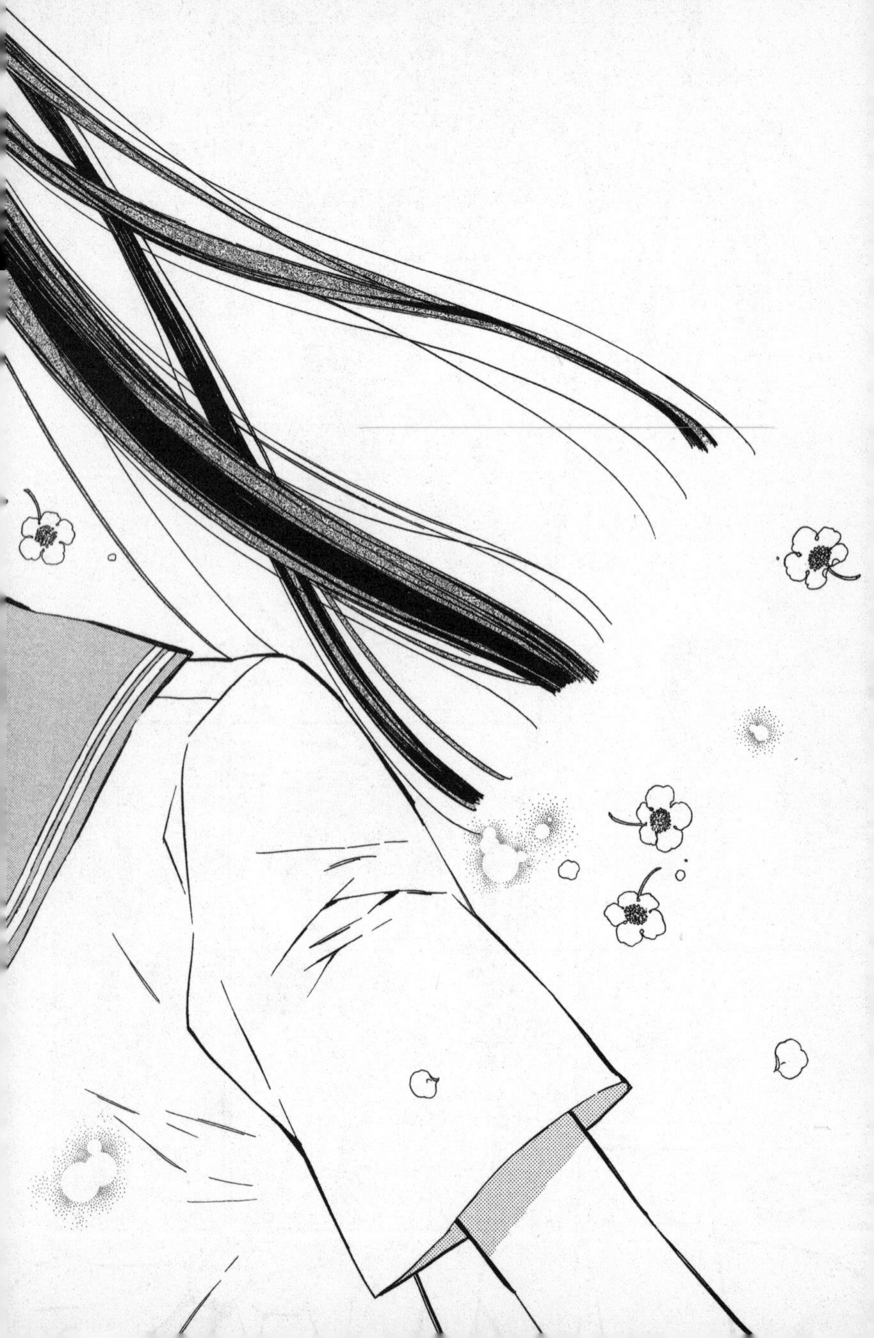

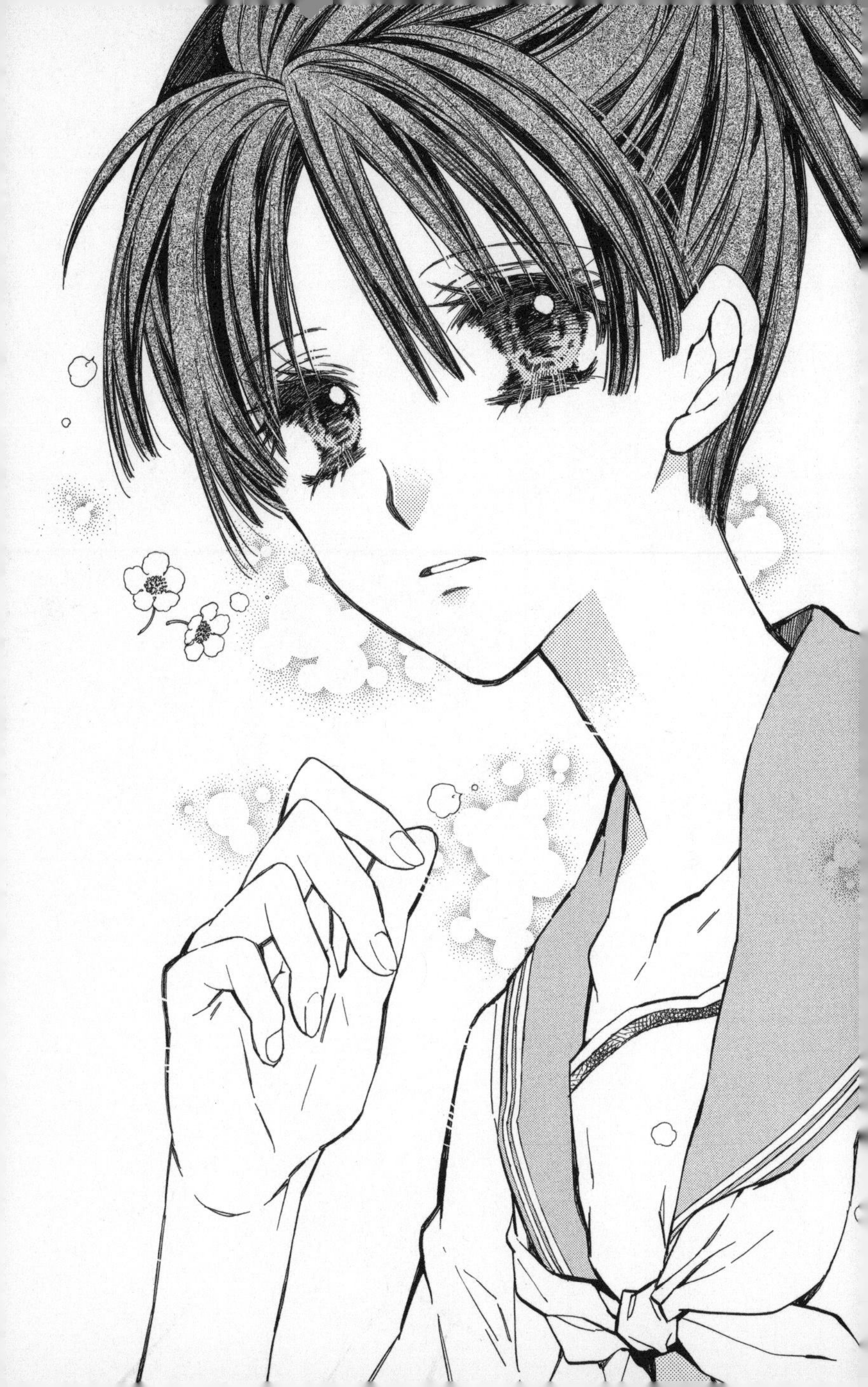

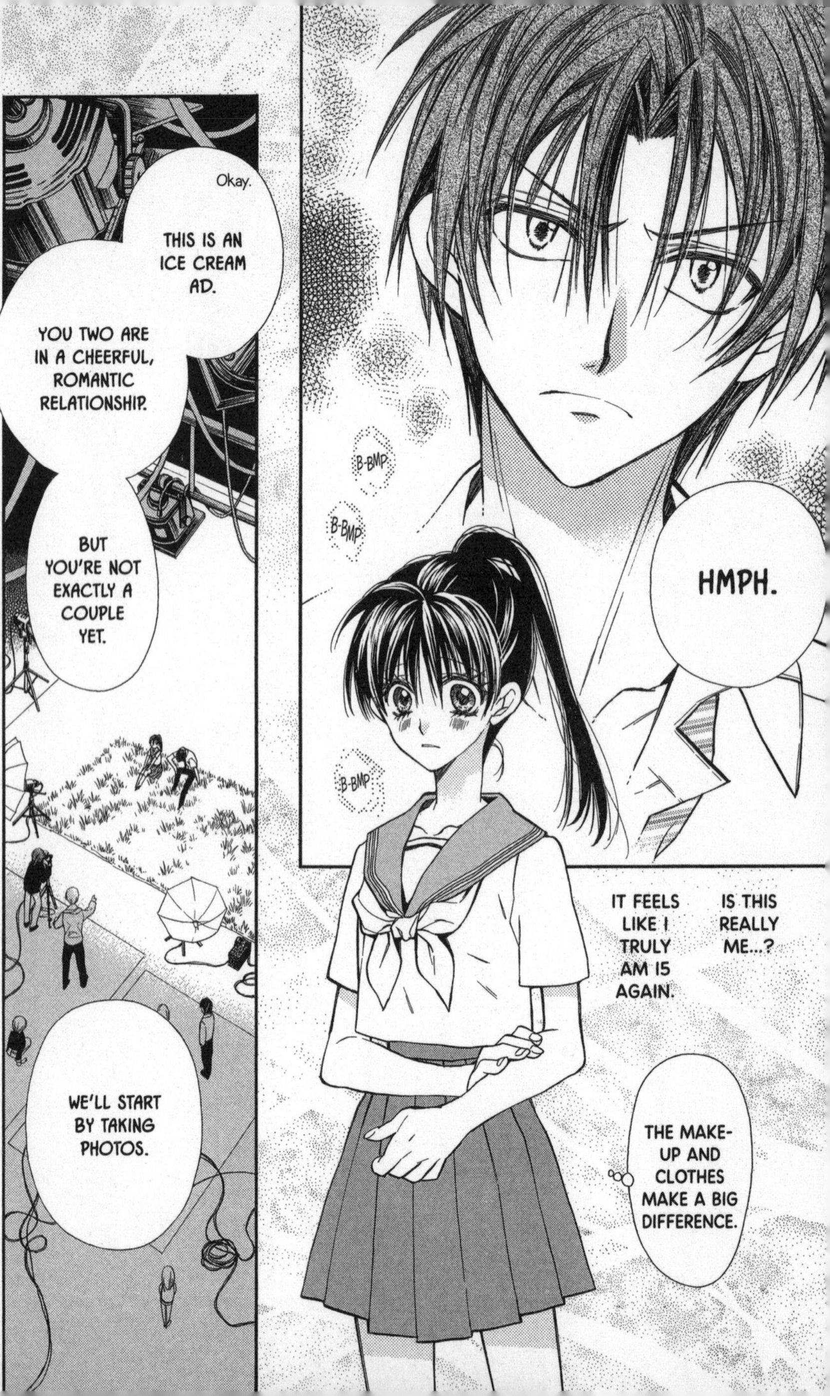
HMPH.
B-BMP
B-BMP
B-BMP
IS THIS REALLY ME...?
IT FEELS LIKE I TRULY AM 15 AGAIN.
THE MAKE-UP AND CLOTHES MAKE A BIG DIFFERENCE.
Okay.
THIS IS AN ICE CREAM AD.
YOU TWO ARE IN A CHEERFUL, ROMANTIC RELATIONSHIP.
BUT YOU'RE NOT EXACTLY A COUPLE YET.
WE'LL START BY TAKING PHOTOS.

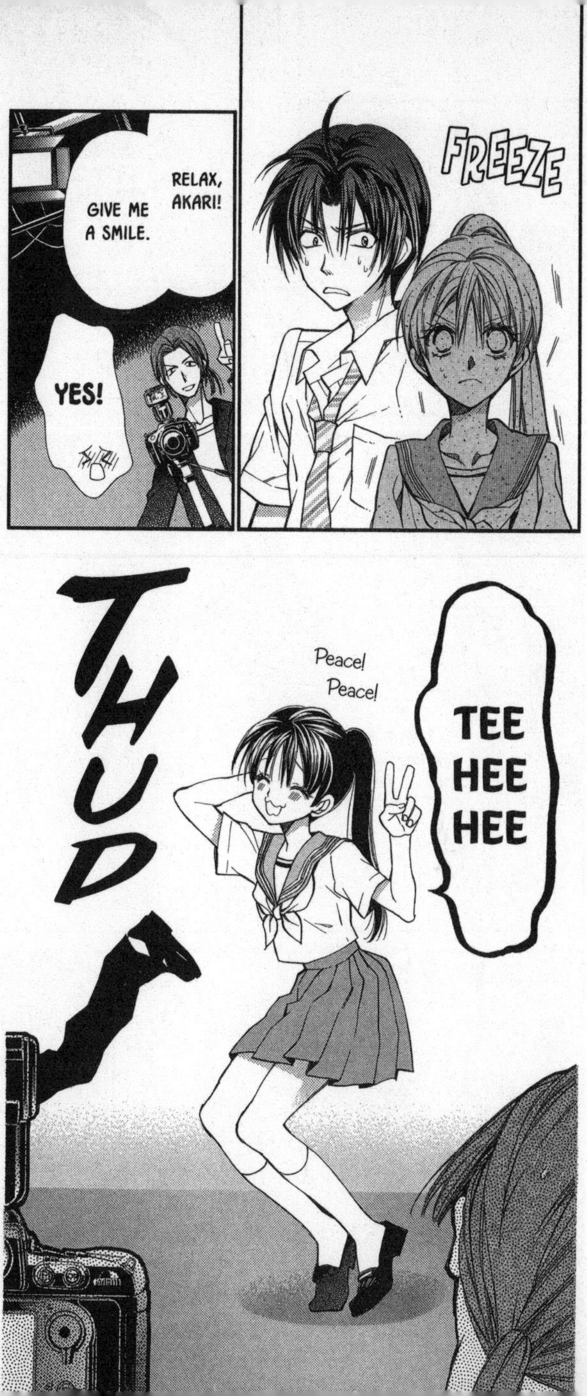
FREEZE
RELAX, AKARI!
GIVE ME A SMILE.
YES!
TEE HEE HEE
Peace! Peace!
THUD

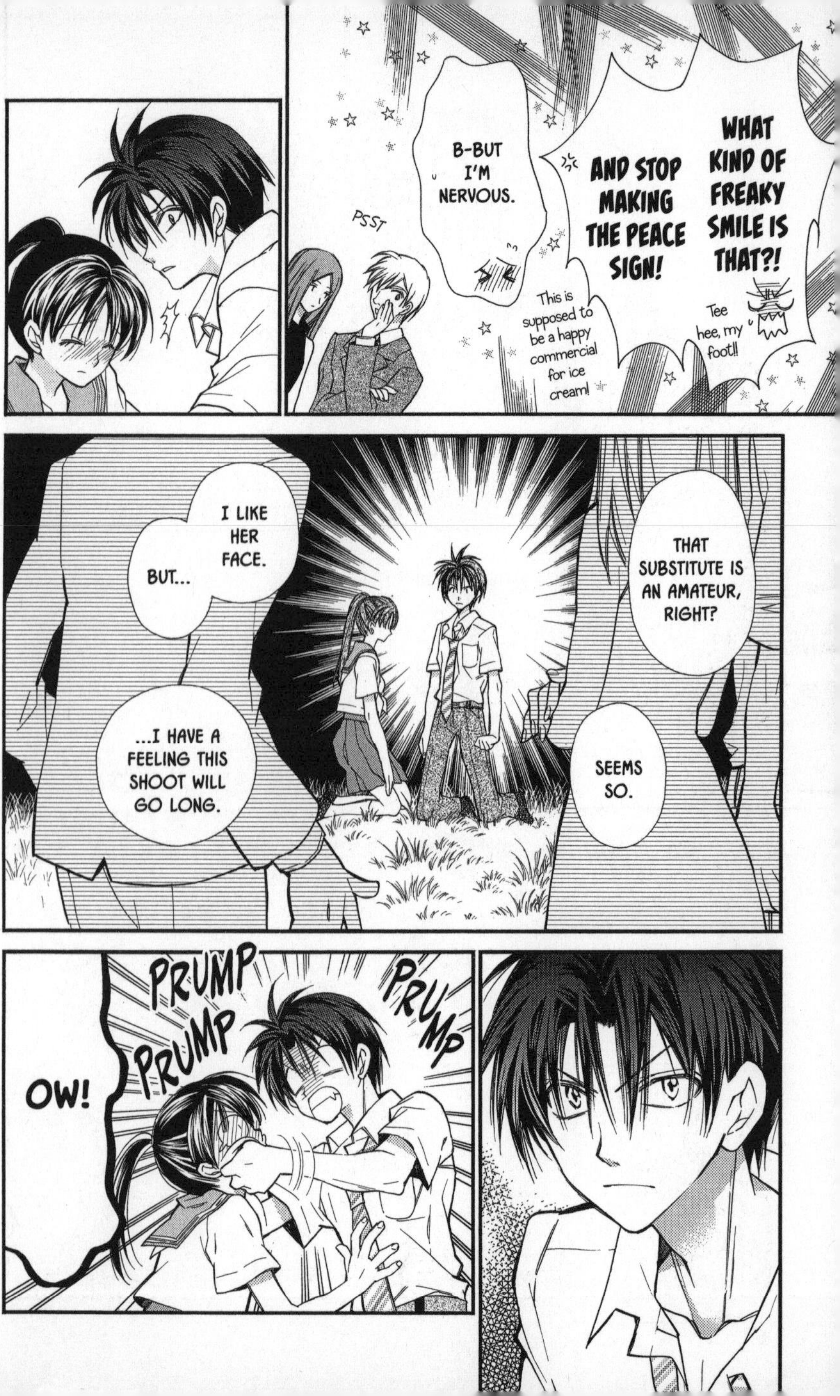
WHAT KIND OF FREAKY SMILE IS THAT?!
AND STOP MAKING THE PEACE SIGN!
Tee hee, my foot!!
This is supposed to be a happy commercial for ice cream!
B-BUT I'M NERVOUS.
PSST
THAT SUBSTITUTE IS AN AMATEUR, RIGHT?
SEEMS SO.
I LIKE HER FACE.
BUT...
...I HAVE A FEELING THIS SHOOT WILL GO LONG.
PRUMP
PRUMP PRUMP
OW!

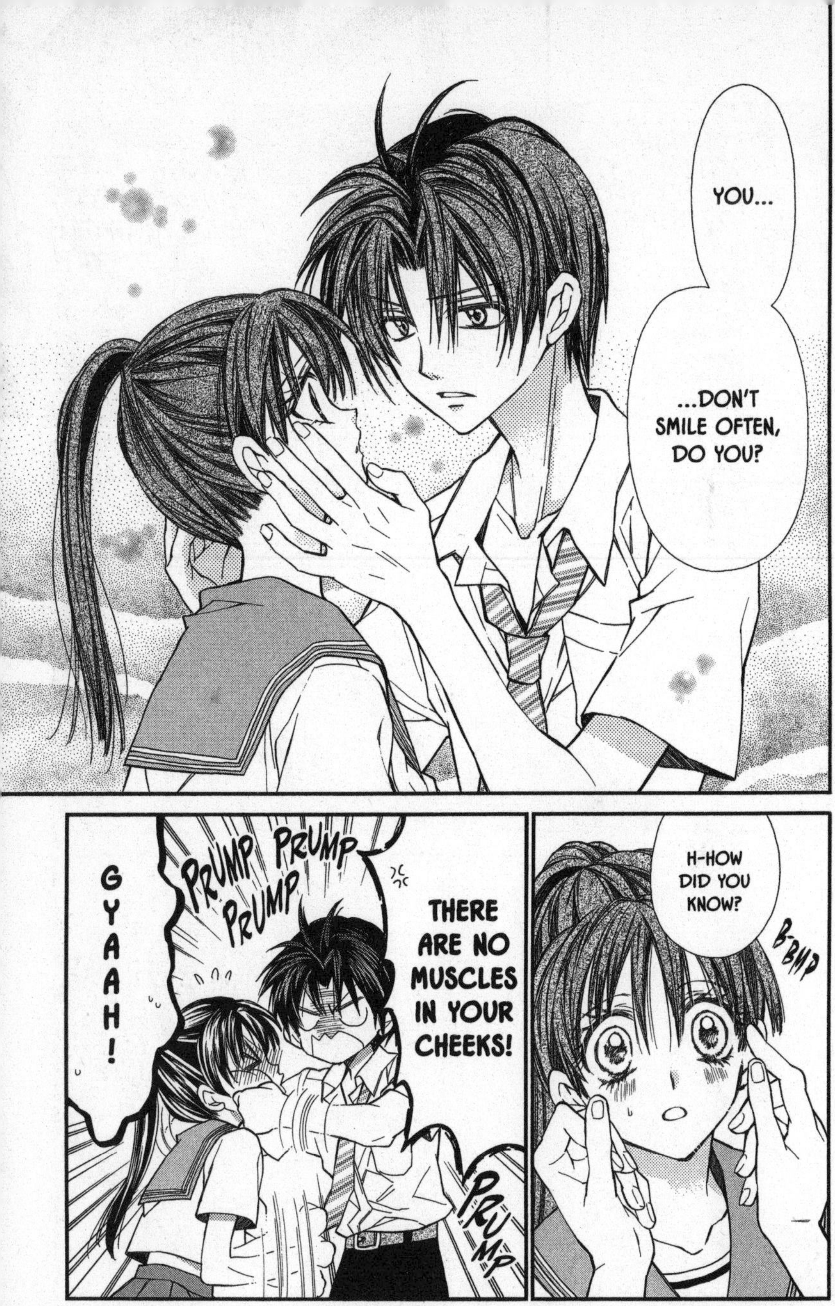
YOU...
...DON'T SMILE OFTEN, DO YOU?
H-HOW DID YOU KNOW?
B-BMP
THERE ARE NO MUSCLES IN YOUR CHEEKS!
PRUMP PRUMP PRUMP
GYAAAH!
PRUMP

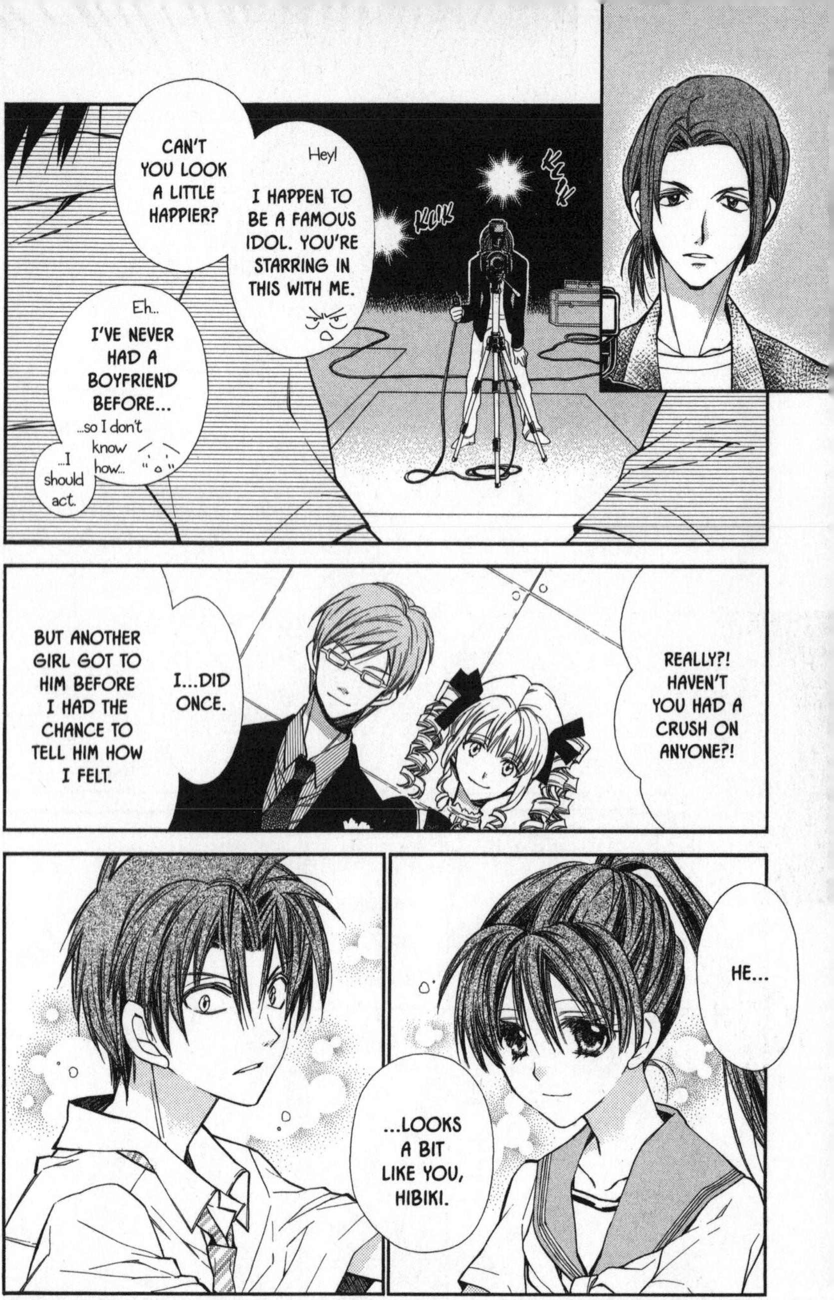
KLIK
KLIK
Hey!
I HAPPEN TO BE A FAMOUS IDOL. YOU'RE STARRING IN THIS WITH ME.
CAN'T YOU LOOK A LITTLE HAPPIER?
Eh...
I'VE NEVER HAD A BOYFRIEND BEFORE...
...so I don't know how...
...I should act.
REALLY?! HAVEN'T YOU HAD A CRUSH ON ANYONE?!
I...DID ONCE.
BUT ANOTHER GIRL GOT TO HIM BEFORE I HAD THE CHANCE TO TELL HIM HOW I FELT.
HE...
...LOOKS A BIT LIKE YOU, HIBIKI.

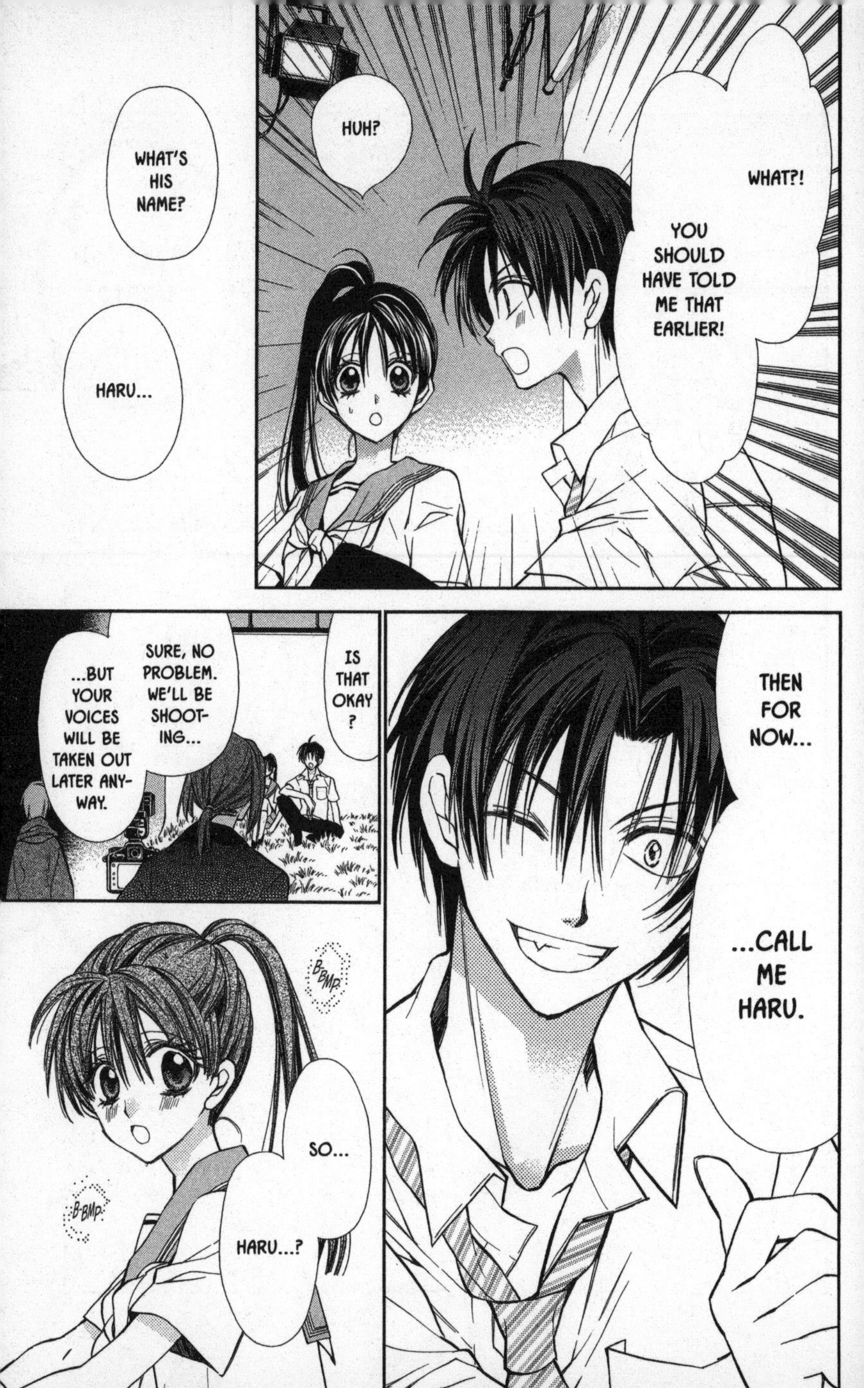
WHAT?!
YOU SHOULD HAVE TOLD ME THAT EARLIER!
HUH?
WHAT'S HIS NAME?
HARU...
THEN FOR NOW...
...CALL ME HARU.
IS THAT OKAY?
SURE, NO PROBLEM. WE'LL BE SHOOTING...
...BUT YOUR VOICES WILL BE TAKEN OUT LATER ANYWAY.
B-BMP
SO...
HARU...?
B-BMP

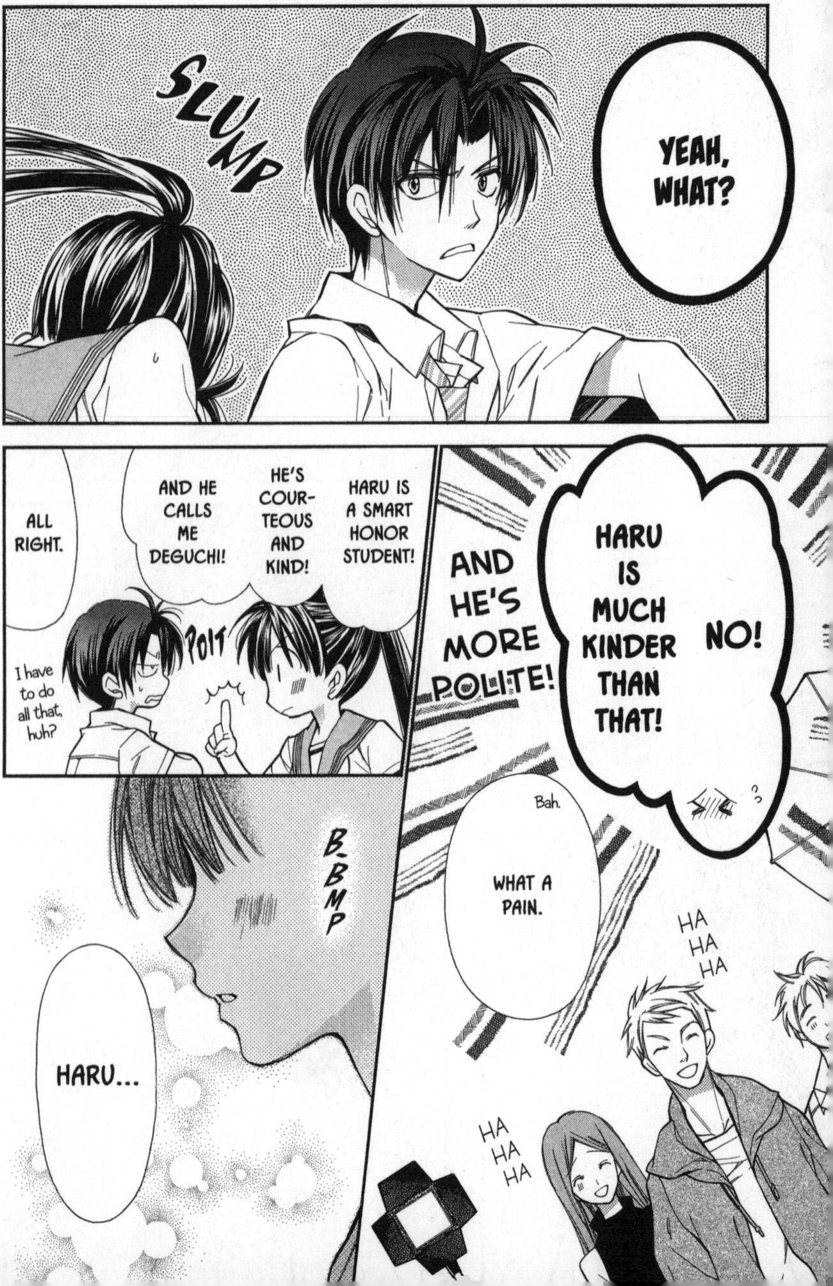
YEAH, WHAT?
SLUMP
NO!
HARU IS MUCH KINDER THAN THAT!
AND HE'S MORE POLITE!
HARU IS A SMART HONOR STUDENT!
HE'S COURTEOUS AND KIND!
AND HE CALLS ME DEGUCHI!
ALL RIGHT.
POIT
I have to do all that, huh?
Bah.
WHAT A PAIN.
HA HA HA
HA HA HA
B-BMP
HARU...

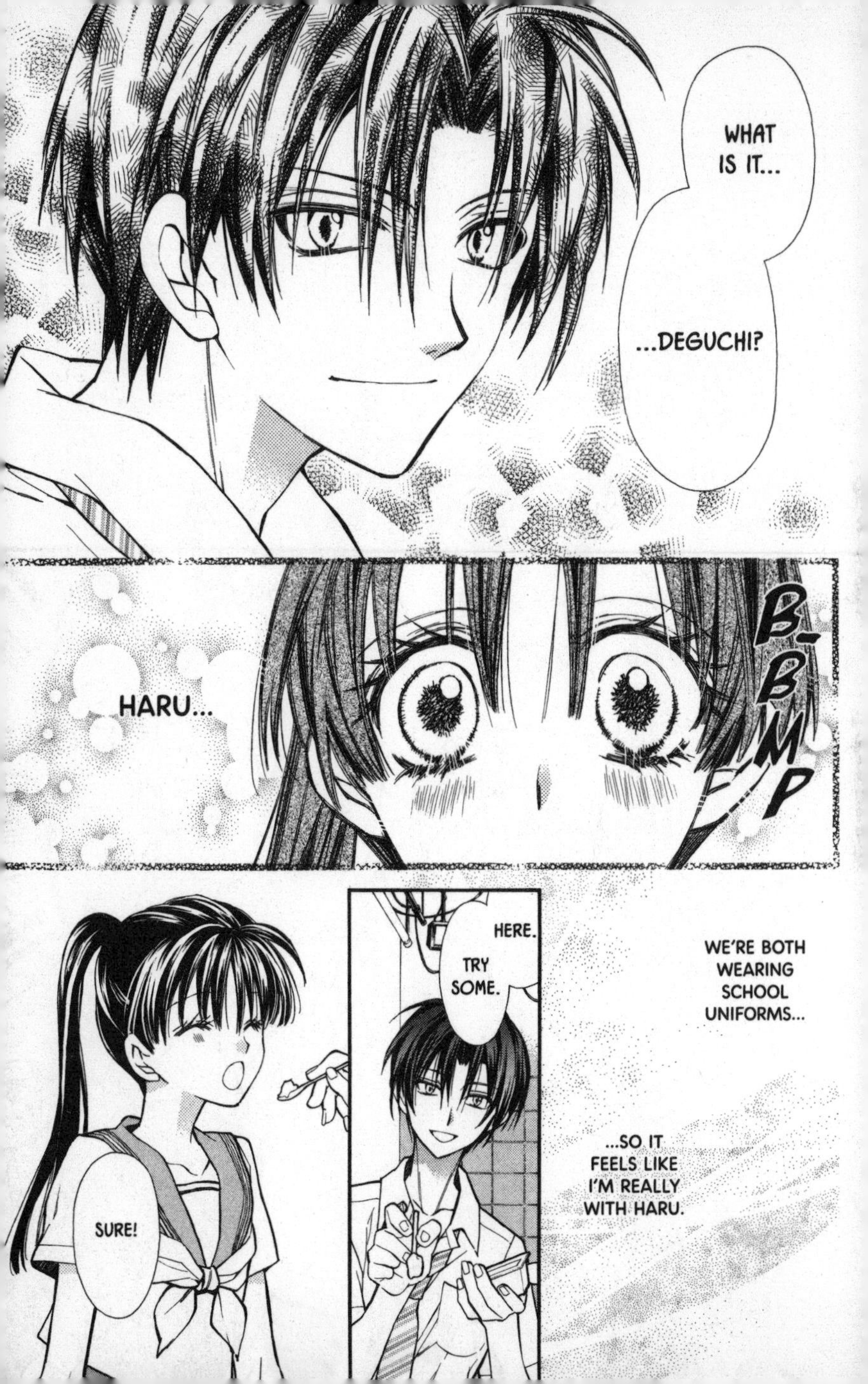
WHAT IS IT...
...DEGUCHI?
B-BMP
HARU...
WE'RE BOTH WEARING SCHOOL UNIFORMS...
...SO IT FEELS LIKE I'M REALLY WITH HARU.
HERE.
TRY SOME.
SURE!

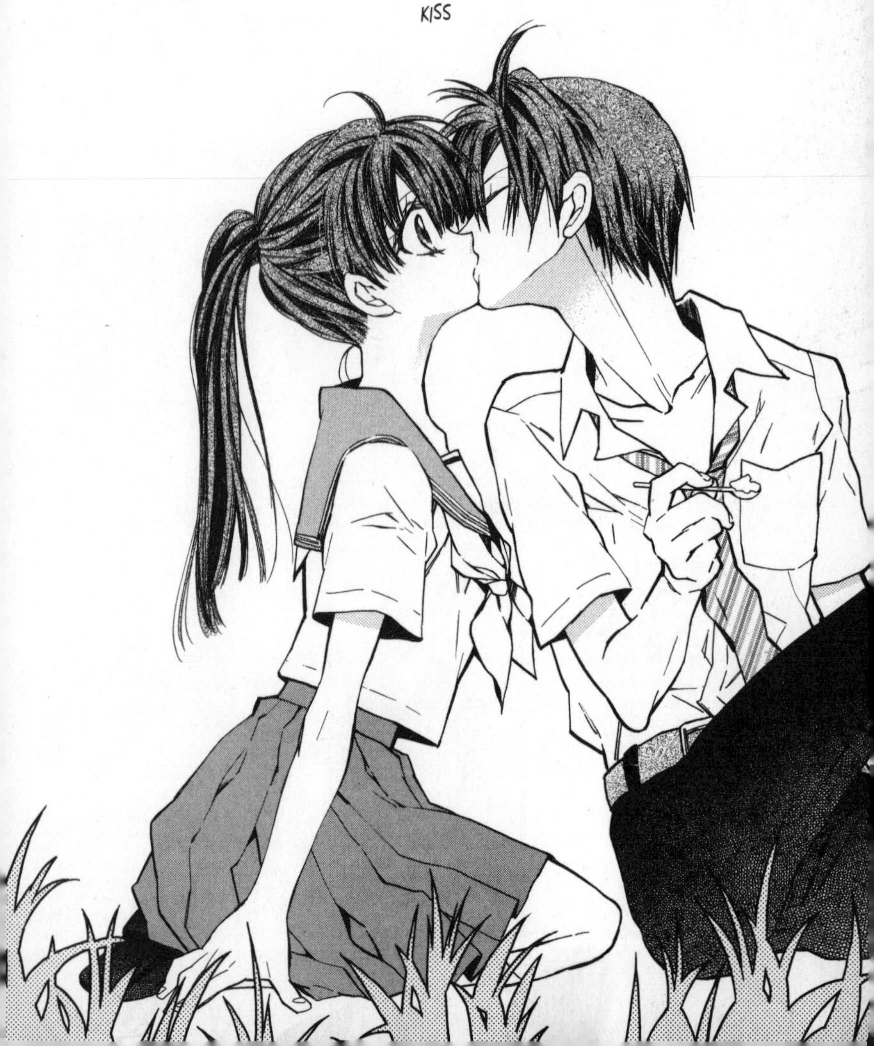
KISS

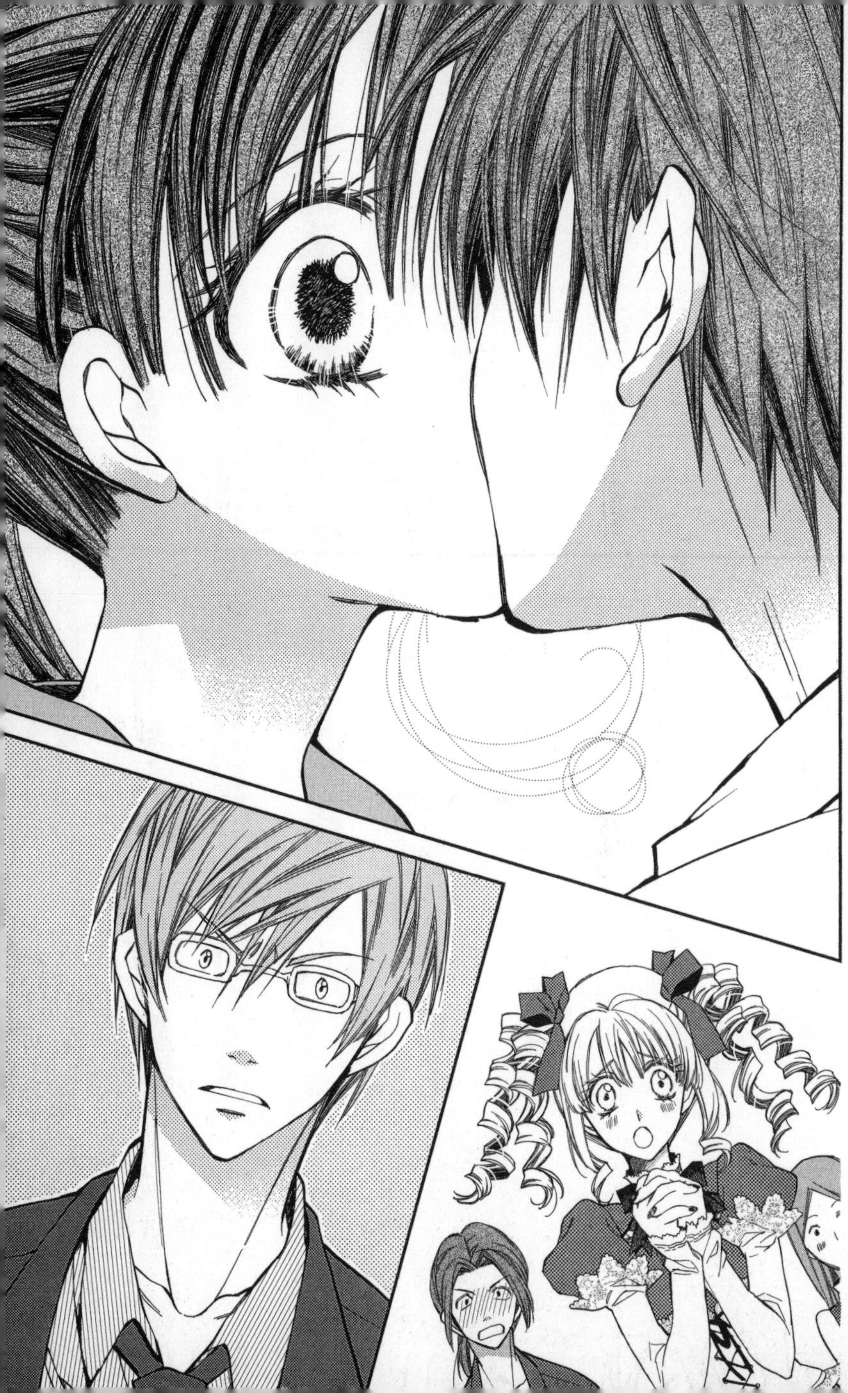

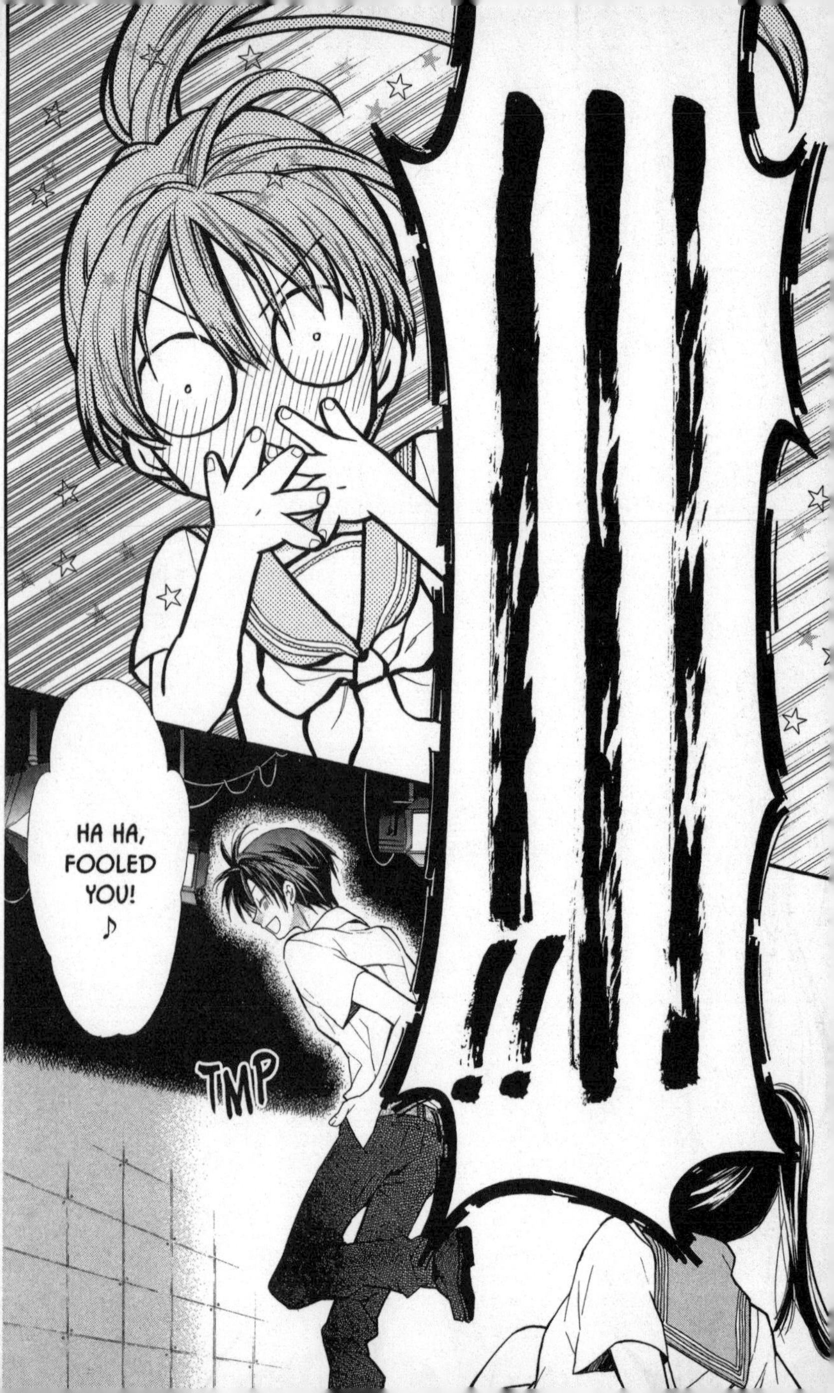
HA HA, FOOLED YOU! ♪
TMP

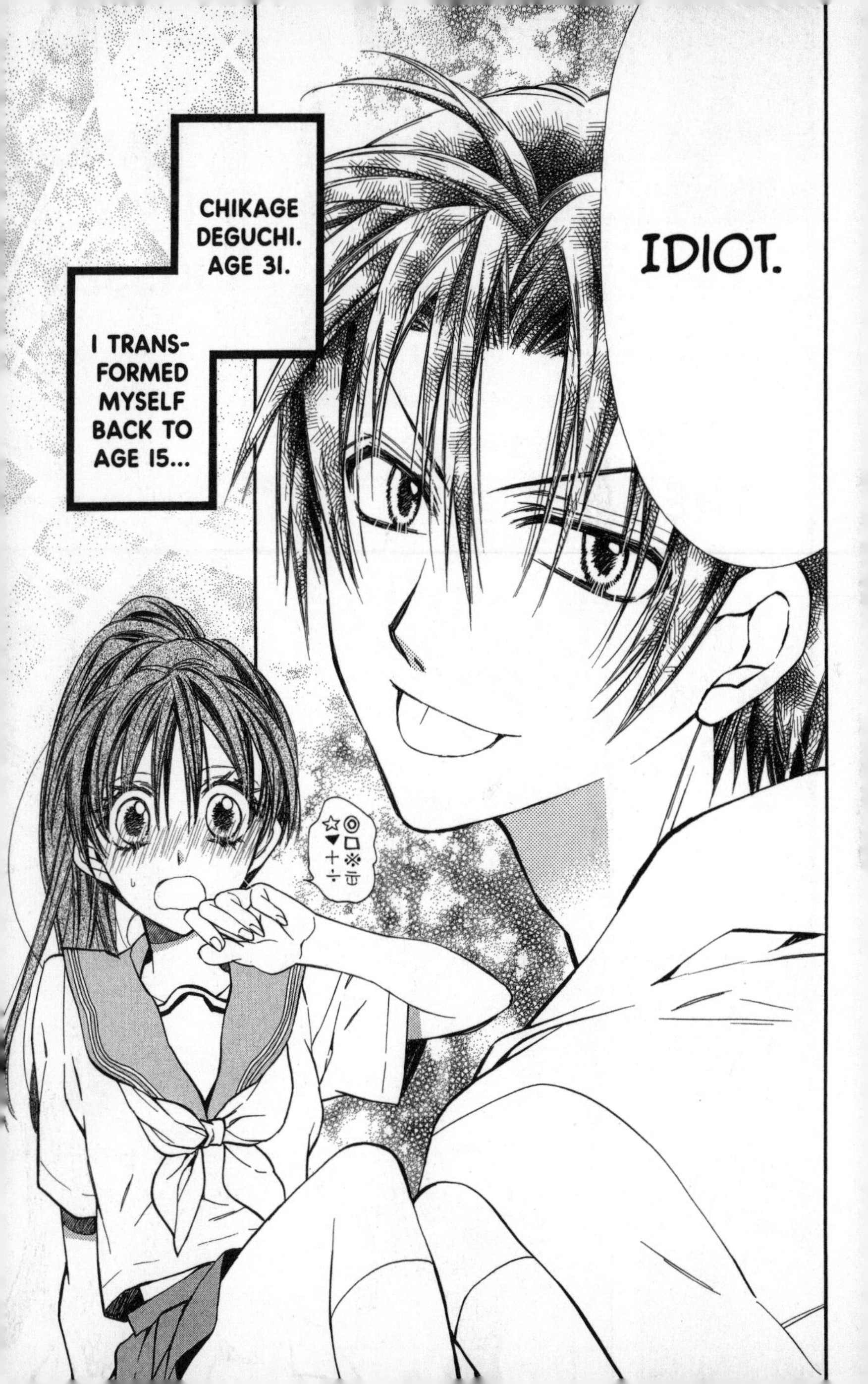
IDIOT.
CHIKAGE DEGUCHI. AGE 31.
I TRANS-FORMED MYSELF BACK TO AGE 15...

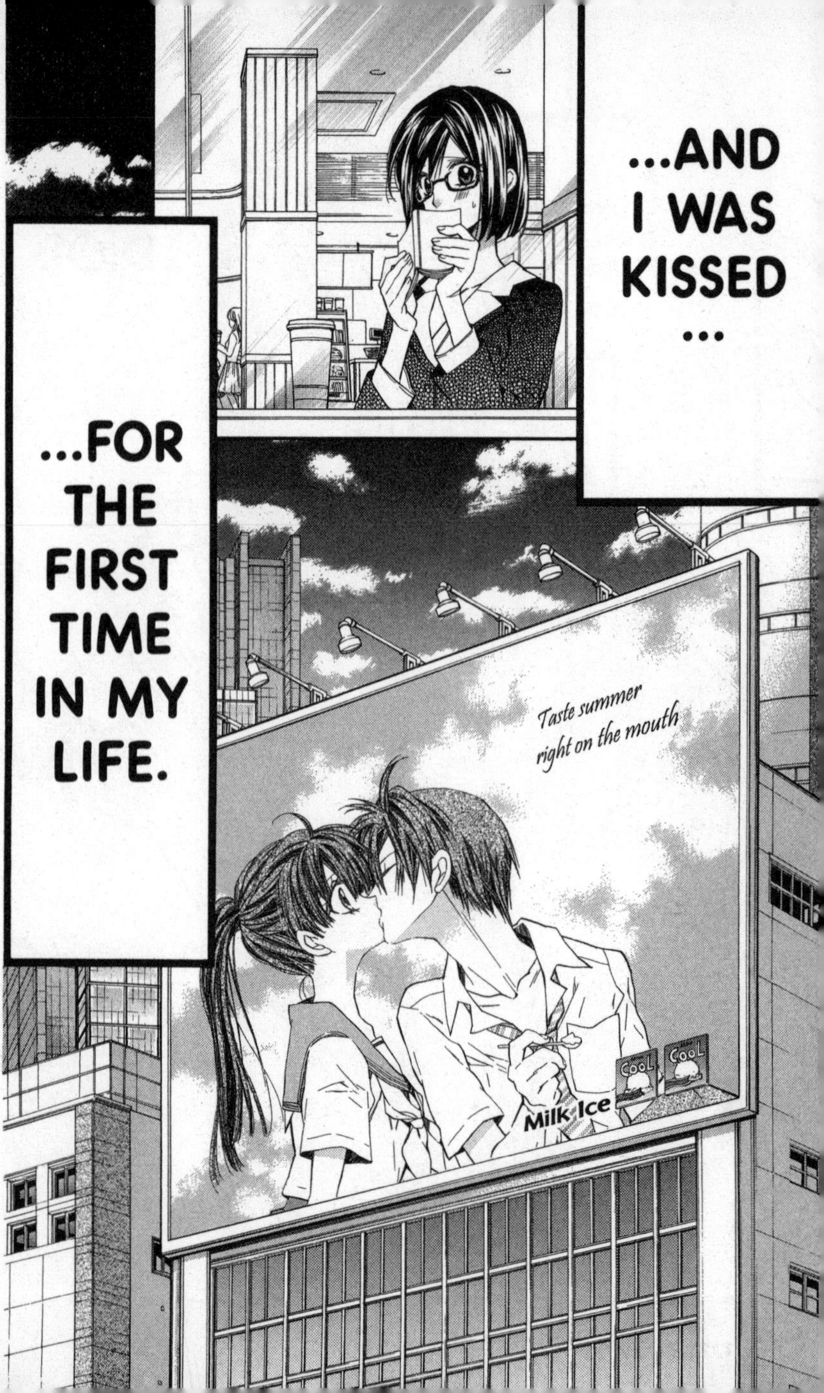
...AND I WAS KISSED ...
...FOR THE FIRST TIME IN MY LIFE.
Taste summer right on the mouth
CooL
CooL
Milk Ice

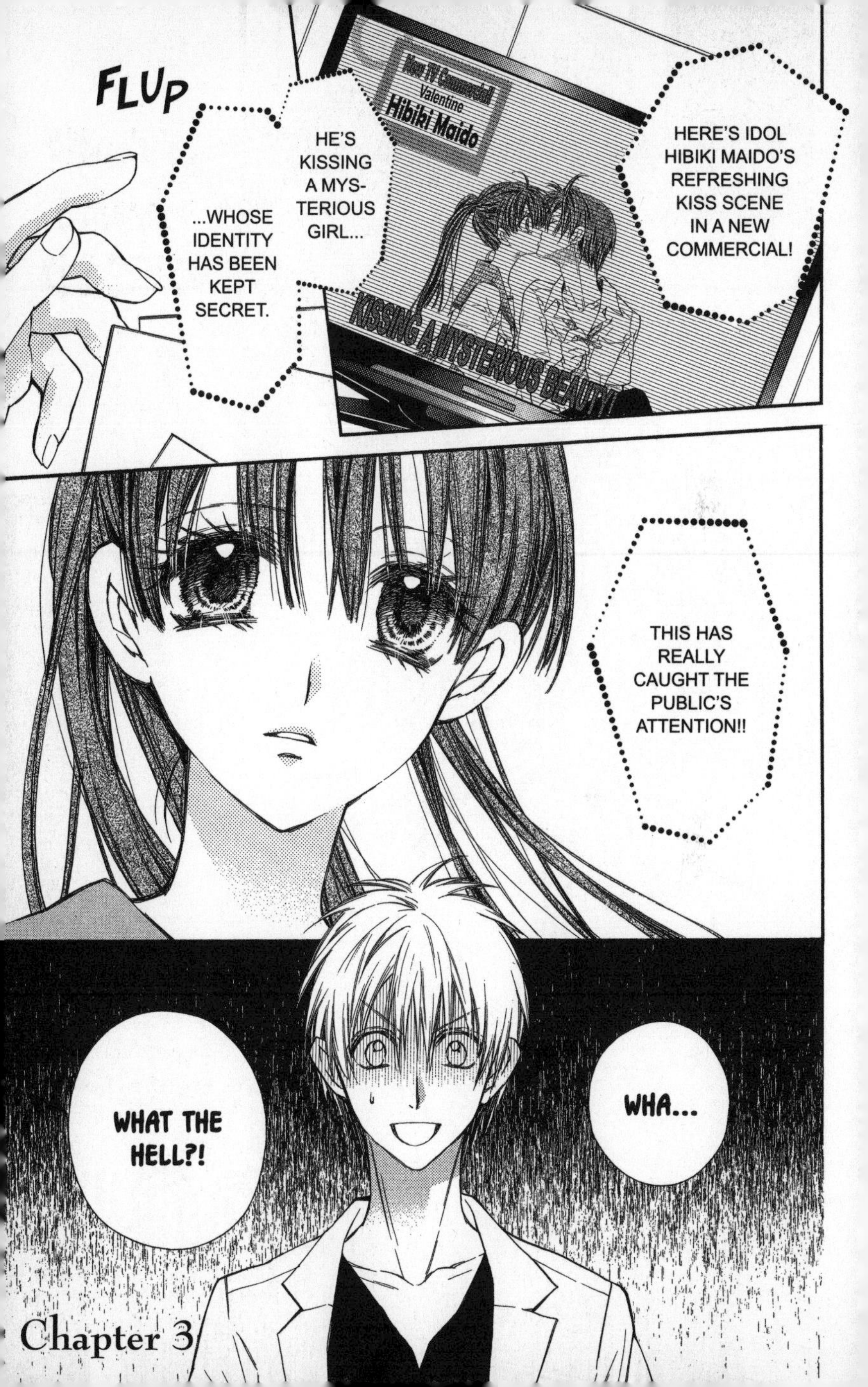
New TV Commercial!!
Valentine
Hibiki Maido
KISSING A MYSTERIOUS BEAUTY!!
HERE'S IDOL HIBIKI MAIDO'S REFRESHING KISS SCENE IN A NEW COMMERCIAL!
HE'S KISSING A MYS-TERIOUS GIRL...
...WHOSE IDENTITY HAS BEEN KEPT SECRET.
FLUP
THIS HAS REALLY CAUGHT THE PUBLIC'S ATTENTION!!
WHA...
WHAT THE HELL?!
Chapter 3

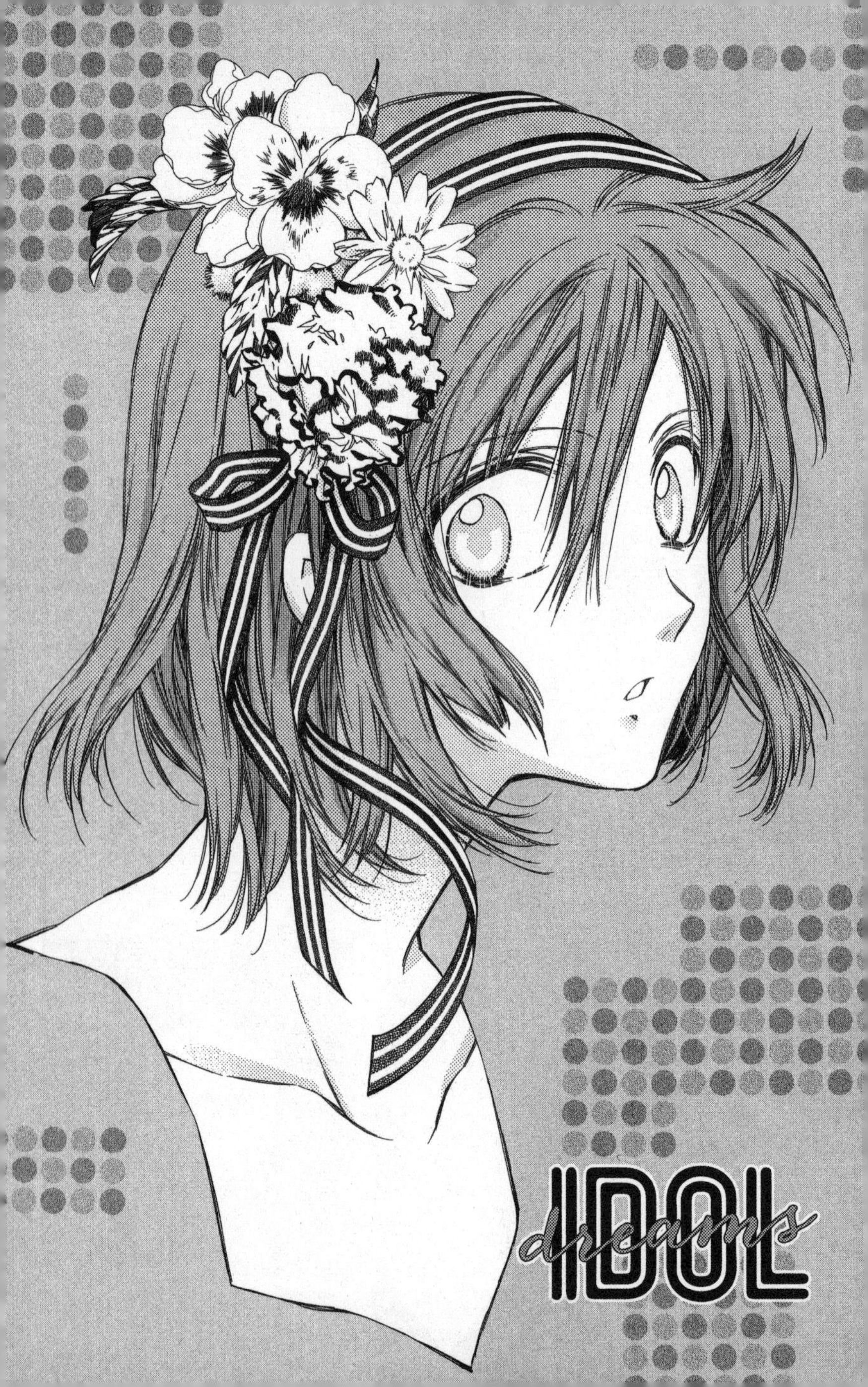
IDOL dreams

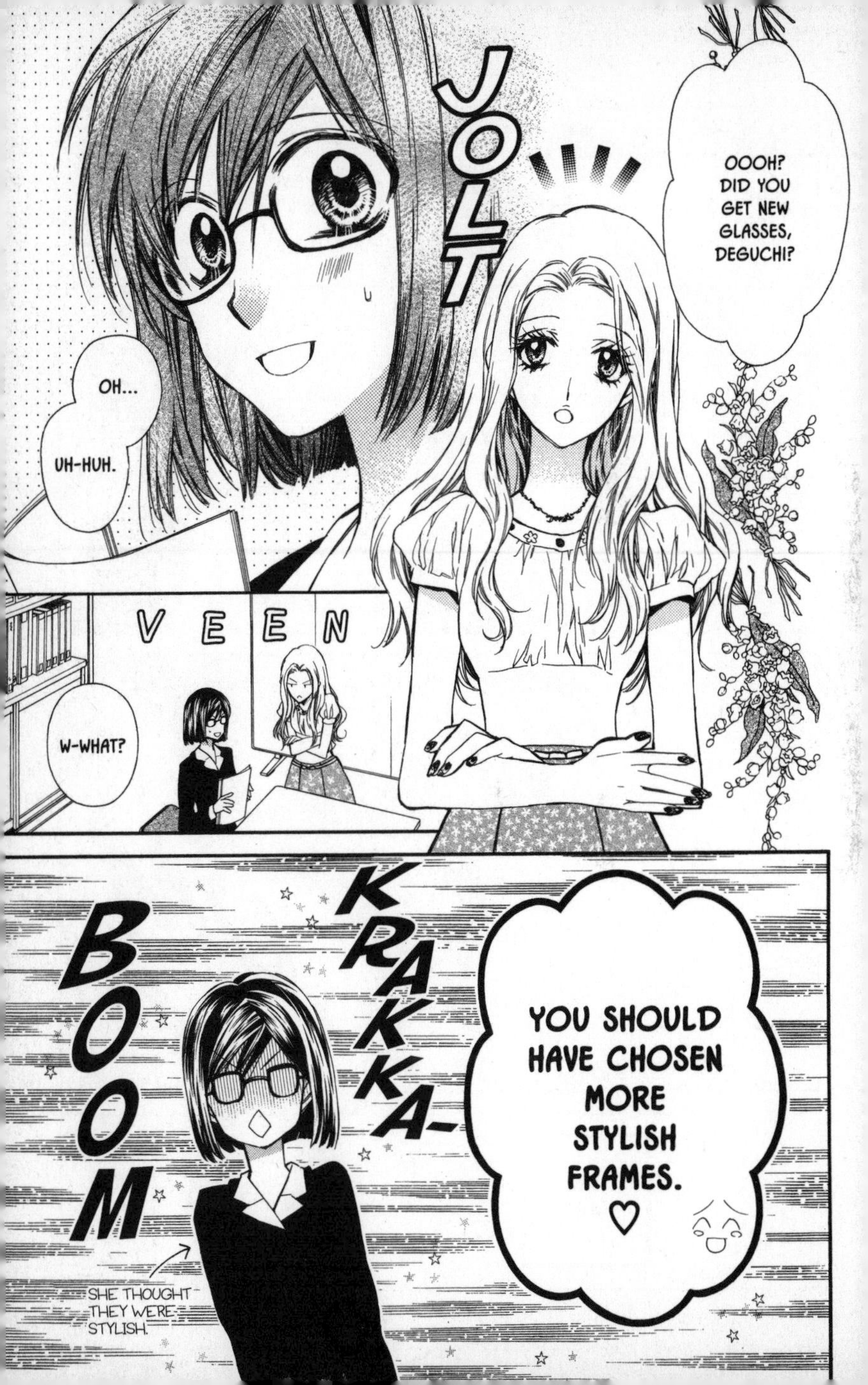
OOOH? DID YOU GET NEW GLASSES, DEGUCHI?
JOLT
OH... UH-HUH.
VEEN
W-WHAT?
YOU SHOULD HAVE CHOSEN MORE STYLISH FRAMES. ♡
KRAKKA-BOOM
SHE THOUGHT THEY WERE STYLISH.

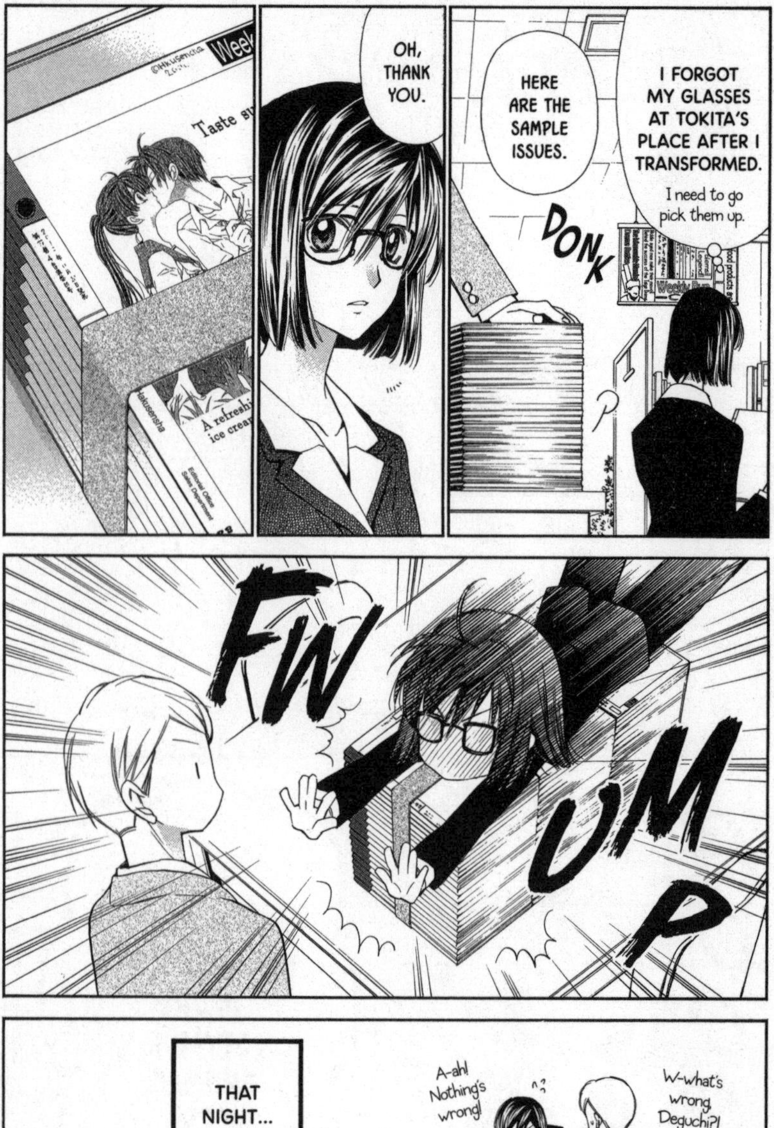
I FORGOT MY GLASSES AT TOKITA'S PLACE AFTER I TRANSFORMED.
I need to go pick them up.
HERE ARE THE SAMPLE ISSUES.
DONK
OH, THANK YOU.
Week
Taste
A refreshi ice cream
Hakusensha
FWUMP
W-what's wrong, Deguchi?!
A-ah! Nothing's wrong!
THAT NIGHT...

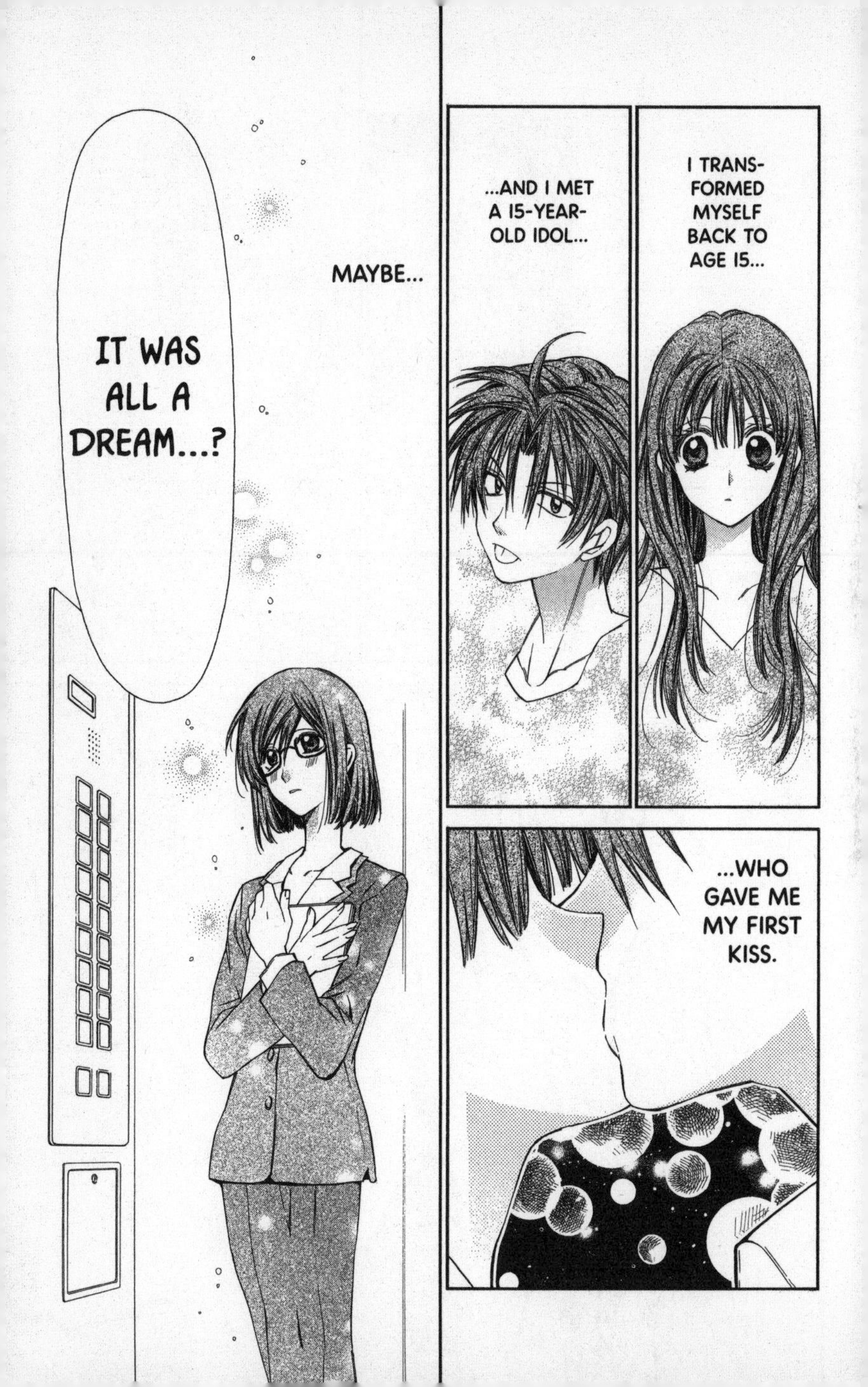
I TRANSFORMED MYSELF BACK TO AGE 15...
...AND I MET A 15-YEAR-OLD IDOL...
...WHO GAVE ME MY FIRST KISS.
MAYBE...
IT WAS ALL A DREAM...?

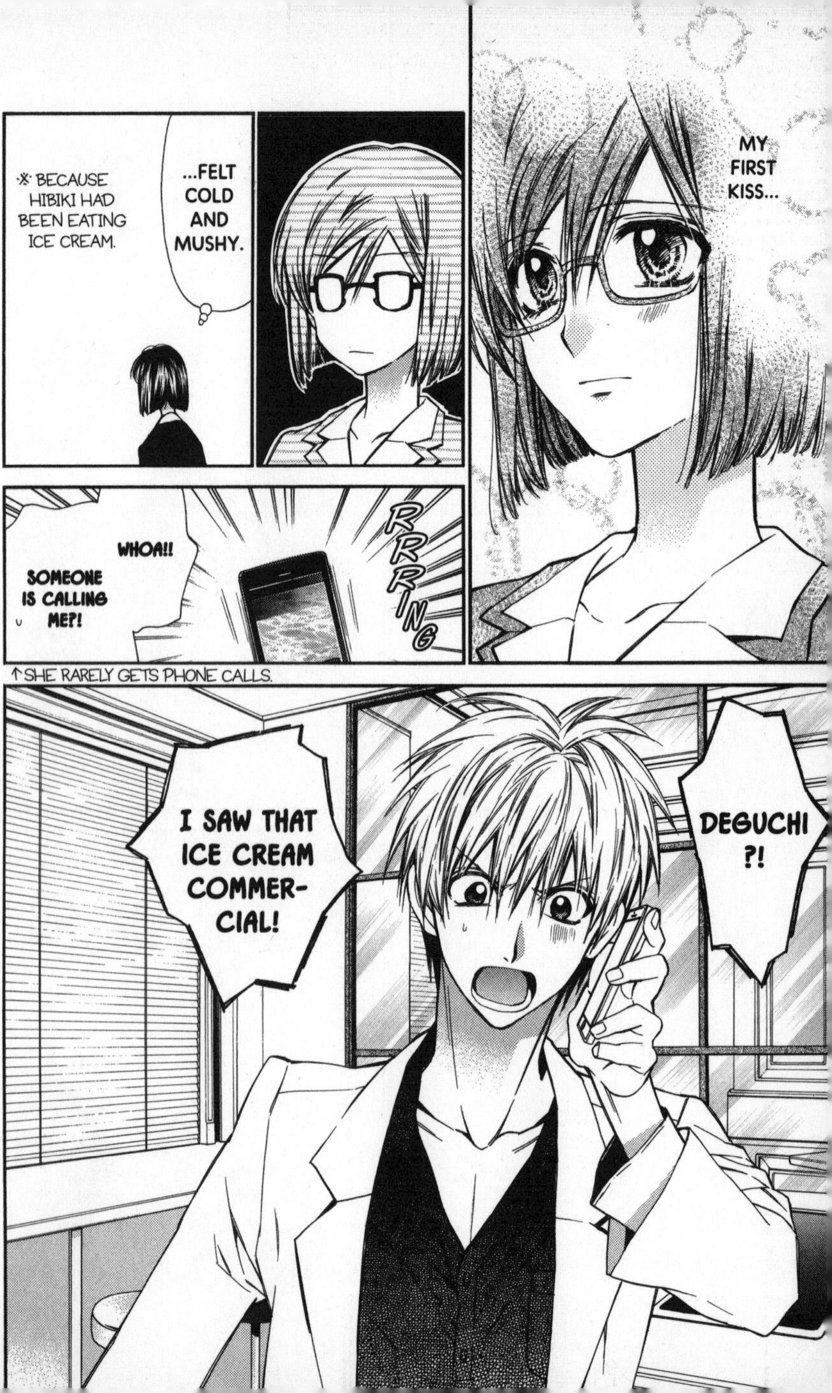
MY FIRST KISS...
...FELT COLD AND MUSHY.
※ BECAUSE HIBIKI HAD BEEN EATING ICE CREAM.
RRRING
WHOA!!
SOMEONE IS CALLING ME?!
↑SHE RARELY GETS PHONE CALLS.
DEGUCHI?!
I SAW THAT ICE CREAM COMMER-CIAL!

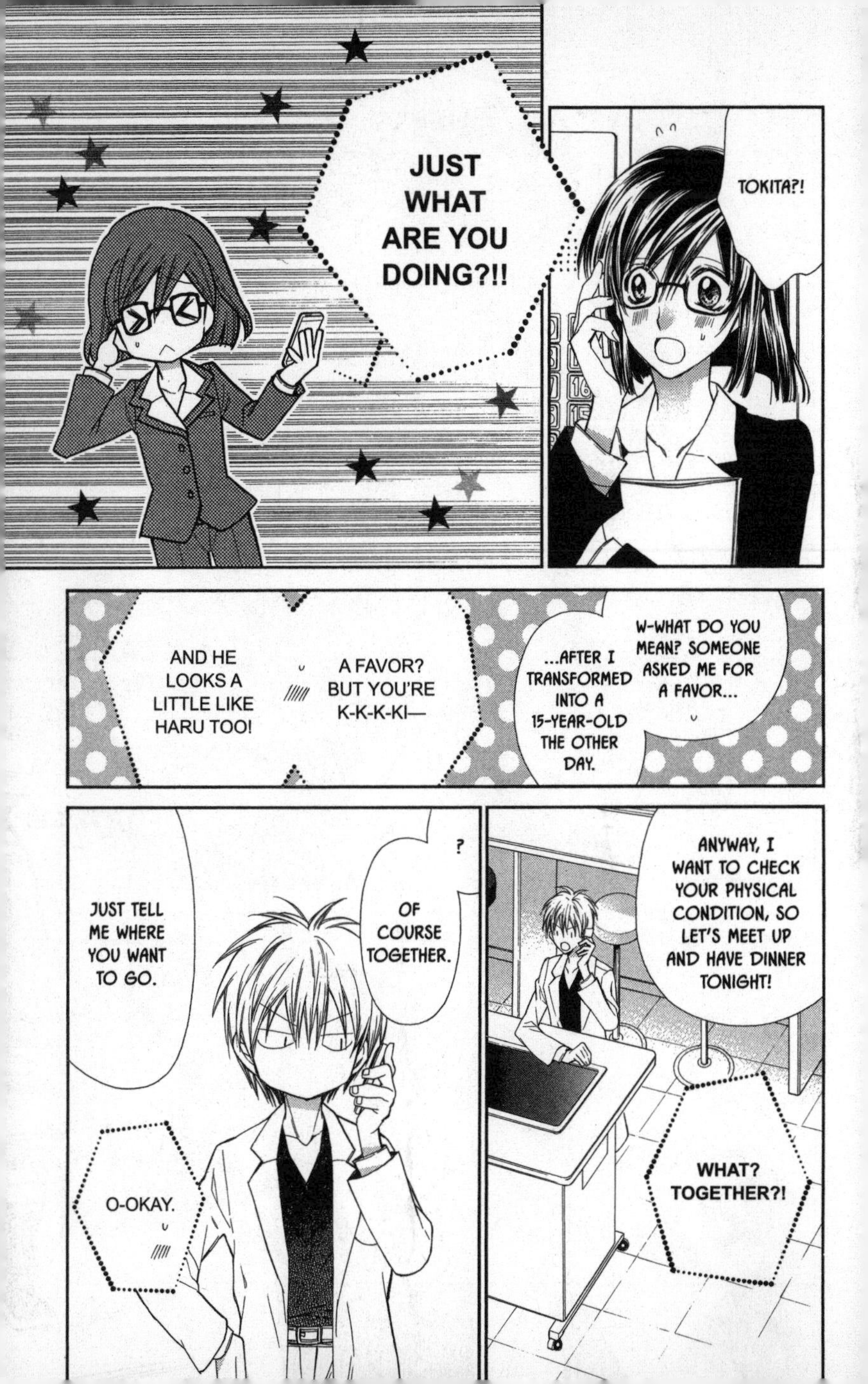
TOKITA?!
JUST WHAT ARE YOU DOING?!!
W-WHAT DO YOU MEAN? SOMEONE ASKED ME FOR A FAVOR...
...AFTER I TRANSFORMED INTO A 15-YEAR-OLD THE OTHER DAY.
A FAVOR? BUT YOU'RE K-K-K-KI—
AND HE LOOKS A LITTLE LIKE HARU TOO!
ANYWAY, I WANT TO CHECK YOUR PHYSICAL CONDITION, SO LET'S MEET UP AND HAVE DINNER TONIGHT!
WHAT? TOGETHER?!
?
OF COURSE TOGETHER.
JUST TELL ME WHERE YOU WANT TO GO.
O-OKAY.

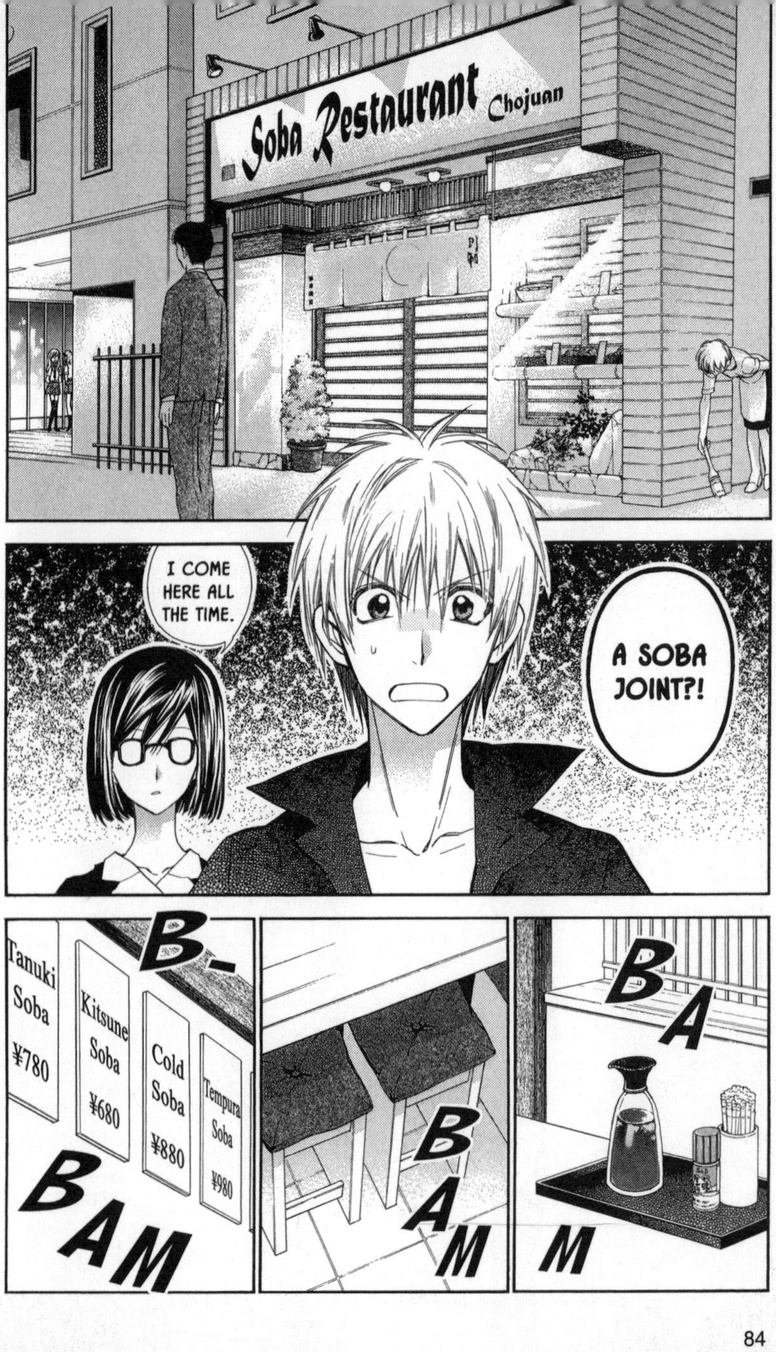
Soba Restaurant Chojuan
A SOBA JOINT?!
I COME HERE ALL THE TIME.
BAM
BAM
B-
Tanuki Soba ¥780
Kitsune Soba ¥680
Cold Soba ¥880
Tempura Soba ¥980
BAM

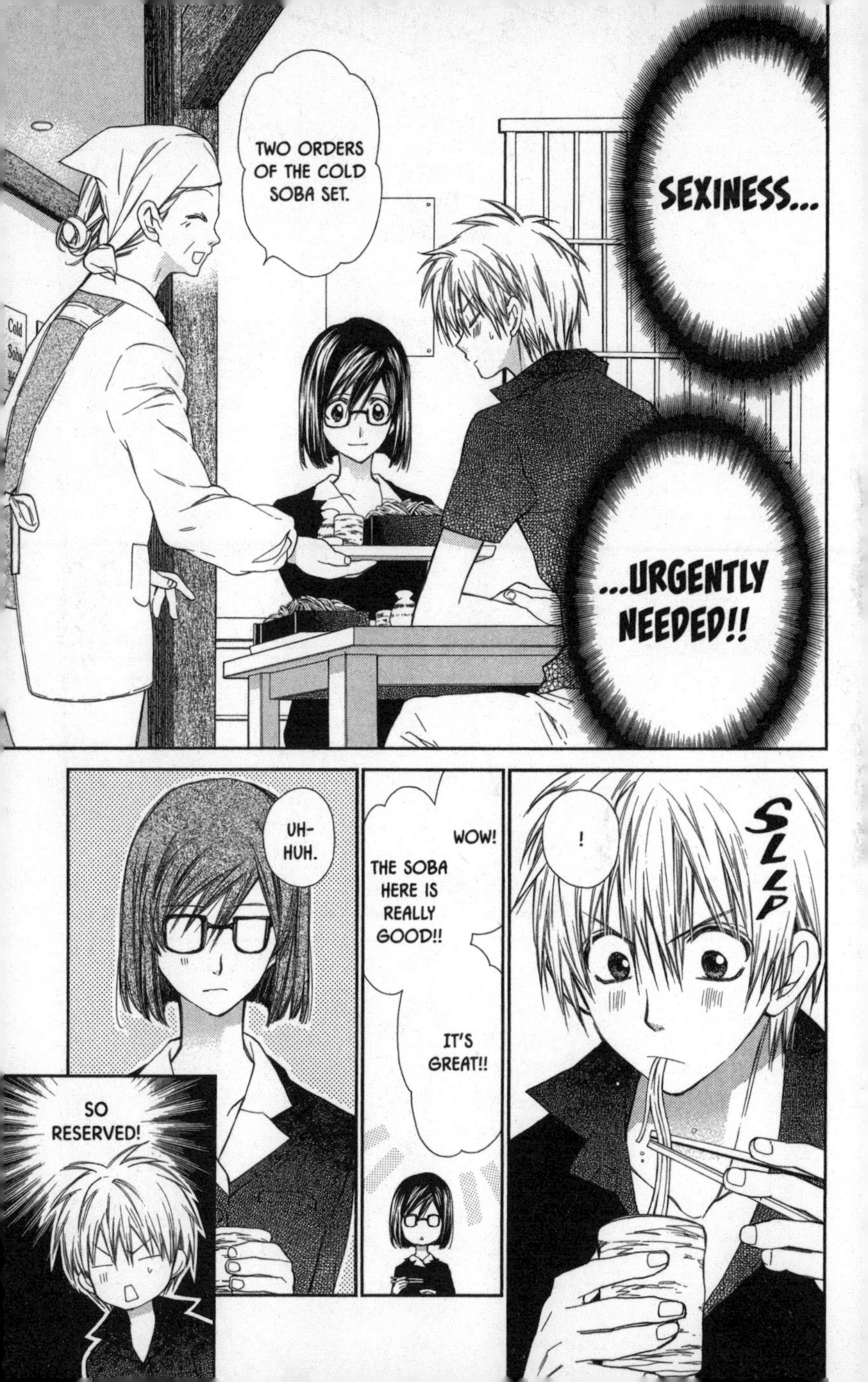
SEXINESS...
...URGENTLY NEEDED!!
TWO ORDERS OF THE COLD SOBA SET.
Cold Soba
SLLP
!
WOW!
THE SOBA HERE IS REALLY GOOD!!
IT'S GREAT!!
UH-HUH.
SO RESERVED!

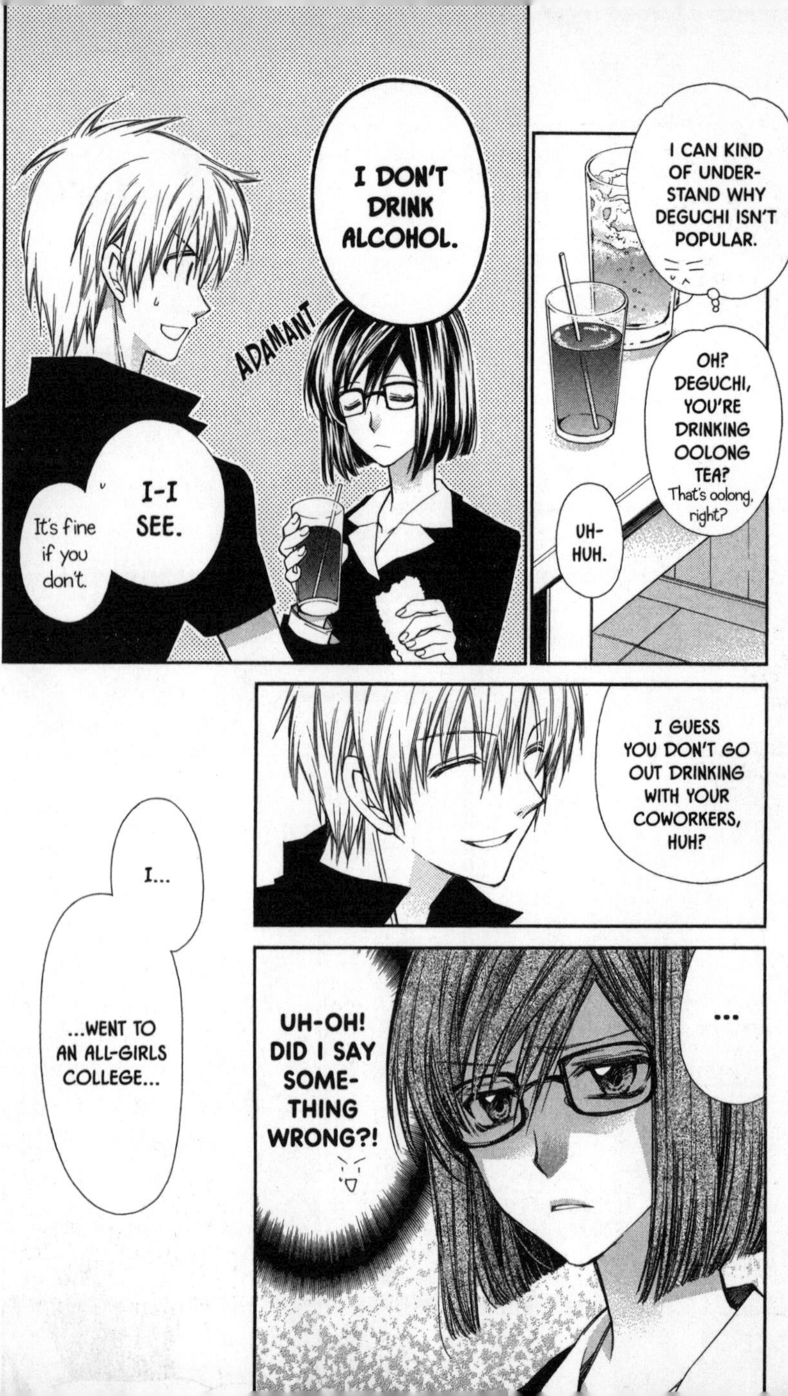
I CAN KIND OF UNDER-STAND WHY DEGUCHI ISN'T POPULAR.
OH? DEGUCHI, YOU'RE DRINKING OOLONG TEA?
That's oolong, right?
UH-HUH.
I DON'T DRINK ALCOHOL.
ADAMANT
I-I SEE.
It's fine if you don't.
I GUESS YOU DON'T GO OUT DRINKING WITH YOUR COWORKERS, HUH?
...
UH-OH! DID I SAY SOME-THING WRONG?!
I...
...WENT TO AN ALL-GIRLS COLLEGE...

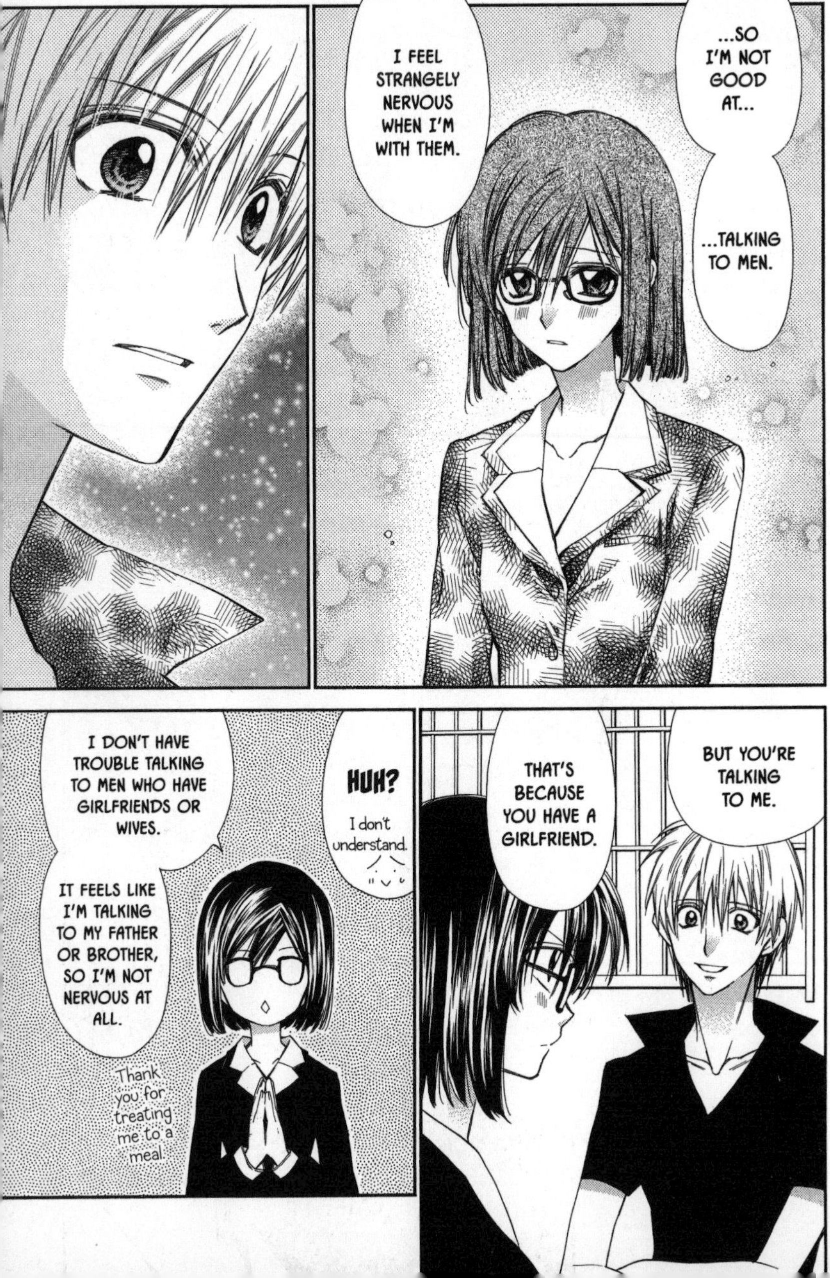
...SO I'M NOT GOOD AT...
...TALKING TO MEN.
I FEEL STRANGELY NERVOUS WHEN I'M WITH THEM.
BUT YOU'RE TALKING TO ME.
THAT'S BECAUSE YOU HAVE A GIRLFRIEND.
HUH?
I don't understand.
I DON'T HAVE TROUBLE TALKING TO MEN WHO HAVE GIRLFRIENDS OR WIVES.
IT FEELS LIKE I'M TALKING TO MY FATHER OR BROTHER, SO I'M NOT NERVOUS AT ALL.
Thank you for treating me to a meal.

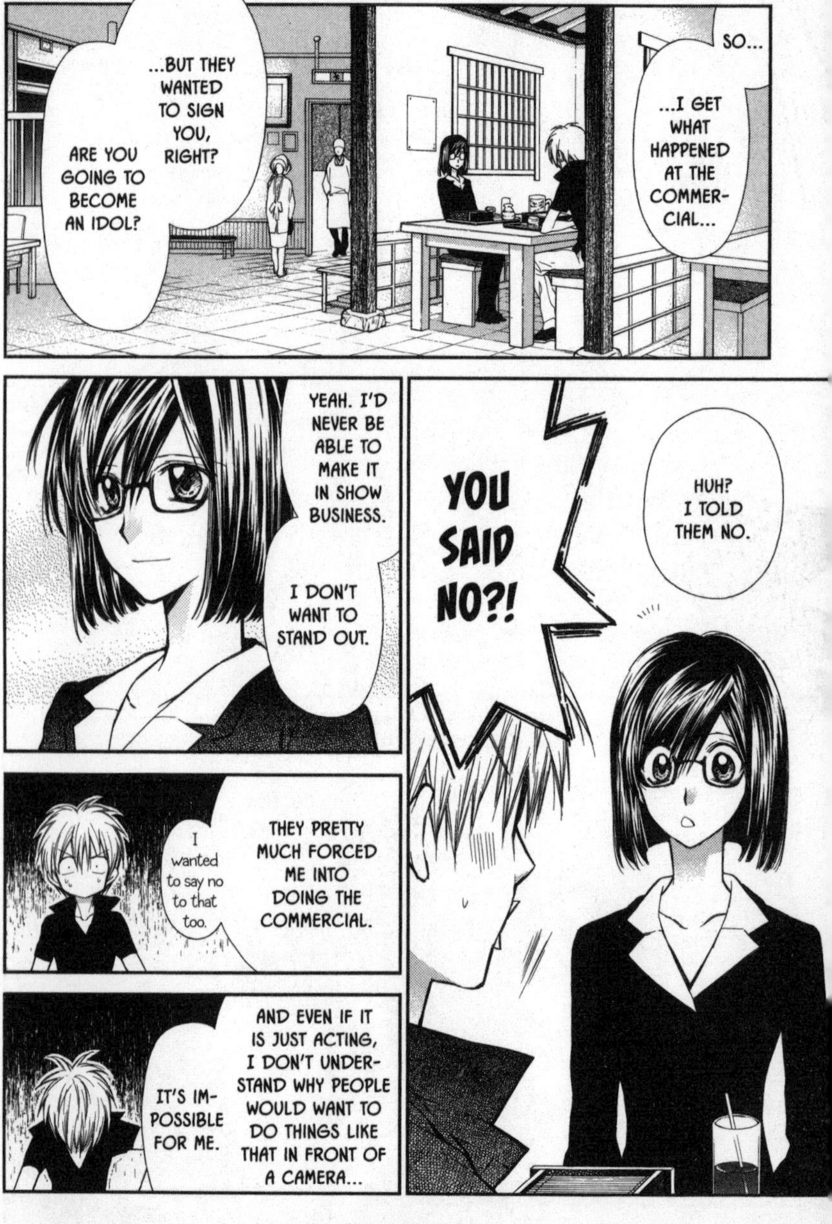
SO...
...I GET WHAT HAPPENED AT THE COMMERCIAL...
...BUT THEY WANTED TO SIGN YOU, RIGHT?
ARE YOU GOING TO BECOME AN IDOL?
HUH? I TOLD THEM NO.
YOU SAID NO?!
YEAH. I'D NEVER BE ABLE TO MAKE IT IN SHOW BUSINESS.
I DON'T WANT TO STAND OUT.
THEY PRETTY MUCH FORCED ME INTO DOING THE COMMERCIAL.
I wanted to say no to that too.
AND EVEN IF IT IS JUST ACTING, I DON'T UNDERSTAND WHY PEOPLE WOULD WANT TO DO THINGS LIKE THAT IN FRONT OF A CAMERA...
IT'S IMPOSSIBLE FOR ME.

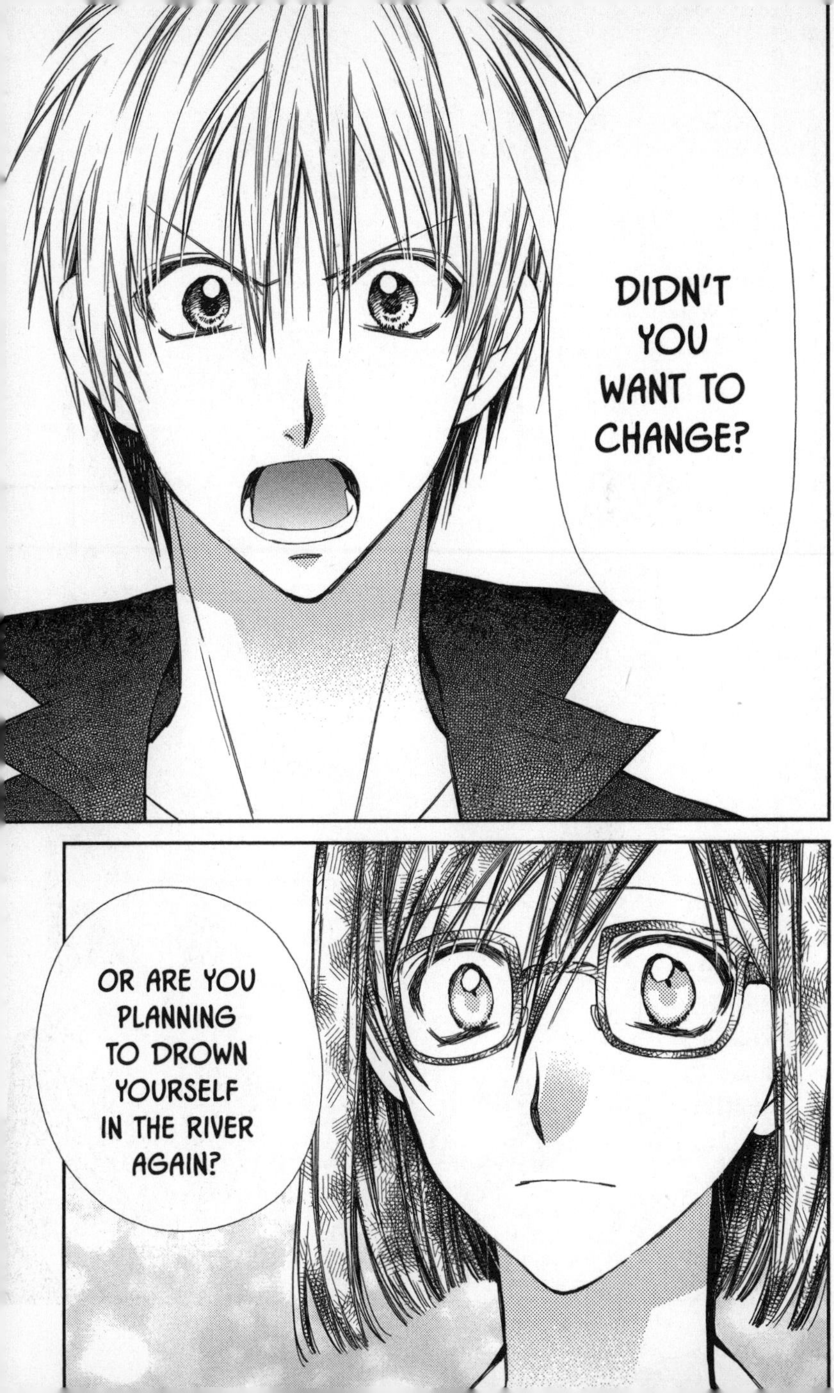
DIDN'T YOU WANT TO CHANGE?
OR ARE YOU PLANNING TO DROWN YOURSELF IN THE RIVER AGAIN?

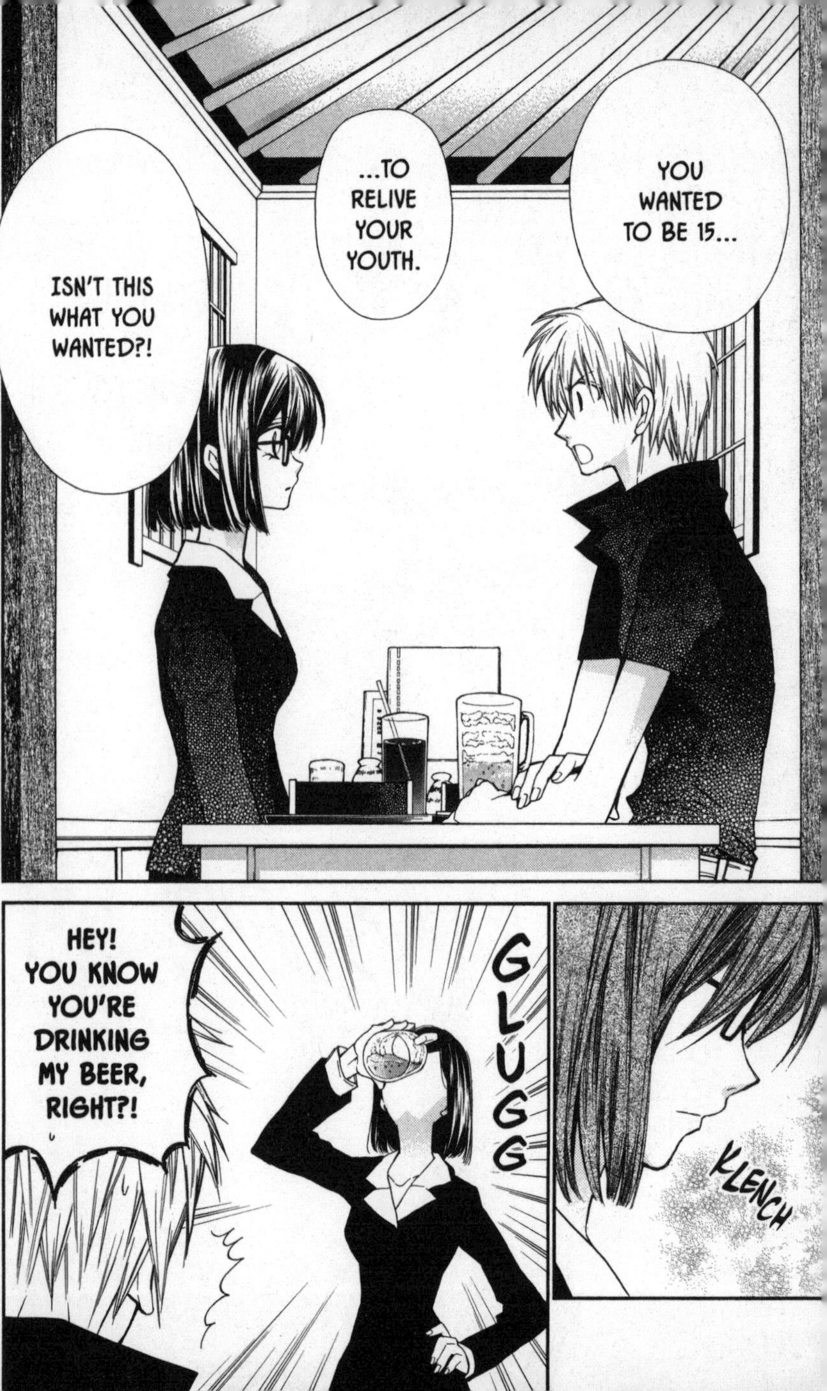
YOU WANTED TO BE 15...
...TO RELIVE YOUR YOUTH.
ISN'T THIS WHAT YOU WANTED?!
KLENCH
GLUGG
HEY! YOU KNOW YOU'RE DRINKING MY BEER, RIGHT?!

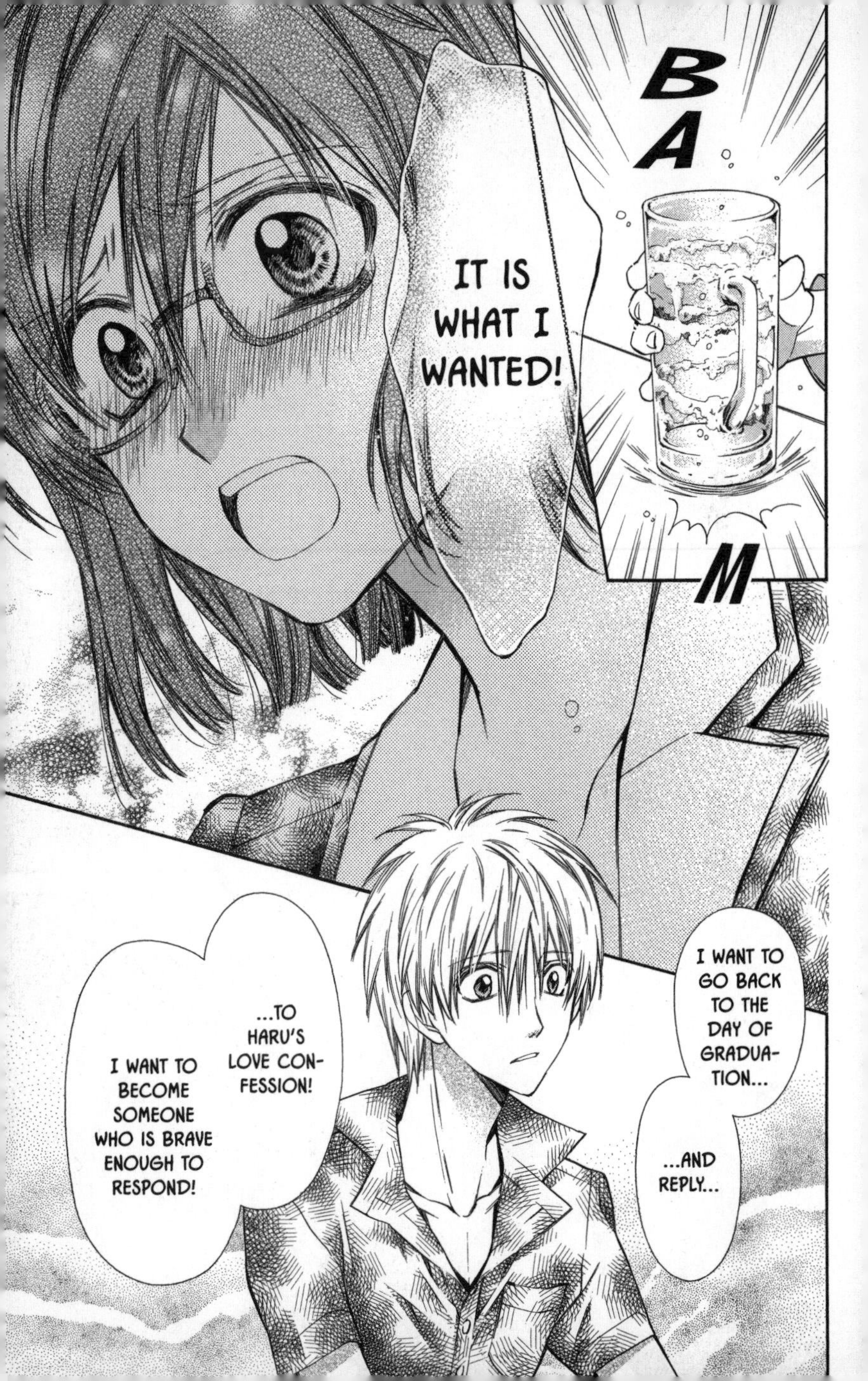
BAM
IT IS WHAT I WANTED!
I WANT TO GO BACK TO THE DAY OF GRADUA-TION...
...AND REPLY...
...TO HARU'S LOVE CON-FESSION!
I WANT TO BECOME SOMEONE WHO IS BRAVE ENOUGH TO RESPOND!

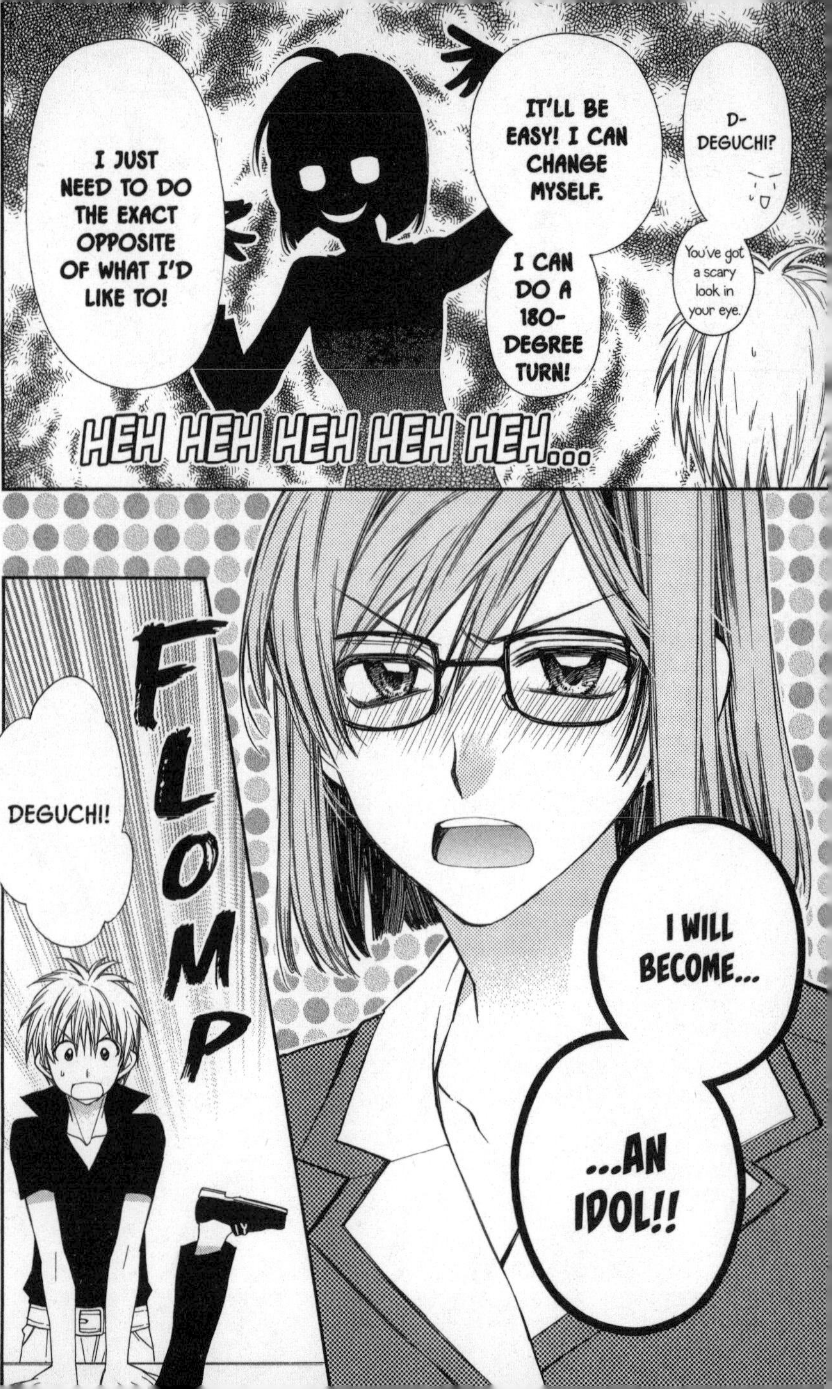
D- DEGUCHI?
You've got a scary look in your eye.
IT'LL BE EASY! I CAN CHANGE MYSELF.
I CAN DO A 180-DEGREE TURN!
I JUST NEED TO DO THE EXACT OPPOSITE OF WHAT I'D LIKE TO!
HEH HEH HEH HEH HEH...
I WILL BECOME...
...AN IDOL!!
FLOMP
DEGUCHI!

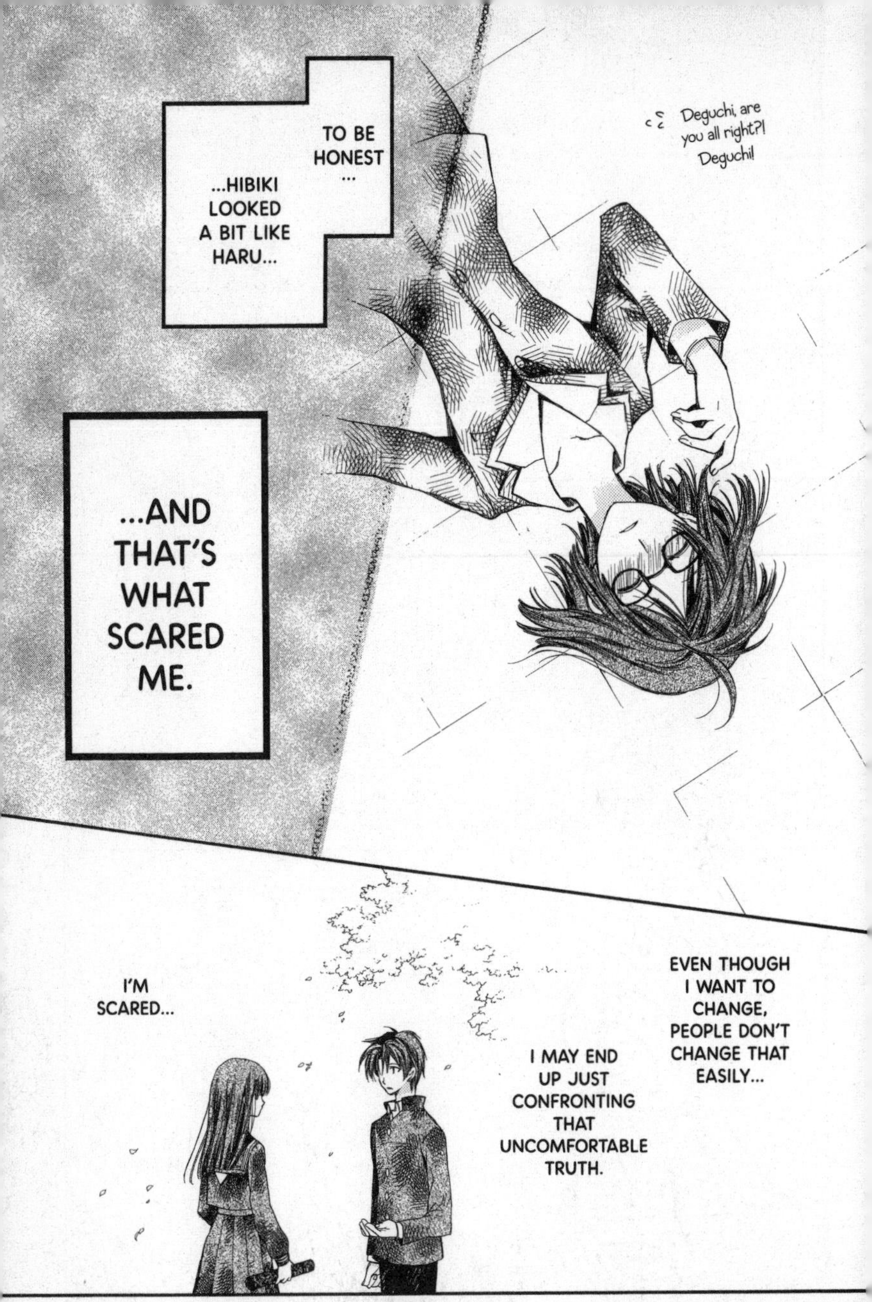
Deguchi, are you all right?! Deguchi!
TO BE HONEST...
...HIBIKI LOOKED A BIT LIKE HARU...
...AND THAT'S WHAT SCARED ME.
EVEN THOUGH I WANT TO CHANGE, PEOPLE DON'T CHANGE THAT EASILY...
I MAY END UP JUST CONFRONTING THAT UNCOMFORTABLE TRUTH.
I'M SCARED...

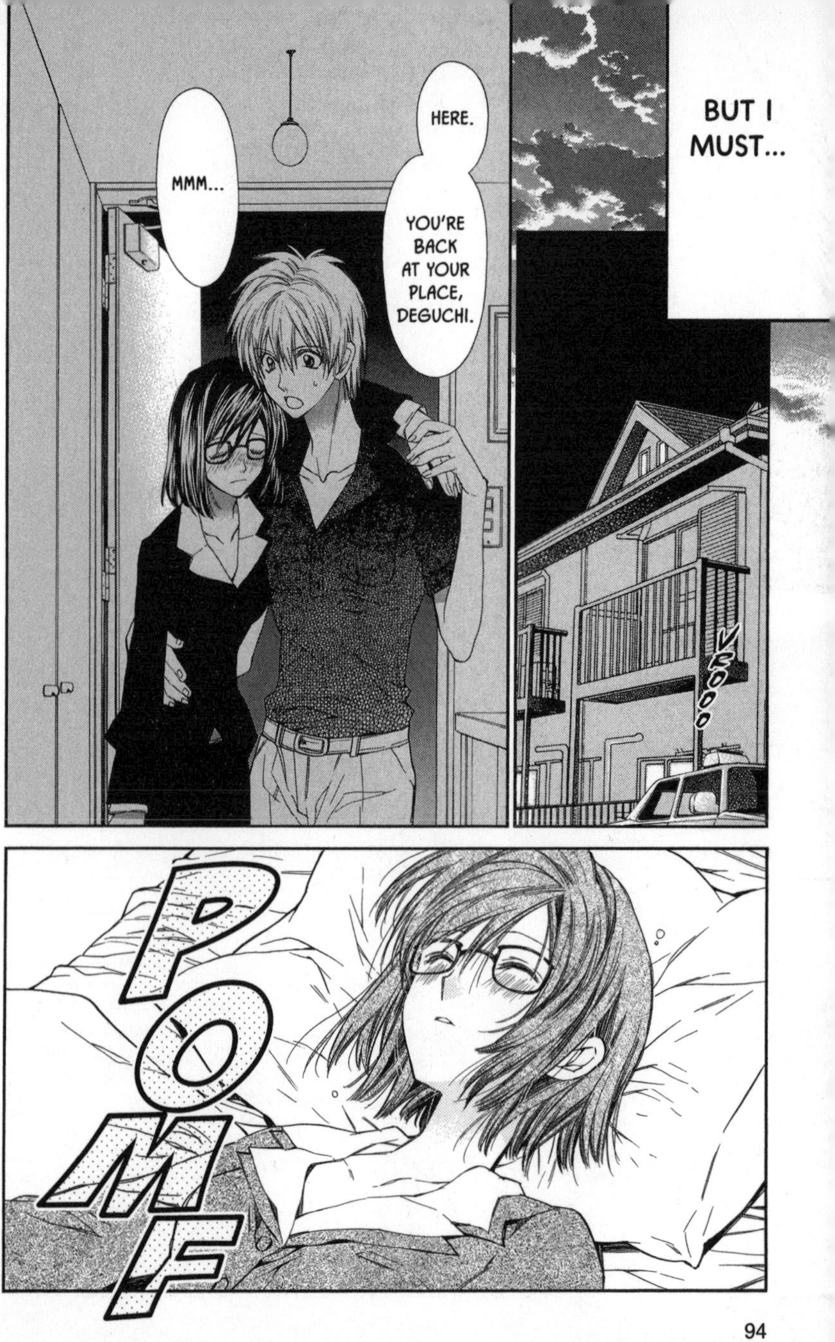
BUT I MUST...
VROOOO
HERE.
YOU'RE BACK AT YOUR PLACE, DEGUCHI.
MMM...
POMF

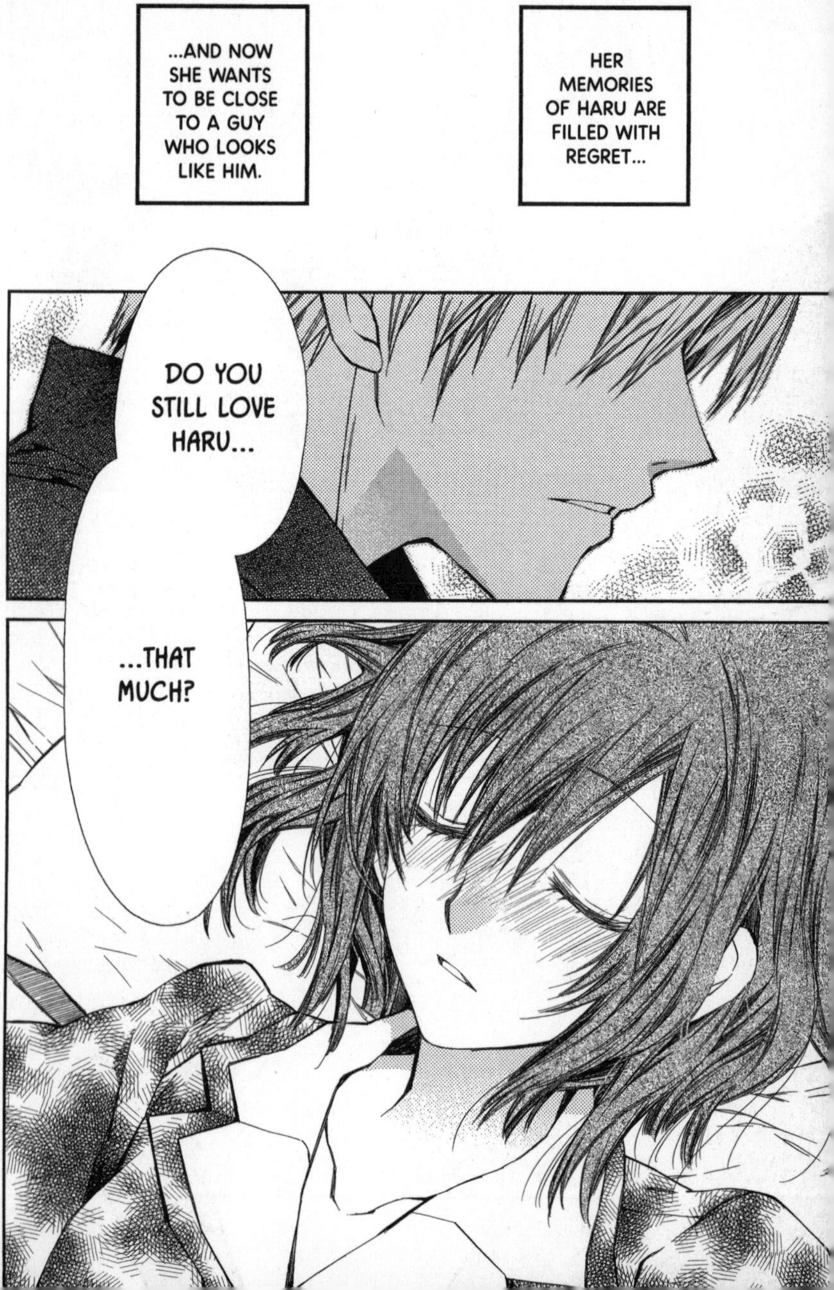
HER MEMORIES OF HARU ARE FILLED WITH REGRET...
...AND NOW SHE WANTS TO BE CLOSE TO A GUY WHO LOOKS LIKE HIM.
DO YOU STILL LOVE HARU...
...THAT MUCH?

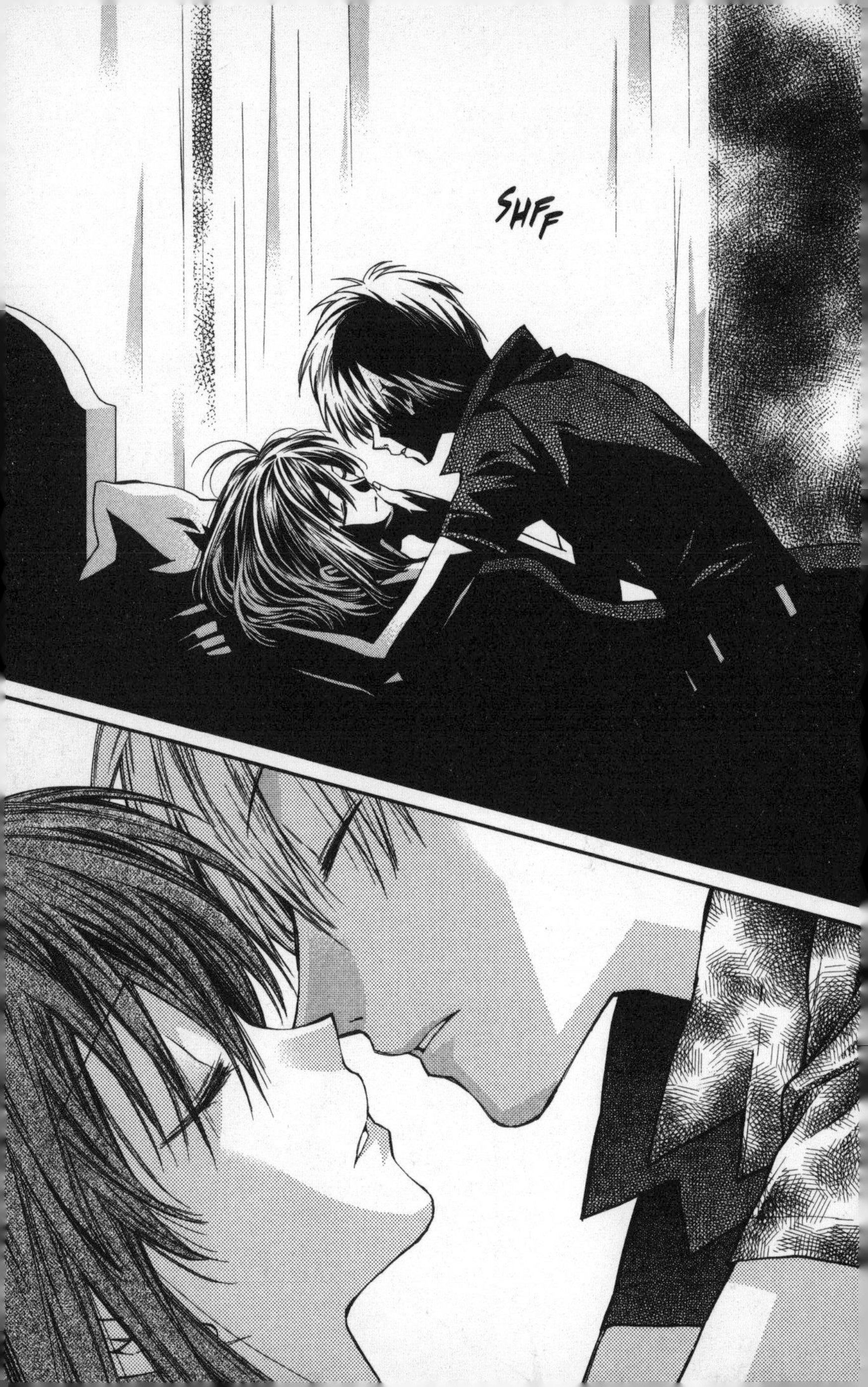
SHFF

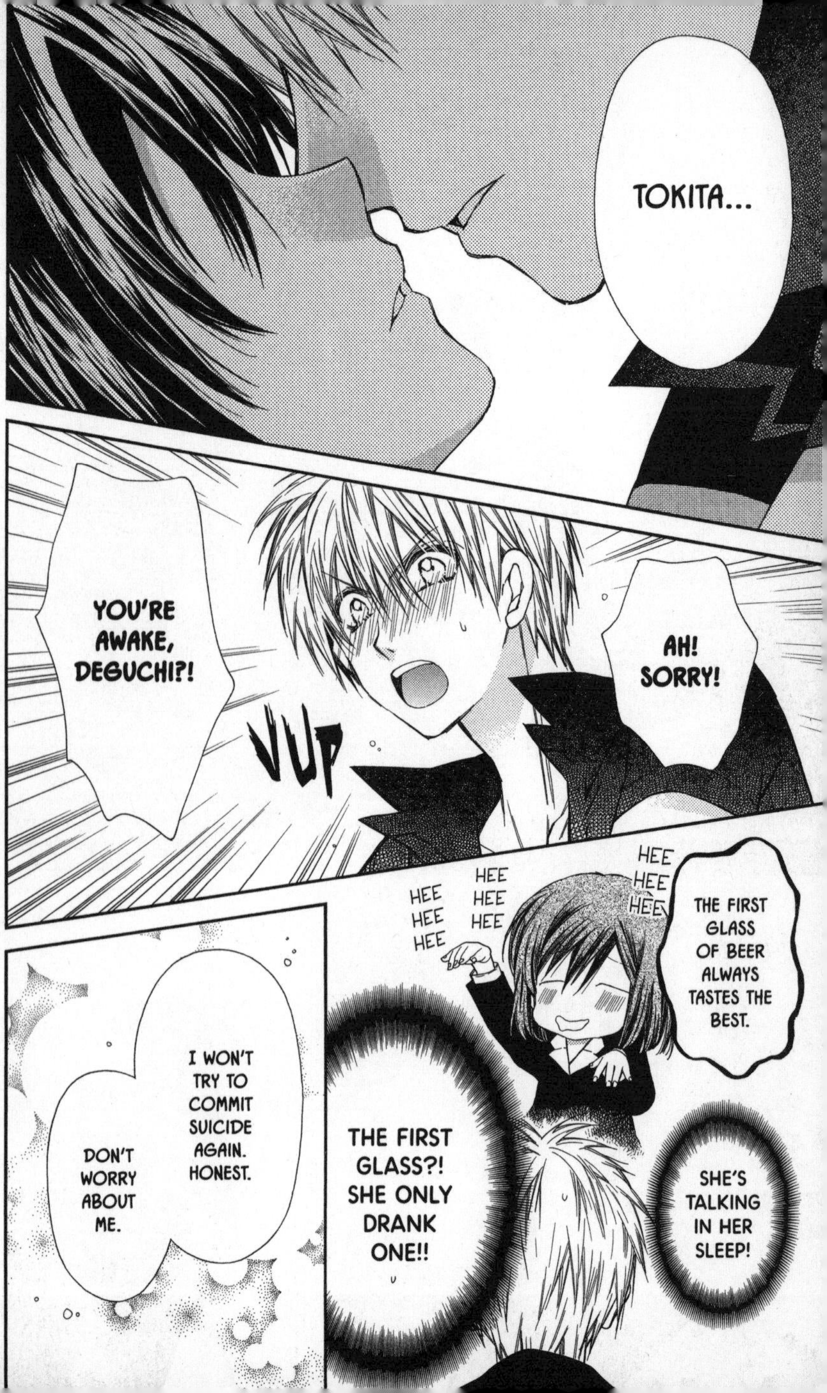
TOKITA...
AH! SORRY!
YOU'RE AWAKE, DEGUCHI?!
VUP
THE FIRST GLASS OF BEER ALWAYS TASTES THE BEST.
HEE HEE HEE
HEE HEE HEE
HEE HEE HEE
SHE'S TALKING IN HER SLEEP!
THE FIRST GLASS?! SHE ONLY DRANK ONE!!
I WON'T TRY TO COMMIT SUICIDE AGAIN. HONEST.
DON'T WORRY ABOUT ME.

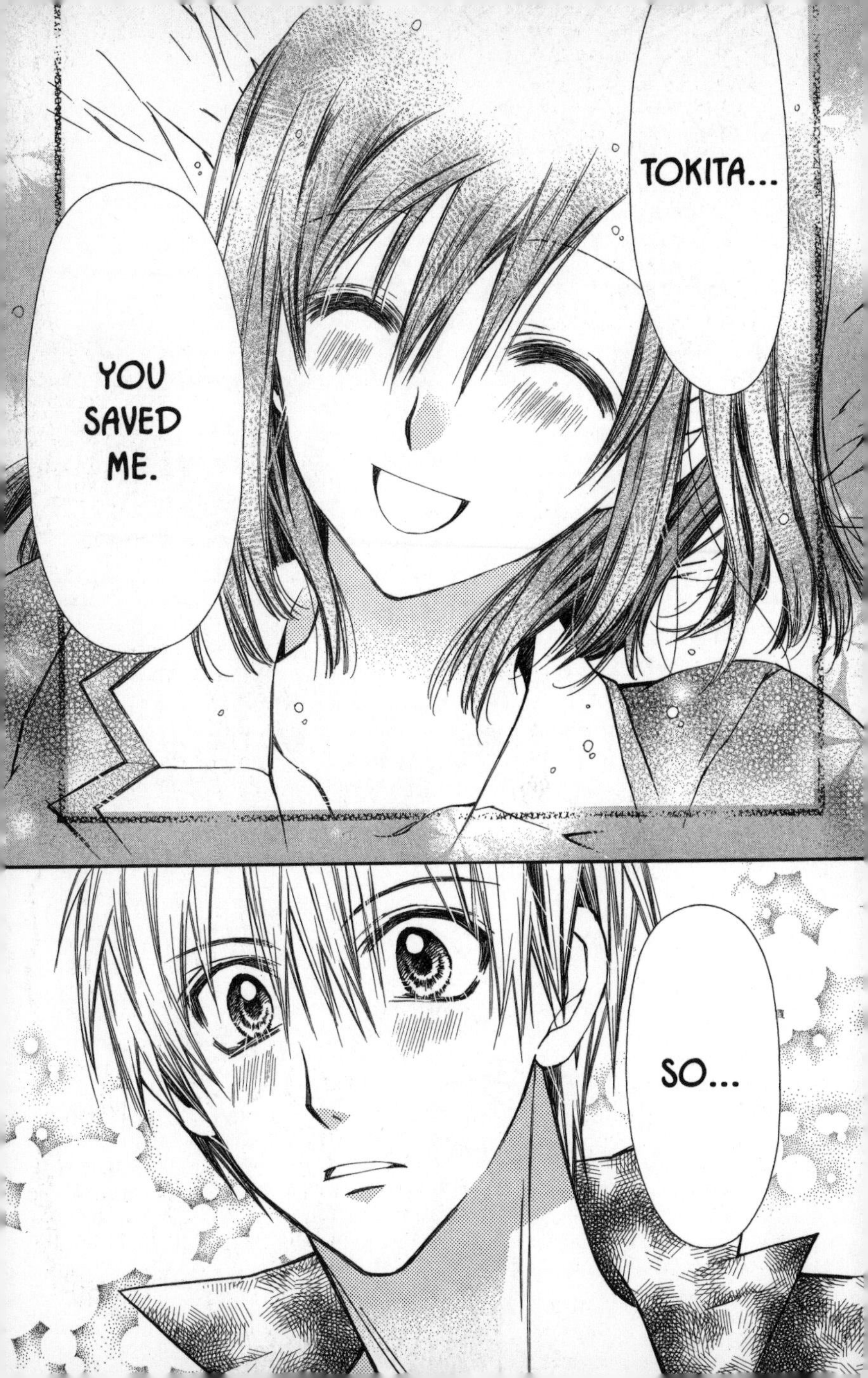
TOKITA...
YOU SAVED ME.
SO...

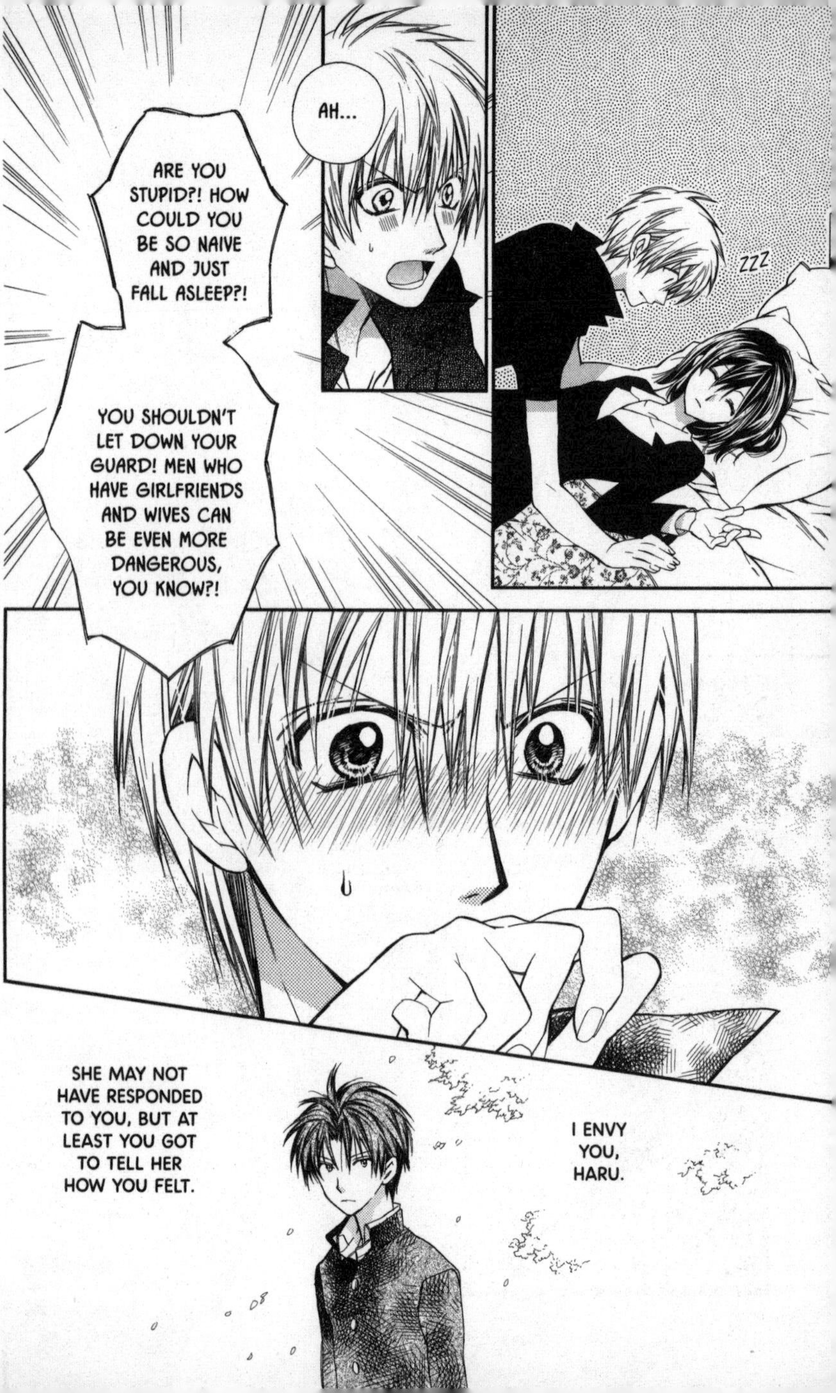
ZZZ
AH...
ARE YOU STUPID?! HOW COULD YOU BE SO NAIVE AND JUST FALL ASLEEP?!
YOU SHOULDN'T LET DOWN YOUR GUARD! MEN WHO HAVE GIRLFRIENDS AND WIVES CAN BE EVEN MORE DANGEROUS, YOU KNOW?!
I ENVY YOU, HARU.
SHE MAY NOT HAVE RESPONDED TO YOU, BUT AT LEAST YOU GOT TO TELL HER HOW YOU FELT.

I NEVER...

...HAD THE COURAGE TO TELL HER I LOVED HER.

WHAT I'M FEELING NOW ISN'T REAL.
I'M JUST CAUGHT UP IN MEMORIES...
...BECAUSE BEING WITH HER STIRS UP OLD FEELINGS.
BUT...
...THAT NIGHT AT THE CLASS REUNION...
...NO ONE RECOGNIZED ME AT FIRST...
...EXCEPT YOU, DEGUCHI. HOW DID YOU AUTOMATICALLY KNOW?

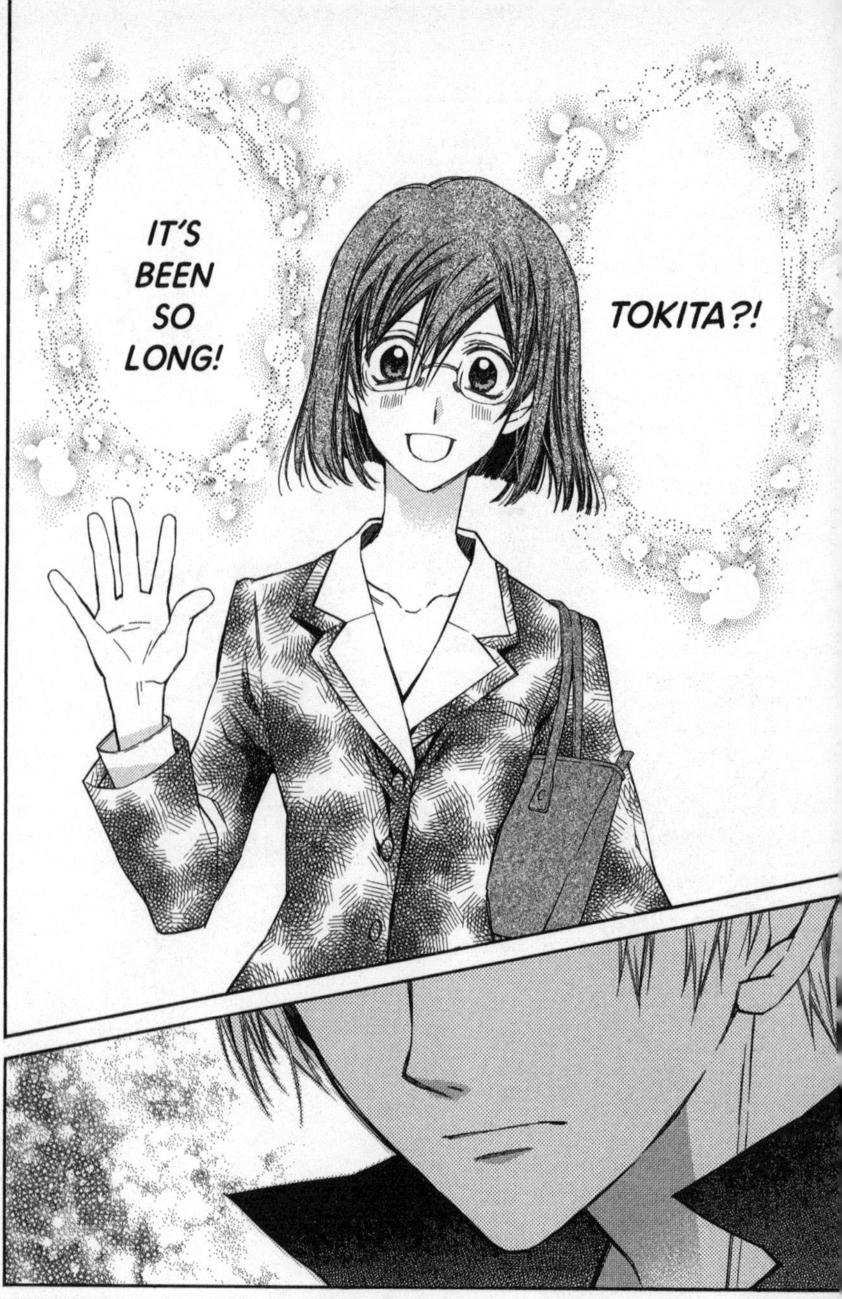
TOKITA?!
IT'S BEEN SO LONG!

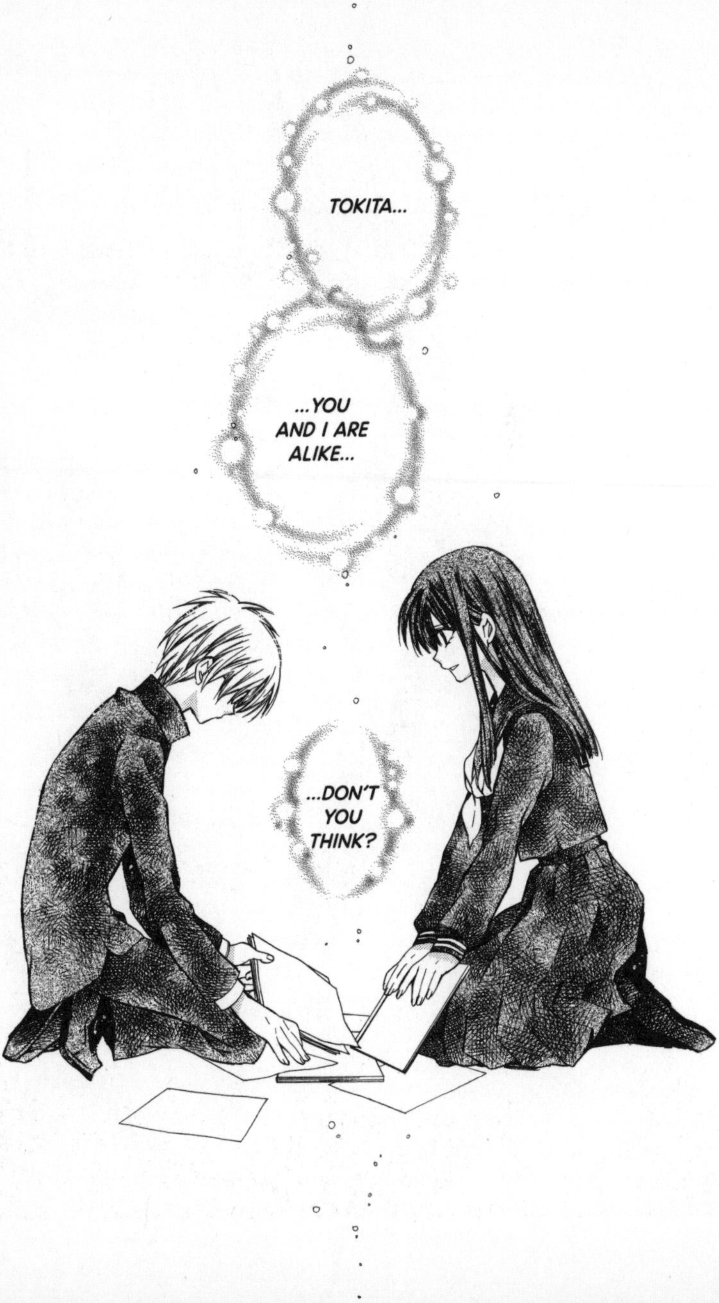
TOKITA...
...YOU AND I ARE ALIKE...
...DON'T YOU THINK?

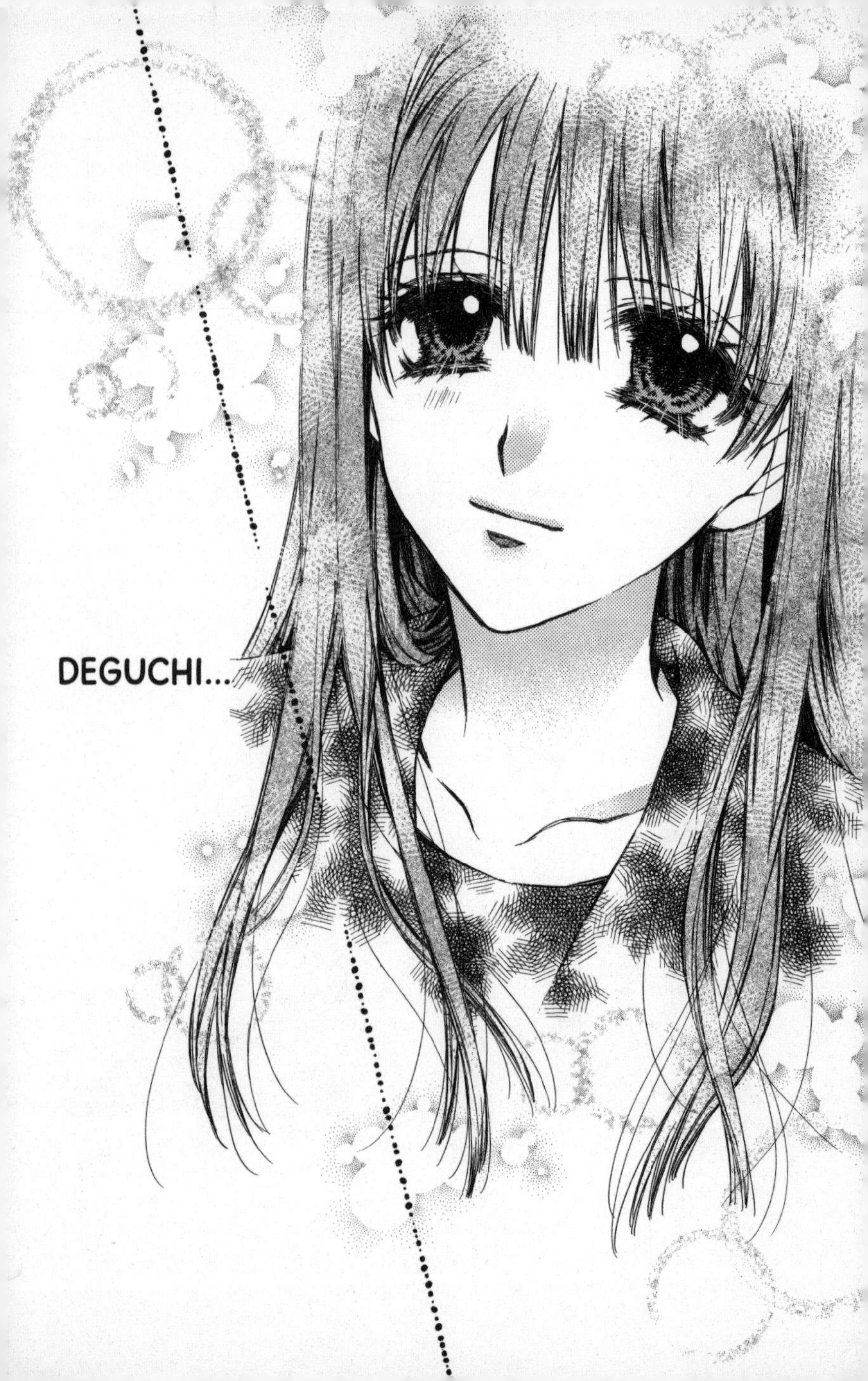
DEGUCHI...

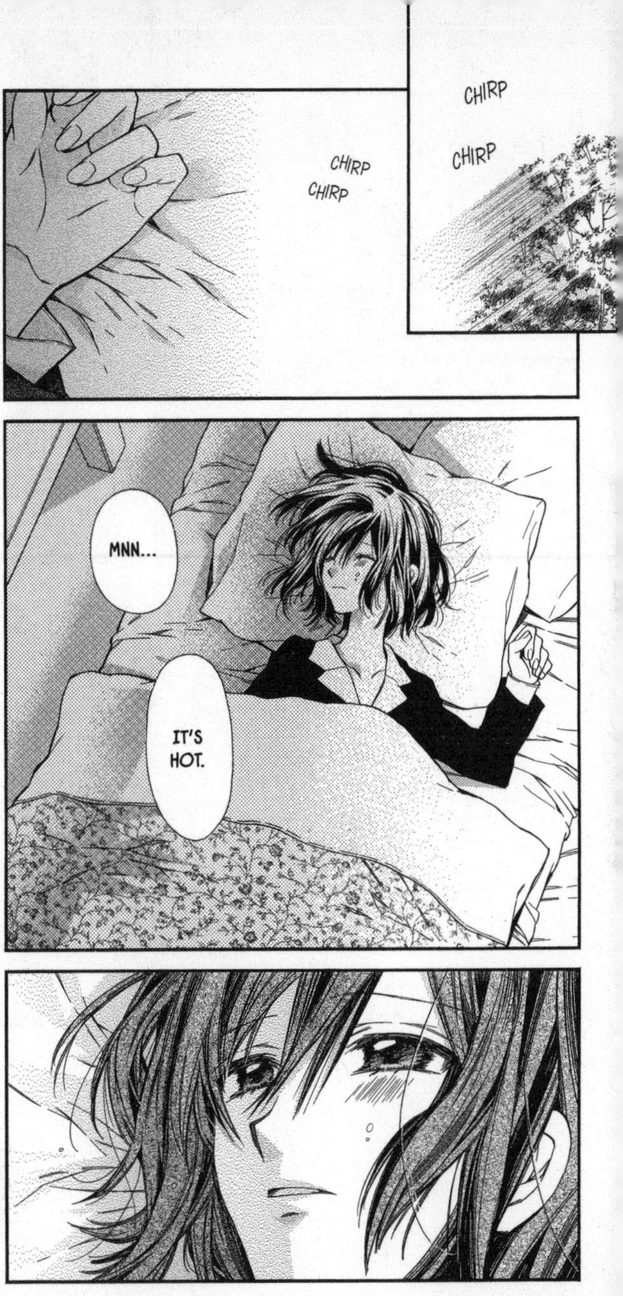
CHIRP
CHIRP
CHIRP
CHIRP
MNN...
IT'S HOT.

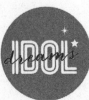

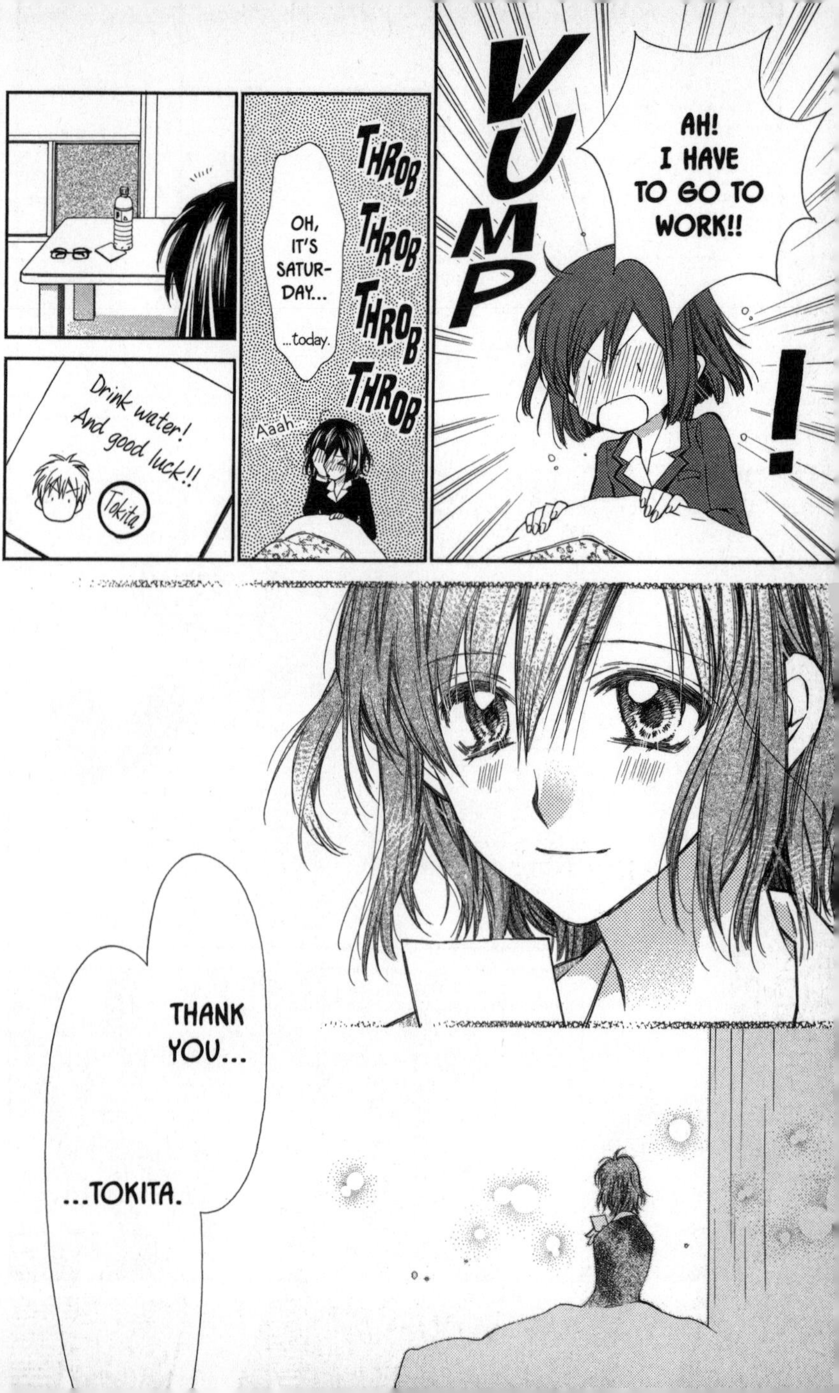
AH! I HAVE TO GO TO WORK!!
VUMP
!
THROB THROB THROB THROB
OH, IT'S SATURDAY... ...today.
Aaah...
Drink water! And good luck!!
Tokita
THANK YOU...
...TOKITA.

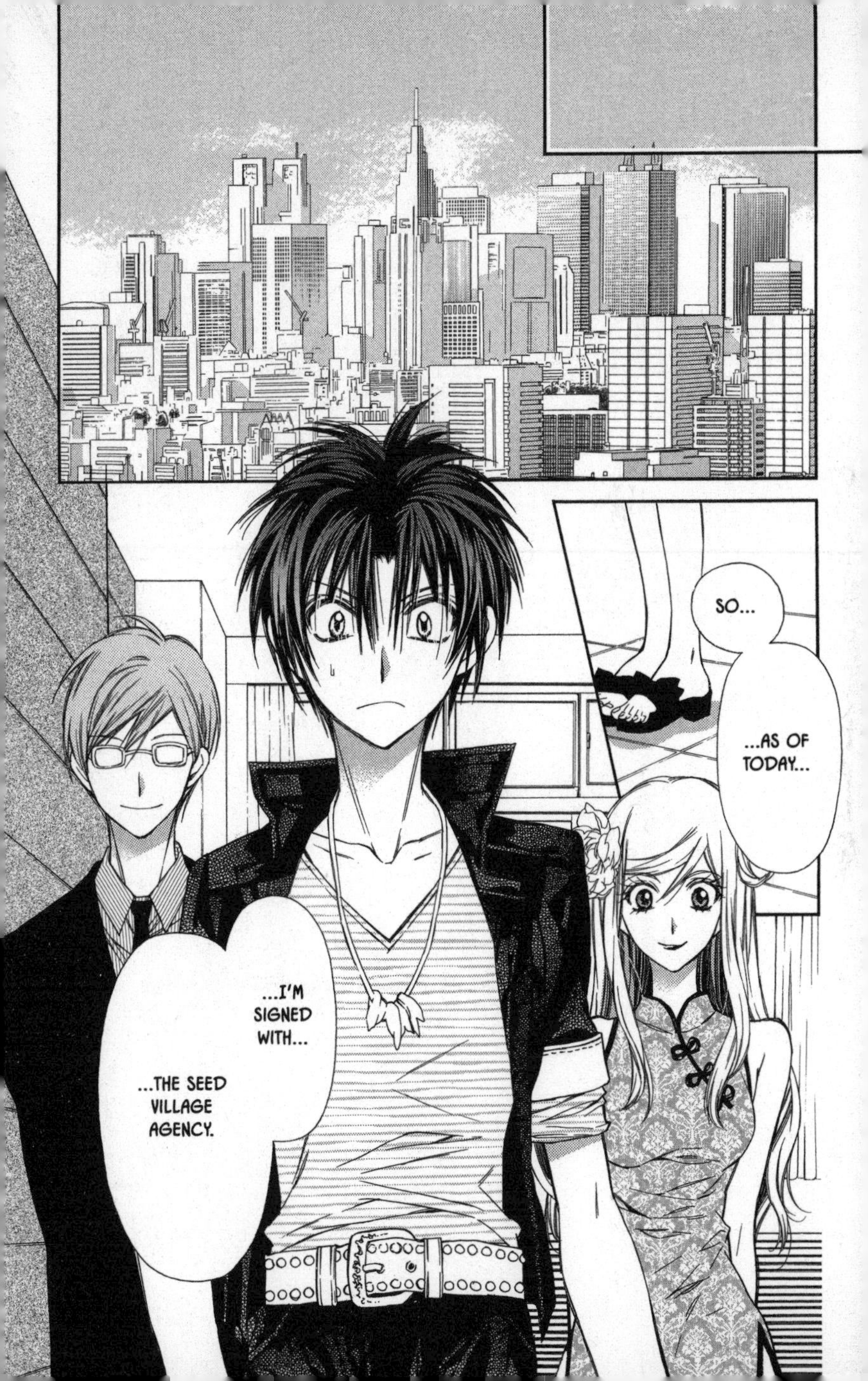
SO...
...AS OF TODAY...
...I'M SIGNED WITH...
...THE SEED VILLAGE AGENCY.

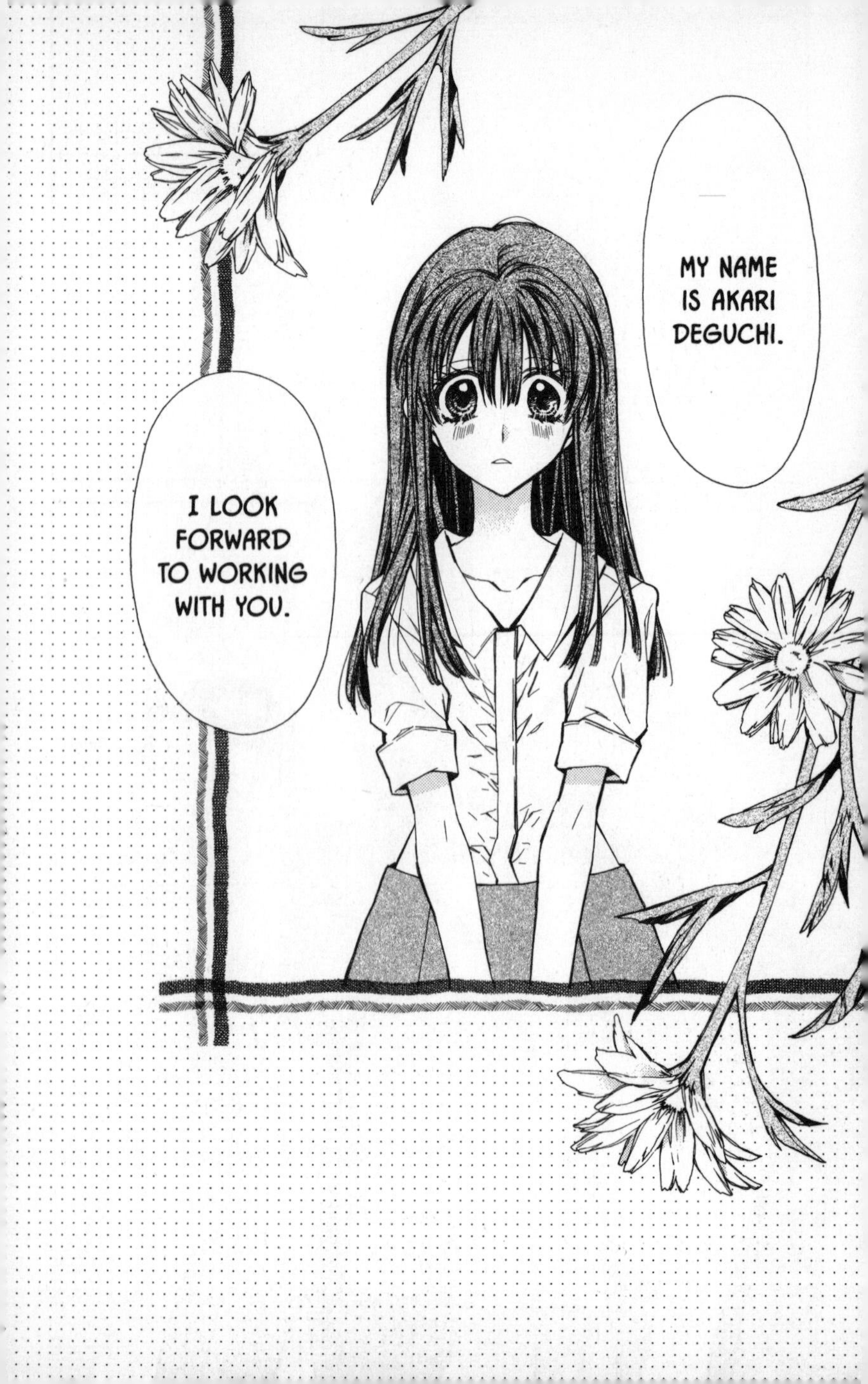
MY NAME IS AKARI DEGUCHI.
I LOOK FORWARD TO WORKING WITH YOU.

Chapter 4

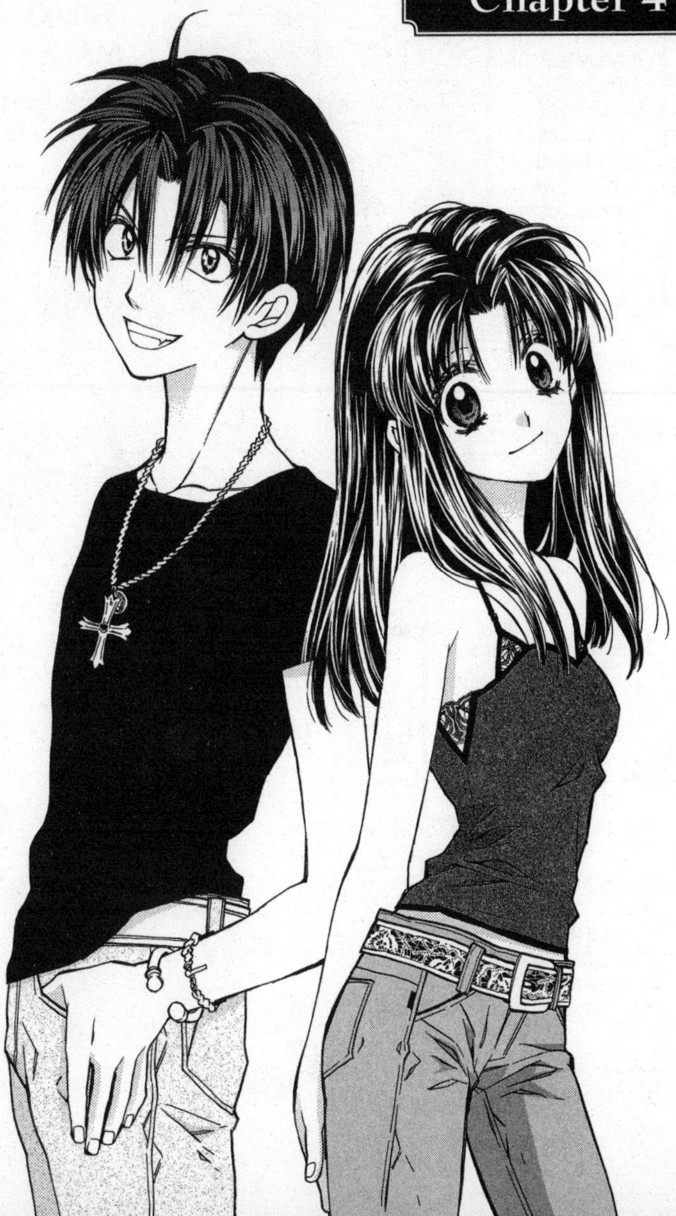

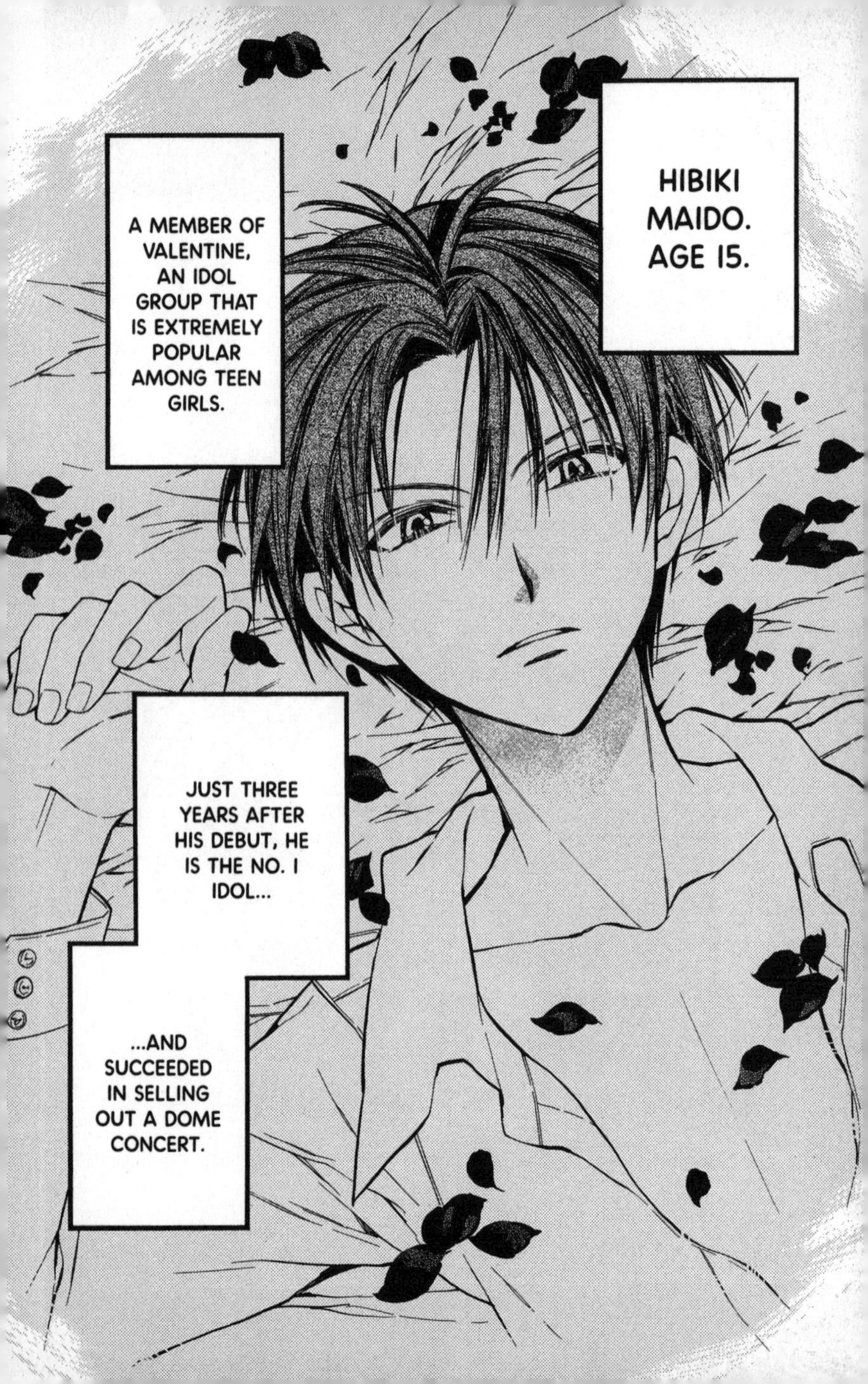
HIBIKI MAIDO. AGE 15.
A MEMBER OF VALENTINE, AN IDOL GROUP THAT IS EXTREMELY POPULAR AMONG TEEN GIRLS.
JUST THREE YEARS AFTER HIS DEBUT, HE IS THE NO. 1 IDOL...
...AND SUCCEEDED IN SELLING OUT A DOME CONCERT.

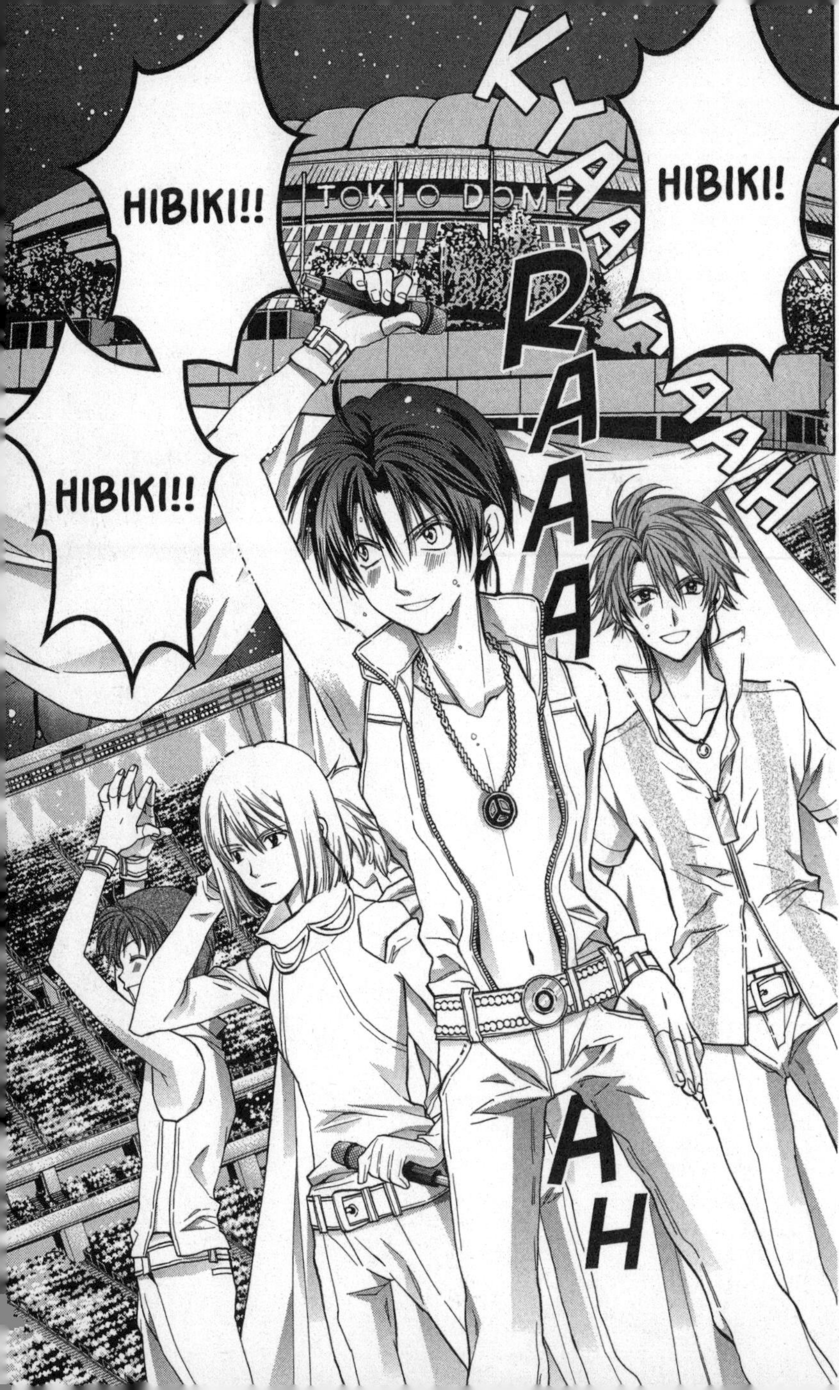
TOKIO DOME
HIBIKI!
KYAAAAAH
RAAAAAH
HIBIKI!!
HIBIKI!!

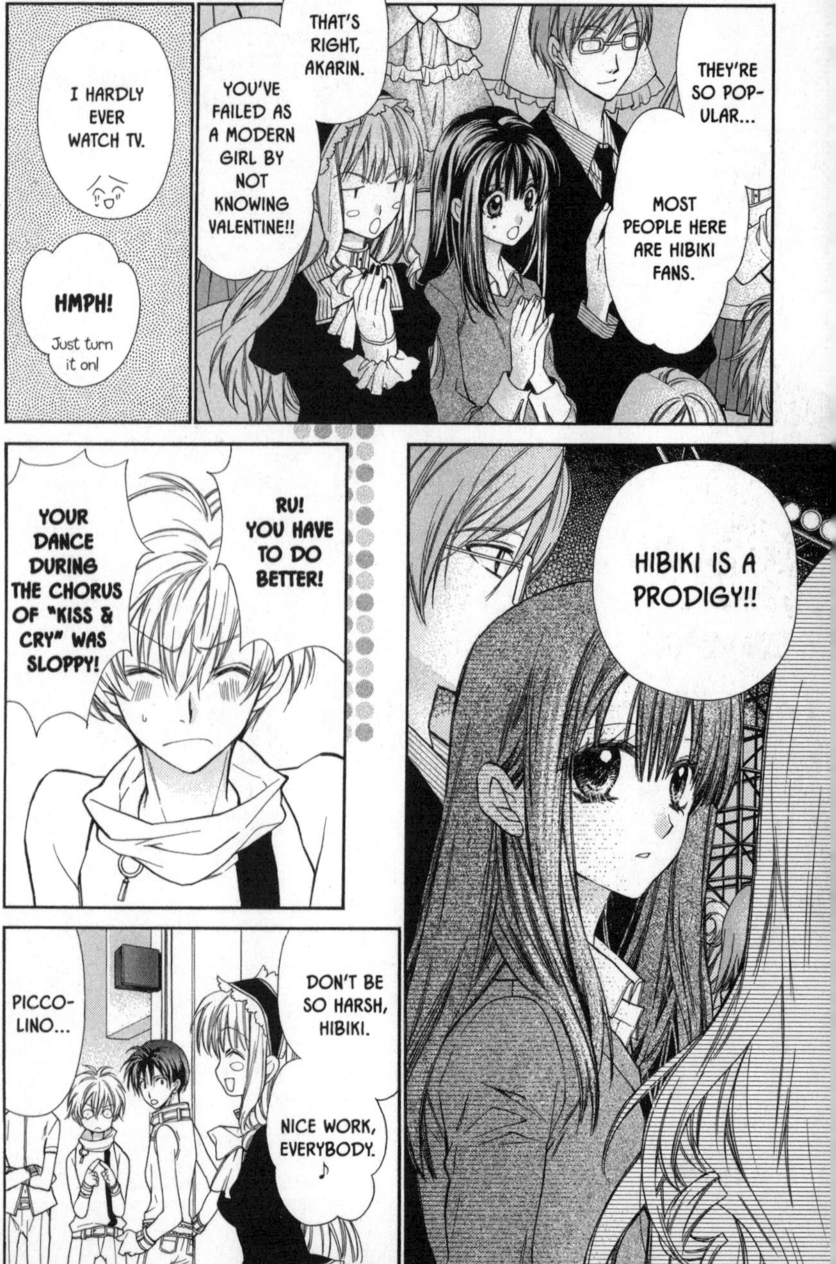
THEY'RE SO POP-ULAR...
MOST PEOPLE HERE ARE HIBIKI FANS.
THAT'S RIGHT, AKARIN.
YOU'VE FAILED AS A MODERN GIRL BY NOT KNOWING VALENTINE!!
I HARDLY EVER WATCH TV.
HMPH!
Just turn it on!
HIBIKI IS A PRODIGY!!
RU! YOU HAVE TO DO BETTER!
YOUR DANCE DURING THE CHORUS OF "KISS & CRY" WAS SLOPPY!
DON'T BE SO HARSH, HIBIKI.
NICE WORK, EVERYBODY. ♪
PICCO-LINO...

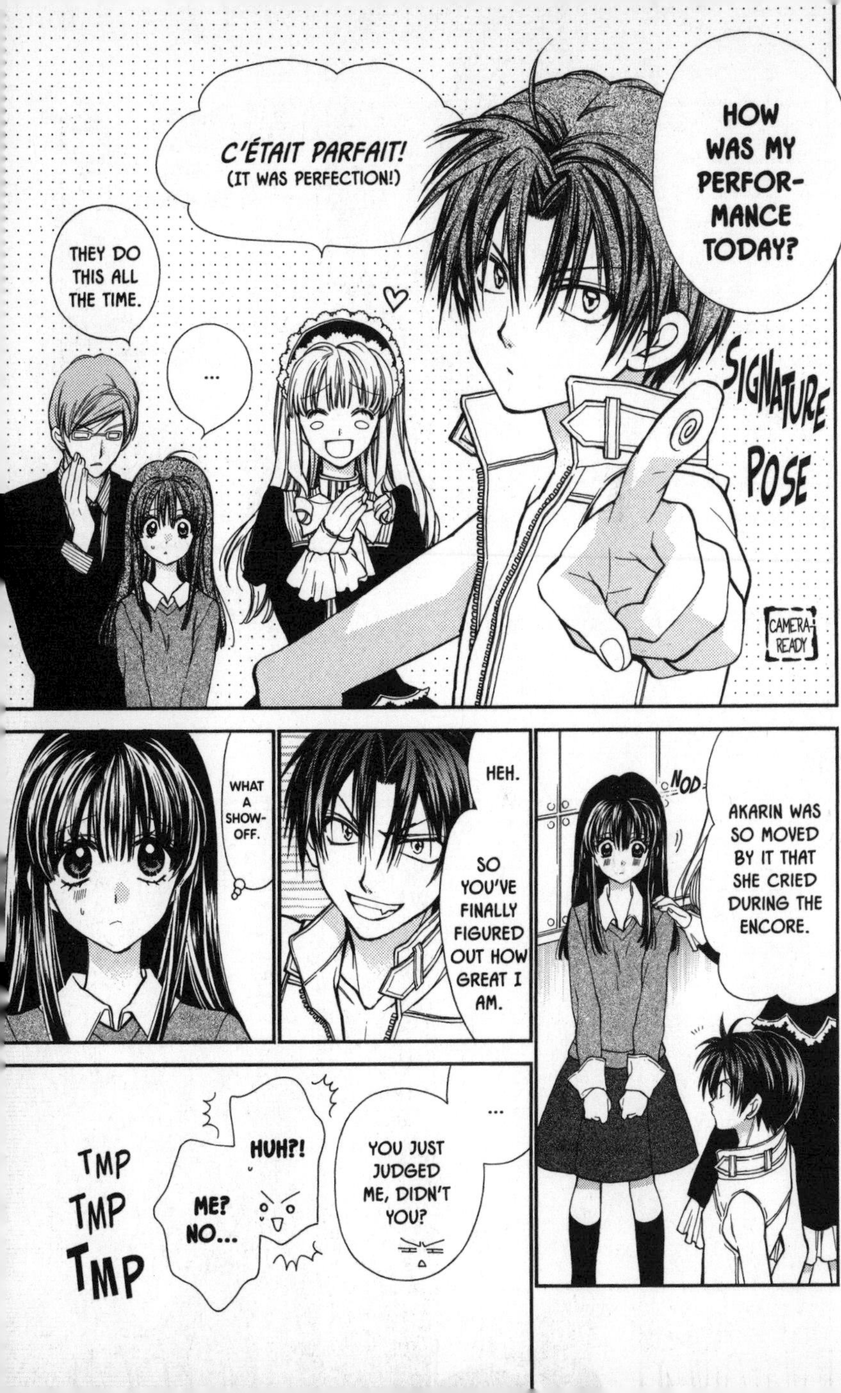
HOW WAS MY PERFOR-MANCE TODAY?
SIGNATURE POSE
CAMERA-READY
C'ÉTAIT PARFAIT!
(IT WAS PERFECTION!)
...
THEY DO THIS ALL THE TIME.
AKARIN WAS SO MOVED BY IT THAT SHE CRIED DURING THE ENCORE.
NOD
HEH.
SO YOU'VE FINALLY FIGURED OUT HOW GREAT I AM.
WHAT A SHOW-OFF.
...
YOU JUST JUDGED ME, DIDN'T YOU?
HUH?!
ME? NO...
TMP TMP TMP

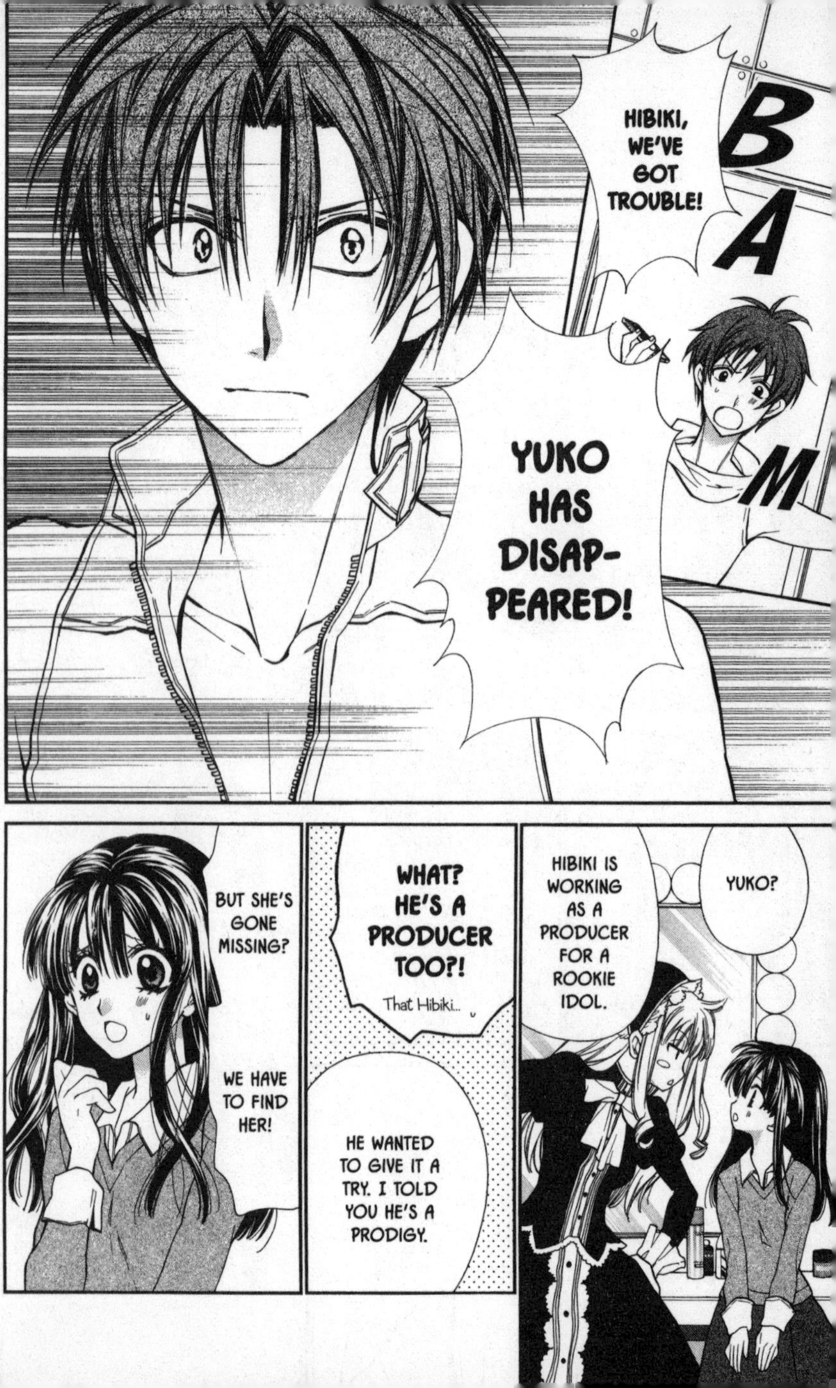
BAM
HIBIKI, WE'VE GOT TROUBLE!
YUKO HAS DISAP-PEARED!
YUKO?
HIBIKI IS WORKING AS A PRODUCER FOR A ROOKIE IDOL.
WHAT? HE'S A PRODUCER TOO?!
That Hibiki...
HE WANTED TO GIVE IT A TRY. I TOLD YOU HE'S A PRODIGY.
BUT SHE'S GONE MISSING?
WE HAVE TO FIND HER!

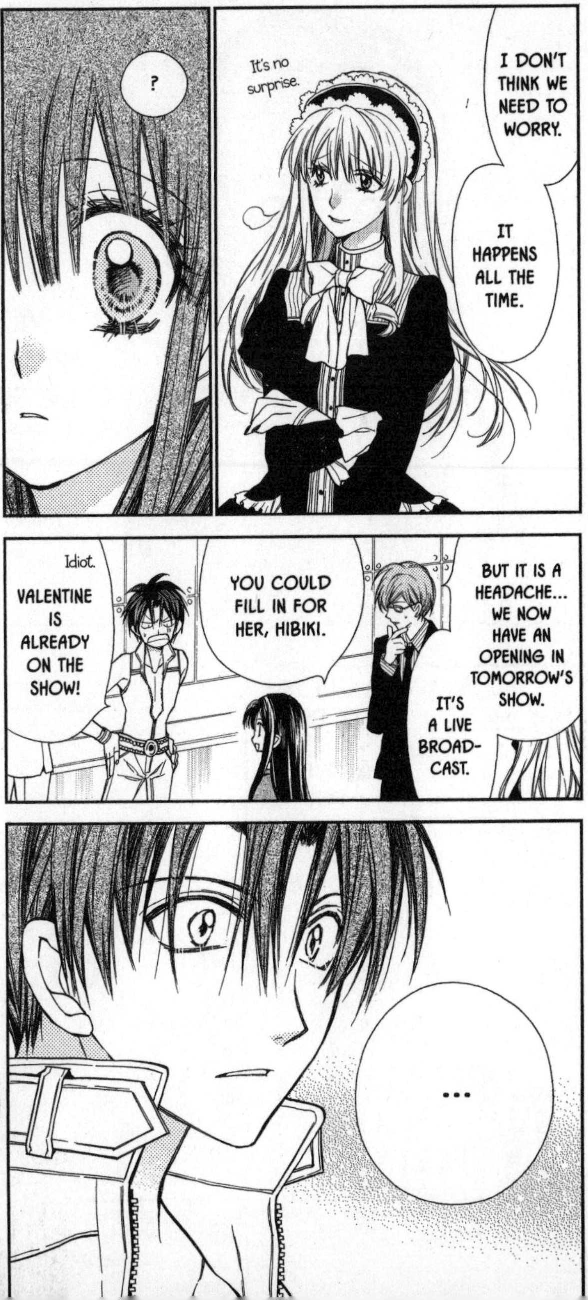
I DON'T THINK WE NEED TO WORRY.
IT HAPPENS ALL THE TIME.
It's no surprise.
?
BUT IT IS A HEADACHE... WE NOW HAVE AN OPENING IN TOMORROW'S SHOW.
IT'S A LIVE BROADCAST.
YOU COULD FILL IN FOR HER, HIBIKI.
Idiot.
VALENTINE IS ALREADY ON THE SHOW!
...

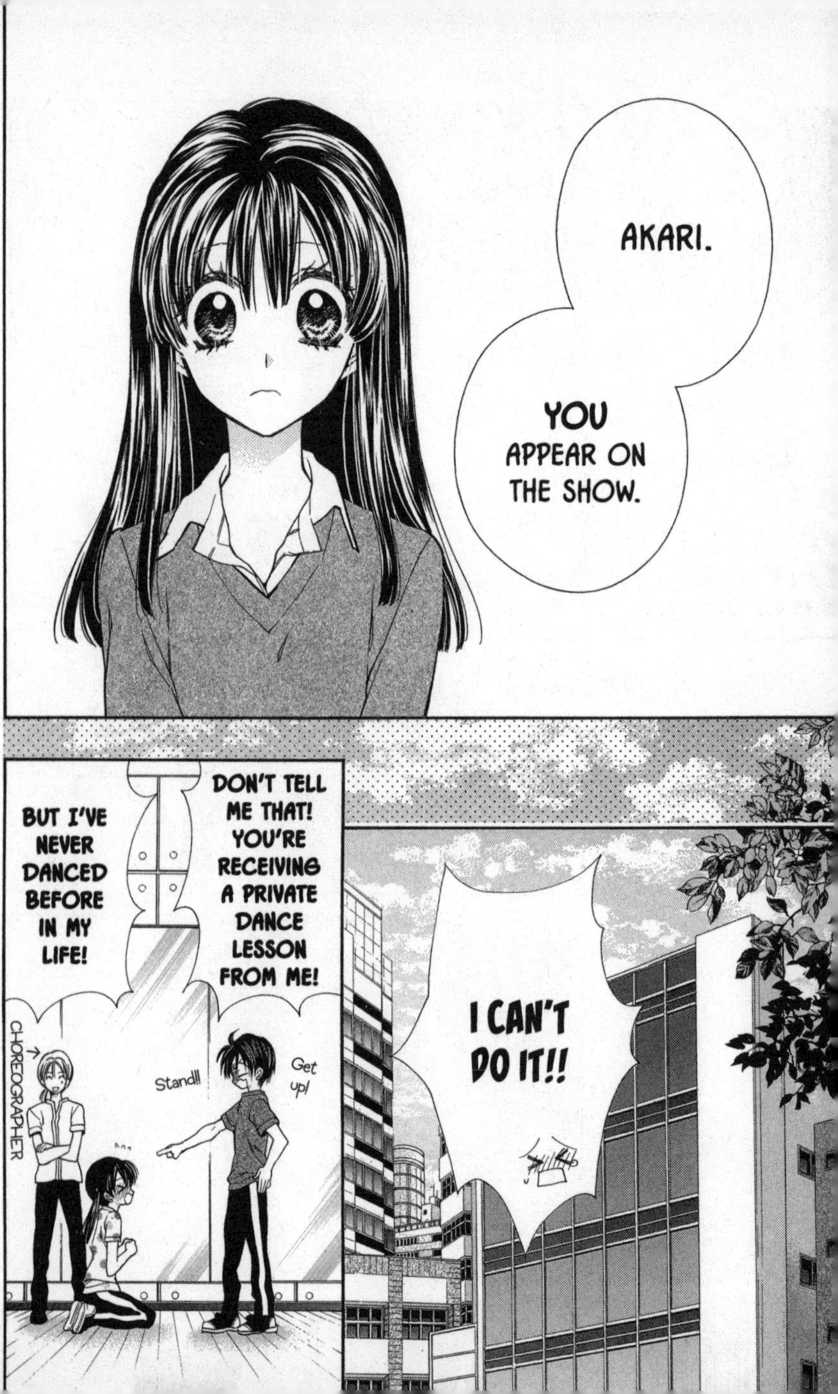
AKARI.
YOU APPEAR ON THE SHOW.
I CAN'T DO IT!!
DON'T TELL ME THAT! YOU'RE RECEIVING A PRIVATE DANCE LESSON FROM ME!
BUT I'VE NEVER DANCED BEFORE IN MY LIFE!
Get up!
Stand!!
CHOREOGRAPHER

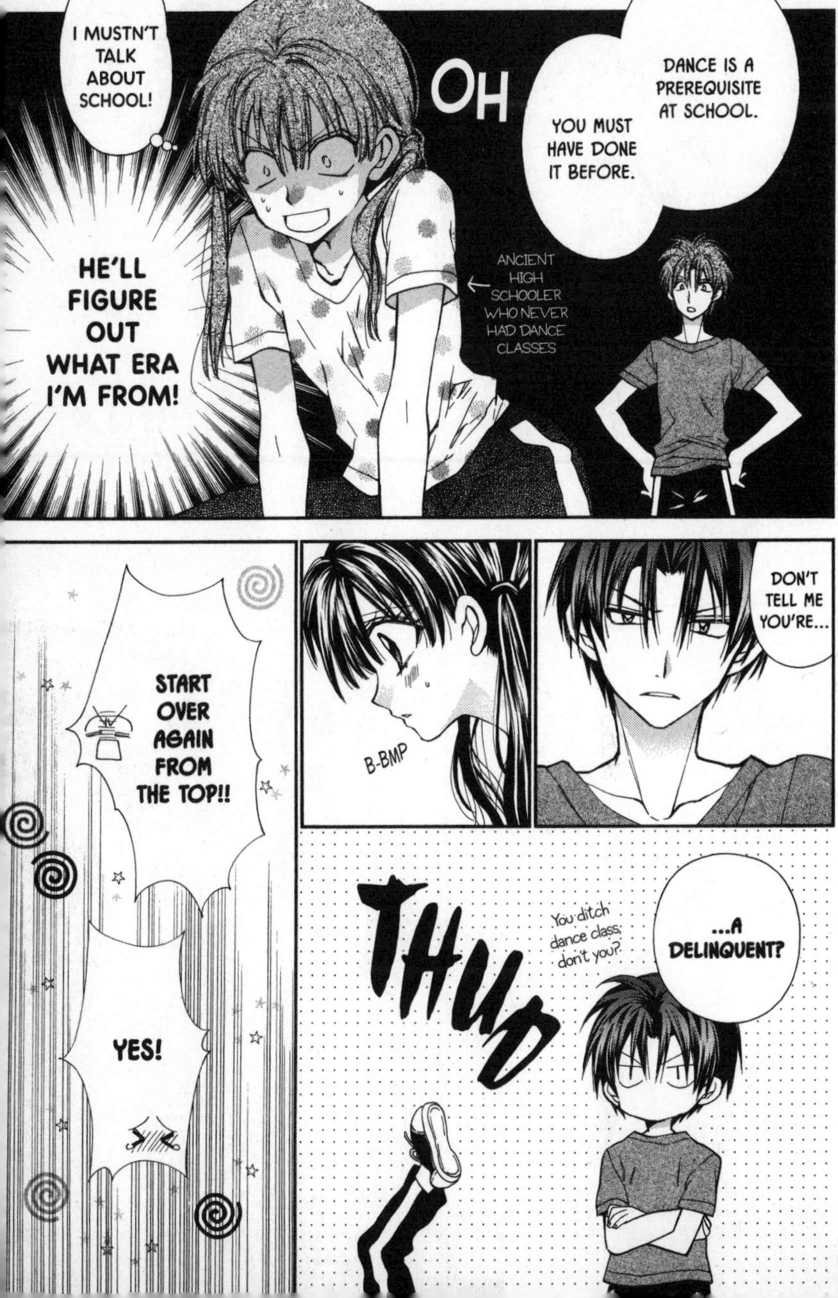
DANCE IS A PREREQUISITE AT SCHOOL.
YOU MUST HAVE DONE IT BEFORE.
OH
ANCIENT HIGH SCHOOLER WHO NEVER HAD DANCE CLASSES
I MUSTN'T TALK ABOUT SCHOOL!
HE'LL FIGURE OUT WHAT ERA I'M FROM!
DON'T TELL ME YOU'RE...
B-BMP
...A DELINQUENT?
You ditch dance class, don't you?
THUD
START OVER AGAIN FROM THE TOP!!
YES!

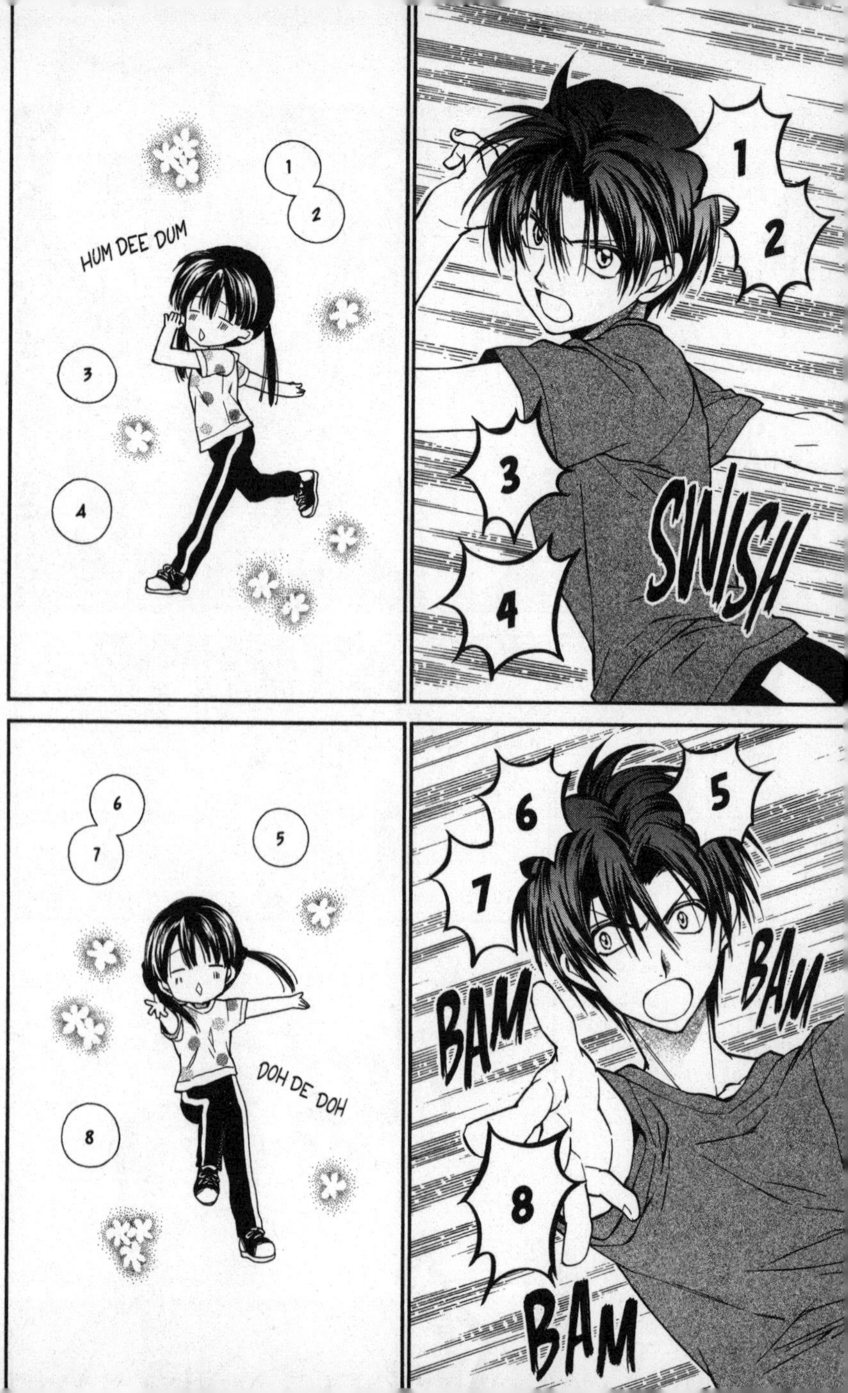
1
2
3
SWISH
4
1
2
HUM DEE DUM
3
4
5
6
7
BAM
BAM
8
BAM
5
6
7
DOH DE DOH
8

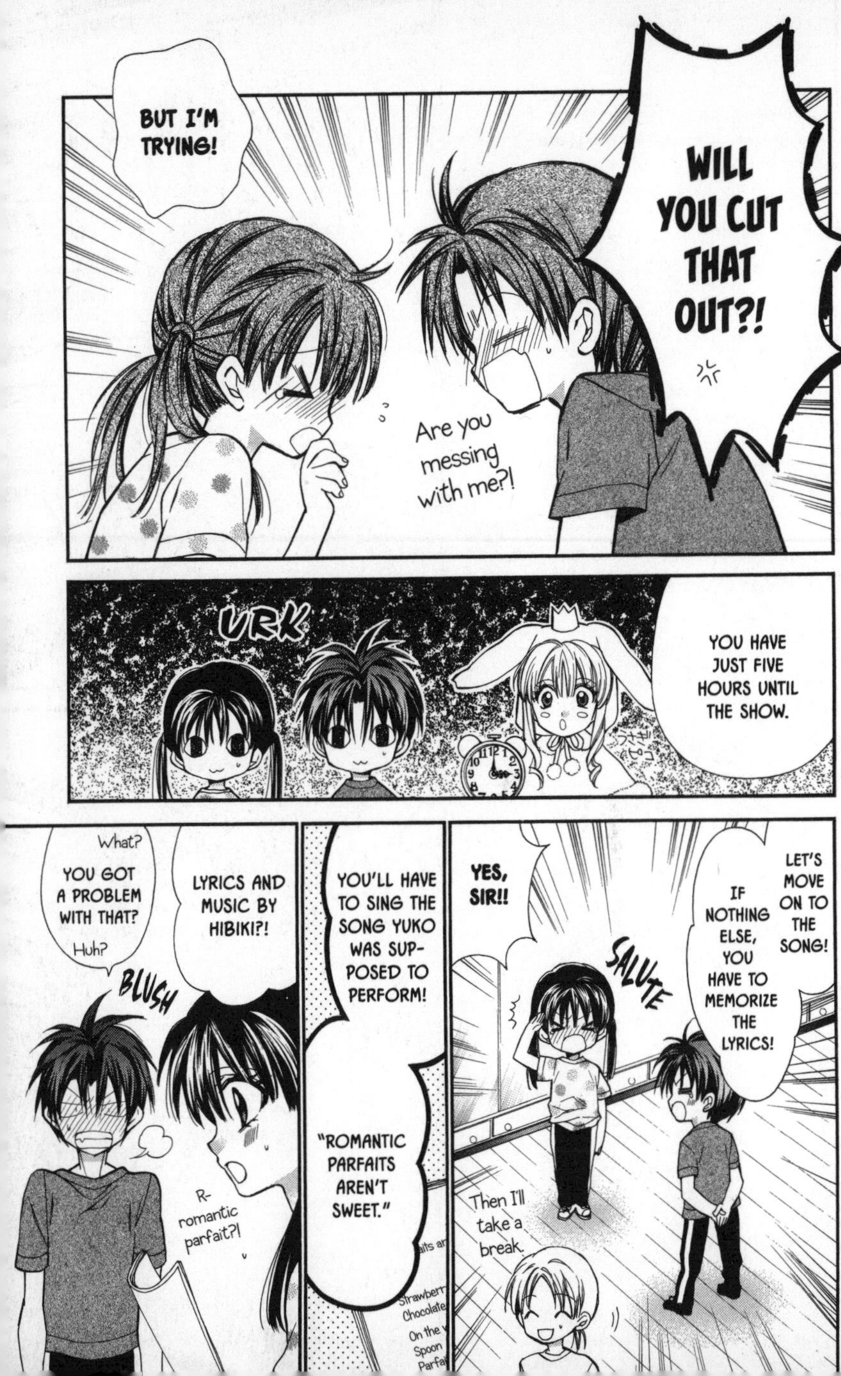
WILL YOU CUT THAT OUT?!
Are you messing with me?!
BUT I'M TRYING!
YOU HAVE JUST FIVE HOURS UNTIL THE SHOW.
URK
LET'S MOVE ON TO THE SONG!
IF NOTHING ELSE, YOU HAVE TO MEMORIZE THE LYRICS!
SALUTE
YES, SIR!!
Then I'll take a break.
YOU'LL HAVE TO SING THE SONG YUKO WAS SUP-POSED TO PERFORM!
"ROMANTIC PARFAITS AREN'T SWEET."
LYRICS AND MUSIC BY HIBIKI?!
What?
YOU GOT A PROBLEM WITH THAT?
Huh?
BLUSH
R-romantic parfait?!

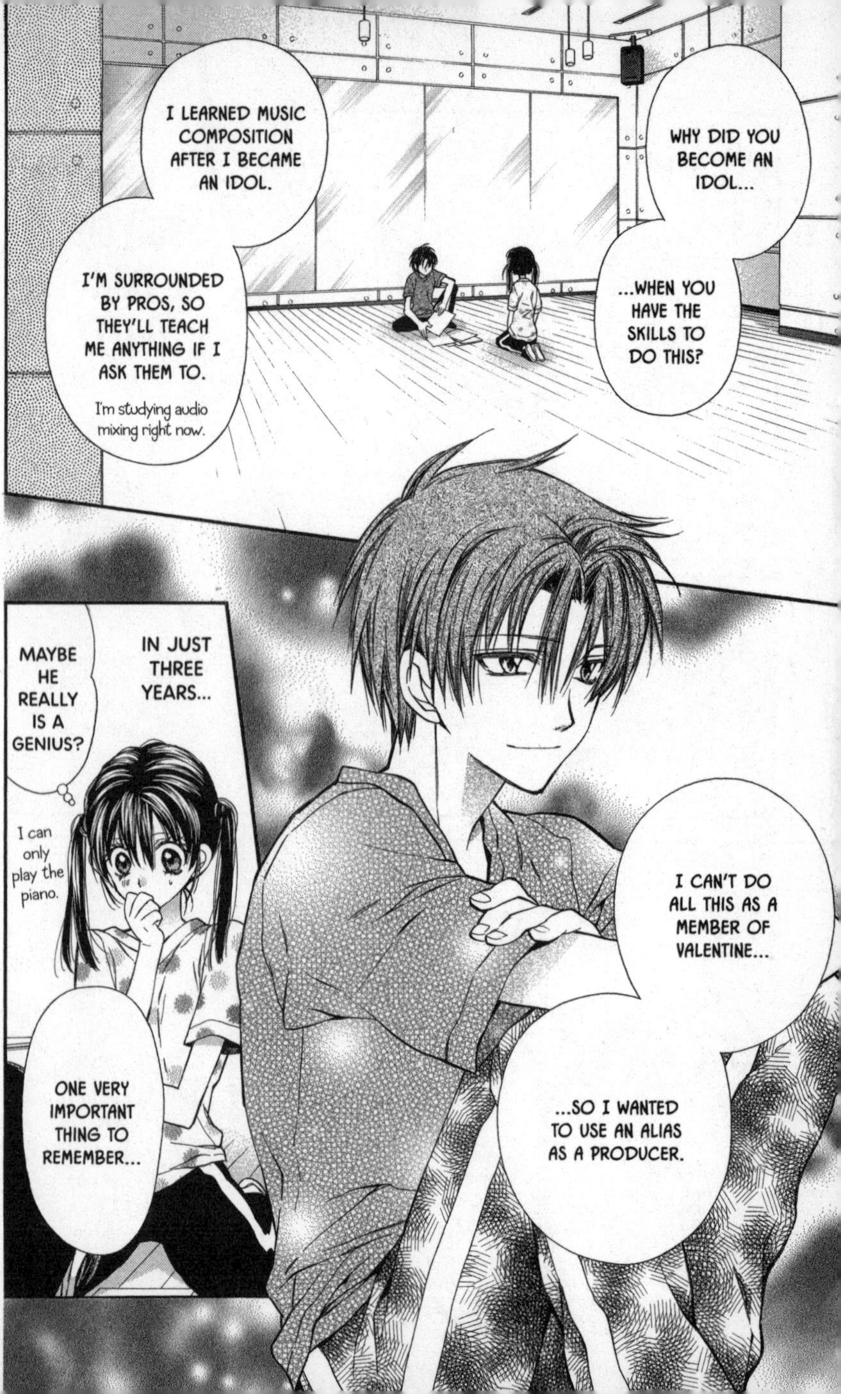
WHY DID YOU BECOME AN IDOL...
...WHEN YOU HAVE THE SKILLS TO DO THIS?
I LEARNED MUSIC COMPOSITION AFTER I BECAME AN IDOL.
I'M SURROUNDED BY PROS, SO THEY'LL TEACH ME ANYTHING IF I ASK THEM TO.
I'm studying audio mixing right now.
I CAN'T DO ALL THIS AS A MEMBER OF VALENTINE...
...SO I WANTED TO USE AN ALIAS AS A PRODUCER.
IN JUST THREE YEARS...
MAYBE HE REALLY IS A GENIUS?
I can only play the piano.
ONE VERY IMPORTANT THING TO REMEMBER...

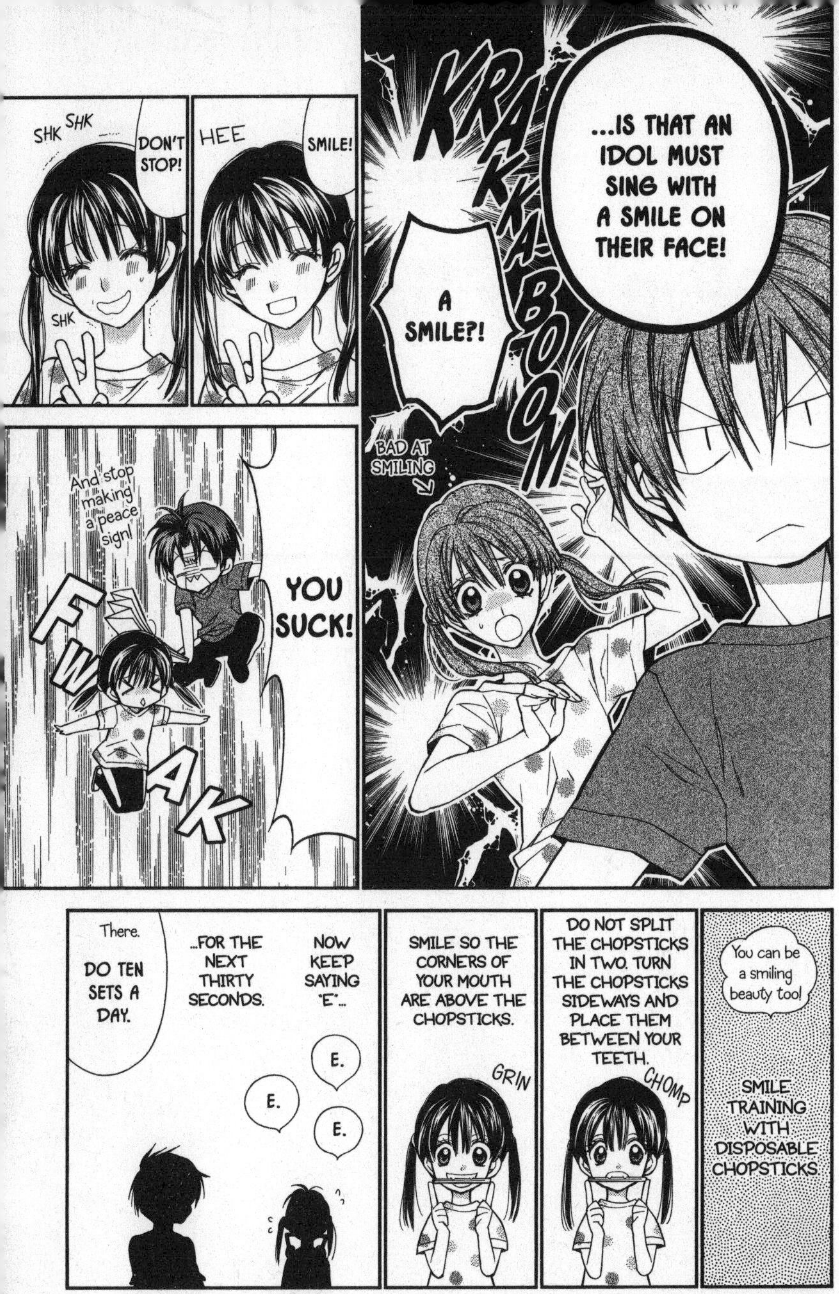
...IS THAT AN IDOL MUST SING WITH A SMILE ON THEIR FACE!
KRAKKABOOM
A SMILE?!
BAD AT SMILING
SMILE!
HEE
DON'T STOP!
SHK SHK
SHK
YOU SUCK!
And stop making a peace sign!
FWAK
You can be a smiling beauty too!
SMILE TRAINING WITH DISPOSABLE CHOPSTICKS
DO NOT SPLIT THE CHOPSTICKS IN TWO. TURN THE CHOPSTICKS SIDEWAYS AND PLACE THEM BETWEEN YOUR TEETH.
CHOMP
SMILE SO THE CORNERS OF YOUR MOUTH ARE ABOVE THE CHOPSTICKS.
GRIN
NOW KEEP SAYING "E"...
E.
E.
E.
...FOR THE NEXT THIRTY SECONDS.
There.
DO TEN SETS A DAY.

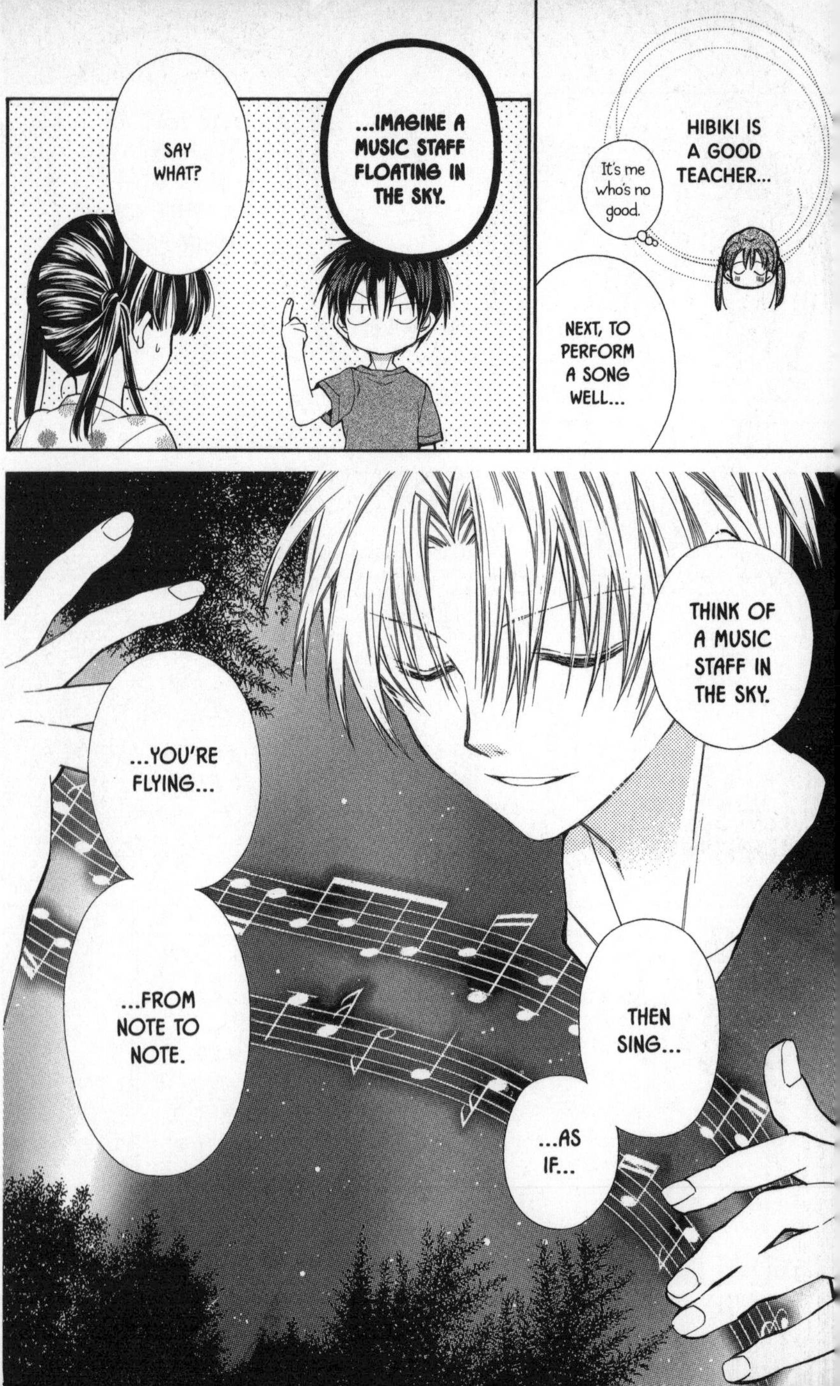
HIBIKI IS A GOOD TEACHER...
It's me who's no good.
NEXT, TO PERFORM A SONG WELL...
...IMAGINE A MUSIC STAFF FLOATING IN THE SKY.
SAY WHAT?
THINK OF A MUSIC STAFF IN THE SKY.
THEN SING...
...AS IF...
...YOU'RE FLYING...
...FROM NOTE TO NOTE.

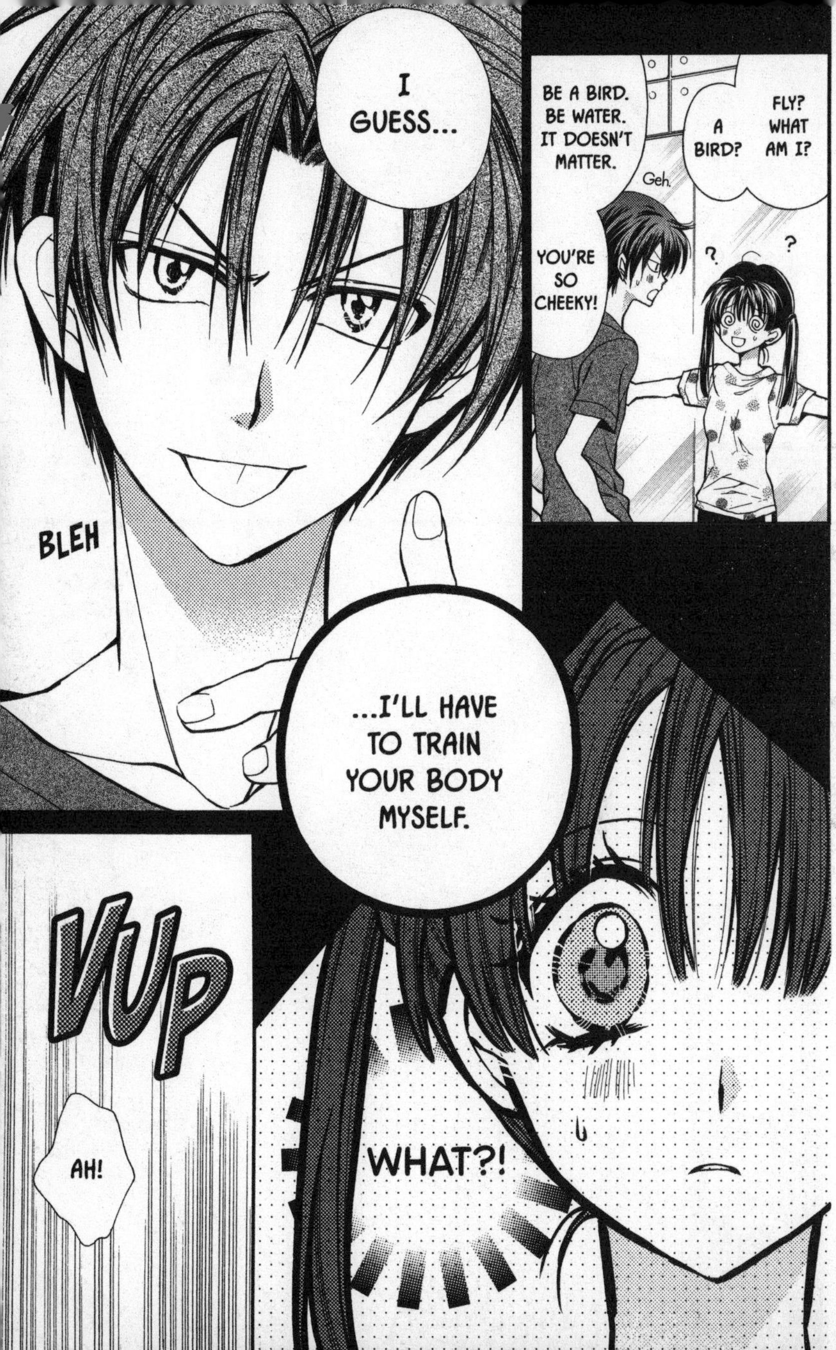
FLY? WHAT AM I?
A BIRD?
BE A BIRD. BE WATER. IT DOESN'T MATTER.
Geh.
YOU'RE SO CHEEKY!
I GUESS...
BLEH
...I'LL HAVE TO TRAIN YOUR BODY MYSELF.
WHAT?!
VUP
AH!

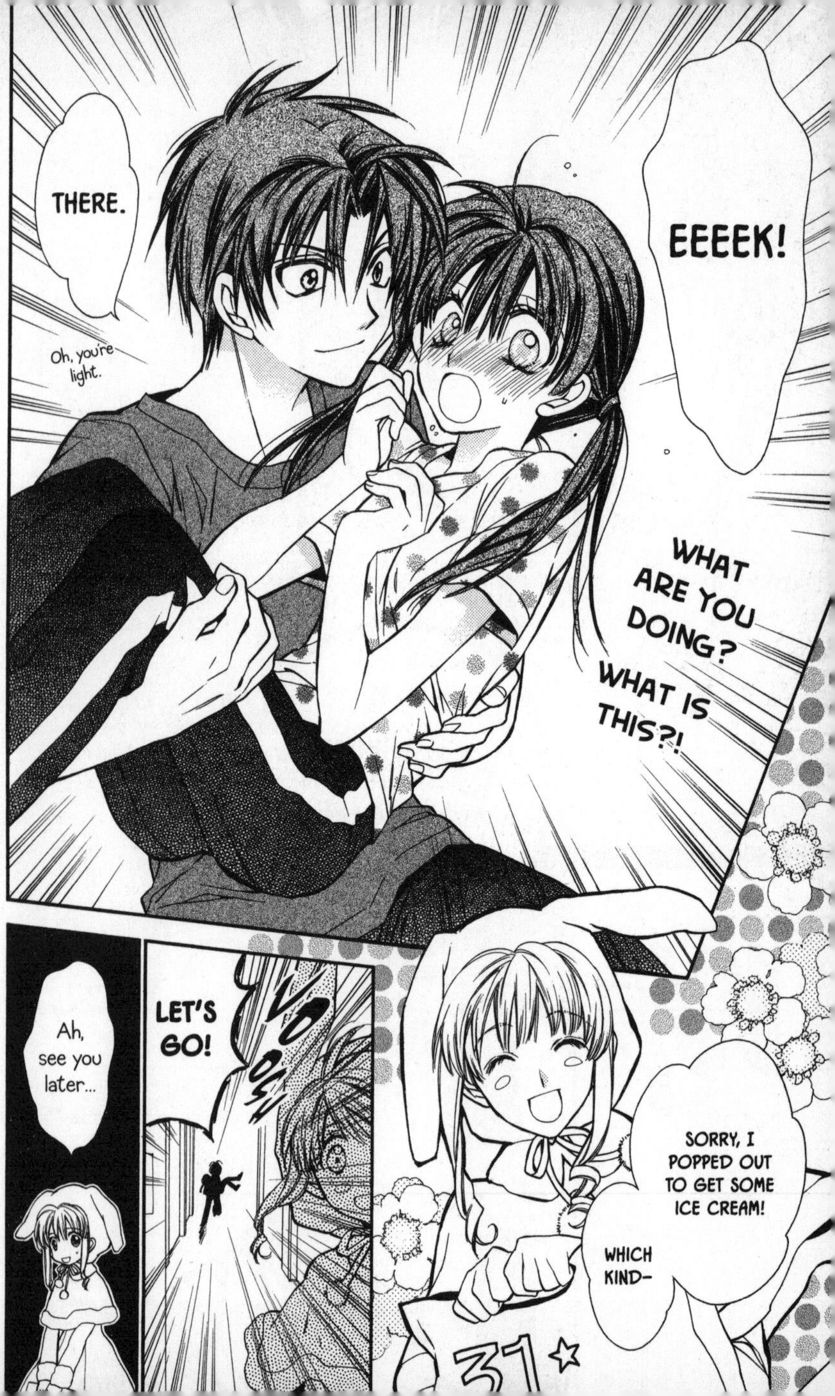
EEEEK!
WHAT ARE YOU DOING? WHAT IS THIS?!
THERE.
Oh, you're light.
SORRY, I POPPED OUT TO GET SOME ICE CREAM!
WHICH KIND-
31☆
VOOSH
LET'S GO!
Ah, see you later...

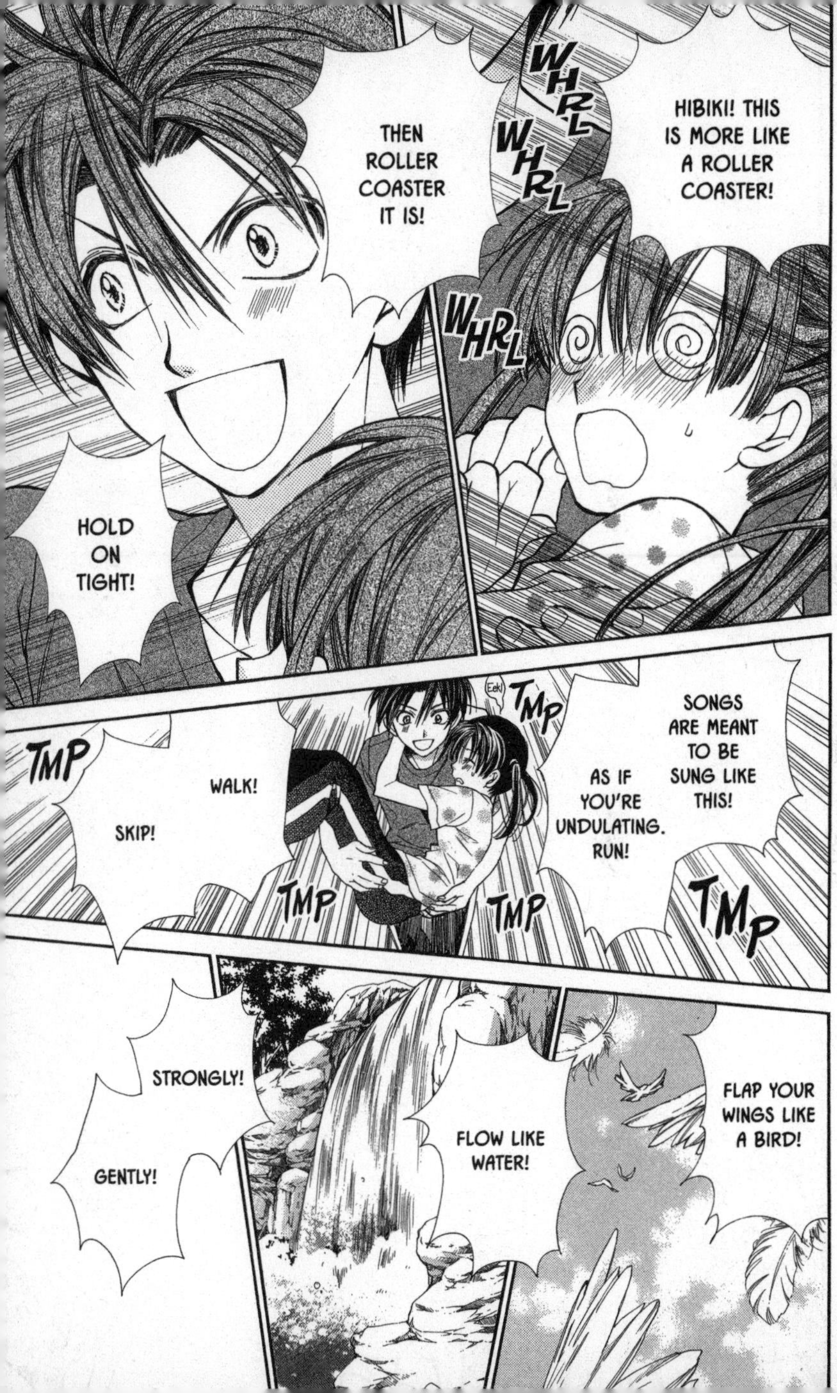
WHRL
WHRL
HIBIKI! THIS IS MORE LIKE A ROLLER COASTER!
WHRL
THEN ROLLER COASTER IT IS!
HOLD ON TIGHT!
SONGS ARE MEANT TO BE SUNG LIKE THIS!
TMP
Eek!
AS IF YOU'RE UNDULATING. RUN!
TMP
TMP
TMP
WALK!
SKIP!
TMP
FLAP YOUR WINGS LIKE A BIRD!
FLOW LIKE WATER!
STRONGLY!
GENTLY!

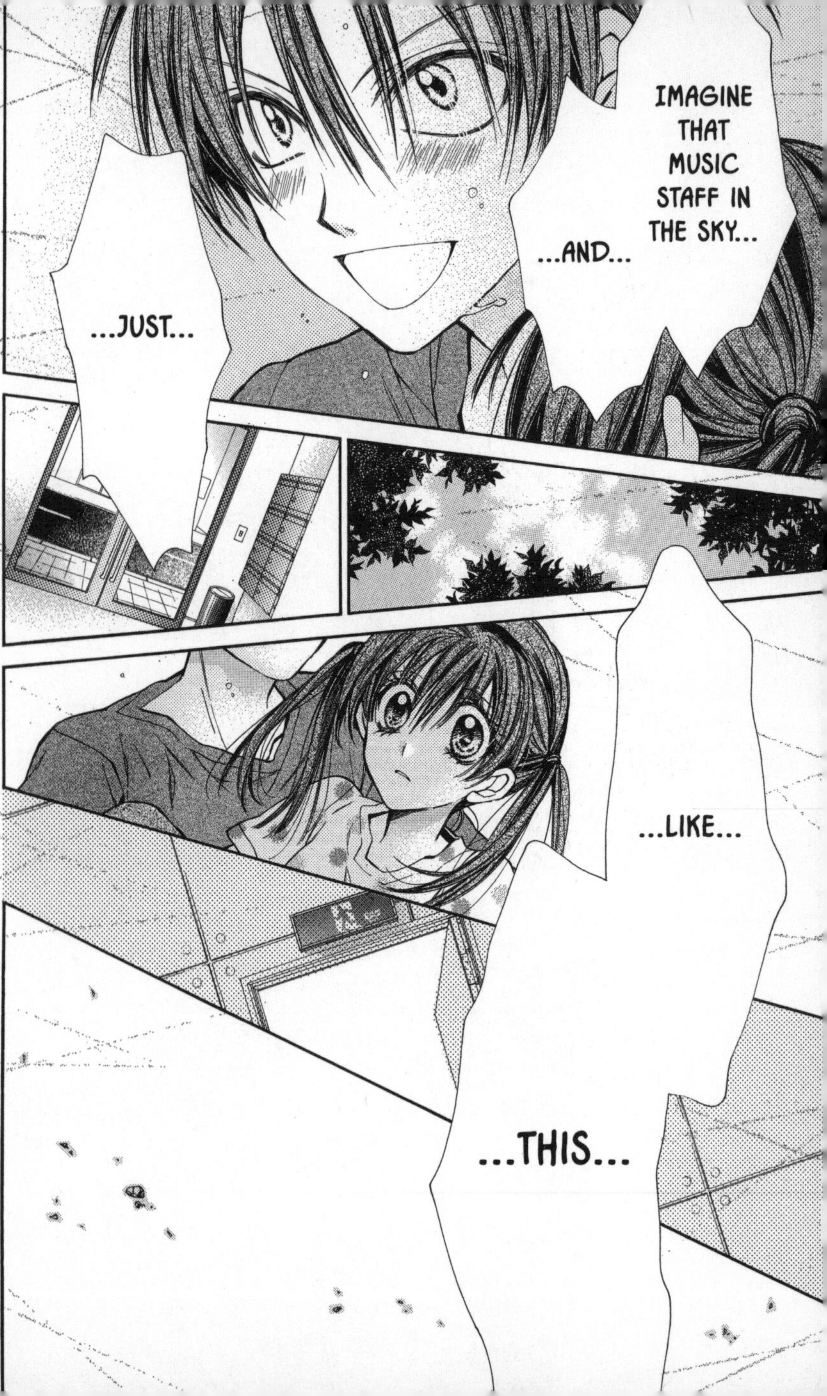
IMAGINE THAT MUSIC STAFF IN THE SKY...
...AND...
...JUST...
...LIKE...
...THIS...

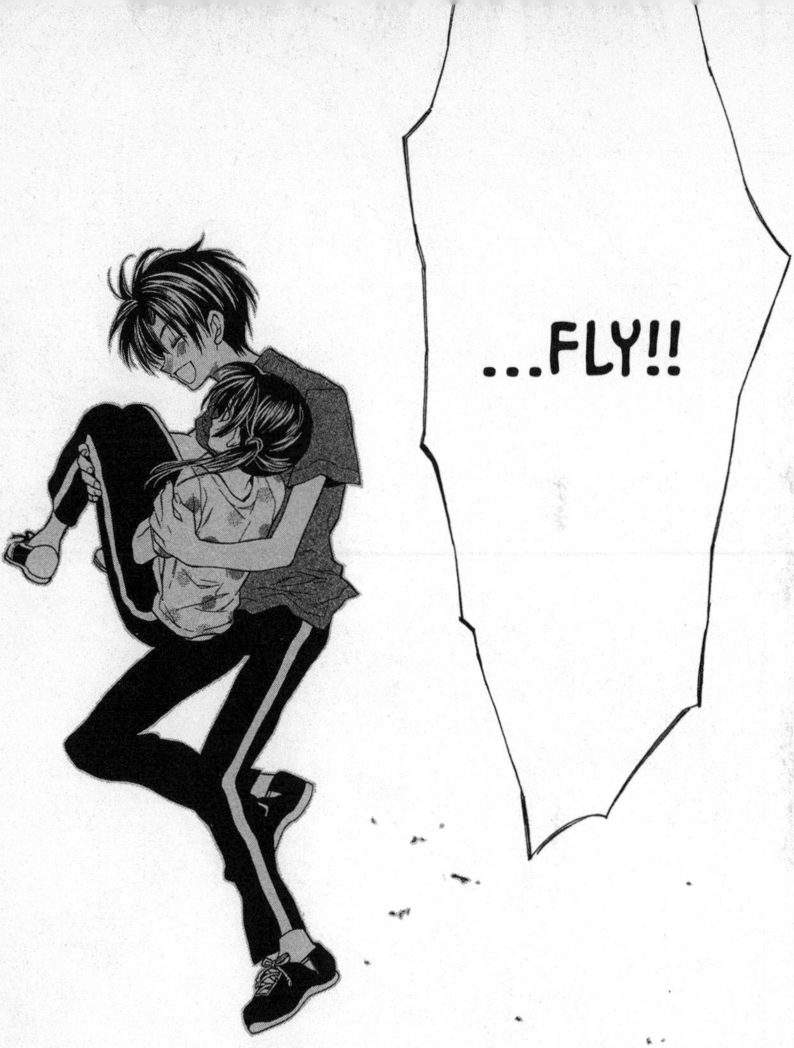
...FLY!!

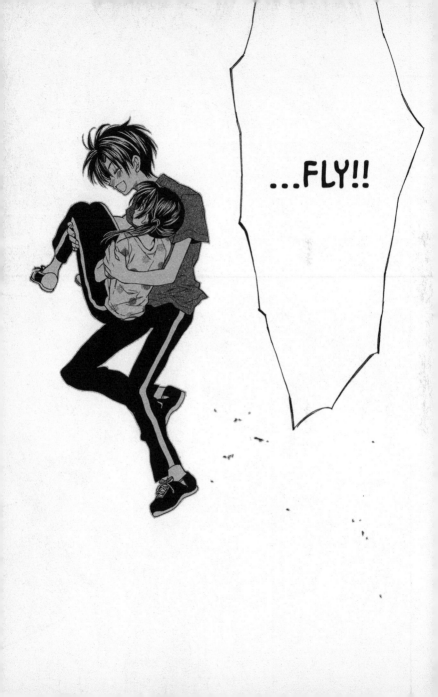

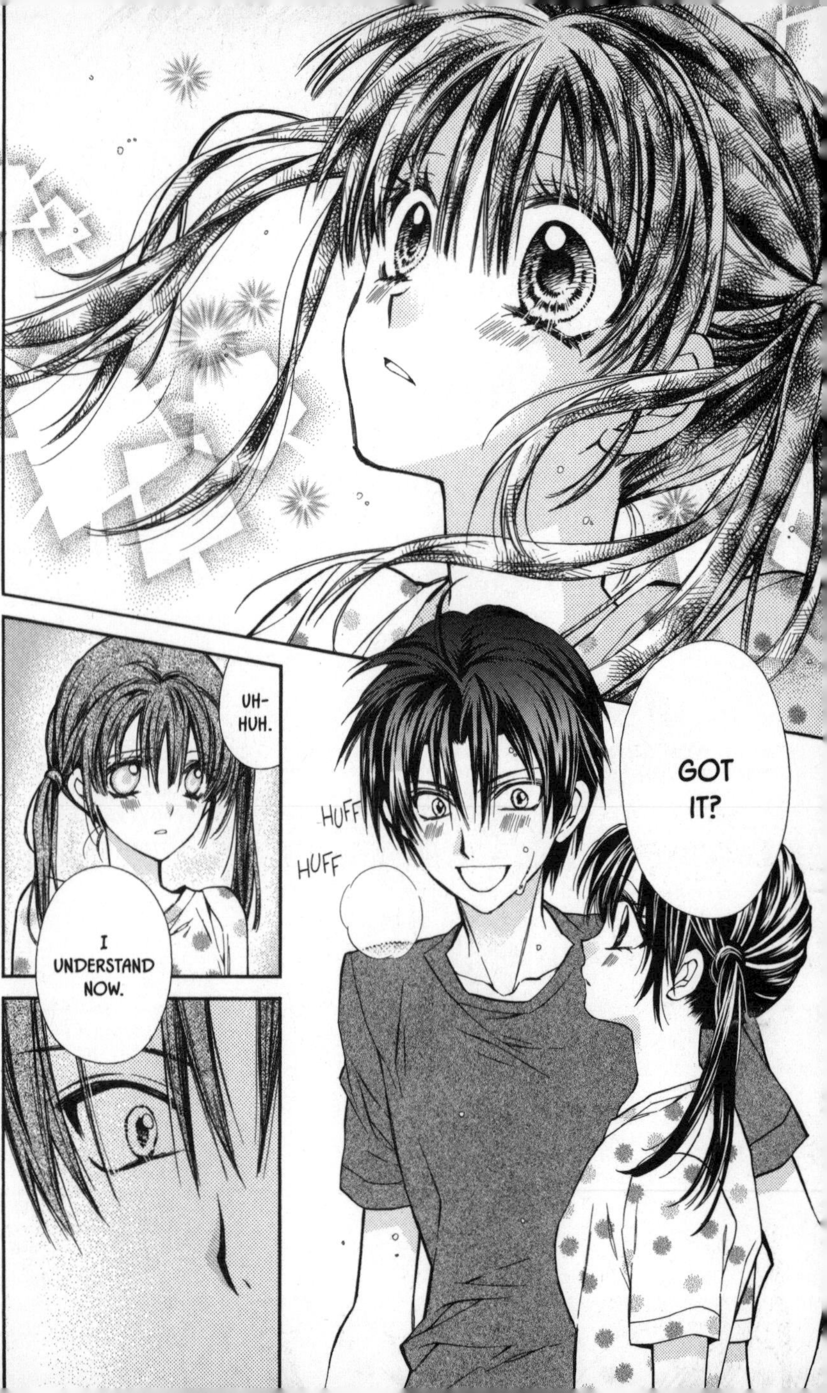
GOT IT?
HUFF
HUFF
UH-HUH.
I UNDERSTAND NOW.

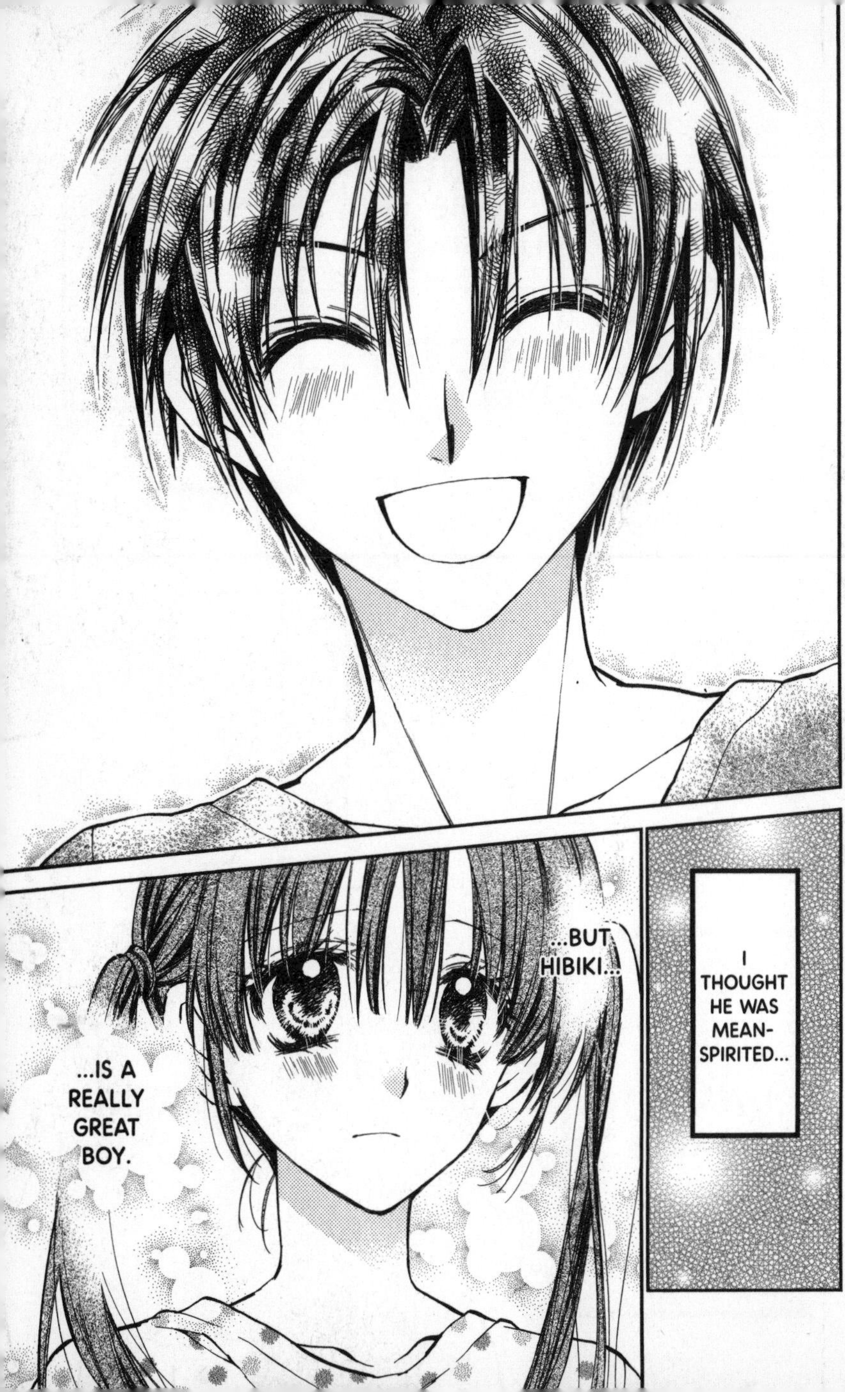
I THOUGHT HE WAS MEAN-SPIRITED...
...BUT HIBIKI...
...IS A REALLY GREAT BOY.

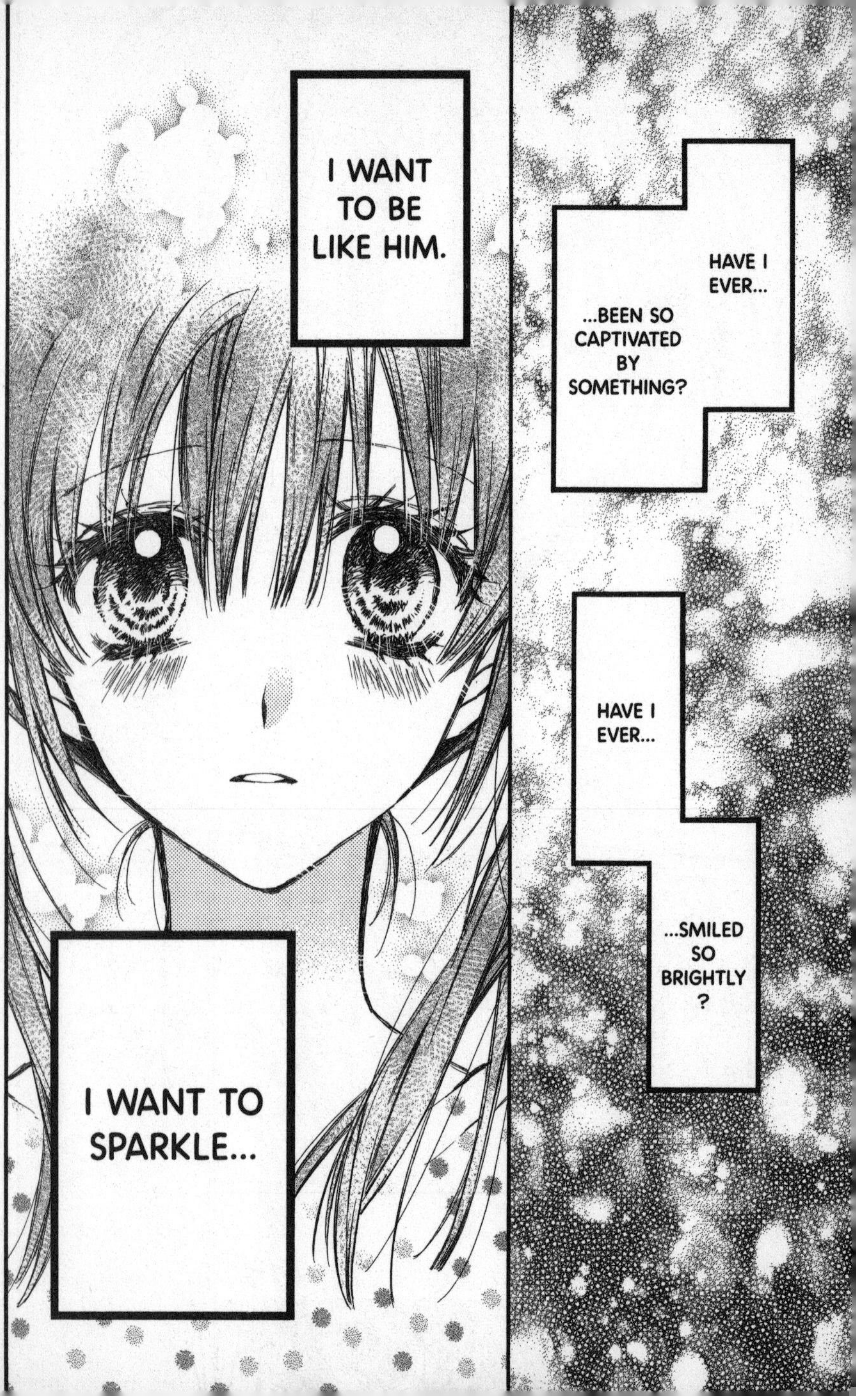
HAVE I EVER...
...BEEN SO CAPTIVATED BY SOMETHING?
HAVE I EVER...
...SMILED SO BRIGHTLY ?
I WANT TO BE LIKE HIM.
I WANT TO SPARKLE...

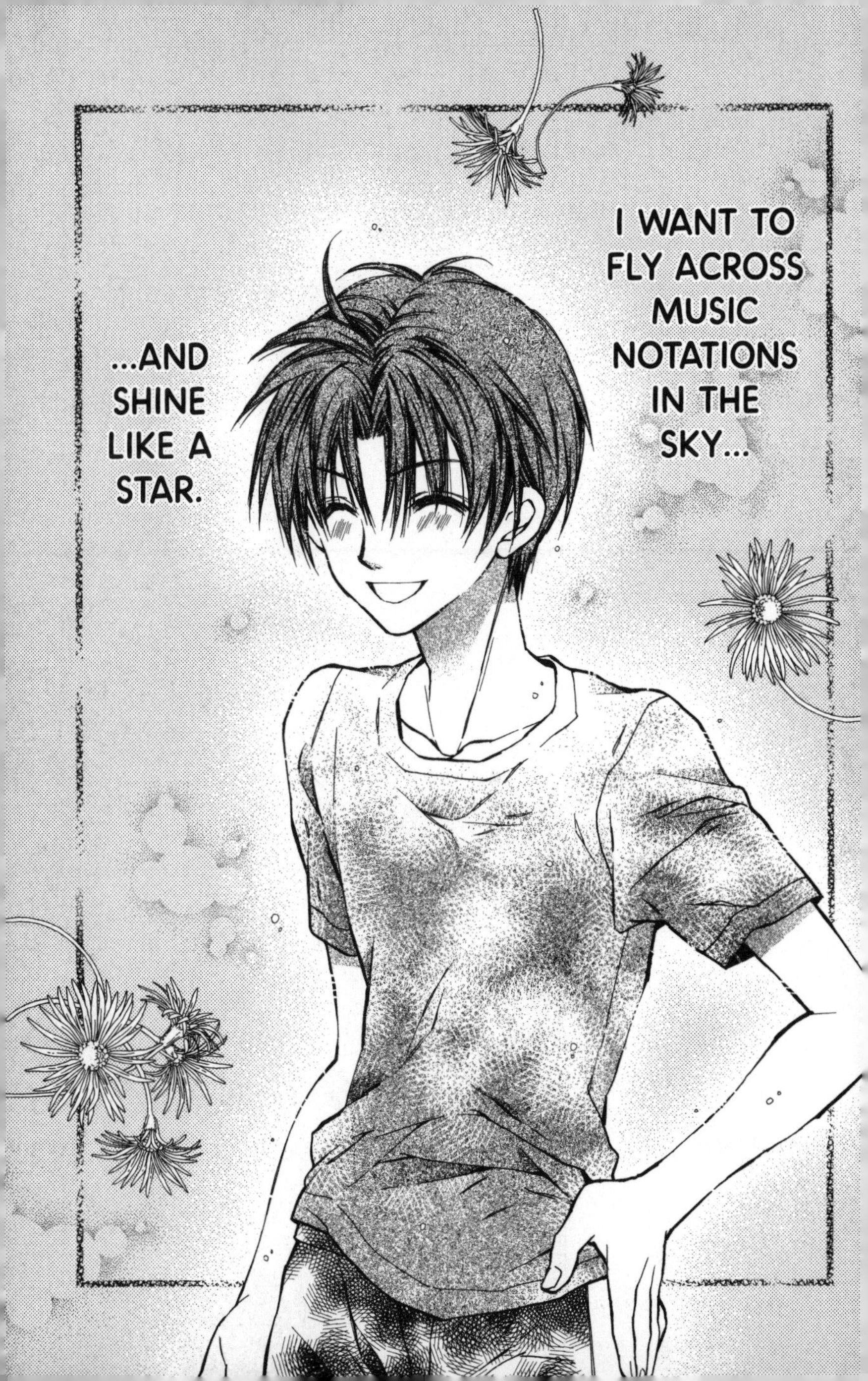
I WANT TO FLY ACROSS MUSIC NOTATIONS IN THE SKY...
...AND SHINE LIKE A STAR.

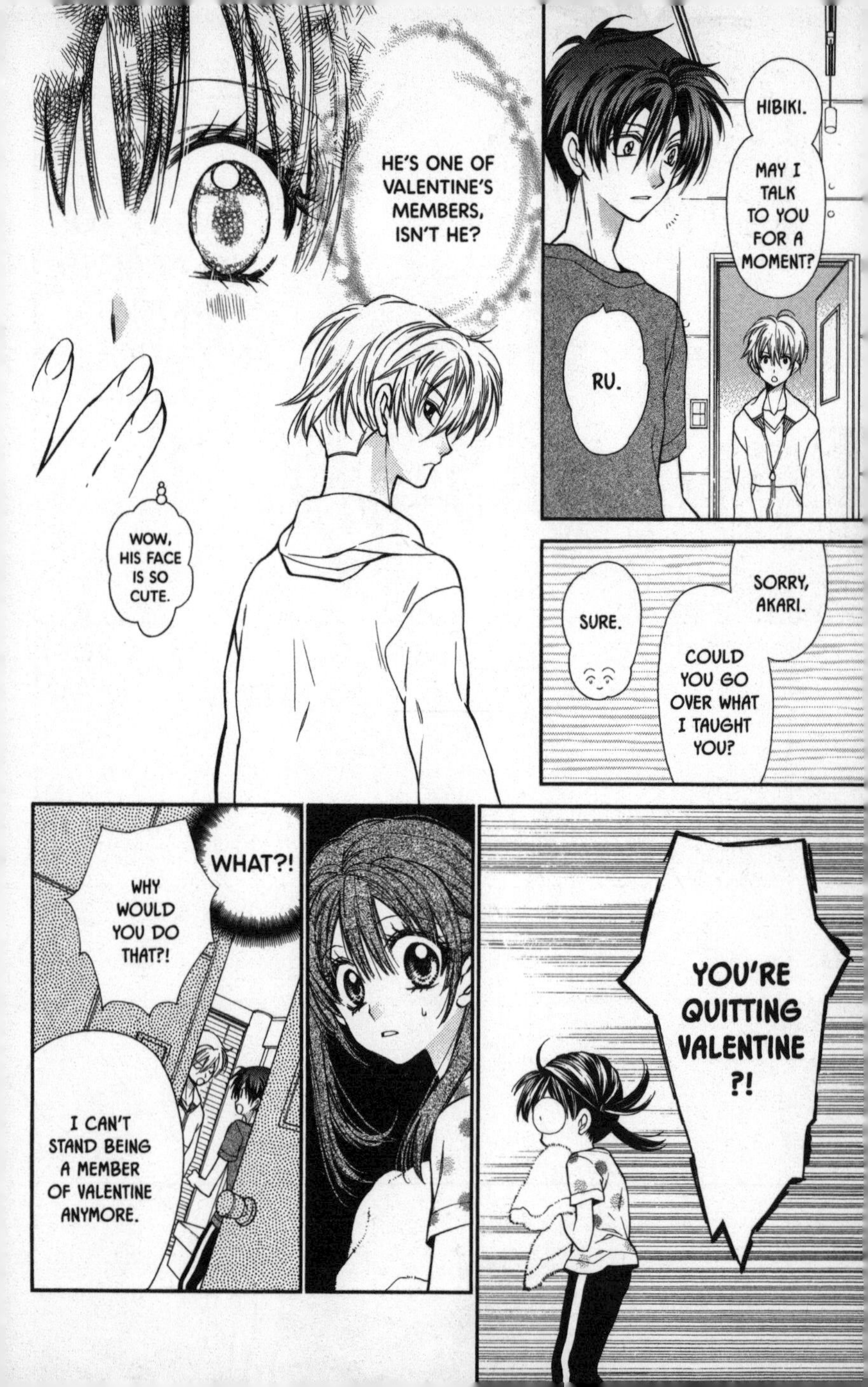
HIBIKI.
MAY I TALK TO YOU FOR A MOMENT?
RU.
SORRY, AKARI.
COULD YOU GO OVER WHAT I TAUGHT YOU?
SURE.
HE'S ONE OF VALENTINE'S MEMBERS, ISN'T HE?
WOW, HIS FACE IS SO CUTE.
YOU'RE QUITTING VALENTINE ?!
WHAT?!
WHY WOULD YOU DO THAT?!
I CAN'T STAND BEING A MEMBER OF VALENTINE ANYMORE.

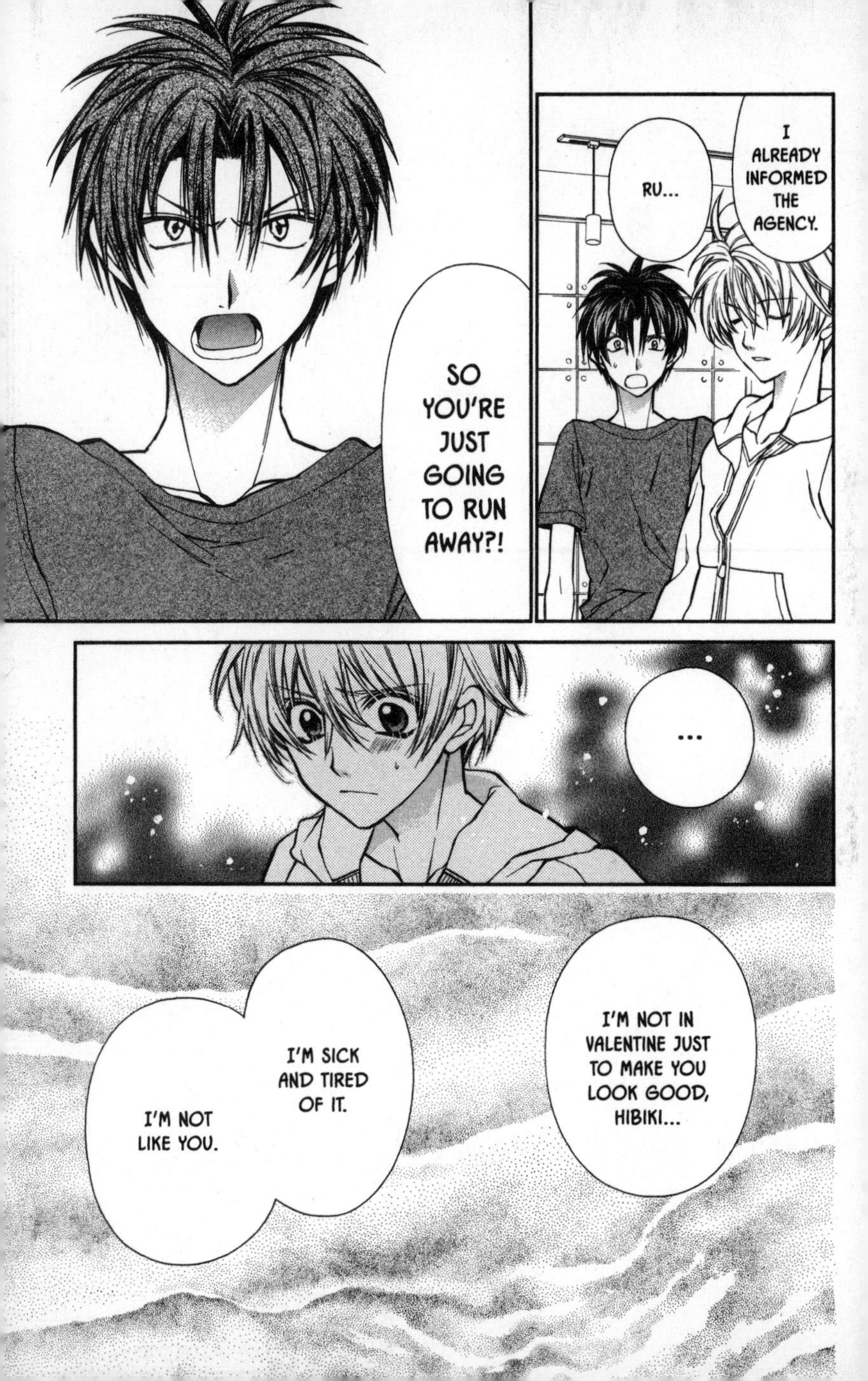
I ALREADY INFORMED THE AGENCY.
RU...
SO YOU'RE JUST GOING TO RUN AWAY?!
...
I'M NOT IN VALENTINE JUST TO MAKE YOU LOOK GOOD, HIBIKI...
I'M SICK AND TIRED OF IT.
I'M NOT LIKE YOU.

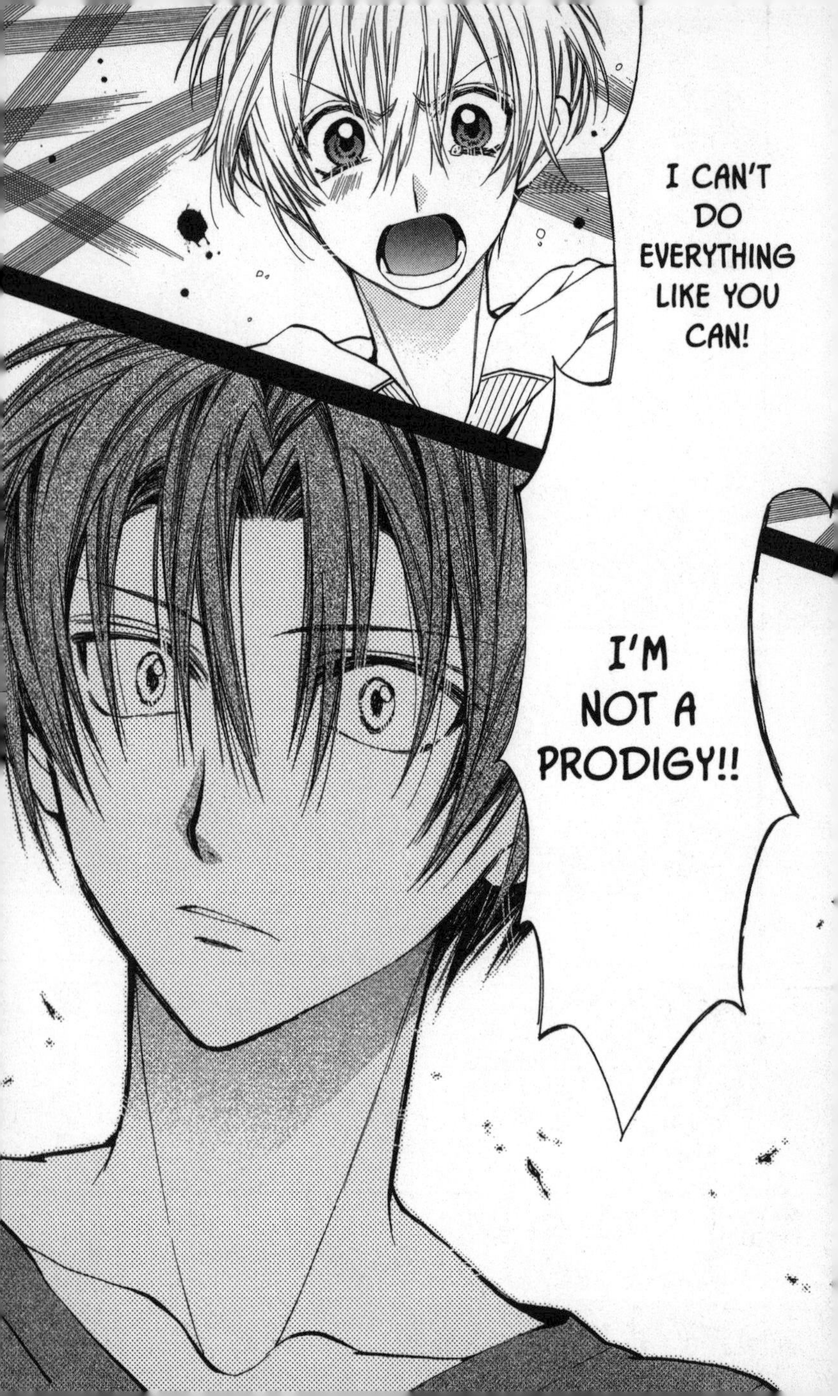
I CAN'T DO EVERYTHING LIKE YOU CAN!
I'M NOT A PRODIGY!!

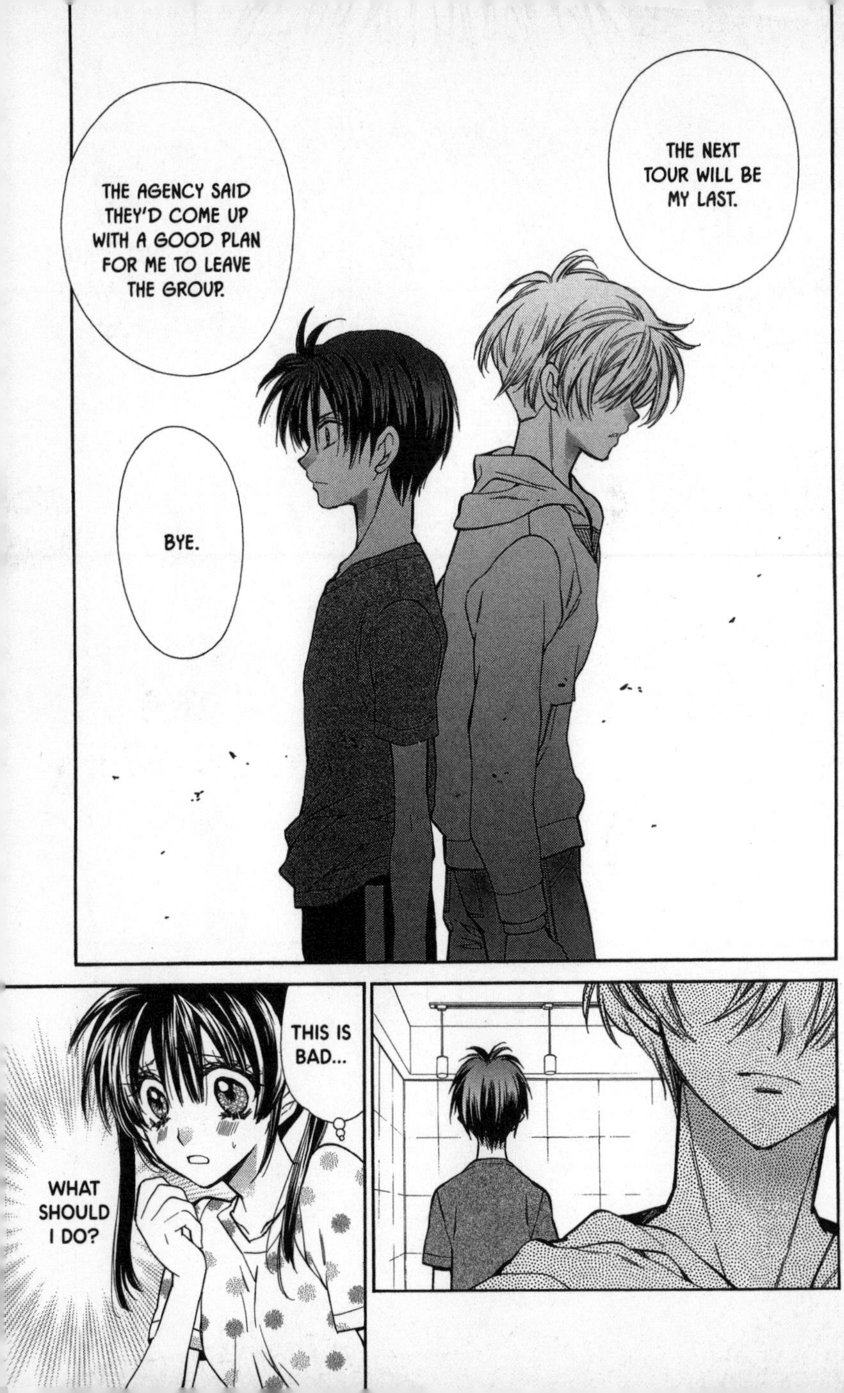
THE NEXT TOUR WILL BE MY LAST.
THE AGENCY SAID THEY'D COME UP WITH A GOOD PLAN FOR ME TO LEAVE THE GROUP.
BYE.
THIS IS BAD...
WHAT SHOULD I DO?

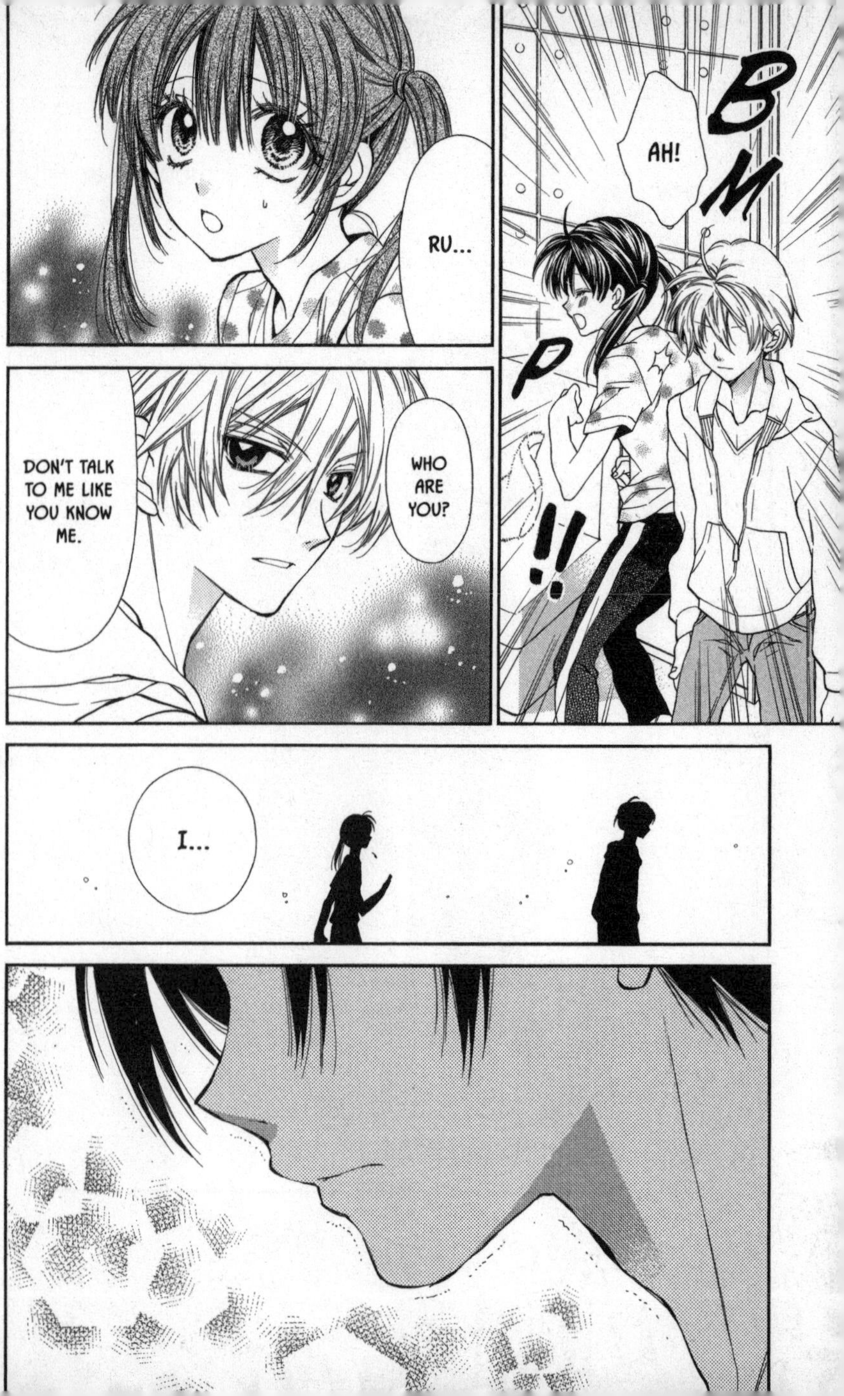
BUMP!!
AH!
RU...
WHO ARE YOU?
DON'T TALK TO ME LIKE YOU KNOW ME.
I...

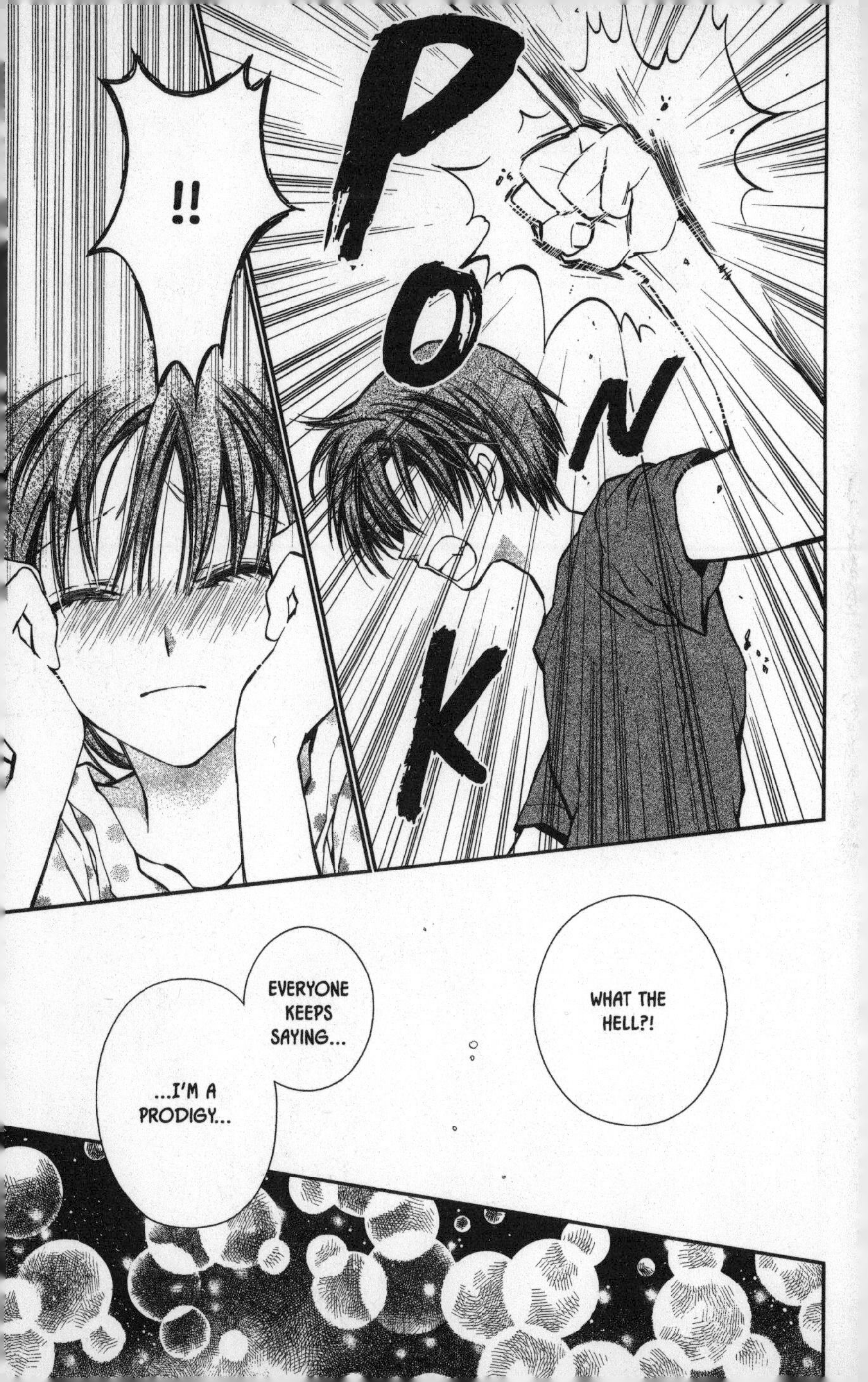
PONK
!!
WHAT THE HELL?!
EVERYONE KEEPS SAYING...
...I'M A PRODIGY...

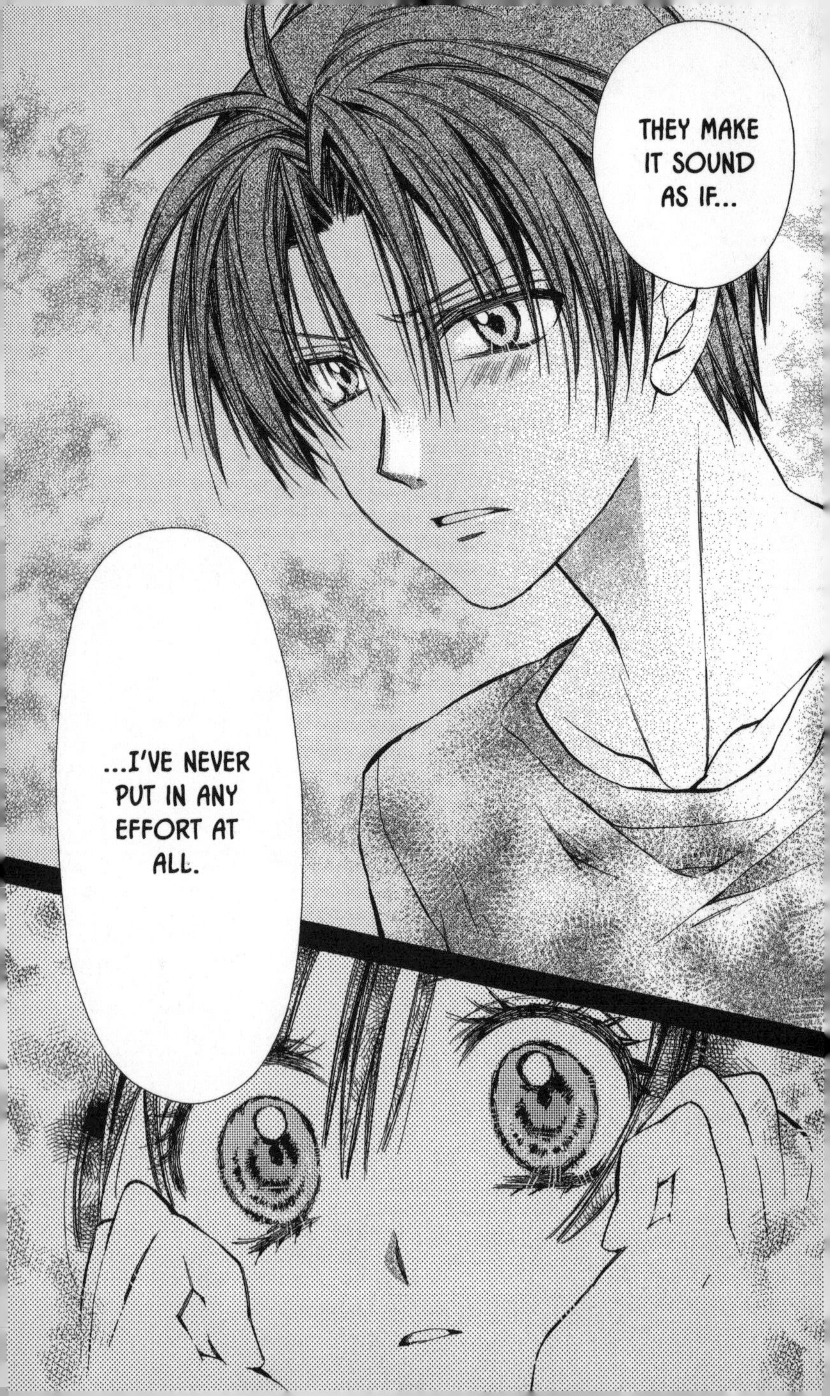
THEY MAKE IT SOUND AS IF...
...I'VE NEVER PUT IN ANY EFFORT AT ALL.

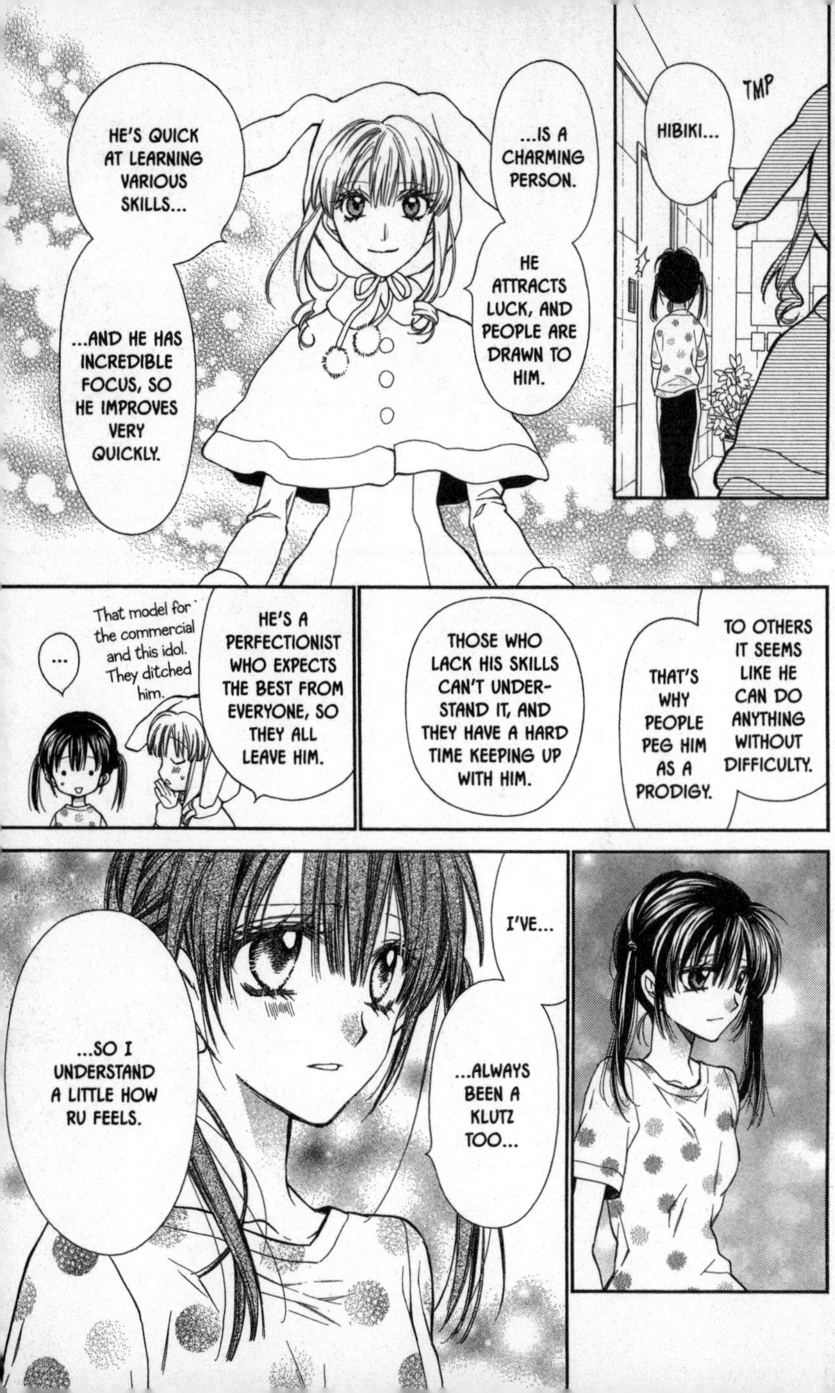
TMP
HIBIKI...
...IS A CHARMING PERSON.
HE ATTRACTS LUCK, AND PEOPLE ARE DRAWN TO HIM.
HE'S QUICK AT LEARNING VARIOUS SKILLS...
...AND HE HAS INCREDIBLE FOCUS, SO HE IMPROVES VERY QUICKLY.
TO OTHERS IT SEEMS LIKE HE CAN DO ANYTHING WITHOUT DIFFICULTY.
THAT'S WHY PEOPLE PEG HIM AS A PRODIGY.
THOSE WHO LACK HIS SKILLS CAN'T UNDERSTAND IT, AND THEY HAVE A HARD TIME KEEPING UP WITH HIM.
HE'S A PERFECTIONIST WHO EXPECTS THE BEST FROM EVERYONE, SO THEY ALL LEAVE HIM.
That model for the commercial and this idol. They ditched him.
...
I'VE...
...ALWAYS BEEN A KLUTZ TOO...
...SO I UNDERSTAND A LITTLE HOW RU FEELS.

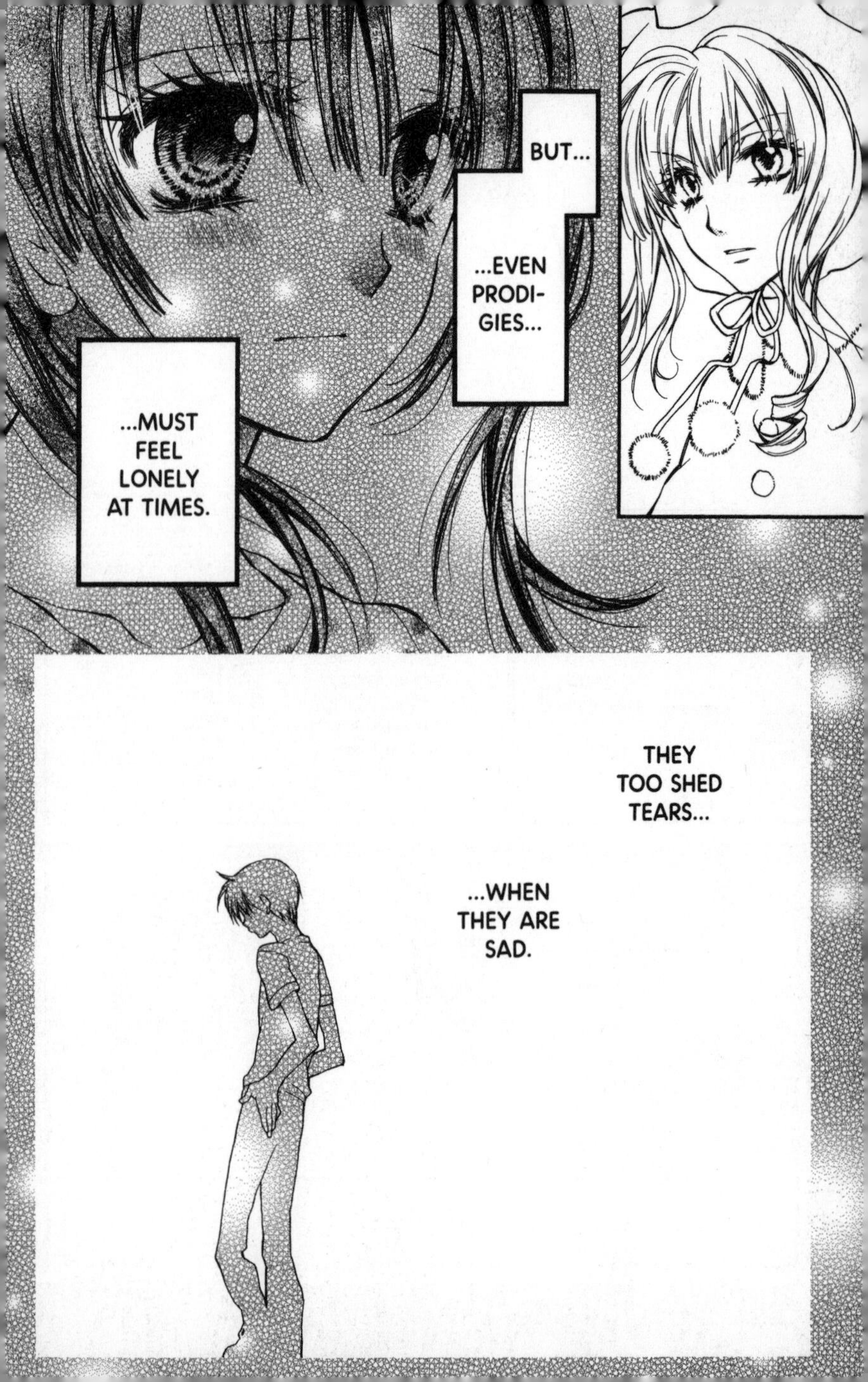
BUT...
...EVEN PRODIGIES...
...MUST FEEL LONELY AT TIMES.
THEY TOO SHED TEARS...
...WHEN THEY ARE SAD.

Chapter 5

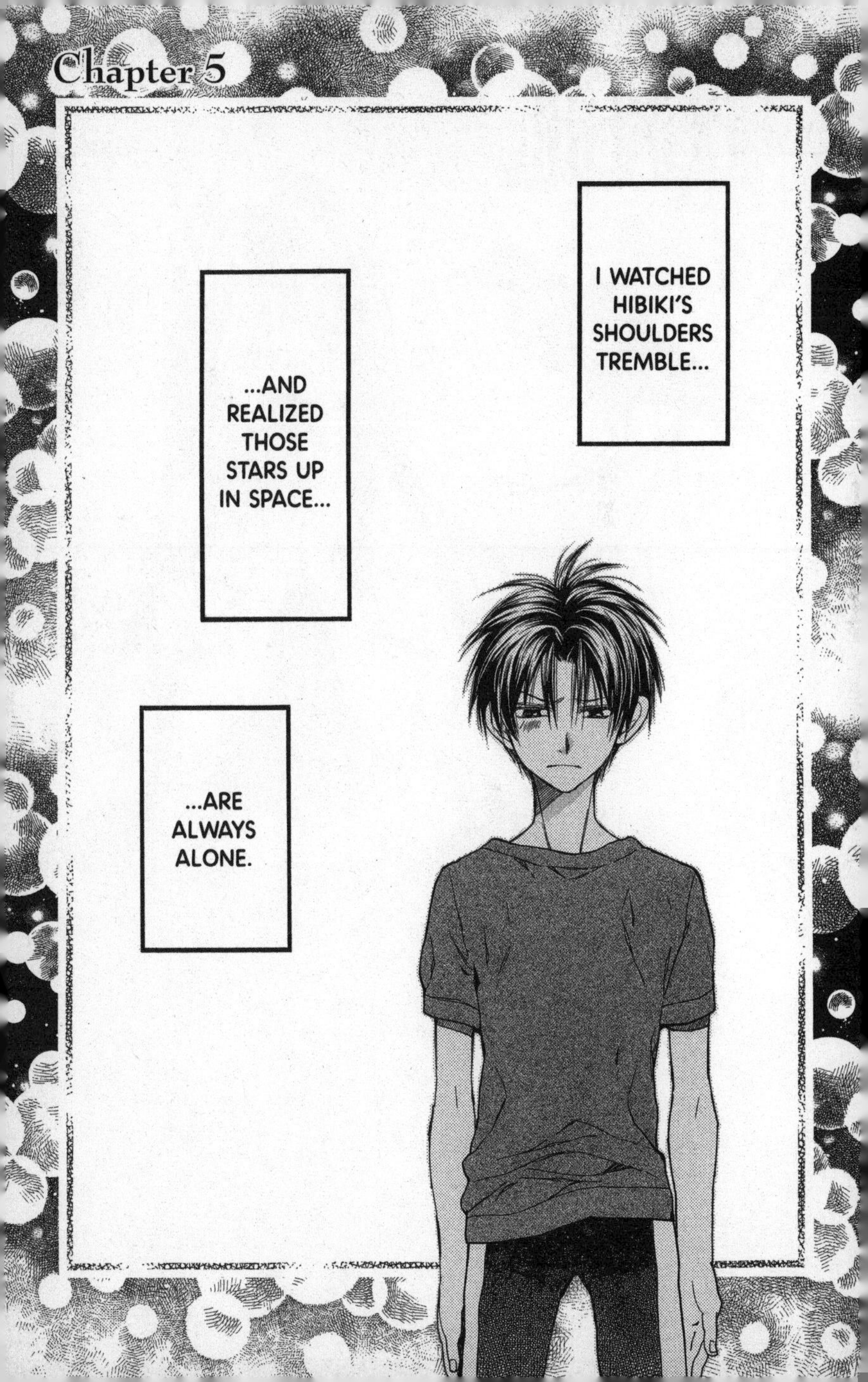
I WATCHED HIBIKI'S SHOULDERS TREMBLE...
...AND REALIZED THOSE STARS UP IN SPACE...
...ARE ALWAYS ALONE.

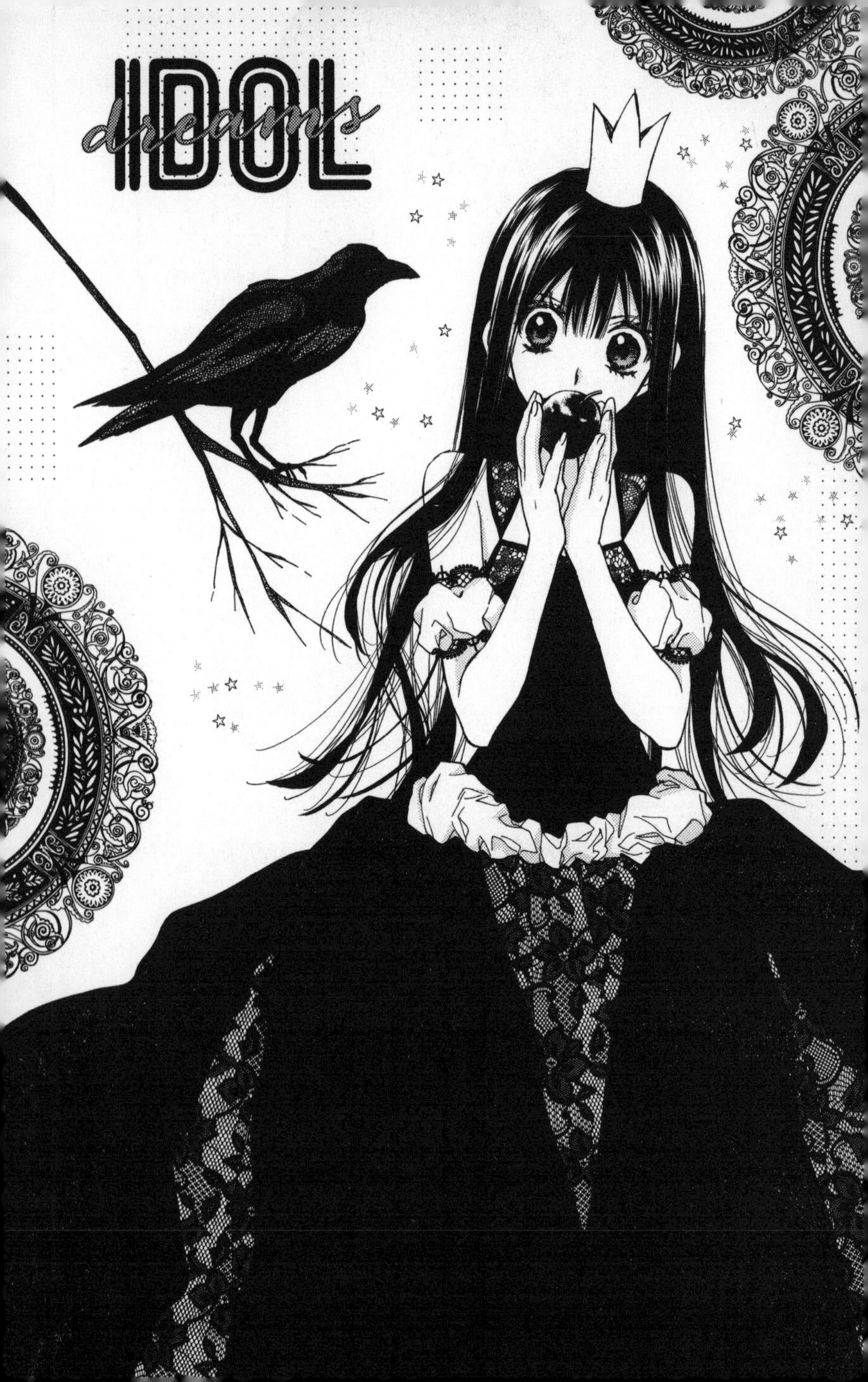
IDOL
dreams

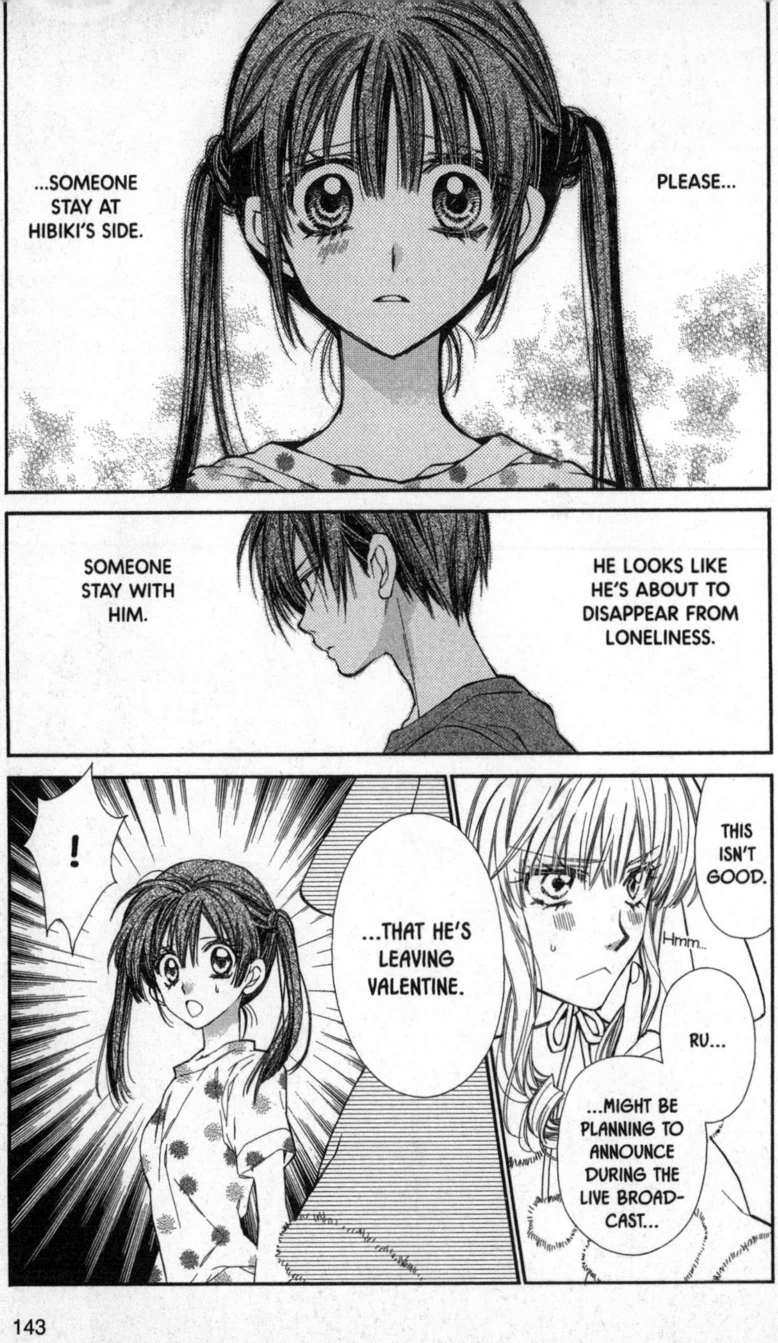
PLEASE...
...SOMEONE STAY AT HIBIKI'S SIDE.
HE LOOKS LIKE HE'S ABOUT TO DISAPPEAR FROM LONELINESS.
SOMEONE STAY WITH HIM.
THIS ISN'T GOOD.
Hmm...
RU...
...MIGHT BE PLANNING TO ANNOUNCE DURING THE LIVE BROAD-CAST...
...THAT HE'S LEAVING VALENTINE.
!

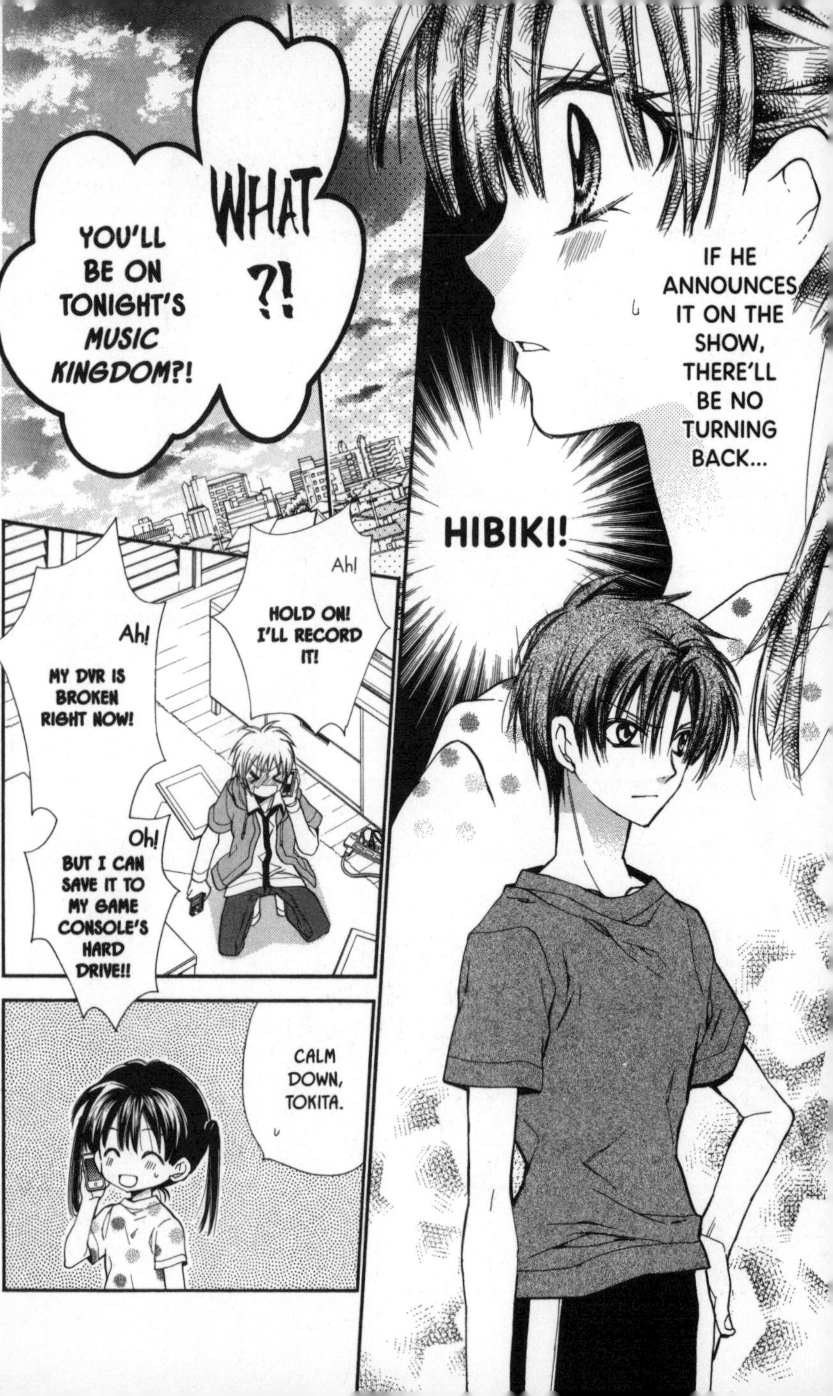
IF HE ANNOUNCES IT ON THE SHOW, THERE'LL BE NO TURNING BACK...
YOU'LL BE ON TONIGHT'S *MUSIC KINGDOM*?!
WHAT ?!
HIBIKI!
Ah!
HOLD ON! I'LL RECORD IT!
Ah!
MY DVR IS BROKEN RIGHT NOW!
Oh!
BUT I CAN SAVE IT TO MY GAME CONSOLE'S HARD DRIVE!!
CALM DOWN, TOKITA.

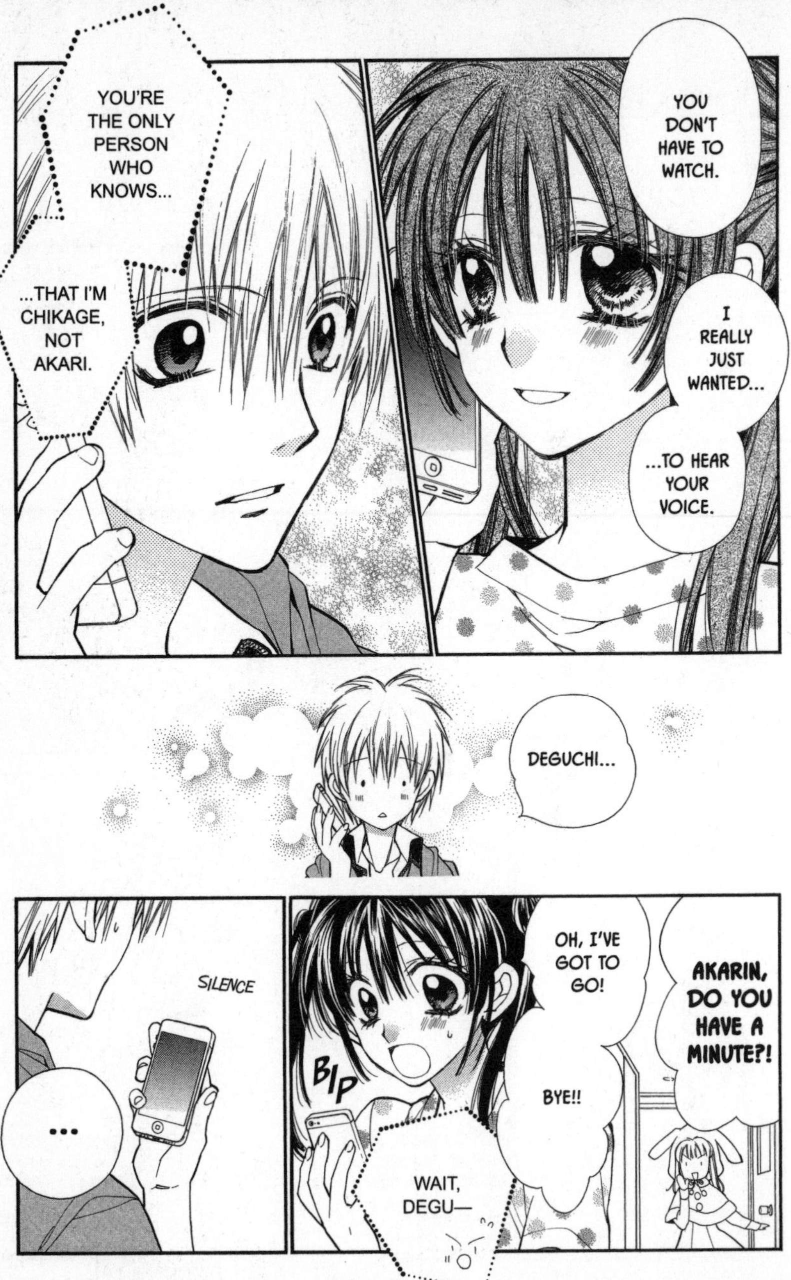
YOU DON'T HAVE TO WATCH.
I REALLY JUST WANTED...
...TO HEAR YOUR VOICE.
YOU'RE THE ONLY PERSON WHO KNOWS...
...THAT I'M CHIKAGE, NOT AKARI.
DEGUCHI...
AKARIN, DO YOU HAVE A MINUTE?!
OH, I'VE GOT TO GO!
BYE!!
BIP
WAIT, DEGU—
SILENCE
...

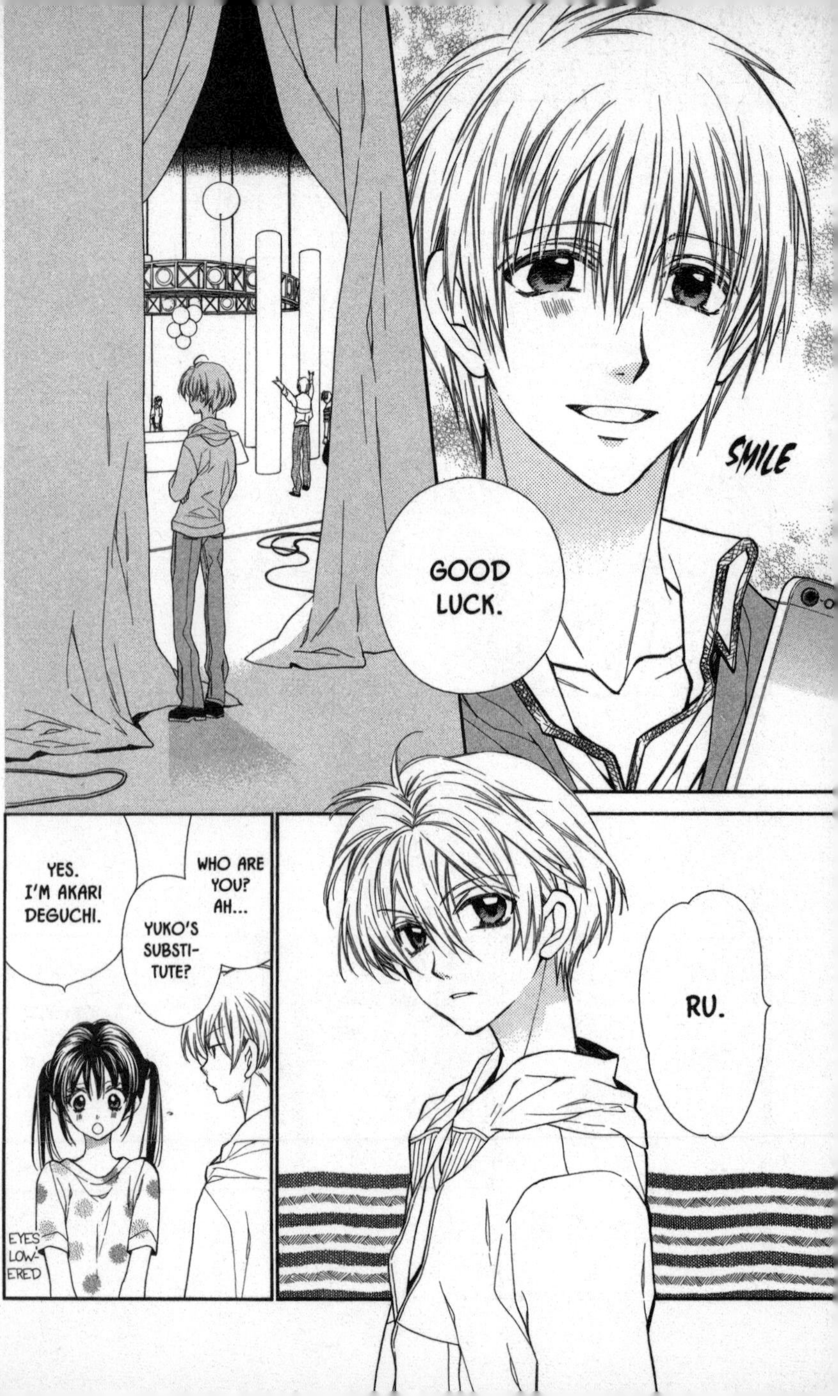
SMILE
GOOD LUCK.
RU.
WHO ARE YOU? AH...
YUKO'S SUBSTITUTE?
YES. I'M AKARI DEGUCHI.
EYES LOWERED

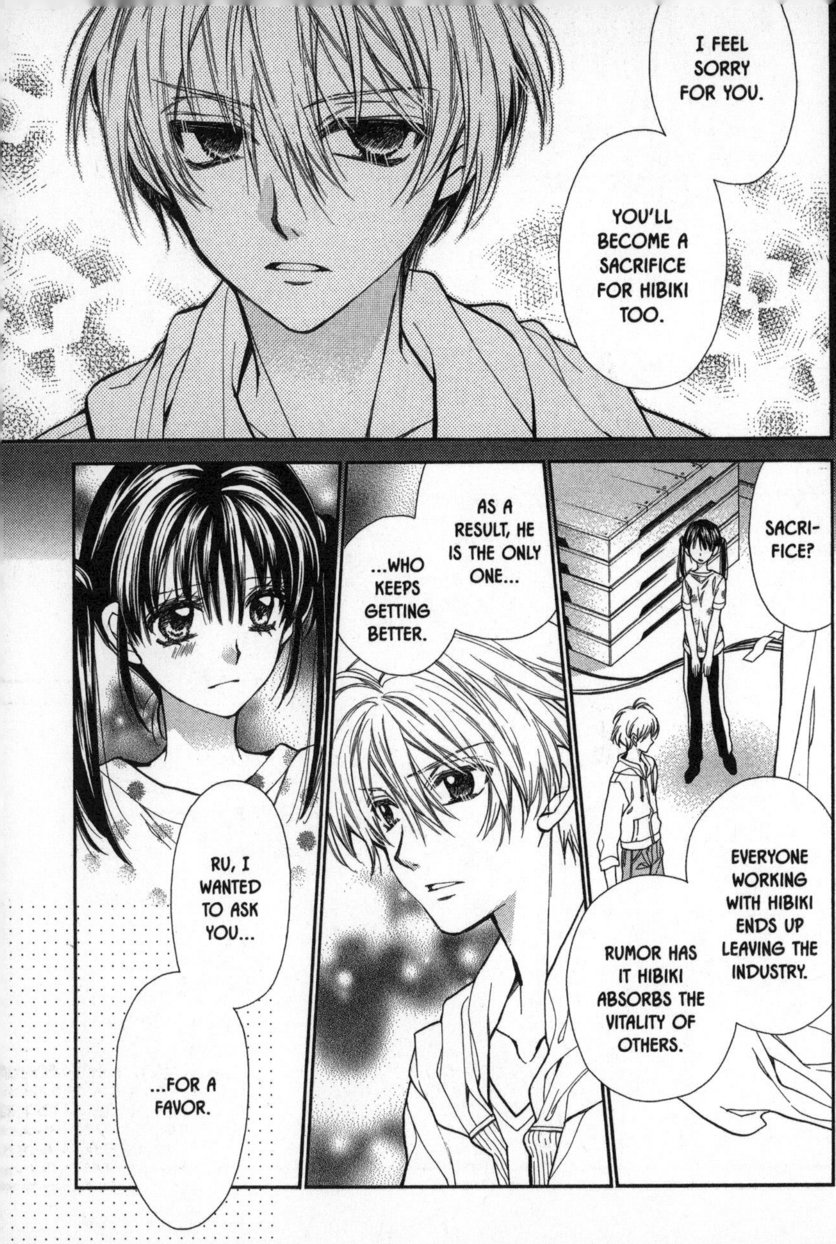
I FEEL SORRY FOR YOU.
YOU'LL BECOME A SACRIFICE FOR HIBIKI TOO.
SACRI-FICE?
EVERYONE WORKING WITH HIBIKI ENDS UP LEAVING THE INDUSTRY.
RUMOR HAS IT HIBIKI ABSORBS THE VITALITY OF OTHERS.
AS A RESULT, HE IS THE ONLY ONE...
...WHO KEEPS GETTING BETTER.
RU, I WANTED TO ASK YOU...
...FOR A FAVOR.

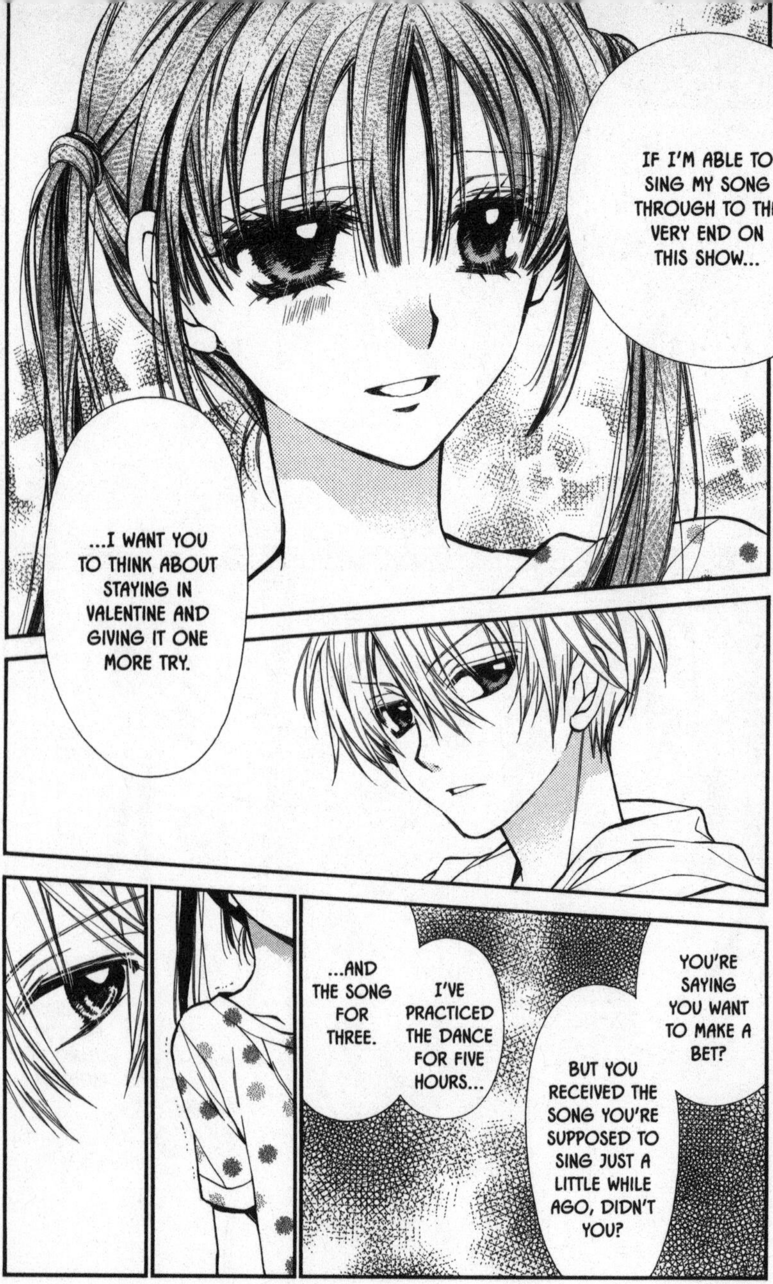
IF I'M ABLE TO SING MY SONG THROUGH TO THE VERY END ON THIS SHOW...
...I WANT YOU TO THINK ABOUT STAYING IN VALENTINE AND GIVING IT ONE MORE TRY.
YOU'RE SAYING YOU WANT TO MAKE A BET?
BUT YOU RECEIVED THE SONG YOU'RE SUPPOSED TO SING JUST A LITTLE WHILE AGO, DIDN'T YOU?
I'VE PRACTICED THE DANCE FOR FIVE HOURS...
...AND THE SONG FOR THREE.

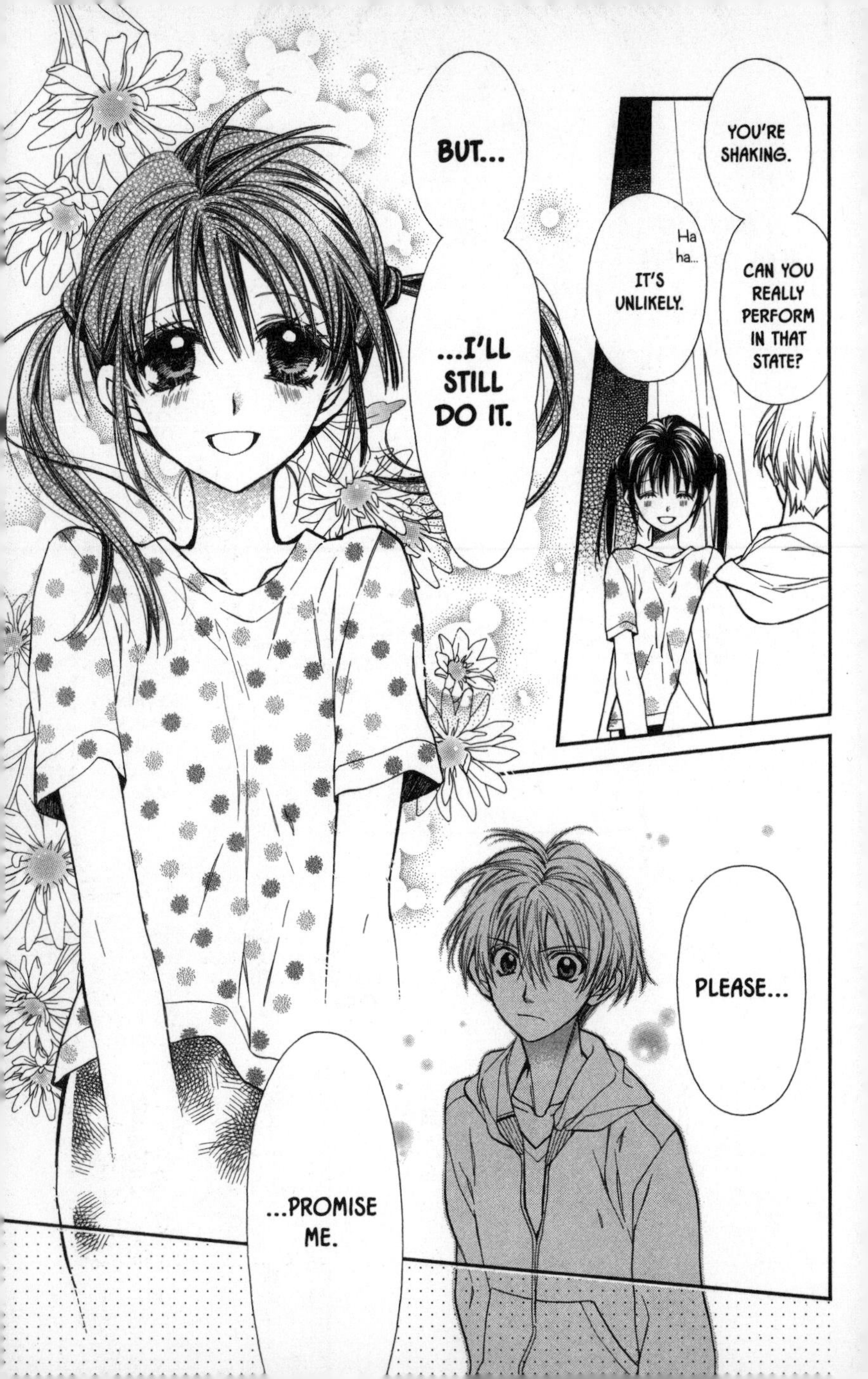
YOU'RE SHAKING.
CAN YOU REALLY PERFORM IN THAT STATE?
Ha ha...
IT'S UNLIKELY.
BUT...
...I'LL STILL DO IT.
PLEASE...
...PROMISE ME.

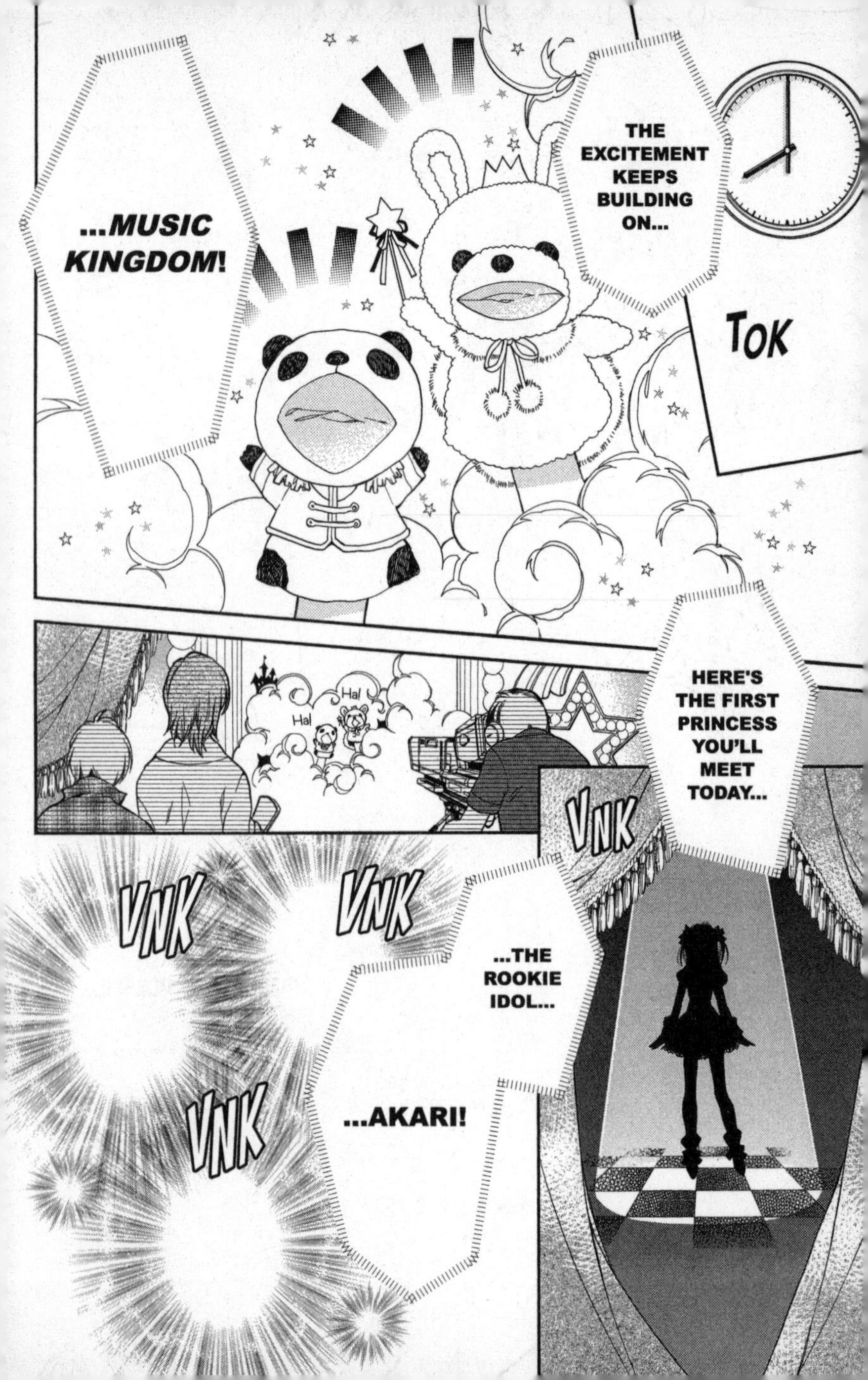
TOK
THE EXCITEMENT KEEPS BUILDING ON...
...MUSIC KINGDOM!
HERE'S THE FIRST PRINCESS YOU'LL MEET TODAY...
Ha!
Ha!
VNK
...THE ROOKIE IDOL...
VNK
VNK
...AKARI!
VNK

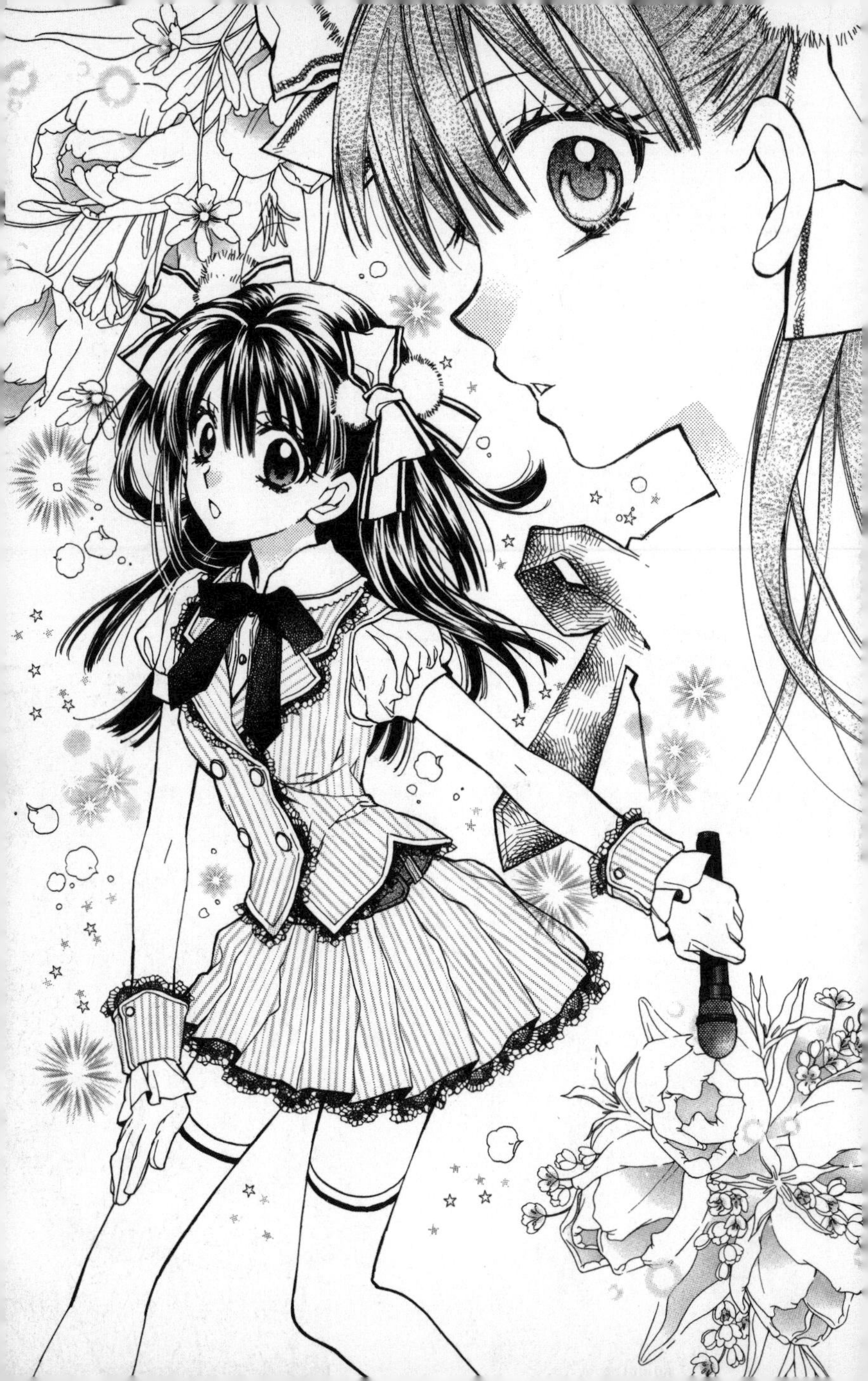

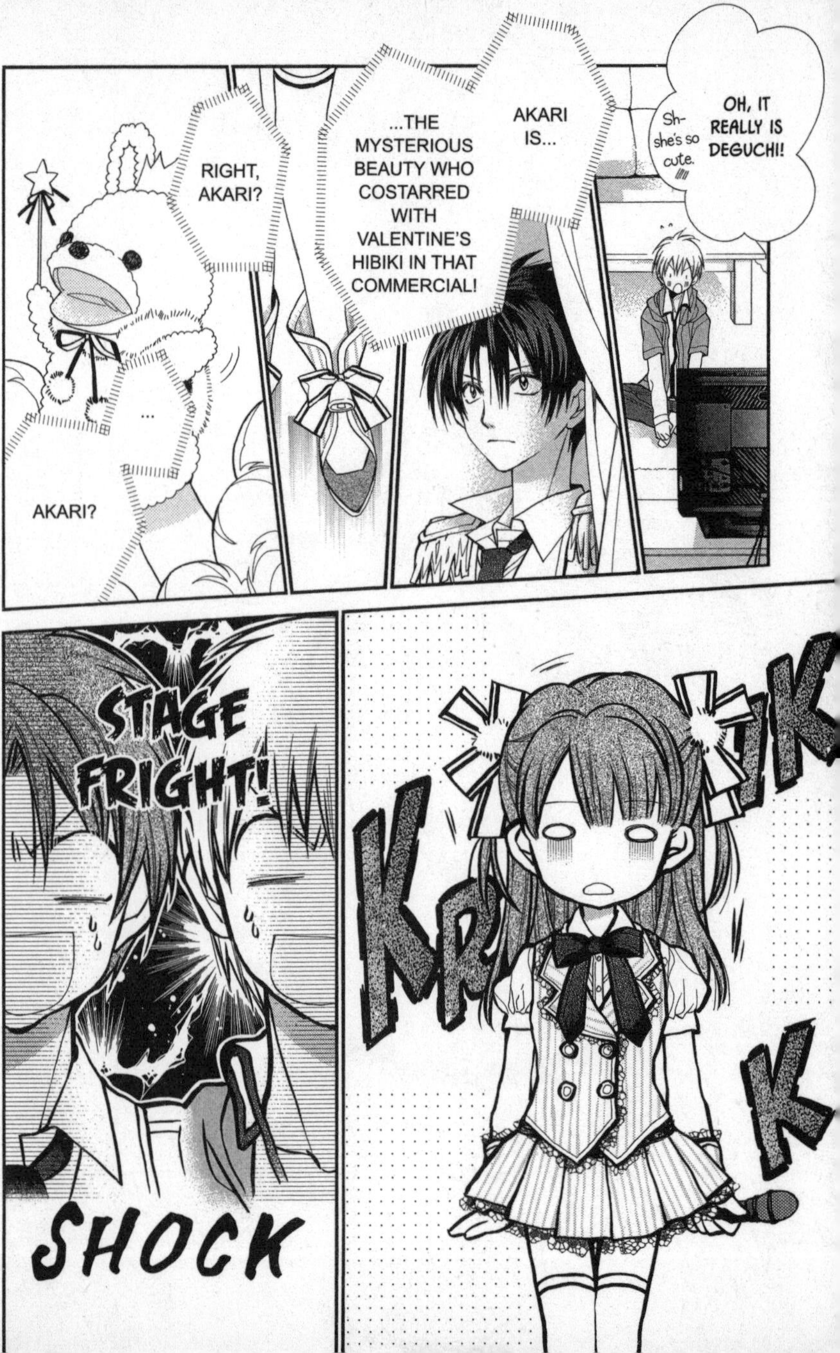
OH, IT REALLY IS DEGUCHI!
Sh-she's so cute.
AKARI IS...
...THE MYSTERIOUS BEAUTY WHO COSTARRED WITH VALENTINE'S HIBIKI IN THAT COMMERCIAL!
RIGHT, AKARI?
...
AKARI?
STAGE FRIGHT!
SHOCK

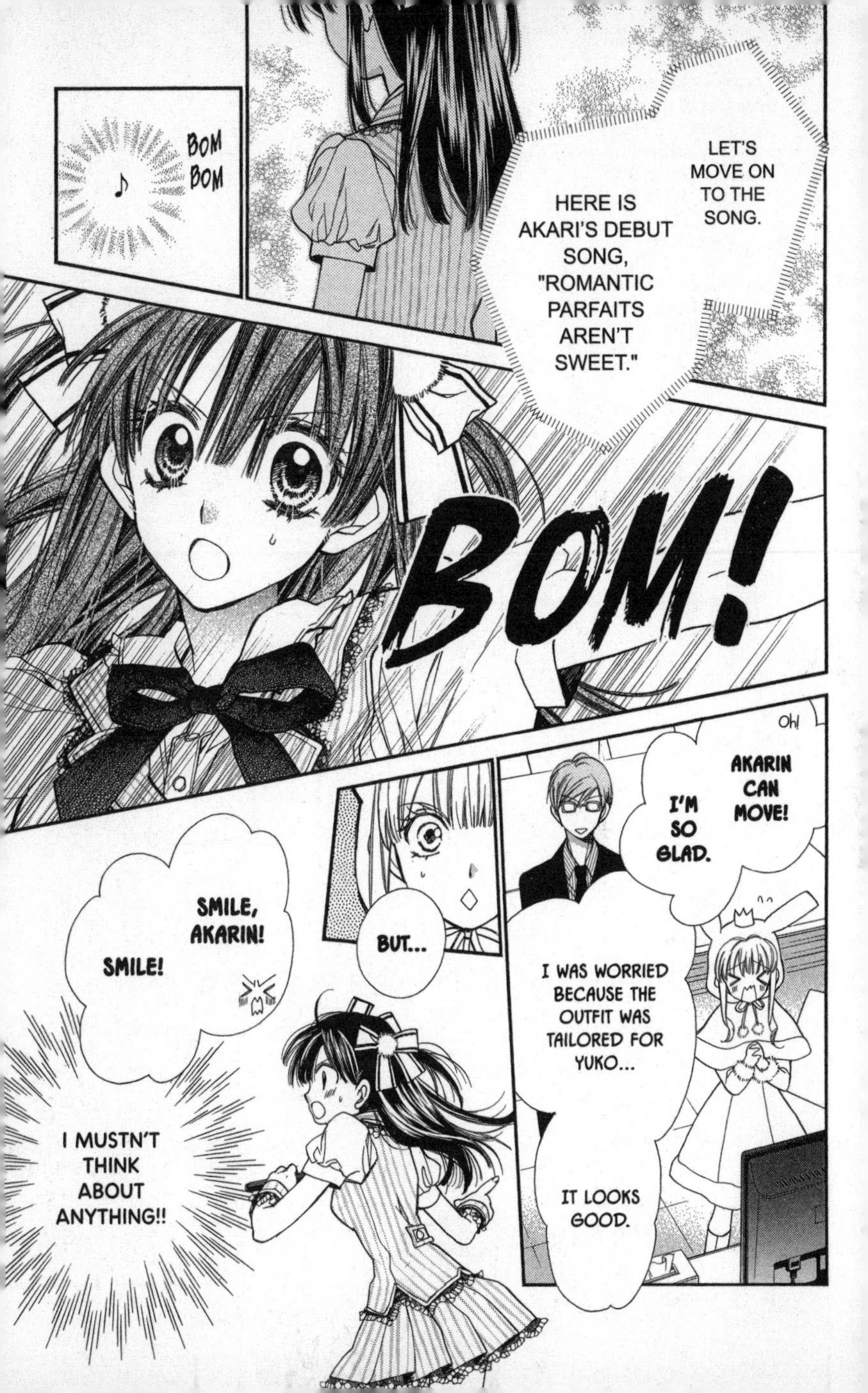
LET'S MOVE ON TO THE SONG.
HERE IS AKARI'S DEBUT SONG, "ROMANTIC PARFAITS AREN'T SWEET."
♪
BOM BOM
BOM!
Oh!
AKARIN CAN MOVE!
I'M SO GLAD.
I WAS WORRIED BECAUSE THE OUTFIT WAS TAILORED FOR YUKO...
IT LOOKS GOOD.
BUT...
SMILE, AKARIN!
SMILE!
I MUSTN'T THINK ABOUT ANYTHING!!

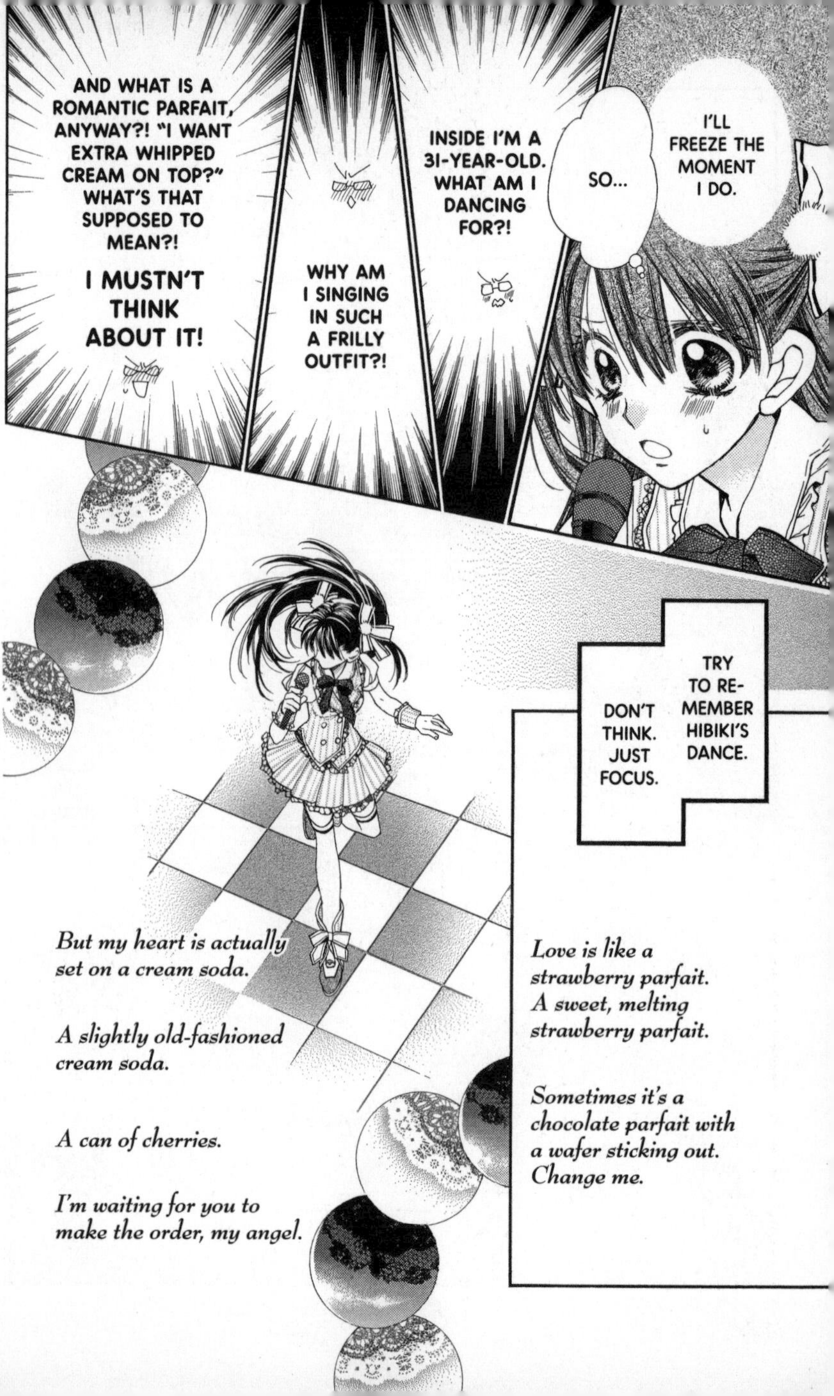
I'LL FREEZE THE MOMENT I DO.
SO...
INSIDE I'M A 31-YEAR-OLD. WHAT AM I DANCING FOR?!
WHY AM I SINGING IN SUCH A FRILLY OUTFIT?!
AND WHAT IS A ROMANTIC PARFAIT, ANYWAY?! "I WANT EXTRA WHIPPED CREAM ON TOP?" WHAT'S THAT SUPPOSED TO MEAN?!
I MUSTN'T THINK ABOUT IT!
TRY TO RE-MEMBER HIBIKI'S DANCE.
DON'T THINK. JUST FOCUS.
Love is like a strawberry parfait. A sweet, melting strawberry parfait.
Sometimes it's a chocolate parfait with a wafer sticking out. Change me.
But my heart is actually set on a cream soda.
A slightly old-fashioned cream soda.
A can of cherries.
I'm waiting for you to make the order, my angel.

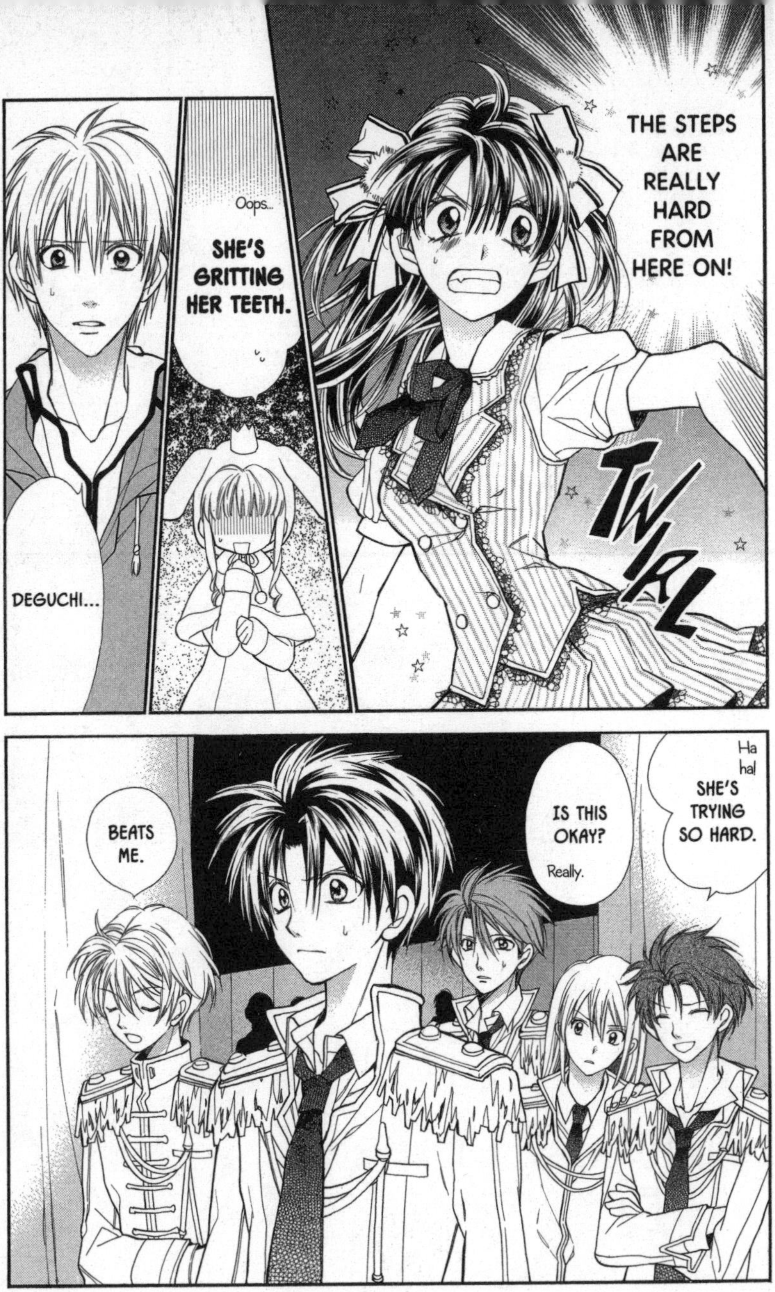
THE STEPS ARE REALLY HARD FROM HERE ON!
TWIRL
Oops...
SHE'S GRITTING HER TEETH.
DEGUCHI...
Ha ha!
SHE'S TRYING SO HARD.
IS THIS OKAY?
Really.
BEATS ME.

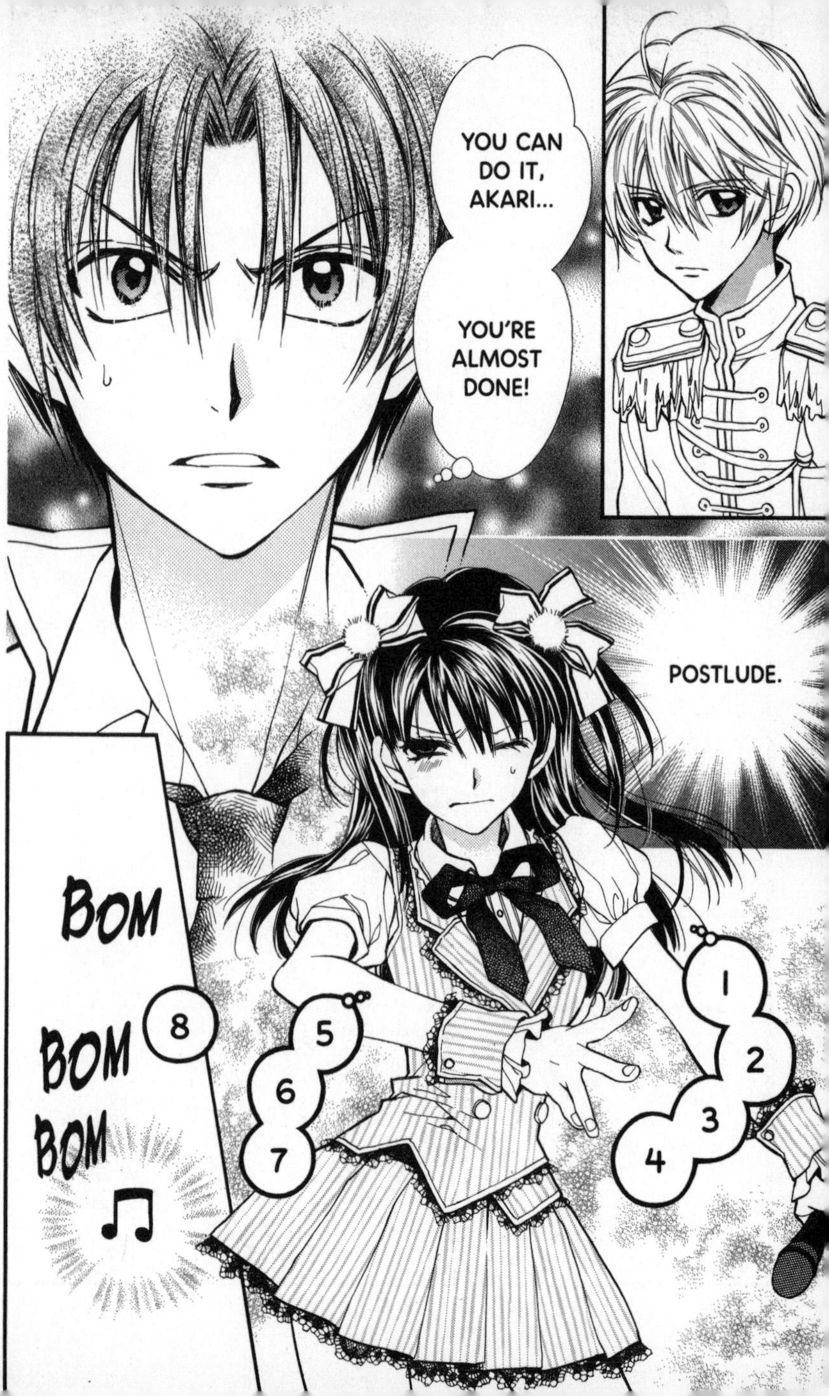
YOU CAN DO IT, AKARI...
YOU'RE ALMOST DONE!
POSTLUDE.
1 2 3 4
5 6 7
8
BOM BOM BOM ♫

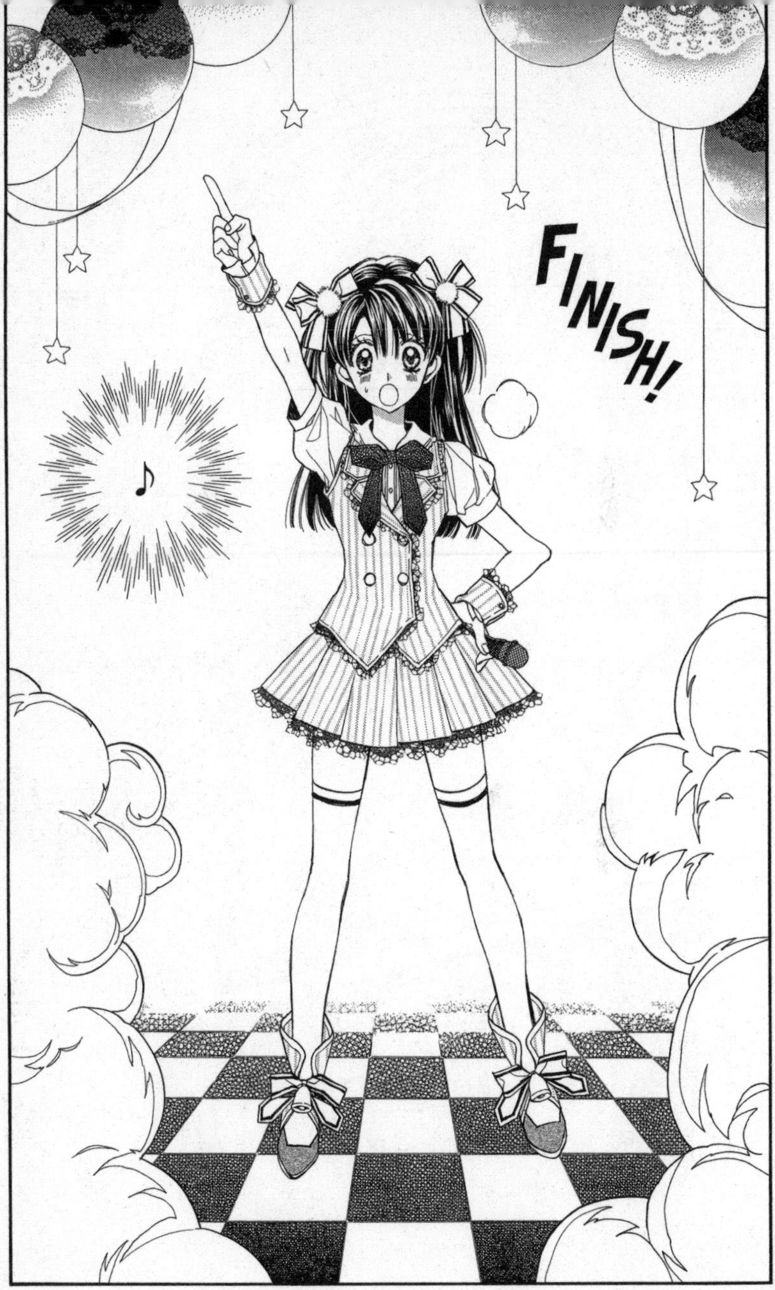
FINISH!

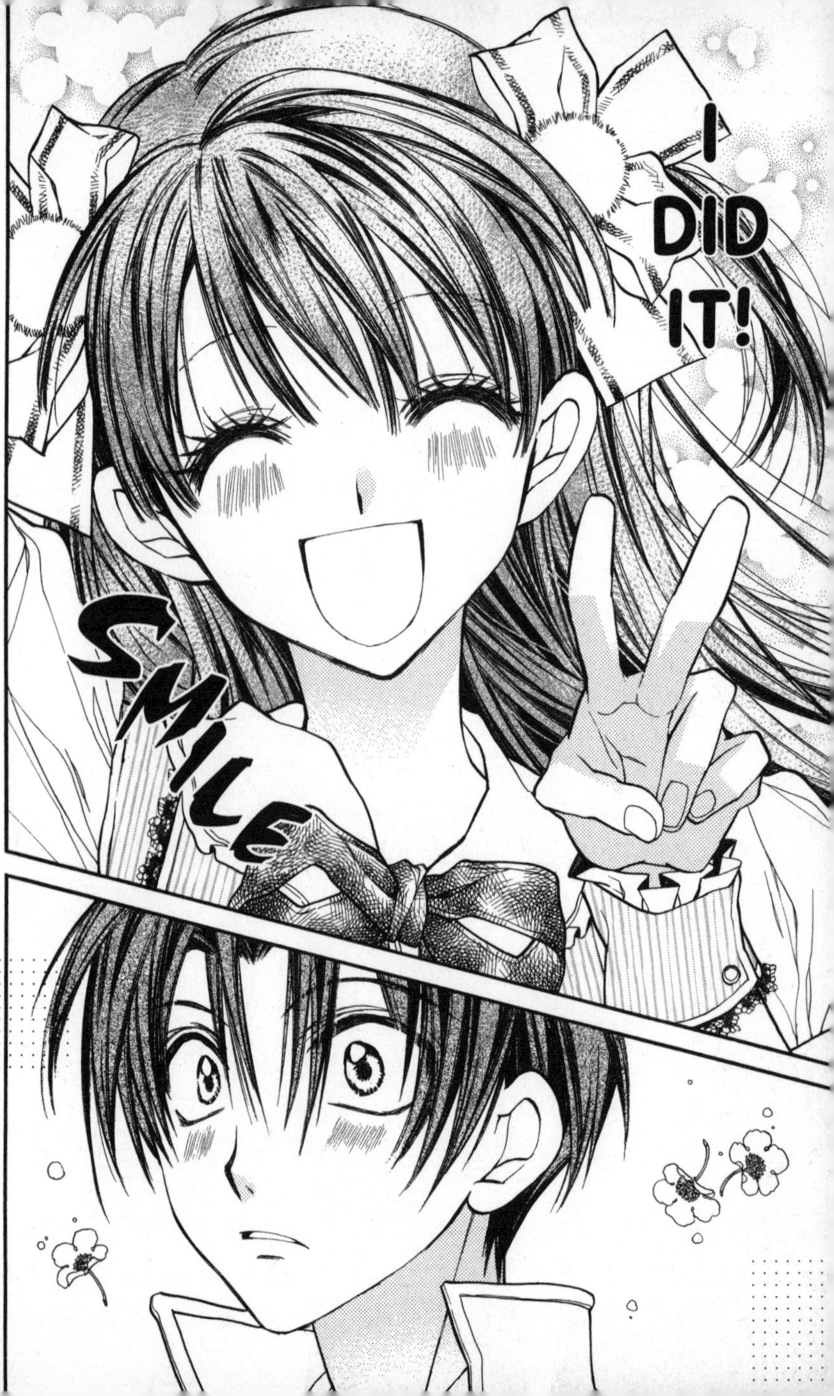
I DID IT!
SMILE

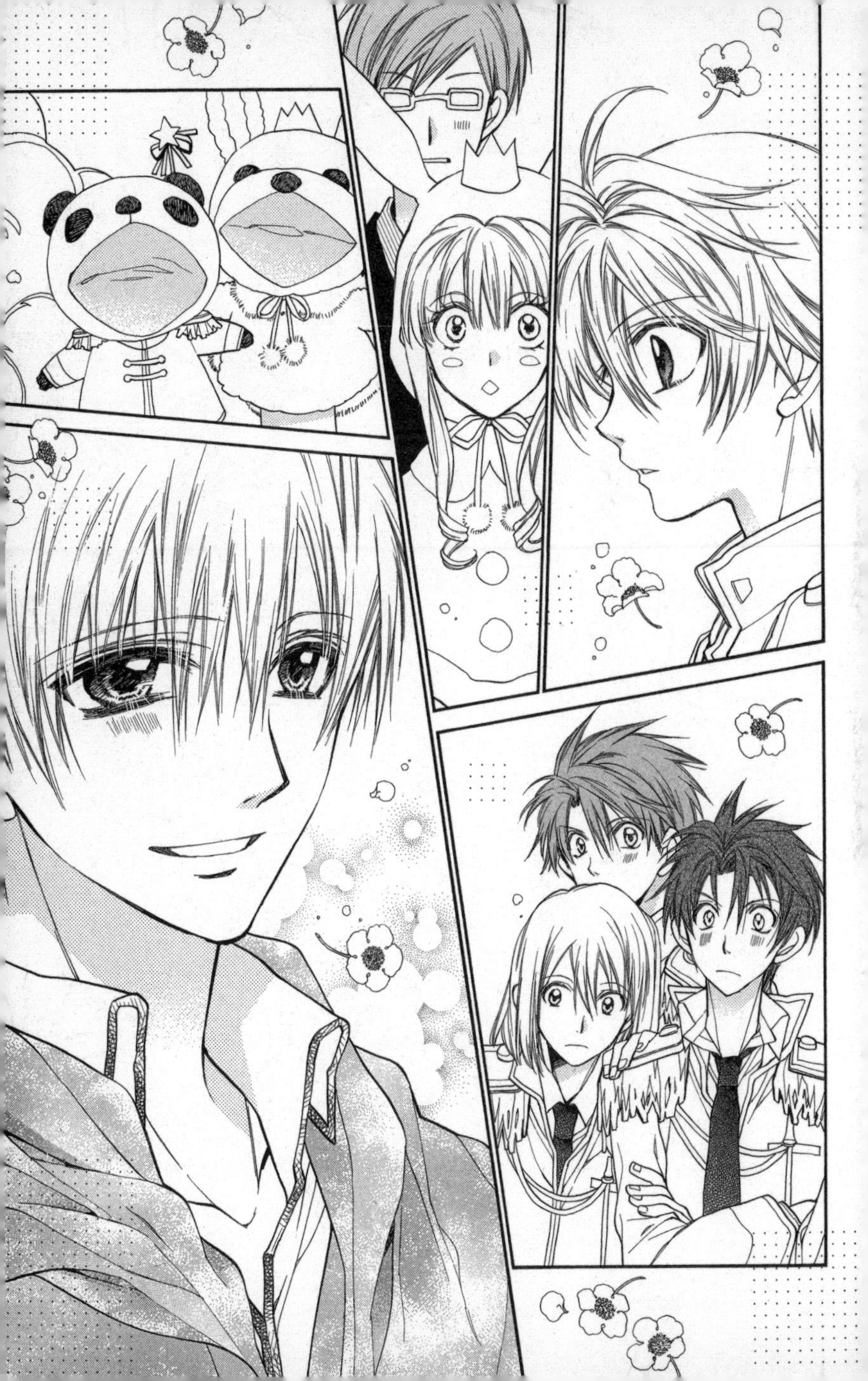

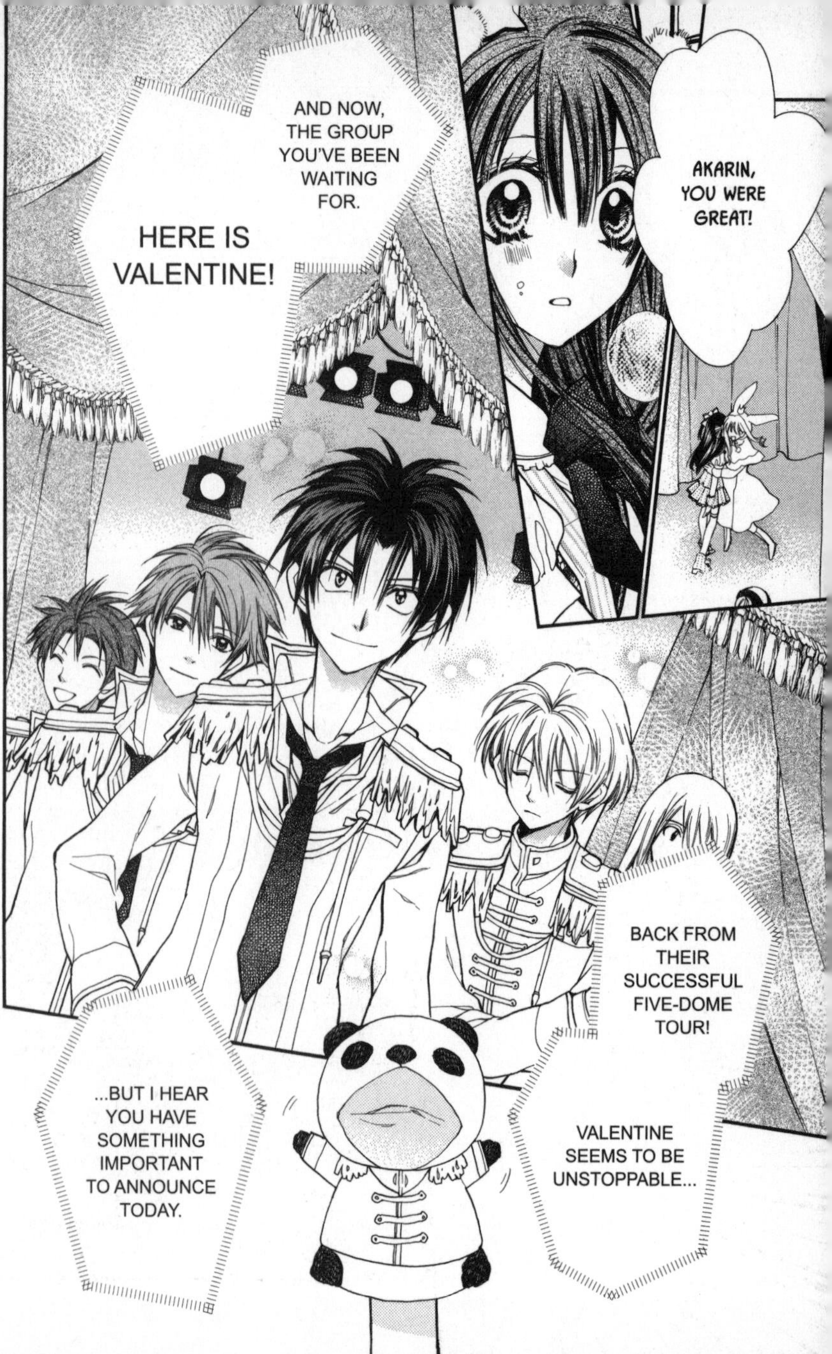
AKARIN, YOU WERE GREAT!
AND NOW, THE GROUP YOU'VE BEEN WAITING FOR.
HERE IS VALENTINE!
BACK FROM THEIR SUCCESSFUL FIVE-DOME TOUR!
VALENTINE SEEMS TO BE UNSTOPPABLE...
...BUT I HEAR YOU HAVE SOMETHING IMPORTANT TO ANNOUNCE TODAY.

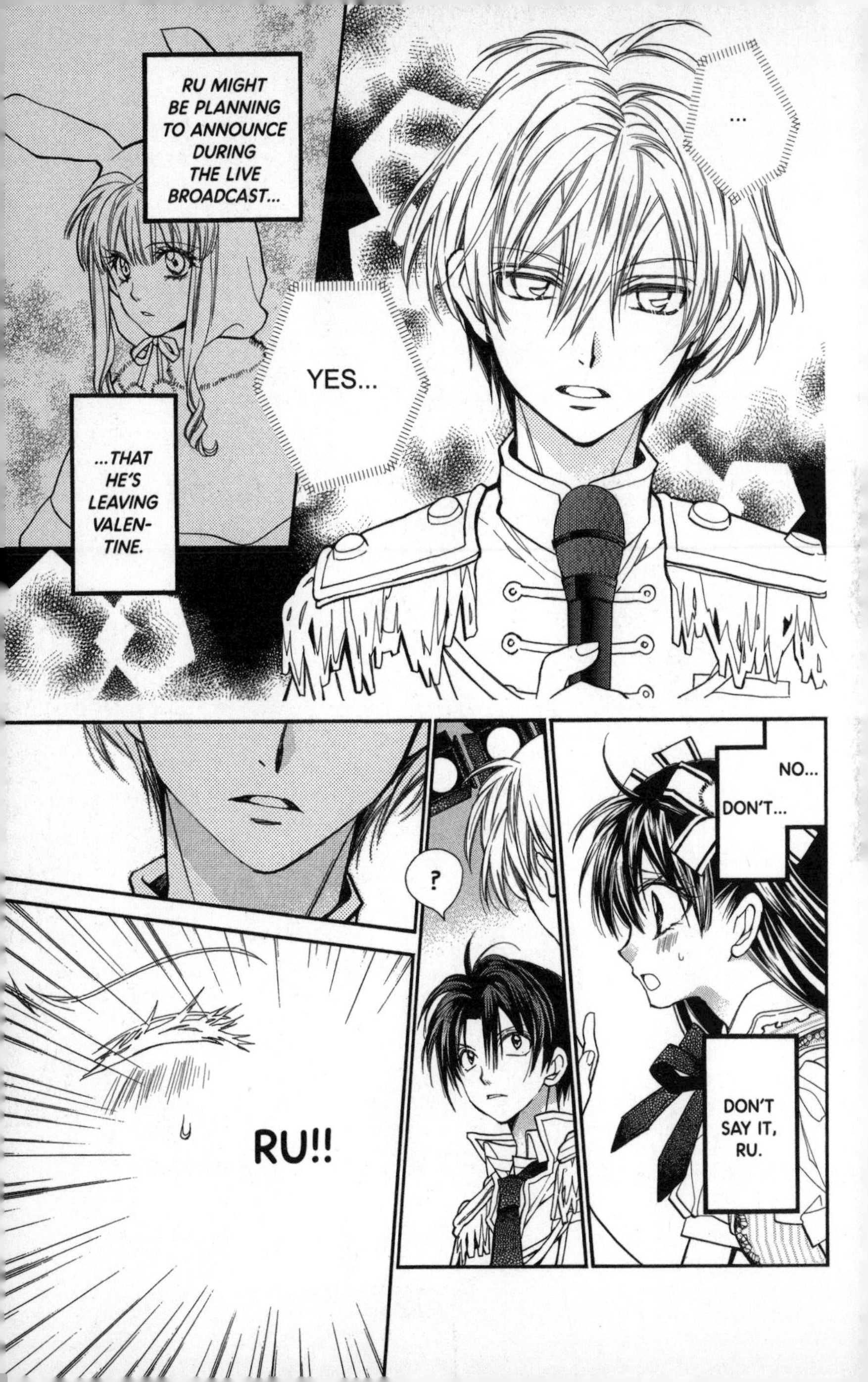
...
YES...
RU MIGHT BE PLANNING TO ANNOUNCE DURING THE LIVE BROADCAST...
...THAT HE'S LEAVING VALEN-TINE.
NO...
DON'T...
DON'T SAY IT, RU.
?
RU!!

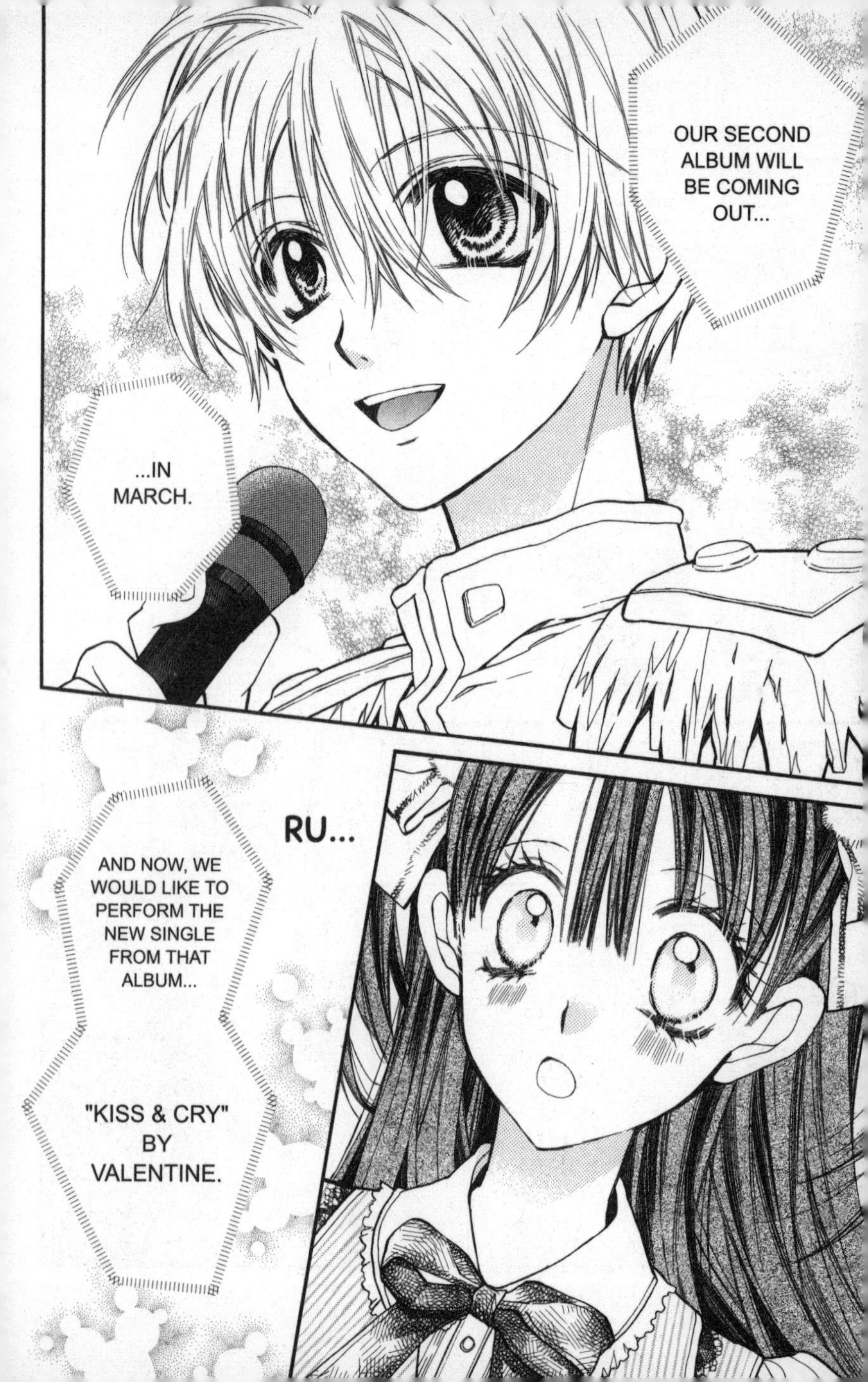
OUR SECOND ALBUM WILL BE COMING OUT...
...IN MARCH.
RU...
AND NOW, WE WOULD LIKE TO PERFORM THE NEW SINGLE FROM THAT ALBUM...
"KISS & CRY" BY VALENTINE.

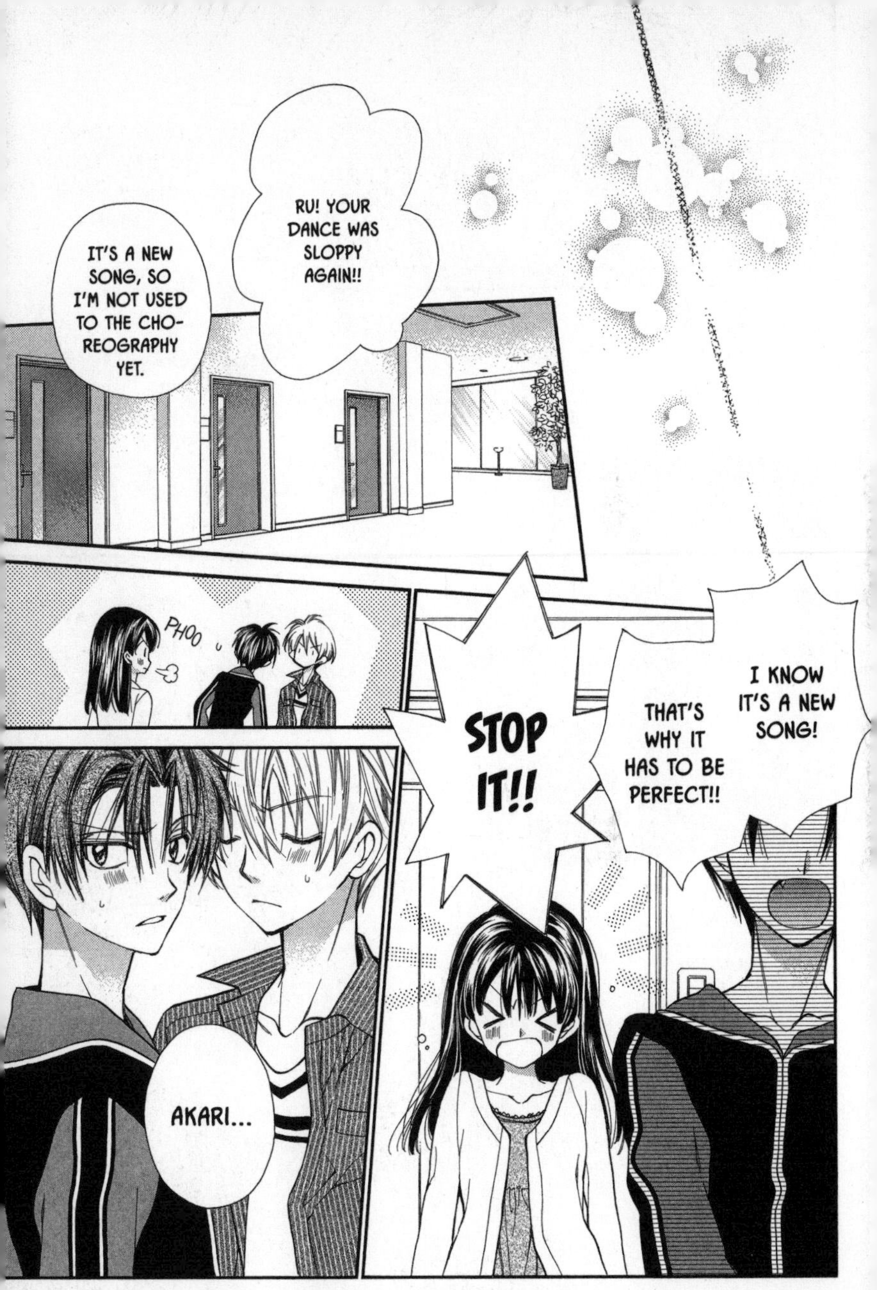
RU! YOUR DANCE WAS SLOPPY AGAIN!!
IT'S A NEW SONG, SO I'M NOT USED TO THE CHO-REOGRAPHY YET.
I KNOW IT'S A NEW SONG!
THAT'S WHY IT HAS TO BE PERFECT!!
STOP IT!!
PHOO
AKARI...

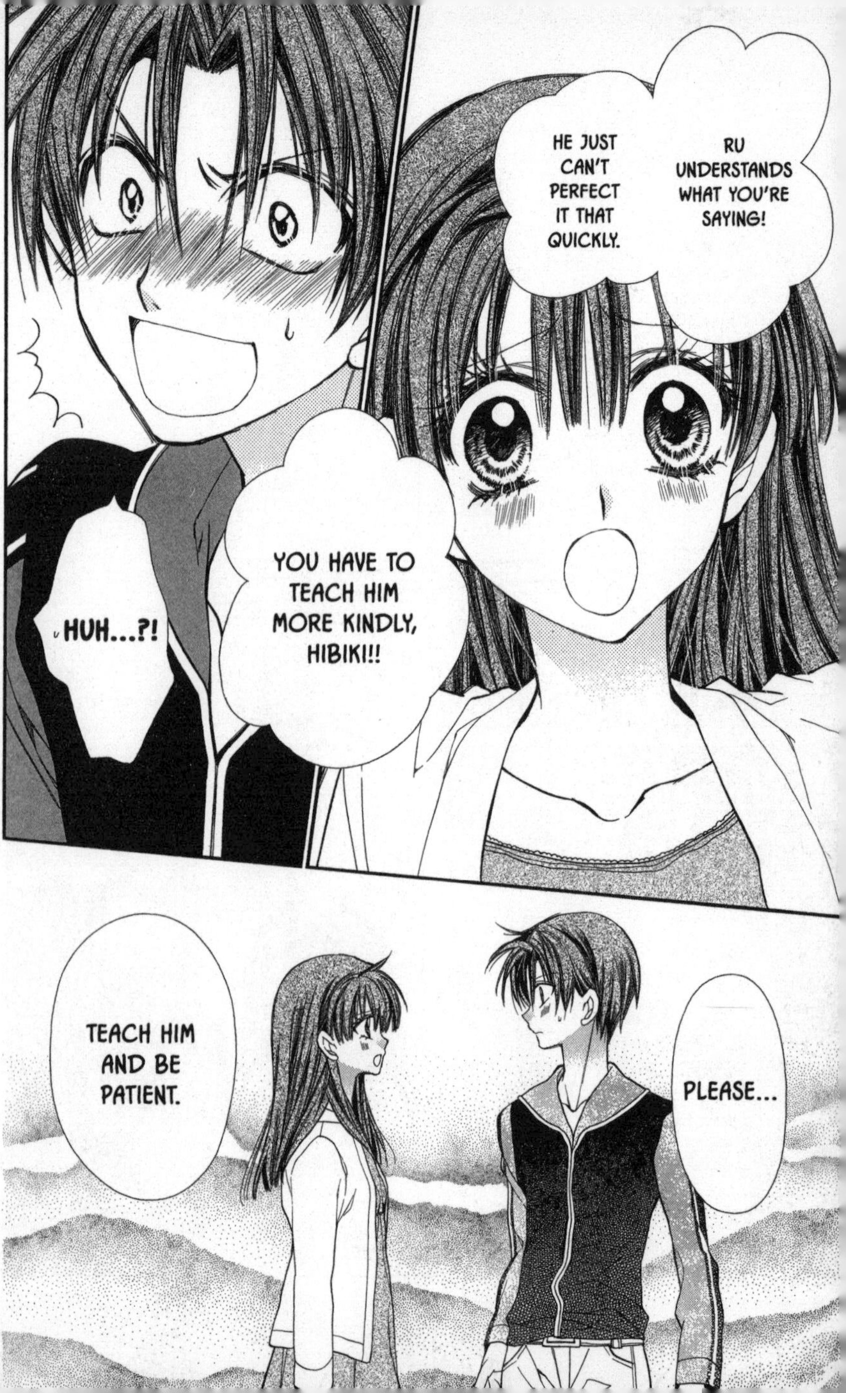
RU UNDERSTANDS WHAT YOU'RE SAYING!
HE JUST CAN'T PERFECT IT THAT QUICKLY.
YOU HAVE TO TEACH HIM MORE KINDLY, HIBIKI!!
HUH...?!
PLEASE...
TEACH HIM AND BE PATIENT.

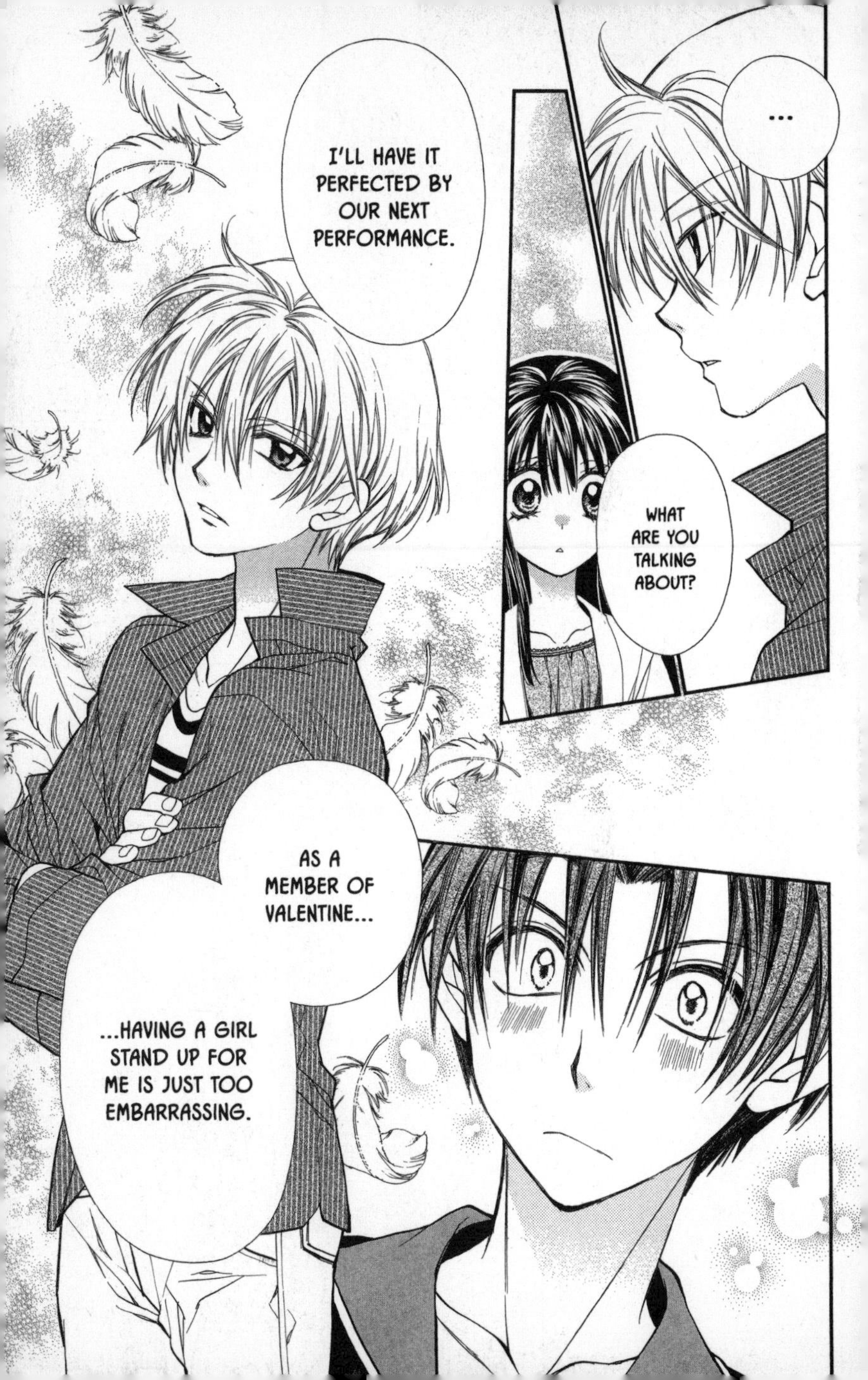
...
WHAT ARE YOU TALKING ABOUT?
I'LL HAVE IT PERFECTED BY OUR NEXT PERFORMANCE.
AS A MEMBER OF VALENTINE...
...HAVING A GIRL STAND UP FOR ME IS JUST TOO EMBARRASSING.

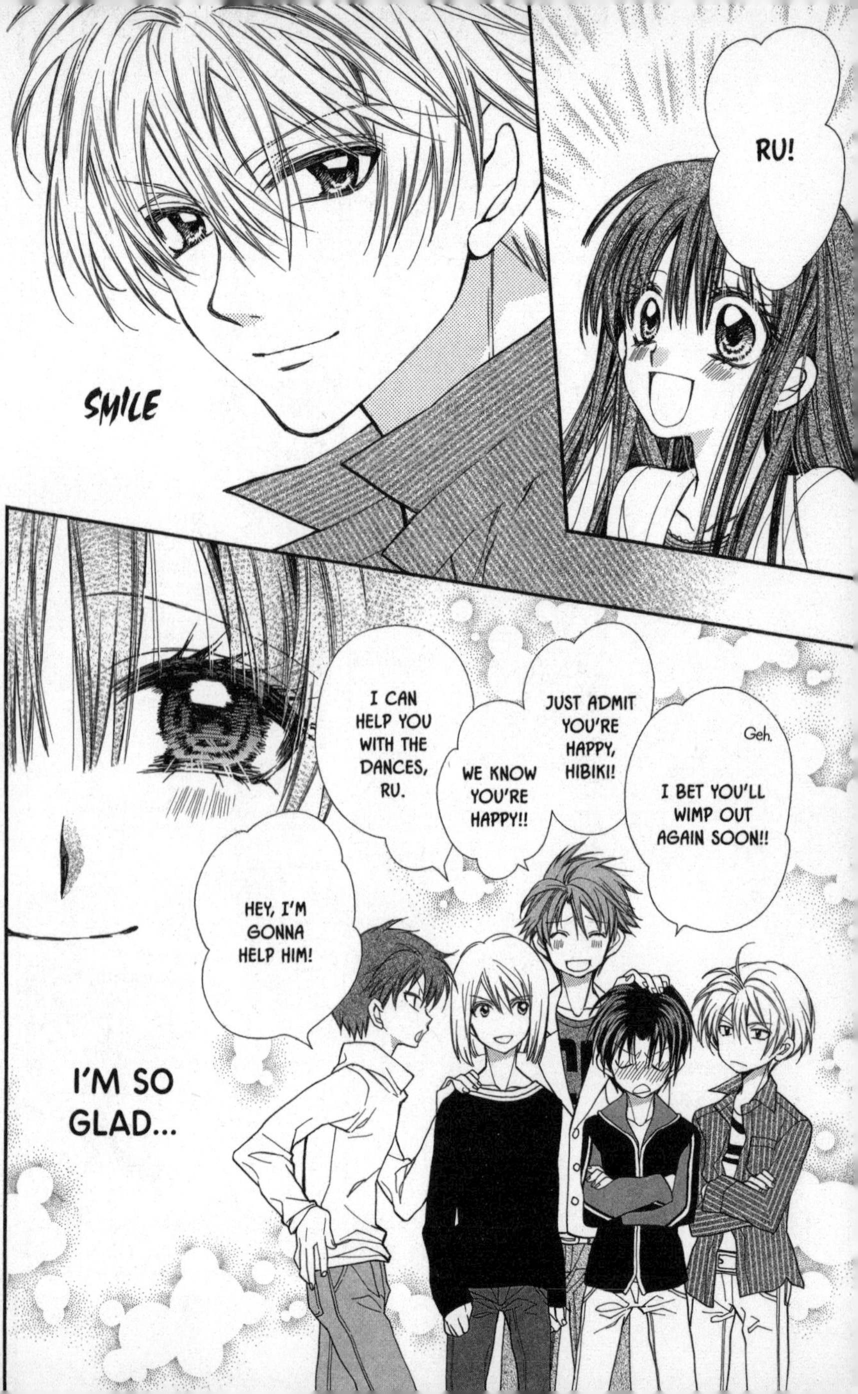
RU!
SMILE
Geh.
I BET YOU'LL WIMP OUT AGAIN SOON!!
JUST ADMIT YOU'RE HAPPY, HIBIKI!
WE KNOW YOU'RE HAPPY!!
I CAN HELP YOU WITH THE DANCES, RU.
HEY, I'M GONNA HELP HIM!
I'M SO GLAD...

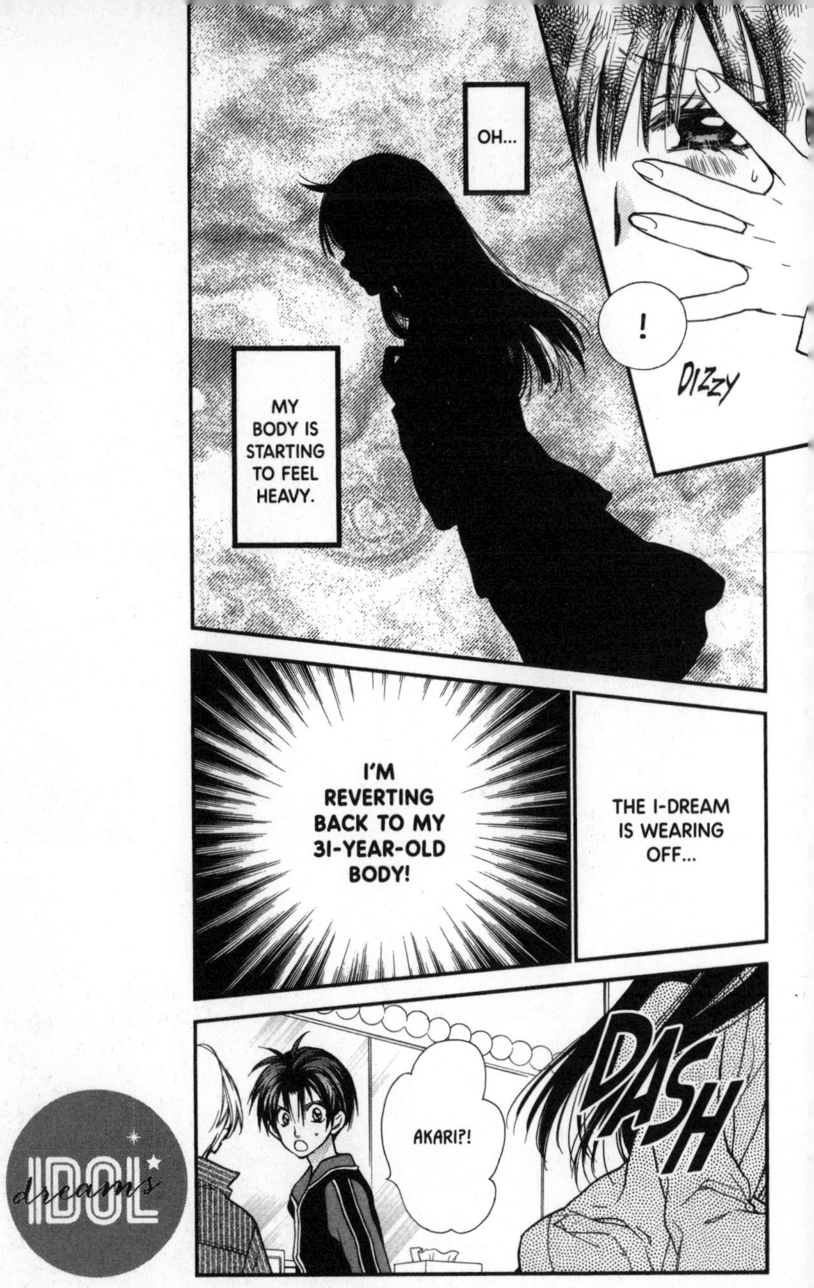
!
DIZZY
OH...
MY BODY IS STARTING TO FEEL HEAVY.
THE I-DREAM IS WEARING OFF...
I'M REVERTING BACK TO MY 31-YEAR-OLD BODY!
DASH
AKARI?!
IDOL dreams

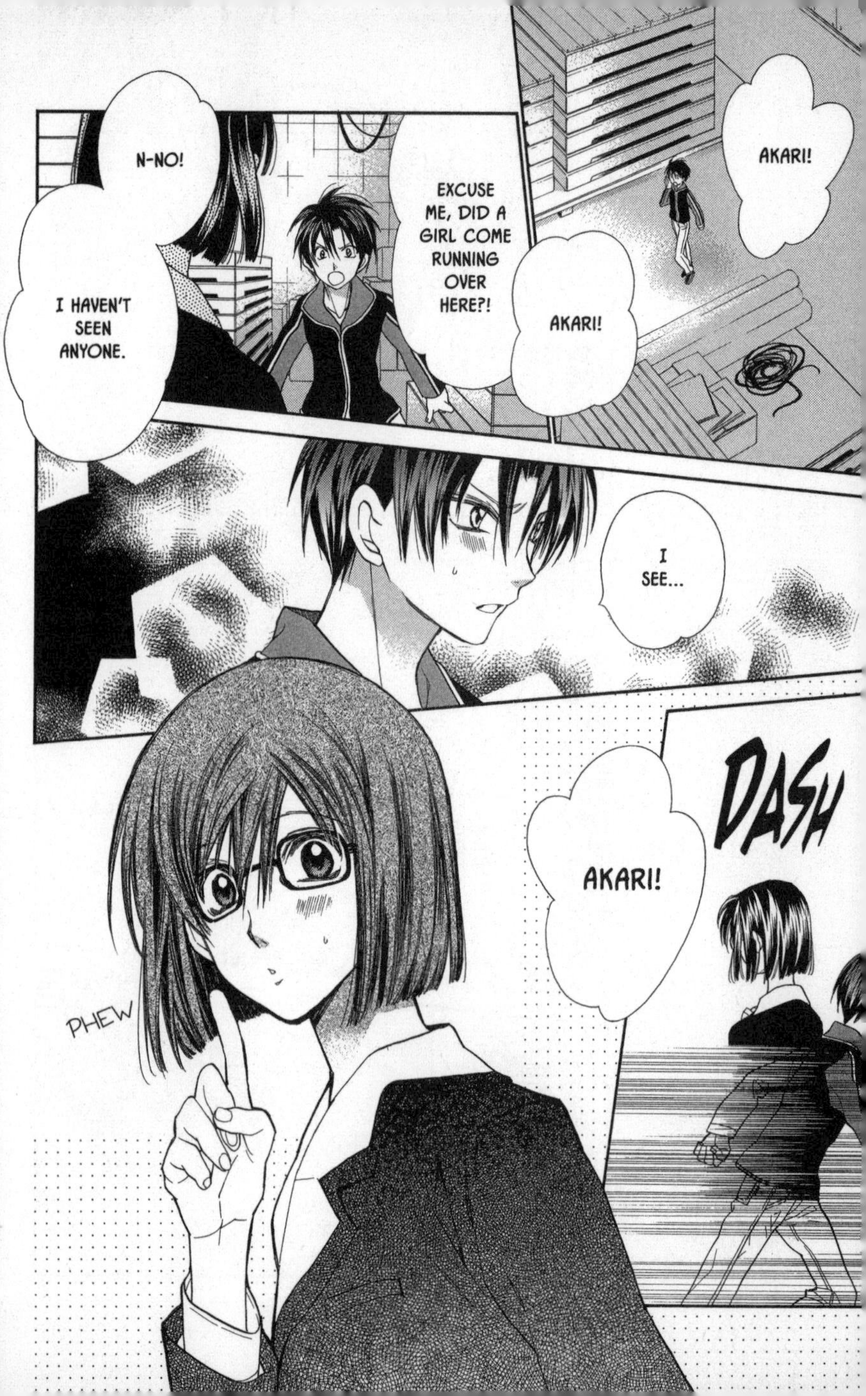
AKARI!
AKARI!
EXCUSE ME, DID A GIRL COME RUNNING OVER HERE?!
N-NO!
I HAVEN'T SEEN ANYONE.
I SEE...
DASH
AKARI!
PHEW

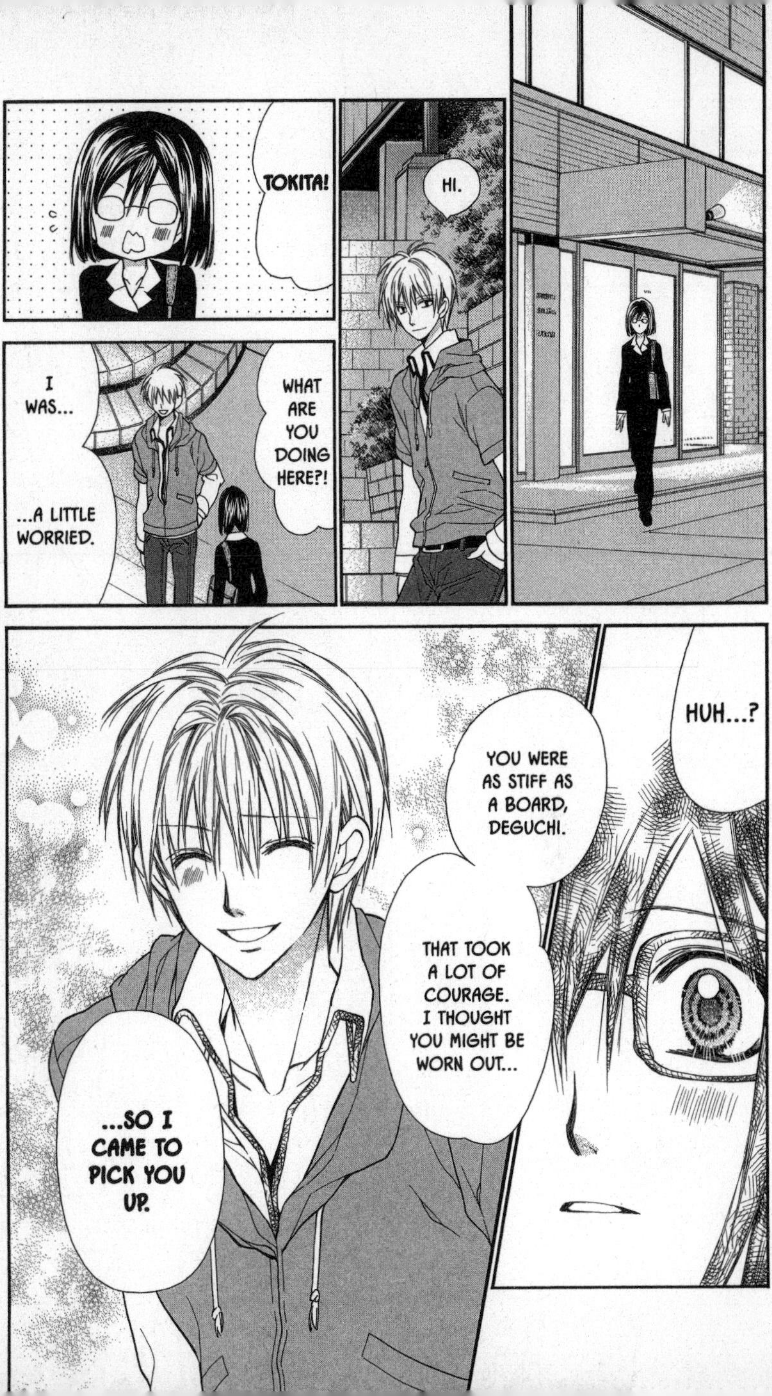
HI.
TOKITA!
WHAT ARE YOU DOING HERE?!
I WAS...
...A LITTLE WORRIED.
HUH...?
YOU WERE AS STIFF AS A BOARD, DEGUCHI.
THAT TOOK A LOT OF COURAGE. I THOUGHT YOU MIGHT BE WORN OUT...
...SO I CAME TO PICK YOU UP.

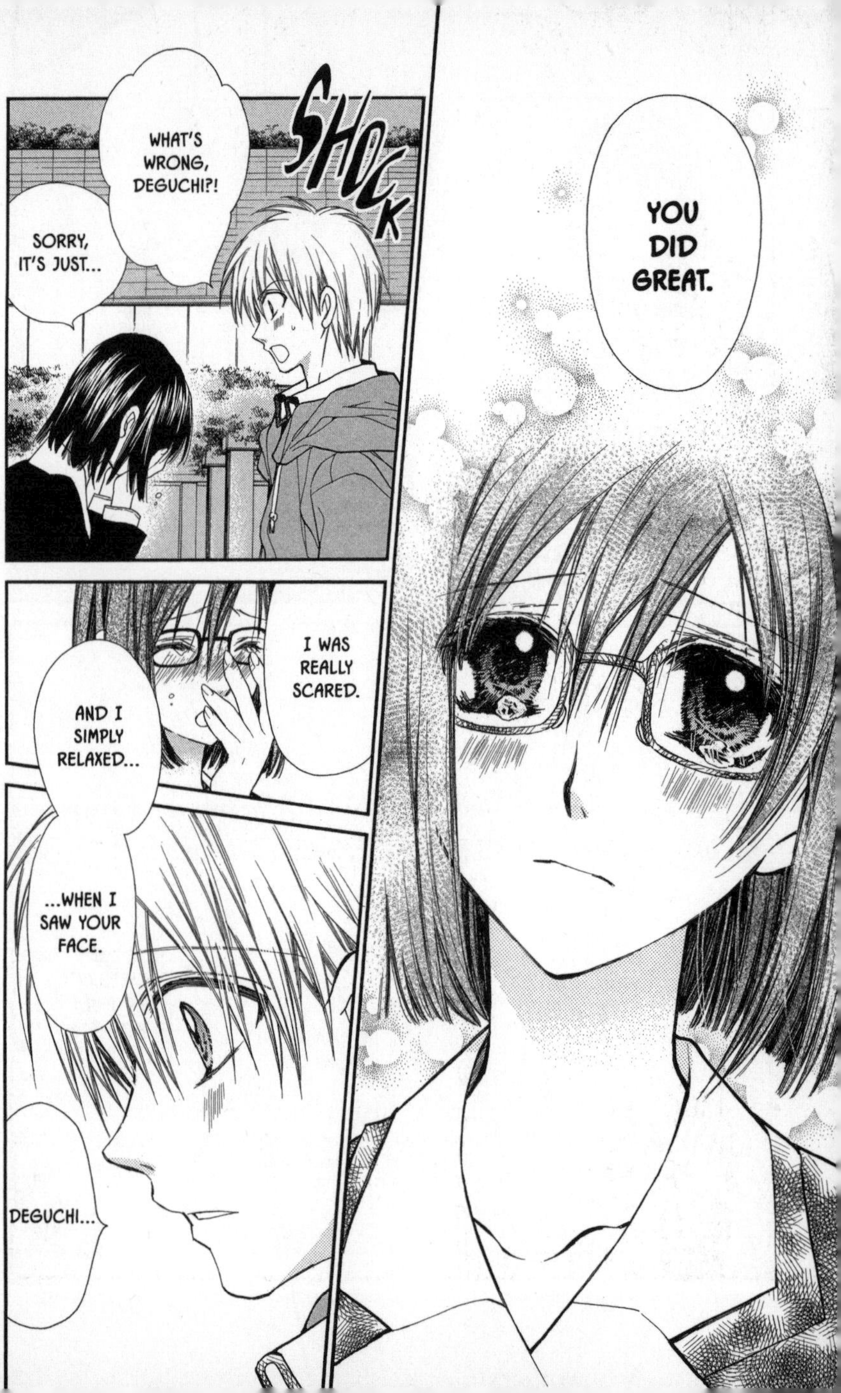
YOU DID GREAT.
SHOCK
WHAT'S WRONG, DEGUCHI?!
SORRY, IT'S JUST...
I WAS REALLY SCARED.
AND I SIMPLY RELAXED...
...WHEN I SAW YOUR FACE.
DEGUCHI...

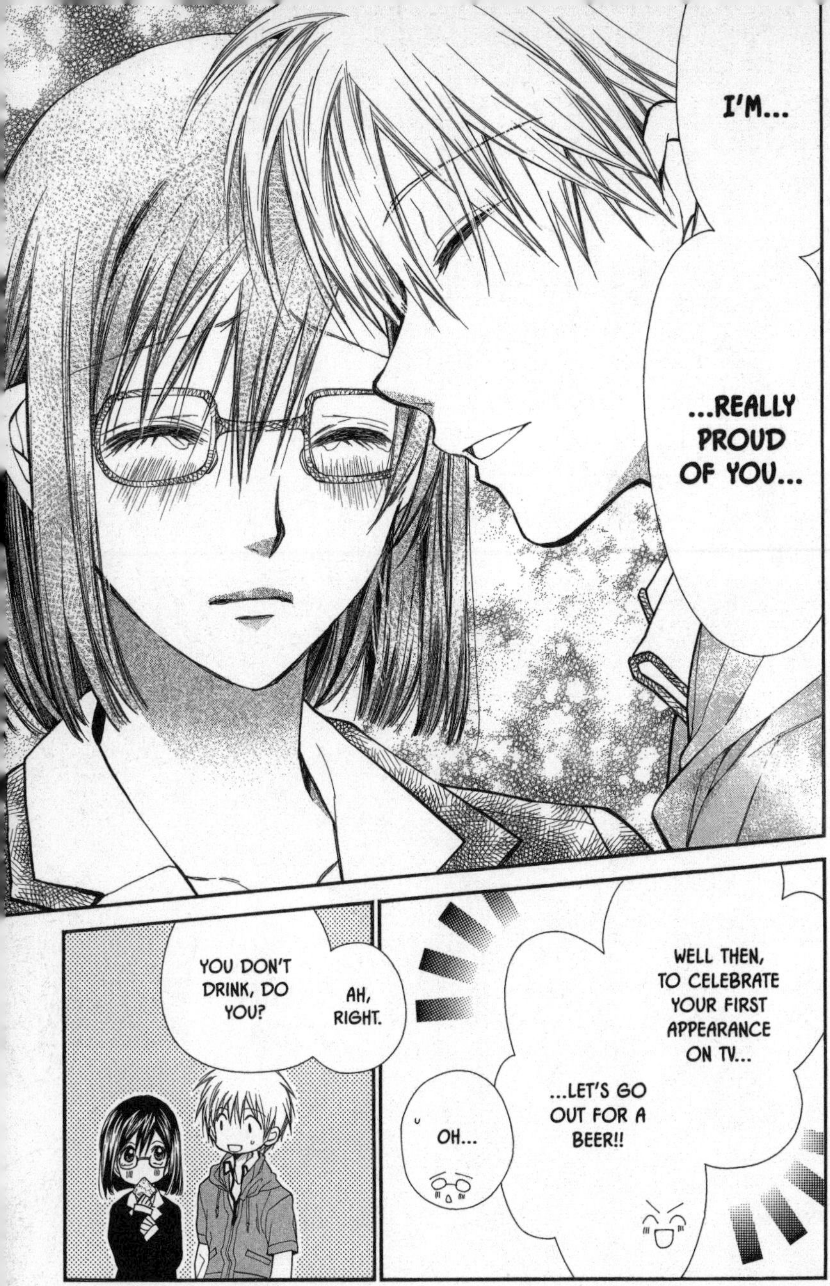
I'M...
...REALLY PROUD OF YOU...
WELL THEN, TO CELEBRATE YOUR FIRST APPEARANCE ON TV...
...LET'S GO OUT FOR A BEER!!
OH...
AH, RIGHT.
YOU DON'T DRINK, DO YOU?

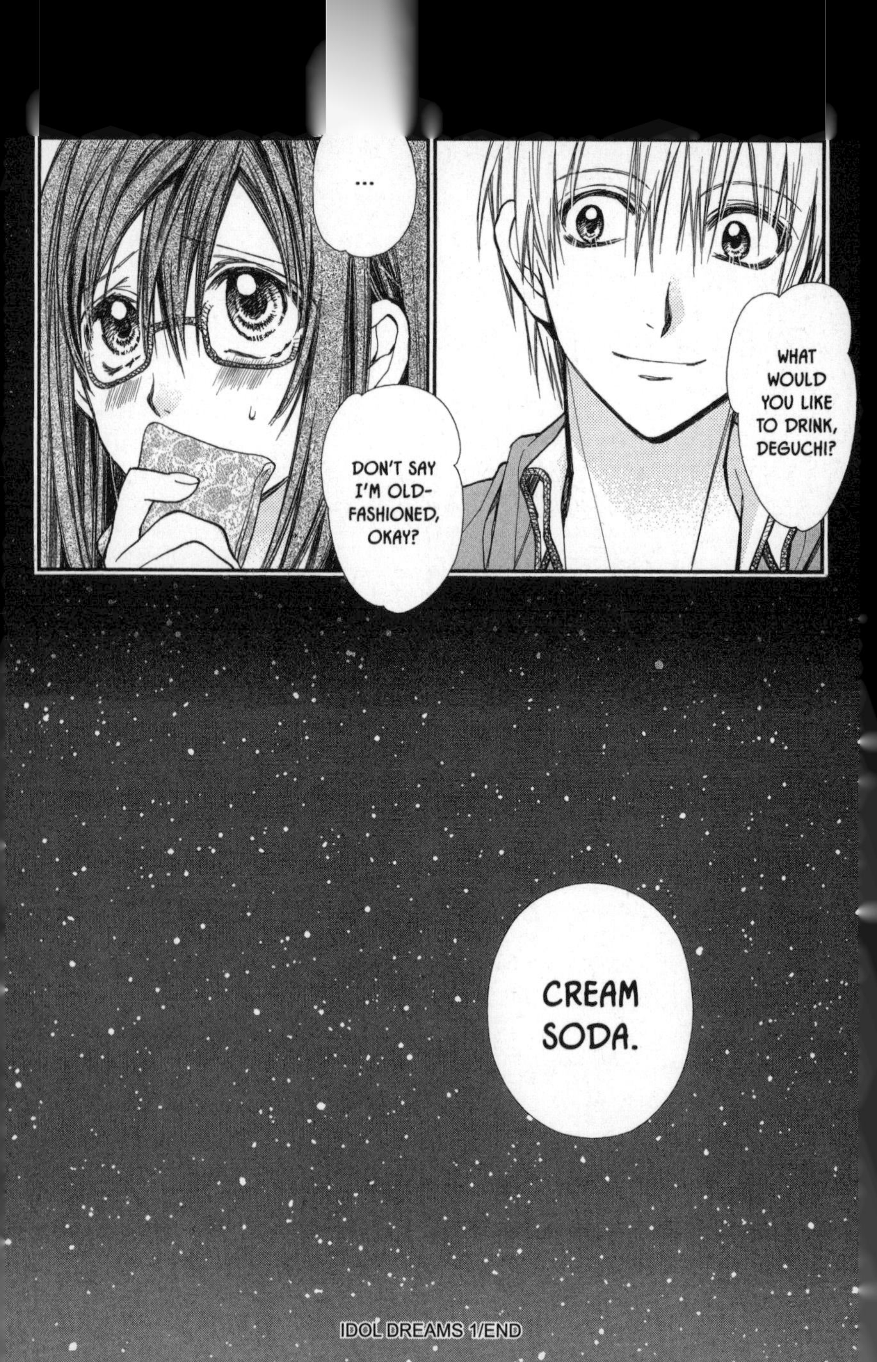
WHAT WOULD YOU LIKE TO DRINK, DEGUCHI?
...
DON'T SAY I'M OLD-FASHIONED, OKAY?
CREAM SODA.

IDOL DREAMS 1/END

IDOL dreams

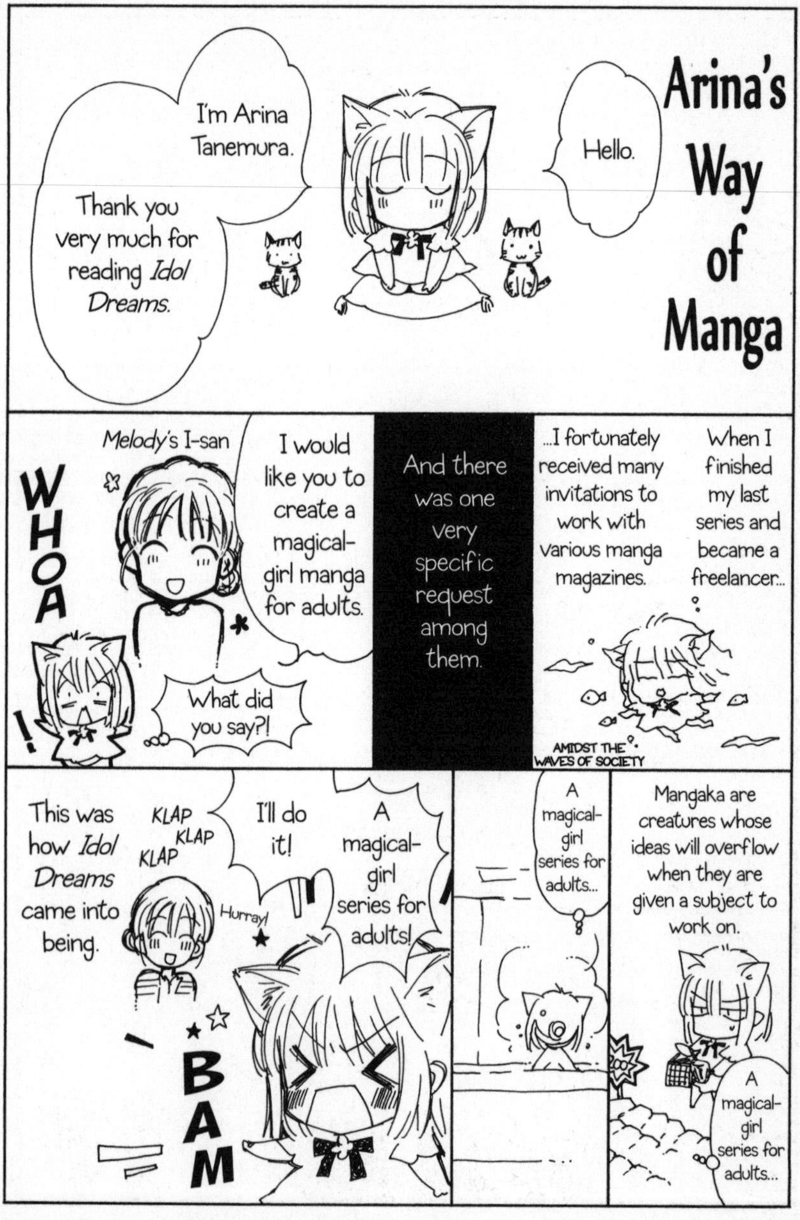
Arina's Way of Manga
Hello.
I'm Arina Tanemura.
Thank you very much for reading *Idol Dreams.*
When I finished my last series and became a freelancer...
...I fortunately received many invitations to work with various manga magazines.
AMIDST THE WAVES OF SOCIETY
And there was one very specific request among them.
I would like you to create a magical-girl manga for adults.
Melody's I-san
WHOA
!
What did you say?!
Mangaka are creatures whose ideas will overflow when they are given a subject to work on.
A magical-girl series for adults...
A magical-girl series for adults...
A magical-girl series for adults!
I'll do it!
BAM
KLAP KLAP KLAP
Hurray!
This was how *Idol Dreams* came into being.

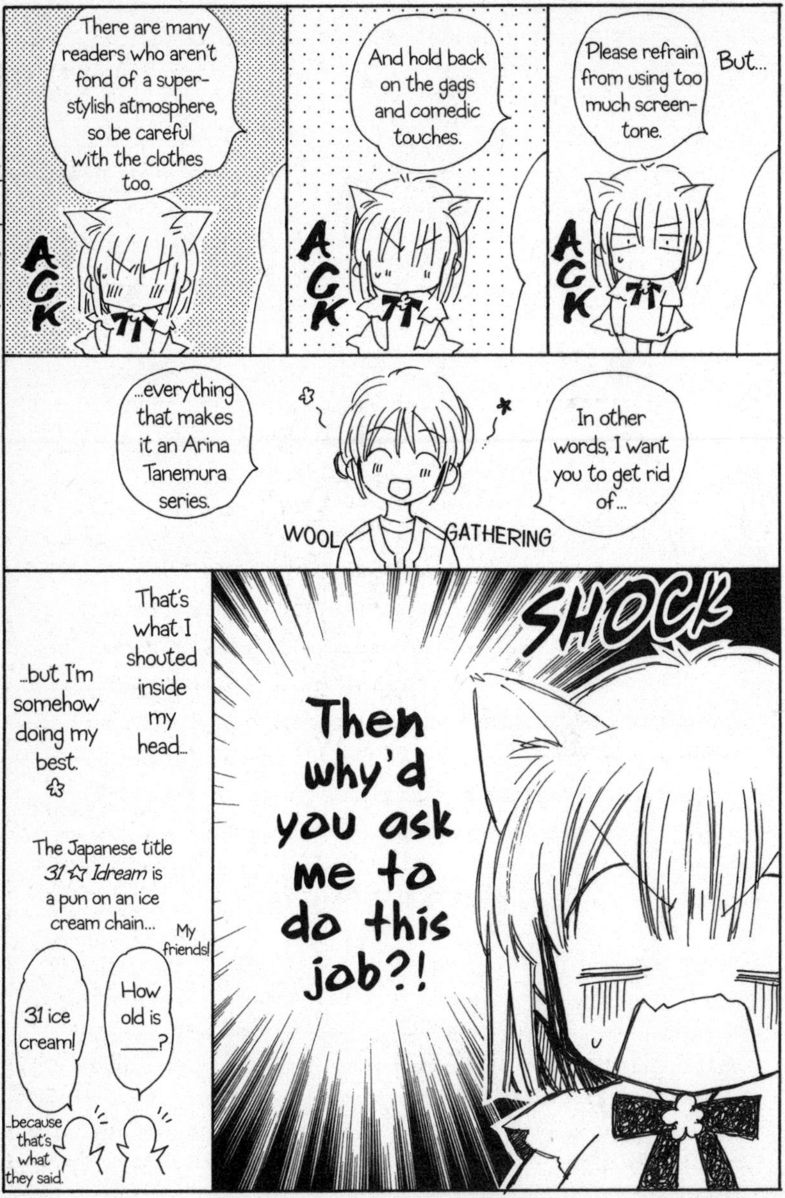
But...
Please refrain from using too much screen-tone.
ACK
And hold back on the gags and comedic touches.
ACK
There are many readers who aren't fond of a super-stylish atmosphere, so be careful with the clothes too.
ACK
In other words, I want you to get rid of...
...everything that makes it an Arina Tanemura series.
WOOL GATHERING
SHOCK
Then why'd you ask me to do this job?!
That's what I shouted inside my head...
...but I'm somehow doing my best. ✿
The Japanese title *31☆Idream* is a pun on an ice cream chain...
My friends!
How old is ____?
31 ice cream!
...because that's what they said.

I'm not stylish in the first place...

ARINA'S WAY OF MANGA/END

When I began working on creating this new series, Chikage
was an office lady with a brash, strong-willed personality.
But I decided to go with a timid, weakhearted personality
following the advice of my editor. All of my previous
heroines were created with the concept in mind of "a girl I
would like to have as my girlfriend if I were a guy," but let's
see how Chikage turns out... I hope you will watch over her
with me as she grows as a character.

ARINA TANEMURA

✳

Arina Tanemura began her manga career in 1996 when her short
stories debuted in *Ribon Original* magazine. She gained fame with the 1997
publication of *I•O•N*, and ever since her debut Tanemura has been a major
force in shojo manga with popular series *Phantom Thief Jeanne*, *Time Stranger
Kyoko*, *Full Moon*, *The Gentlemen's Alliance †* and *Sakura Hime: The Legend of
Princess Sakura*. Both *Phantom Thief Jeanne* and *Full Moon* have been adapted
into animated TV series.

IDOL dreams 1

SHOJO BEAT EDITION

STORY & ART BY **ARINA TANEMURA**

TRANSLATION **Tetsuichiro Miyaki**
TOUCH-UP ART & LETTERING **Inori Fukuda Trant**
DESIGN **Shawn Carrico**
EDITOR **Nancy Thistlethwaite**

Thirty One Idream by Arina Tanemura
© Arina Tanemura 2014
All rights reserved.
First published in Japan in 2014 by HAKUSENSHA, Inc., Tokyo.
English language translation rights arranged with HAKUSENSHA, Inc., Tokyo.

The stories, characters and incidents mentioned
in this publication are entirely fictional.

No portion of this book may be reproduced or
transmitted in any form or by any means without
written permission from the copyright holders.

Printed in the U.S.A.

Published by VIZ Media, LLC
P.O. Box 77010
San Francisco, CA 94107

10 9 8 7 6 5 4 3 2 1
First printing, November 2015

PARENTAL ADVISORY
IDOL DREAMS is rated T for Teen and
is recommended for ages 13 and up.
This volume contains sexual themes.
ratings.viz.com

www.viz.com

www.shojobeat.com

Kamisama Kiss

Story and art by **Julietta Suzuki**

What's a newly fledged godling to do?

Now a hit anime series!

Nanami Momozono is alone and homeless after her dad skips town to evade his gambling debts and the debt collectors kick her out of her apartment. So when a man she's just saved from a dog offers her his home, she jumps at the opportunity. But it turns out that his place is a shrine, and Nanami has unwittingly taken over his job as a local deity!

Available now!

VIZ MEDIA
viz.com

Shojo Beat

RATED TEEN
ratings.viz.com

Kamisama Hajimemashita © Julietta Suzuki 2008/HAKUSENSHA, Inc.

Ouran High School

Host Club

BOX SET

Story and Art by
Bisco Hatori

Escape to the world of the young, rich and sexy

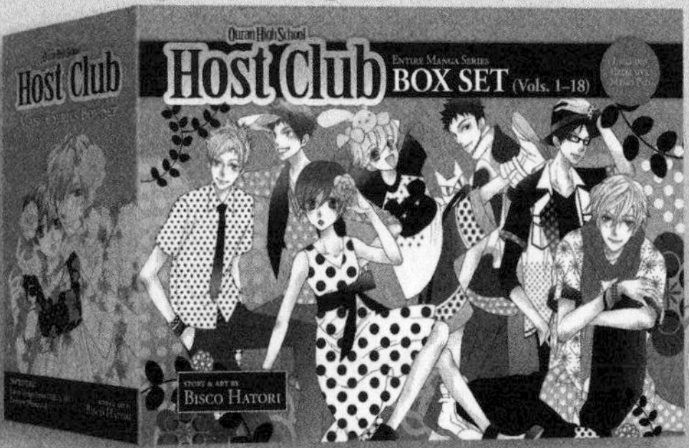

All 18 volumes
in a collector's box
with an Ouran High
School stationery
notepad!

In this screwball romantic
comedy, Haruhi, a poor girl at
a rich kids' school, is forced to
repay an $80,000 debt by working
for the school's swankiest, all-
male club—as a boy! There she
discovers just how wealthy the six
members are and how different
the rich are from everybody else...

viz
MEDIA
www.viz.com

Shojo Beat

RATED T TEEN
ratings.viz.com

Ouran Koko Host Club © Bisco Hatori 2002/HAKUSENSHA, Inc.

Natsume's
BOOK of FRIENDS

STORY and ART by
Yuki Midorikawa

Make Some Unusual New Friends

The power to see hidden spirits has always felt like a curse to troubled high schooler Takashi Natsume. But he's about to discover he inherited a lot more than just the Sight from his mysterious grandmother!

Available at your local bookstore or comic store.

www.shojobeat.com

Natsume Yujincho © Yuki Midorikawa 2005/HAKUSENSHA, Inc.

www.viz.com

OTOMEN

by AYA KANNO

Despite his tough jock exterior, Asuka Masamune harbors a secret love for sewing, shojo manga, and all things girly. But when he finds himself drawn to his domestically inept classmate Ryo, his carefully crafted persona is put to the test. Can Asuka ever show his true self to anyone, much less to the girl he's falling for?

Find out in the *Otomen* manga—buy yours today!

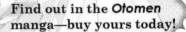

Don't Hide What's *Inside*

Available at your local bookstore or comic store.

OTOMEN © Aya Kanno 2006/HAKUSENSHA, Inc.

www.viz.com

Kyoko Mogami followed her true love Sho to Tokyo to support him while he made it big as an idol. But he's casting her out now that he's famous enough! Kyoko won't suffer in silence— he's going to get her sweet revenge by beating Sho in show biz!

Vol. 1 ISBN: 978-1-4215-4226-3

Vol. 2 ISBN: 978-1-4215-4227-0

Vol. 3 ISBN: 978-1-4215-4228-7

Only **$14.99** for each volume! ($16.99 in Canada)

Show biz is sweet...but revenge is sweeter!

Skip·Beat!

Story and Art by YOSHIKI NAKAMURA

In Stores Now!

kip•Beat! © Yoshiki Nakamura 2002/HAKUSENSHA, Inc.

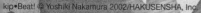

www.viz.com

...and STILL kick some butt?!

ORESAMA TEACHER

Story & art by Izumi Tsubaki

Determined to make the best of the situation and make her mother proud, Mafuyu decides to turn over a new, feminine, well-behaved leaf. But her fighting spirit can't be kept down, and the night before school starts she finds herself defending some guy who's getting beaten up. One slip wouldn't have been a problem, except the guy is *...her teacher?!* How can Mafuyu learn to be a good girl if her teacher won't let her forget her wicked past?

Oresama Teacher, Vol. 1
ISBN: 978-1-4215-3863-1 • $9.99 US / $12.99 CAN

IN STORES NOW!

ORESAMA TEACHER © Izumi Tsubaki 2008/HAKUSENSHA, Inc.

www.viz.com

STOP!
YOU MAY BE R… …RONG WAY!

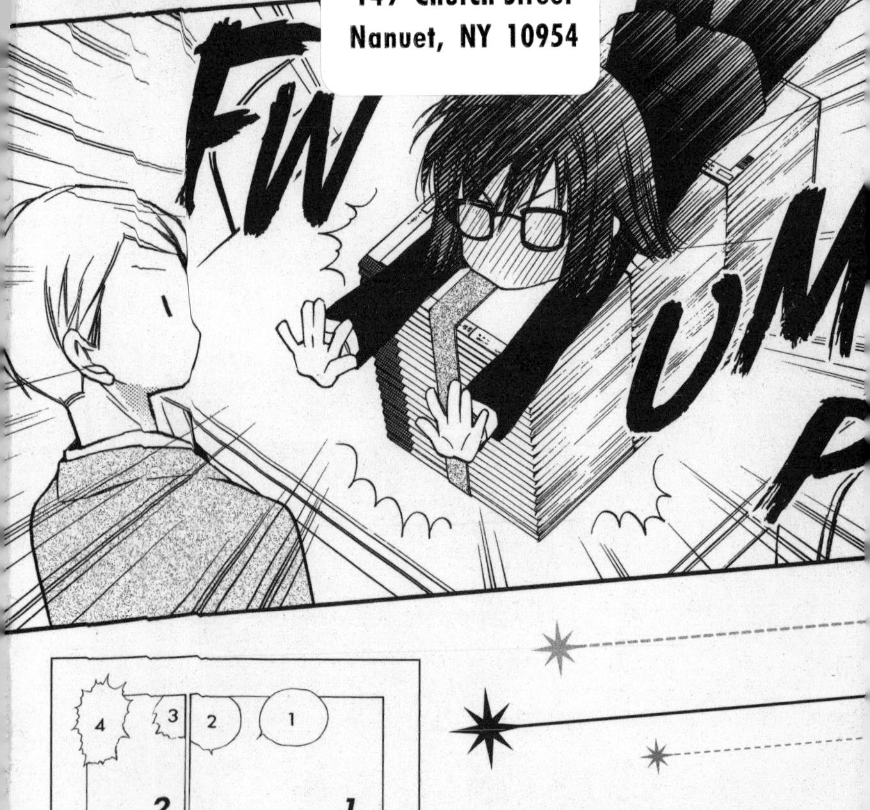

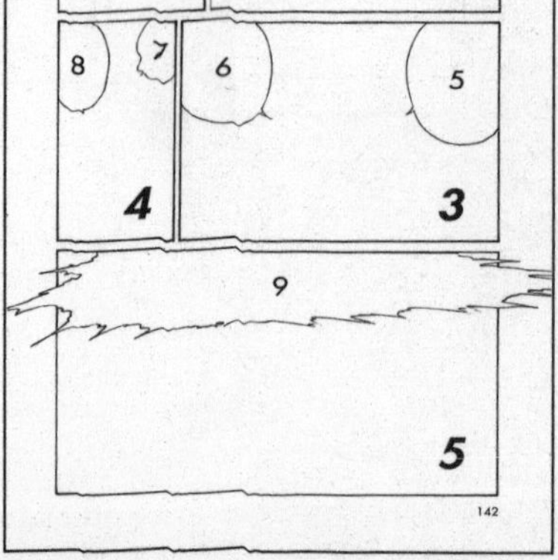

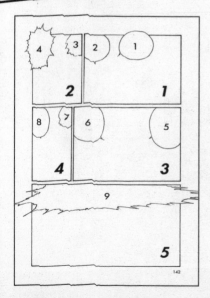

In keeping with the original Japanese comic format, this book reads from right to left—so action, sound effects and word balloons are completely reversed to preserve the orientation of the original artwork.

Check out the diagram shown here to get the hang of things, and then turn to the other side of the book to get started!